MASTERING

Homebrew

RANDY MOSHER

MASTERING
Homebrew

THE COMPLETE GUIDE TO BREWING DELICIOUS BEER

CHRONICLE BOOKS
SAN FRANCISCO

Library of Congress Cataloging-in-Publication Data:

Mosher, Randy.
  Mastering Homebrew : the Complete guide to brewing delicious
beer /
Randy Mosher.
    pages cm
 Includes bibliographical references and index.
  ISBN 978-1-4521-0551-2
1. Brewing—Amateurs' manuals. I. Title.

  TP577.M676 2015
  641.87'3—dc23

                    2013010255

Manufactured in China

Designed and typeset by Nick Steinhardt, Smog Design, Inc.
Illustrations by Randy Mosher and Nick Steinhardt
Unless otherwise noted, all photographs by Randy Mosher.

Briess is a registered trademark of Briess Industries, Inc. Bairds
Malt is a registered trademark of Bairds Malt Limited. Carafa is a
registered trademark of Mich. Weyermann GmbH & Co. Caramu-
nich is a registered trademark of Mich. Weyermann GmbH & Co.
Cara-Pils is a registered trademark of Breiss Industries, Inc. Palisade is a registered trademark of Select Botanicals Group, LLC.
Simcoe is a registered trademark of Select Botanicals Group, LLC.
Ribena is a registered trademark of Glaxo Group Limited. Sinamar
is a registered trademark of Mich. Weyermann GmbH & Co.

10 9 8 7 6 5 4 3 2 1

Chronicle Books LLC
680 Second Street
San Francisco, California 94107
www.chroniclebooks.com

Facing page: Fred Eckhardt at the 1998 AHA
National Homebrewers Conference in Portland,
OR, in 1998. Photo by Edward Bronson.

To FRED ECKHARDT,

the grand gentleman of American homebrewing, who did so much to set us all on a civilized and irreverent path.

LAFLEUR BREWING COMPANY
EVANSTON, ILLINOIS

BAD BREEER BREWERY
Birra ad ata fermentazione non pastorizzata rifermentata in bottiglia

Prodotto ed imbottigliato ad.Gr.grano, for ho

4 PERE
QUADRUP
CON PE
MARTIN S
33 cl e
alc. 10 % vol
OG 1092
BU 30

mbottigliato i

Ingredienti: acqua, malto d'o
Martin Sec damonted 50 %,
malto di frumento, lupo
Conservare in ancaro ci in lu
ci tra deposito naturale

MOCHACHINO MILK STOUT
Frankenbarley Brewery

THE LONELY MOUNTAIN BREWERY
ROBUST PORTER
BLG: 15,5   IBU: 27   ALK: 5,4%
#3   23.04.2014

REPELLER
HIGH WATER BREWERY

JAM SESSIONS
4.8%
2014
PEANUT BUTTER BROWN ALE WITH BLACKBERRIES & RASPBERRIES

BROWAR ABSZTYFIKANT
16° BLG   6.8% ALK
71 IBU
CZARNA OWCA
BLACK IPA
CHINOOK, CASCADE, WILLAMETTE, CITRA
24.02.13

EMPYREAN ALES • BEER QUEST • 18 NOV
WITH THE OIL OF AFRO-DYTEE
Kristl Bol
THEESEN
COSMIC DEBRIS
ASTHMA CURING LOW-GRAVITY WINTER ALE
Mystery Robe
PORTER
AN' THE DUST OF THE GRAND WAZOO
Reach Nervonna T'nigh

American Stout
hultaj
Alk. 5,6°   Blg 15,0°

busted prop
melk stout
BANG

Drunken Poodle
the Mutt's Nuts
Hazelnut
Brown ale

Acknowledgments

Thanks to Lyn Kruger and Keith Lemcke of the Siebel Institute for giving me a platform, along with their support and encouragement. Thanks also to Ray Daniels, Chris White, Chris Graham, Stan Heironymous, Penny Pickart, and Ron Pattinson. A special thanks to my friends in Brazil, Argentina, Australia, Italy, and Denmark who sponsored several trips that really opened my eyes to the possibilities of global beer. And, of course, deep gratitude to my partners in 5 Rabbit Cerveceria for letting me share and help shape their journey. Thanks to all my friends in the brewing world who shared their secrets with amazing quotes. Thanks to my ferocious copyeditor, Molly Jackel, for making me look like a real writer. An extra-special thank-you to Tom Schmidlin, whose eagle eye and learned brain saved me from many a misstep.

Facing page, row by row from top left: Homebrew labels by Jim LaFleur, Matteo Pellis/Alberto Bodritti, Jason McLaughlin, Piotr "ThoriN" Jurkiewicz, Dave Gallagher, Kim Leshinski, Łukasz Szynkiewicz, Kim Theesen, Łukasz Szynkiewicz, Eric Monson, and Robert Alvord.

CONTENTS

CONTENTS

Foreword

People often ask, "What made the American Craft Beer Revolution happen?" There's an old saying, often attributed to President Kennedy, "Success has many fathers, and failure is an orphan." In craft brewing, I think there's no doubt that homebrewers are the "many fathers" of the explosion of craft brewing. Just about all the pioneering craft brewers started as homebrewers, myself included. Thirty years ago the American commercial beer landscape was a bland horizon of watered-down mass domestics and stale imports. The only way to get a flavorful beer was to brew it yourself. Back then, nobody thought American brewers were even capable of brewing great beer.

Certainly one individual who was a key catalyst to the homebrew revolution was President Jimmy Carter, who, bless him, legalized homebrewing in 1978. The homebrewers of the 1970s and 1980s were passionate and indefatigable. They faced an uphill struggle. Few homebrew clubs or stores existed. Ingredients were often hard to find. No Internet meant no chat rooms, websites, beer blogs, or easy resources for recipes. The available books about brewing were few and mostly focused on commercial brewing. As often as not, early homebrewers had to make it up as we went along. The challenges for homebrewers twenty-five years ago remind me of the challenges our Colonial era–brewing forebears endured. Samuel Adams and the other brewers of his day concocted recipes on the spot to make use of available, harvestable ingredients.

As the American beer landscape has expanded from about 50 breweries in the United States in 1984 to more than 2,000 breweries in 2012, people have often asked me to name the biggest competitors to Samuel Adams. From Day One, my standard answer has been the same. My biggest obstacles are ignorance and apathy. People who don't know about beer and don't care about beer.

Mastering Homebrew holds the promise of extinguishing this ignorance and apathy. No one who reads this book will come away unenlightened or unenthusiastic. In the early years of the Boston Beer Company, I ran up against the long-held assumption that beer is a beverage of the masses that has none of the complexity and nobility of wine. Those days, mercifully, are behind us. Restaurateurs tell us that their beer list says as much about their establishments as their wine list. This is probably the best time in history to be a beer lover, and Randy Mosher is just the person to be our Pied Piper of good beer.

Today there's a brave new world in homebrewing, and that world just got a whole lot better with the publication of this book. Randy has become a worthy literary heir to the late Michael Jackson, the Bard of Beer. Randy is a walking encyclopedia of beer and brewing, and his palate and taste are impeccable. One of Randy's great gifts as a teacher is to communicate basic information in a way that is fascinating both to neophytes and experienced brewers.

If you're standing in your kitchen right now holding this book, just about to start homebrewing for the first time, let me make a recommendation. Stop what you're doing! Open your refrigerator and select a bottle of your favorite beer. Leave the kitchen. Sit down in your favorite chair. Open the beer. Open this book to chapter 1. Close your eyes and take a sip of your beer. To my mind, there is nothing like the first sip of my first beer of the day. *Aaaah!*

Now, this is how you start the process of homebrewing. Read, then drink, and then brew. I urge you to drink in this book and learn everything you can before you even start sterilizing your brewing equipment. It will make you thirsty, but it will make you a better brewer. This book will teach you the art and the science of brewing, the chemistry and the mystery, the sensations and the sensational.

Oh, how I wish I had had this book in 1984 when I brewed my first batch of Samuel Adams in my kitchen. The wallpaper might have survived. The beer would have been better, and I would have been better able to evaluate and appreciate my brew. This book might just be the only brewing book most homebrewers will ever need.

So, let me bid you bon voyage as you embark on the wonderful journey Randy has laid out for you.

Cheers!

JIM KOCH
chairman and cofounder, the Boston Beer Company

CHAPTER

1

Introduction

TO

BEER

❧ What is it about brewing beer? Holding this book in your hand, you are as much as admitting that there is some special fascination with it, but what?

Is it about creating a beer for its practical qualities as a thirst-quenching and refreshing beverage, or perhaps for its suppleness as a dining companion (one that doesn't dominate or dismiss its partners), or as a tasty and temperate path to relaxation if not abused?

Is it beer's willingness to bend to the needs and moods of the seasons, offering a meaningful way to engage in the flow of time—as sustenance and succor in a dark, cold winter, as hearty harbinger of spring, as celebration of the mindless joy of summer, or as autumn's rich and toasty counterpoint to the harvest's bounty? Beer suits the moment like no other drink.

Maybe it's that every glass portends a vast range of possibilities. Dozens of ingredients creating unlimited possibilities in terms of strength, color, and flavor, topped off by a universe of amazing aromas. It's easy to be drawn in by the sense of endless creativity as each new brew offers its delicious rewards.

Perhaps it's beer's ability to draw people into an easy camaraderie. Every brewery, no matter how small, starts to build a community around it. It is a highly social hobby because the product creates sociability—inescapably so. I promise that brewing will draw people to you.

Maybe it's the empowerment you feel as a maker of beer to provoke, entertain, surprise, seduce, and satisfy people. To brew well certainly invites a heaping plateful of rewards, but brewing great beer is not a simple pursuit. Creating art at a high level never is. Learning to master brewing means understanding the many biochemical, sensory, and practical aspects of beer, brewing, and tasting. Like any pursuit, brewing's returns are proportionate to what you put into it. The good news is that you can make really tasty beer right from the beginning. Then, you'll have plenty to sustain you as you improve your skills.

QUICK START GUIDE

I love to hear the sound of my words rattling around in your head as much as the next author, but I'd like to suggest you jump ahead and get a brew going. Hands-on learning is the best; everything makes so much more sense when you can see it, taste it, touch it. If you're not yet brewing, I urge you to do so at the earliest possible opportunity.

Purchase the items listed on page 118. If you're really in a hurry, go to your nearest homebrew store and buy an equipment kit. Just be sure to get a 6.5-gallon/25-L carboy, as these don't always come with the kits and I think they make better beer and less mess. You will also need a stainless-steel pot of 4- to 5-gallon/ 14- to 19-L capacity, and a stove or burner capable of heating it to boiling. And start saving bottles (non-twist-off preferred) to fill with your beer when the time comes (see the Bottling Gear, page 187).

Pick out a recipe, use The Amazing Shape-Shifting Beer Recipe on page 116, or, if you're in a hurry, get a kit. Just make sure it's not pure extract and if there is sugar in it, that there's just a little. Also shoot for something in the normal alcohol range (4.5 to 6 percent). Higher-alcohol beers are more challenging to brew and take longer to mature into a drinkable state.

3

Don't forget the yeast. There's nothing really wrong with dry yeast, but if you're serious, go for the liquid, which offers genuine brewing pedigrees and a lot more strains to choose from. Pick an ale yeast appropriate for the style you're brewing, or just go crazy and pick a yeast strain that sounds interesting to you. When in doubt, use Chico, a.k.a. California Ale. Forget about lager for now.

BASIC KIT OF HOMEBREW GEAR

A typical beginner's brewing kit will include the following (clockwise from top right): carboy for conditioning, racking hose (in this example with a siphon starter as part of it), stirring paddle or spoon, hydrometer, thermometer, bottling wand, fermentation lock, bottle and carboy brushes for cleaning, a bottle capper, a stick-on thermometer for the carboy, a plastic fermenter, and a bottling bucket with a spigot. A stainless-steel brewing pot is also necessary, but is usually sold separately.

TYPICAL BATCH OF HOMEBREWING INGREDIENTS

A basic kit of homebrewing ingredients contains dry or liquid malt extract, priming sugar, crushed grains, hops, and yeast, plus hop and grain bags and caps.

Follow the Extract Plus Steeped-Grain Procedure on page 119. The whole thing should take about 3 hours. Don't forget to measure the original gravity and write everything down on a worksheet (see page 241). When the wort, or unfermented beer, is cooled, add, or "pitch," the yeast. Place the beer in a location with a fairly constant temperature of 58 to 70°F/14 to 21°C, away from bright light.

Watch your beer go through the stages of fermentation (see Fermentation from Start to Finish, page 218). After a few days of vigorous activity, the foam will subside and the surface will clear. At this point the beer is in the conditioning phase, which should take 1 to 2 weeks. When the beer clears and appears to darken, it's ready for bottling.

Follow the bottling directions on page 226. Store at the same temperature as fermentation, or possibly a little warmer if you want the beer to carbonate faster.

Give it a week or more to ferment, chill one, then open a bottle and taste the beer to check the carbonation. If the beer's nicely sparkly, this will be one of the more exciting moments of your life. If it's not, wait another week for your moment of ecstasy.

8

Now you can get back to this book while you plan your next brew.

The late Bill Friday's buttons summed up the spirit of the hobby. Photo by Ed Bronson.

ABOUT THIS BOOK

This handbook is intended to be a comprehensive guide to homebrewing with a special focus on how to understand, manipulate, and control the flavor of beer. The choice of ingredients, the way they are blended and processed at every step, the many variables of fermentation, and, finally, packaging, serving, and aging all have roles to play in what ends up in the glass. While there are almost always technical reasons behind the many decisions in brewing a beer, each choice nearly always has an artistic reason to consider as well—or should have if you're doing it right.

Fortunately, beer is quite forgiving. If you pay attention to just a few things—first among them sanitization—you can easily make some delicious beer. Jump in, get some brews in the tanks, and become the big beer celebrity of your circle of friends; once you're having a ton of fun with it, start pushing yourself to understand and manage all the technical aspects. Your beers will rise in quality as your ambitions do. It's a fascinating and rewarding challenge, the perfect recipe for a great hobby.

I have spent a career as a graphic designer and a writer, and I believe that beer is art, period. It lives in the sensory, emotional, and conceptual parts of our brains. Beer's purpose is to tickle people, and there is no equation for that. No amount of brewing science can tell you *what* to brew. That takes imagination, creativity, and a well-developed sense for the flavors and aromas of both raw ingredients and the finished product—art, art, art!

The road to creating art can feel a bit vague, partly because it's a more internal process and for sure it can't be reduced to numbers. But that doesn't mean it's all moonbeams and unicorns. There are some methodical, practical, and even scientific aspects to the art of brewing, and I'm going to lay those out for you in some detail.

One of my main goals is to get you completely comfortable formulating your own recipes. The tools for calculation are here, but beyond that, I've tried to give you some ways to think about the structure of the recipes: from the top-down concept to the way ingredients are layered to do particular jobs to the roles of process and fermentation. With a little study, anyone should be able to conjure up a vision of their next beer, then create a recipe and work out the details so the finished brew nails the concept.

On the technical side, I have tried to get the latest points of view on important controversial topics. For most hotly debated issues (like hot-side aeration, for instance), it turns out that good, general practice when you brew is enough to keep you out of trouble. Special brews or circumstances sometimes demand special procedures; but otherwise, it's useful to remember that brewers before industrialization made beer good enough to be celebrated in poetry and song using little more than wooden tubs and sticks—along with keen senses and some well-honed experience.

Why Homebrew?

I've got my reasons to homebrew, but I thought it would be fun to pose this question to some of the best brewers and beer thinkers I know from around the world. They have answered this far better than I could have.

> **To make beer is to make happiness.**

MARCO FALCONE, owner and brewmaster, Falke Bier, Belo Horizonte, Brazil

> **Homebrewing is the often-invisible roots of the more visible tree of craft brewing. Homebrewers are among the most innovative breweries in America and there are millions of them. They can try crazy things in five-gallon batches.**

JIM KOCH, cofounder and chairman, the Boston Beer Company, Boston, MA

The grand pooh-bah of American homebrewing, Charlie Papazian, has a catchphrase: "Relax. Don't worry. Have a homebrew." And he's right. Relaxing means broadening your focus and keeping in mind what the purpose of all the effort is. If you don't have time to dig deeply into the pleasures of beer, to know them in a most intimate way, how will you ever know what beer is capable of and what science can do for you?

For me, this is the real compelling thing about brewing: it requires discipline and imagination in both the empirical and the lyrical spheres. Brewing offers rewards far beyond what ends up in your cup. It can push us places we wouldn't go without it.

Homebrewing is important for the same reason that home cooking is important. It is an act of creation that keeps us connected to our natures as creatures. After all, beer is liquid bread, a food, sustenance for both body and soul, which is probably why for most of civilization the person in charge of the domestic hearth tended to both the stew and the brew.

SABINE WEYERMANN, Weyermann Malting, Bamberg, Germany

Members of the Tampa Bay BEERS homebrew club get happy at a recent American Homebrewers Association Conference. Photo by Edward Bronson.

WHAT'S IN HERE?

We start with a brief introduction to beer and the ways it is measured and described, including an overview of the human sensory apparatus as it relates to beer—becoming a good taster is a hugely important aspect of being a brewer. After that, you'll find sections on ingredients, the brewing process through fermentation, and the equipment you'll need to start your home brewery. Then we'll dig into recipe formulation from a predictive and conceptual standpoint. The recipes start in chapter 7. First is a whirlwind tour of beer styles with plenty of recipes, including the classic brewing traditions of Europe and the beers inspired by those traditions, like the new American beers. Next are some of the fascinating beers folks around the world are brewing with local flavors and creative approaches, followed by beers with alternate ingredients. Then comes a personal approach to a year of beer, season by season. I've devoted a chapter to problem solving and, finally, there is a guide to books, groups, and other resources to aid in your quest for the perfect beer.

This work is peppered with pithy bits of wisdom from the world's brewing elite. Some you have heard of, others maybe not; they offer this book a perspective you could never get from just me. Wherever possible, I have tried to present information visually to show the relationships that might be less gripping in paragraph form.

My goal is to bring an interested novice quickly up to speed, so that he or she is able to produce varied and delicious brews right from the start. This book is also a practical tool, helping the brewer understand the ingredients, methods, and variables of the brewing process in order to make decisions that benefit the broth in your kettle.

BREWING *with* BOTH HALVES *of* YOUR BRAIN

Brewing, if you do it right, will use your whole brain. The range of technical details is vast, covering everything from metallurgy to biochemistry, which requires some informed and systematic thinking. Ingredient characteristics, beer styles, and recipes must be worked out with numbers. There is a good deal of engineering to it.

Beer is far more than numbers, though. Brewing well is about the impact it can have on the human psyche. It triggers memories, creates emotion, and tells stories. This is where art lives. Science has nothing to say about these subjects. It is just a tool of the artist to achieve a particular end.

Most of us, because of our inclinations, schooling, and career paths, are stuck in one cubbyhole or the other, but brewing offers us the opportunity to give the less-used hemisphere a workout. With brewing, artists can play mad scientist, engineers can dabble in the arts. Brewing makes us whole.

Even if I could go to a Michelin three-star restaurant nightly, on occasion I would prefer to stay home and cook. Homebrewers enjoy brewing, and enjoy pleasing their friends with the fruits of their labors even more. Homebrewing is like making love; the simplest success is exciting.

CHARLES FINKEL, founder, Merchant Du Vin Beer Importers, and co-owner, Pike Brewing Company, Seattle, WA

THINKING LIKE *a* SCIENTIST

The field of science has developed a framework of ideas, definitions, and relationships over the last few centuries to describe the world around us and how it functions. This system depends on specialized language as building blocks to an understanding of the nature of things. To non-scientists this language can seem arcane and daunting. But in order to dive in to the technical side of brewing and fermentation, it will be helpful to have a refresher course in some of the terms and concepts.

Physics, chemistry, and biology are all involved in the brewing process. Physics describes the mechanical, electrical, and other physical aspects of the universe. In brewing, heat transfer, gas behavior, liquid flow, and other phenomena fall in this category. Chemistry involves the interaction of molecules and their component atoms and ions, of which there are a bewildering variety in the brewing process. Biology is a mix of chemistry and physics applied to the specialized world of living things—in beer's case, grain and yeast. Biochemistry is the unique chemistry of living organisms. It drives many of the important facets of brewing, from enzyme activity to fermentation.

As a brewer, it's your job to monitor and manipulate the physical and biochemical activity of brewing and get it to do your bidding—no more, no less. Science provides the framework that allows us to think empirically, using numbers to describe physical processes. This makes it possible to predict things like color and gravity in our recipes, and have some control over the brewing process. At the same time, it's important to cultivate a sense of what's meaningful and useful. Most brewing calculations focus on a few key variables and ignore a host of other parameters, so they're only approximate. As you work with them over time, you get a feel for how accurate they can be and how to get the greatest benefit with the least amount of stressing out over insignificant details.

Mad Zymurgists Club booth at a Homebrewing Conference. Science is something you take very seriously—or you don't.

WHAT *to* WORRY ABOUT

As a new brewer, there are a thousand things you imagine can go wrong, turning all your hard work into a slimy disgusting mess, ruining your reputation, and poisoning the neighborhood in the process. Relax. You won't poison anybody; pathogens can't live in beer. The chances of a flavor disaster are slim, too. Most likely, you will make tasty beer right from the start. Making it better will be a long march of incremental changes. Every added piece of knowledge put into practice will make your beer a little bit better.

If there's one thing to be obsessive about, it's cleaning and sanitization—well, okay, that's two things—because dirty equipment and sloppy sanitization will ruin a beer in many creatively horrifying ways. It's best to develop good habits about cleanliness in the brewery, and get good, brewery-grade cleaning and sanitizing chemicals. It's also important to follow manufacturer's recommendations on the dilution and use of these chemicals to ensure they work right and don't have harmful effects on the beer.

Homebrewing is a good school.

YVAN DE BAETS, brewmaster and founder, Brasserie de la Senne, Sint-Pieters-Leeuw, Belgium

Precision is a subject of endless debate in the homebrewing community, and it's easy to understand why. Small things can add up to better beer to drink. When confronted with numbers, as we often are in brewing, it is easy to focus on them and lose sight of their true meaning, which is how they relate to what's in the glass.

Chasing a certain mash pH or predicting hop bitterness to the second decimal place can be fun, but we are not trying to launch a spacecraft into orbit around Saturn. Hop bitterness, for example, can be reliably predicted only within about 10 percent, perhaps less. This seems pretty rough, but it turns out that we can distinguish bitterness only in 5 BU (Bitterness Units, sometimes called IBU or International Bitterness Units), and this is for bitterness below about 20 BU; it gets worse at higher numbers. So, 10 percent accuracy in your hop predictions turns out to be plenty good enough. The same tolerance of imprecision applies to color calculations, and for most people, alcohol percentage as well.

Yeast likes ideal conditions, but it's hardy and adaptable and will produce perfectly fine beer even if things are a wee bit off. So if you're inclined to get carried away with the technical details, make sure one of them is the notion of scale, and check to make sure you're not just pursuing numbers for numbers' sake.

Fine-tuning certain specifics can have great effect in some circumstances. The question is, which specifics? For the answer, I refer you to Mr. Ray Daniels, quoted at right. The range of options in brewing is so vast that it's almost impossible to master or control every one. Futile, too, because a packaging lager brewery, a monastery in Belgium, a real-ale-focused craft brewery, and the guy in his garage with the amazing setup (you, eventually) all need different things—or rather the beer does.

For brewery predictions, repeatability is perhaps the better goal to focus on. Because unless you buy some expensive laboratory equipment, you probably never will know what color or hop bitterness you're getting. Absolute precision is kind of a false idol unless you're a nut for analysis. As a product for the senses, beer has to meet the expectations of sight, smell, and taste—machines be damned. We're all flawed, with limited resolution and accuracy, so a rough calculation is all we really need.

I'm a scientist and engineer by training but I submit to the world of faith and the unknowable. One should be disciplined yet open to simple experiences. Still the brewing process follows the laws of nature, so we must embrace the clarity of science while appreciating the chaos. What can we create? What happens when we make subtle changes in process or material? That's the marriage of art and science.

DAN CAREY, cofounder and brewmaster, New Glarus Brewing Company, New Glarus, WI

The answer to any technical brewing question is "It depends."

RAY DANIELS, founder and CEO, Cicerone Certification Program, and author of *Designing Great Beers*

CHEMICAL *and* BIOCHEMICAL CONCEPTS

A full understanding of the complexities of brewing requires some familiarity with the various players and processes. The following list of terms may seem like highly technical jargon, but specialized language is required to describe the highly specific concepts involved in beer brewing.

pH

This is a measure of the acidity or alkalinity of a substance. The *H* refers to hydrogen ions, which are actually protons that carry a positive electrical charge. The more hydrogen ions, the more acidity; the more they are lacking (an excess of electrons), the more alkaline, or basic. It's a logarithmic scale; each full step represents a tenfold increase over the last. Neutral pH is at 7, indicating neither an excess nor dearth of hydrogen ions and electrons. Above 7 becomes more alkaline, and below, more acidic.

MOLECULE

Two or more atoms held together in a stable configuration through chemistry.

pH SCALE

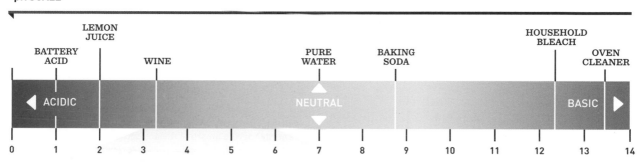

A pH scale is helpful in measuring the acidity or alkalinity of your beer, wort, or mash.

ION

An electrically charged atom or group of atoms. It is useful to think of brewing water ions such as carbonate or calcium as half-molecules, because when mineral salts dissolve in water they come apart, or dissociate into their individual ions, which are attracted to other ions in the solvent according to their electrical charges. These dissociated ions can be manipulated in various ways to achieve the desired water chemistry for a specific brew.

IONS IN AND OUT OF SOLUTION

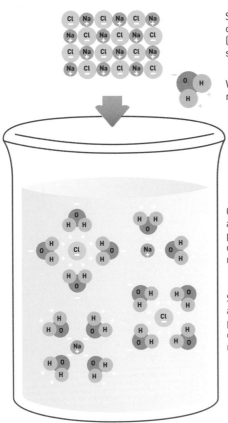

Sodium chloride (NaCl) in solid state

Water (H_2O) molecule

Chlorine (-) attracted to positive end of water molecules

Sodium (+) attracted to positive end of water molecules

Mineral salts dissociate into their individual ions when they dissolve in brewing water that can then be manipulated in various ways to achieve the desired water chemistry for a specific brew.

BUFFERING

The ability of certain molecules to soak up acids or bases even if they are not themselves strongly basic or acidic. This is an important aspect of mash chemistry, as a number of chemicals in that process have strong buffering capabilities.

REACTION

In order for matter to be transformed from one chemical state to the other, it must undergo a reaction. At the beginning, each molecule has a particular energy state, and the reaction will turn the reactants into different chemicals with a higher or lower energy level. But in order to do so, the reaction has to have energy put into the system. You can think of this energy as a hill: On one side is before the reaction, and the other side is after. In order to get to the other side, a push is needed up the hill so it can roll down the other side. Some reactions, like the splitting of starch molecules into sugar in the mash, may require a good deal of energy input to make the transformation.

ENZYME

A specialized type of protein molecule that can act as a catalyst, which is a substance that aids in chemical reactions by lowering the energy barrier, and thus the amount of energy needed to make the reaction happen. Enzymes seem miraculous, often lowering the required energy by a factor of a millionfold or more. There are hundreds of them involved in brewing and yeast physiology. Life would be quite impossible without them.

Every enzyme has temperature, pH, water concentration, and other parameters that determine its level of activity. Enzymes are named for the chemicals they act upon, and generally end in *ase*. Amylase is the type of enzyme that breaks apart the barley starches known as amylose and amylopectin, hence the name, meaning "starch-attacking enzyme."

POLYMER

A type of organic molecule formed by combining smaller subunits. They are ubiquitous in living things. We will be most interested in two types: proteins and starches.

CARBOHYDRATES

This is a large class of compounds built from five- or six-sided ring-shaped molecules. The simplest forms in this large class of compounds are monosaccharide sugars such as glucose (dextrose) and fructose. Two sugar units attached to one another become a disaccharide; in brewing, this is mostly maltose. Somewhat longer chains are known as oligosaccharides or dextrins, and when the chain becomes longer than about ten units, it is known as starch.

SOME SUGARS AND OTHER COMMON CARBOHYDRATES IN BREWING

GLUCOSE/DEXTROSE
Simple sugar released during malting. Less than 10% of extract. Also sometimes used as an adjunct.

MALTOSE
A two-unit sugar, the main fermentable in wort, created during mashing. Less than 10% of extract.

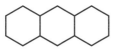

MALTOTRIOSE
A three-unit sugar, a minor wort component. Fermentable by lager yeast but not ale yeast.

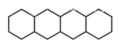

MALTOTETRAOSE
A four-unit sugar unfermentable by any brewers' yeast.

DEXTRINS
Longer sugars (up to 10 units), unfermentable by any brewers' yeast. Depending on brewing process, varying amounts can end up in beer.

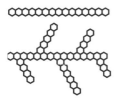

STARCH
Longer straight-chain (amylose) or branched (amylopectin) carbohydrates. Generally, beer contains no starch.

The sugars and carbohydrates involved in brewing vary in complexity and structure.

AMINO ACID

A class of nitrogen-bearing molecules that are the building blocks of proteins. There are just twenty of them in most living things. We will not be concerned much about specific ones, but as a group, they are a critical aspect of yeast nutrition derived from malt.

PROTEIN

A specialized class of polymeric molecules composed of amino acids. They play many different roles in living things, from structural roles as sheets and tubes to highly complex and chemically active molecules that serve as enzymes, signaling chemicals, and more. Proteins are so much a part of life that they are what our DNA encodes for—literally, what we're made of.

POLYPEPTIDE

A chain of amino acids not large enough to be a protein, but that connect to form proteins.

BREWING LIKE *an* ARTIST

Ultimately, beer has to interact with the senses and the mind, which are mostly beyond our ability to quantify. Making delicious, interesting, and resonant beers requires a good deal of self-awareness as well as a keen perception of the way others experience the world.

In my view, art is all about messing with people's heads. At the highest level, this is what brewing is about—our ability to get in there and affect people. It's a huge power and a privilege, ultimately quite an intimate act. We are plucking the sensory notes and emotional associations people have built up over a lifetime of happy moments—candy, bread, cake, cookies, chocolate, raisins, citrus, grass, pine trees, sagebrush, fruit—and we're just waiting for the beer to pour in and push those buttons.

To do this in brewing, as with any art, requires an intuitive grasp of the qualities of the raw materials and the way they interact and transform into the finished product. It's important to be able to focus on the sensations offered by beer and its ingredients, and build up an internal library of qualities and impressions about them. This is something you never stop learning. Try walking around your neighborhood just paying attention to the smells. It's an amazing experience. Do the same with malts and hops every time you have the chance.

It's important to know your drinkers as well. As a homebrewer, your beer usually stays close to home, so there's not a lot to think about. But when you take it to a different audience, you have to do a little research. I love to brew beer for weddings and other celebrations because it forces me to think about the beer in fresh terms, from the point of view of a new audience. This is as fun as it is challenging. Those of you who are interested in competitive brewing will have to consider the judges, who have a very particular point of view thrust on top of their personal likes and dislikes. It is helpful to see the beer through their eyes, which is one of the reasons it's so useful to become a judge yourself.

Art is not entirely intuitive. There are rules, or rather tools, like contrast, layering, hierarchy, counterpoint, and others, that give artists many different ways to construct and organize their work. If you have experience with any other art form, you will recognize these immediately. I'll have plenty more to say about these in chapter 7.

Brewing has encouraged me to seek out a social network of like-minded curious, generous, passionate, and kind people, and it has re-ignited my desire to learn more about history, alchemy, biology, and chemistry. I now seek out others' opinions about the challenges it poses. In short, I believe brewing has made me a better, more rounded (figuratively as well as literally) person.

CHRIS P. FREY chairman, American Homebrewers Association governing committee

GETTING STARTED *and* GETTING BETTER

A top goal of a new homebrewer is to get set up and get brewing really tasty beers as soon as possible, and this is a realistic goal. We are lucky to have so many different ways to make beer, from super simple to crazy complicated. With the right equipment and skills, an advanced brewer can control every tiny detail of the brewing process and create beers on a par with any in the world. Beginners give up a bit of control and accept limitations in exchange for speed and simplicity. The typical pattern is to get comfortable with the basics, then as confidence and resources allow, move to more complicated brewing procedures that allow them to use the same full range of ingredients and techniques as professional brewers.

Most homebrewers start brewing with an extract method incorporating steeped grains, like the one at the beginning of chapter 4. It's an easy method that takes just 2 to 3 hours, and requires minimal equipment and space. Typically, you'll boil only 3 gallons/11 L, and this is mixed with sanitized water in the fermenter. For these reasons, many people will stick to this procedure for making beer and never feel the need to make brewing any more complicated.

This method does have its limitations. Without mashing—the cooking procedure that breaks down malt starches into sugars—the brewer is relying heavily on the malt manufacturer and is limited to crushed grains like caramel malt that yield extract without a proper mash. Not all beer types can be brewed using this procedure.

The next step up incorporates a mini mash of specialty grain, giving you many more choices in the recipe. This process uses the same time and temperature profile—usually an hour at 150°F/66°C—as a full-scale brew, but the mash is limited to a portion of the recipe, and malt extract forms the majority of the base, which adds about an hour to the brew session but allows you to use nearly any kind of specialty malts for a far larger range of possible beers. This method requires a small, insulated container with some sort of false bottom or screen to separate the liquid from the solids when done. As in the extract-plus-steeped-grain method, the full volume of the wort need not be boiled.

Me and my original brewing partner, Ray Spangler, bottling batch number two, c. 1985. Photo by Nancy Cline.

The biggest step up is to go to full grain. This gives you the same control over your recipe and process as the largest commercial breweries and allows you to make totally authentic versions of any beer style on Earth. The drawback is a little more equipment, including a kettle capable of boiling the full volume of the brew and a mash tun that is typically twice the volume of the brew. Setups for mashing range from super simple to rocket-science complicated. For many of us, making equipment is every bit as fun as brewing. However, simple equipment with a skilled brewer will make beer just as good as the most elaborate and costly system. The other investment you have to consider is time. A typical 5-gallon/19-L batch of full-mashed beer will take between 4 and 6 hours; larger batches take a little longer.

These three methods typically represent a progression as a brewer gains more confidence and is corrupted by this seductive and soul-stealing hobby. A brewer might start with extract and a little caramel malt, switch to mini mashes, then after a year or so, move to full mashes. Some people start mashing right away; others are perfectly happy using extract and some specialty grains. It's a matter of personal choice, but you don't have to decide right away. Most of the recipes in this book can be brewed with either an all-grain mash or an extract method.

Extract Brewing Overview

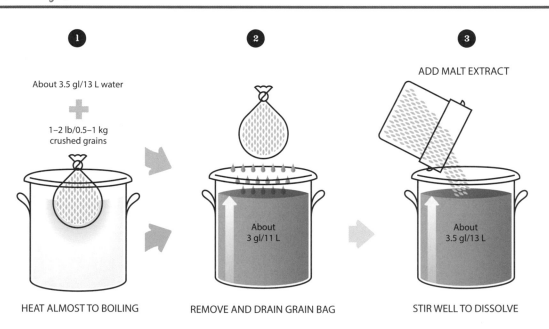

1 About 3.5 gl/13 L water

+

1–2 lb/0.5–1 kg crushed grains

HEAT ALMOST TO BOILING

2 About 3 gl/11 L

REMOVE AND DRAIN GRAIN BAG

3 ADD MALT EXTRACT

About 3.5 gl/13 L

STIR WELL TO DISSOLVE

The extract + steeped grains procedure is a simple 2- to 3-hour extract method that requires minimal equipment and space.

I highly recommend hooking up with a homebrewing club in your area. There are hundreds of them around the world, and places without a thriving club are increasingly rare. Even if you're not normally a joining kind of person, try to make contact anyway. Homebrew clubs are among the friendliest, most supportive, and enjoyable communities on the planet; an invaluable source of advice as well as camaraderie. Being connected to a club will definitely improve your beer and your brewing experience.

Entering competitions and judging them will also improve your brewing. Even if you're not a competitive person, every beer you enter receives a detailed judging form filled out by two or three judges, providing valuable feedback that is well worth the cost of entry. The narrow strictures of brewing to style, even if you chafe at them, are a real test of your ability to control the process for a specific result. Becoming a judge gives you insight into beer's flavors and styles that is nearly impossible to achieve any other way.

Be sure you maintain a fun, positive, and relaxed attitude about this hobby. It's easy to become obsessed with the many technical aspects of brewing, and if you let them, they can turn brewing into a frustrating chore. No matter what, keep the big picture in mind. Beer is about pleasure, sharing, and fun. Watching someone taste your beer and break into a wide smile is one of life's great, soul-satisfying joys.

Ready to start brewing right now?

Turn to page 116

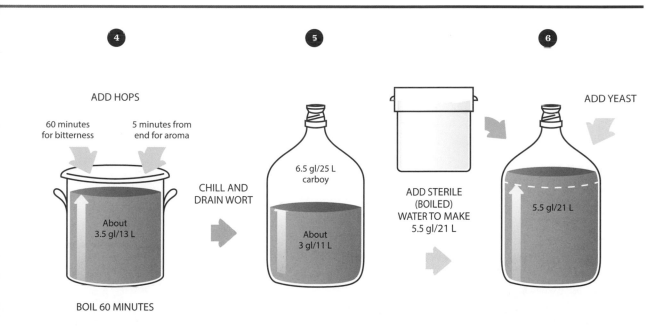

4

ADD HOPS

60 minutes for bitterness

5 minutes from end for aroma

About 3.5 gl/13 L

BOIL 60 MINUTES

CHILL AND DRAIN WORT

5

6.5 gl/25 L carboy

About 3 gl/11 L

ADD STERILE (BOILED) WATER TO MAKE 5.5 gl/21 L

6

ADD YEAST

5.5 gl/21 L

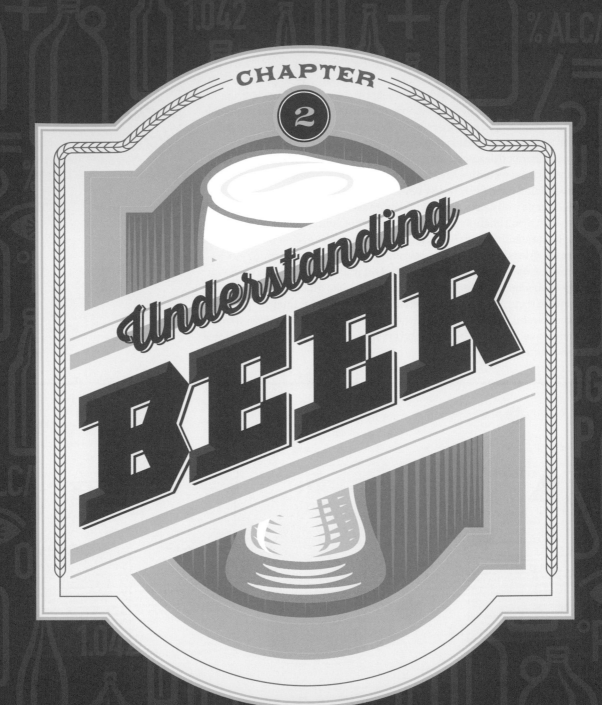

CHAPTER

2

Understanding

BEER

❧❧ The first question is an existential one: Why is there beer? The answer will depend very much on your point of view.

For the people who created it, beer was something a bit magical, a gift of the gods that provided nutrition and safe water, and engendered a relaxed feeling of intoxication that relieved the pains of a hard life and brought the community closer together—"meat and drink and cloth," as it was described centuries ago in England. For some early people, the transformation of the soil, through barley, into beer was a metaphor for human domination of the earth. This is represented in the familiar image of a man we know today as St. George, on horseback slaying a dragon. But he is a late substitution; the rider was actually the god Sabazios, beloved of the barbarians in the Greek world, who associated him with beer and barley. Beer, we could say, is the serpent's blood.

For us today, beer is no less magical, but our needs are different. Three thousand years later, nature has been so thoroughly "conquered" that we are in fear of losing it altogether. The long march of progress has produced many benefits, but has created a land of sorry side effects as well. Modern industrial foods and beverages are mostly pale imitations of their natural counterparts, "food facsimiles," as Brooklyn Brewery's brewmaster Garrett Oliver calls them. Hand-brewed beer can serve as an antidote to this sad state of affairs. So while we long for the good old days, our need for community is as strong as ever. Beer answers the call as it always has, generously lubricating human interactions and making, where it is allowed to, a more civilized world in which to live.

Besides being nutritious, flavorful, easily preserved, and more, beer relieves the cares of everyday life, fosters an esprit de corps (breaking down social barriers), and contributes to a joie de vivre. But it is preeminently a mind-altering substance, tapping into the mysteries of our existence (fermentation itself is magic) and the otherworldly functioning of our minds.

PATRICK E. MCGOVERN, molecular anthropologist and author of *Uncorking the Past* and *Ancient Wine*

ANATOMY of a BEER

Before we start putting a beer together, it might be helpful to take one apart. Beer is a liquid solution of water and alcohol, infused with carbon dioxide, flavored and colored with small amounts of carbohydrates, proteins, minerals, melanoidins, and hundreds of aromatic compounds derived from malt, hops, and yeast. The specific quantities of all these substances—perhaps a thousand or more—give every beer its unique character and appeal.

MEASURABLES

The parameters that follow are the most commonly used numerical descriptors of beer. Many of these qualities can be accurately measured and are commonly used to analyze beer for quality control and other purposes. We will also use these numbers to describe beers and calculate recipes based on quantities of ingredients and other variables. Brewing organizations like the American Society of Brewing Chemists and the European Brewery Convention set the procedures and standards for analyzing beers, measurement units, and other specifics.

GRAVITY

This is the density of wort, or unfermented beer, a measure of dissolved substances, mostly sugar that will be turned into alcohol, plus some miscellaneous unfermentable carbohydrates, proteins, and other material. It is a general indicator of the strength of the soon-to-be beer. Two systems are used to express this density: degrees Plato (°P) and original gravity (OG).

Plato expresses gravity as a percentage by weight. A 10°P wort contains 10 percent by weight of dissolved matter. Degrees Balling is an earlier measure corrected by Dr. Plato, but as Dr. Balling was Czech, you still see his name on the scale relative to Czech brewing. Winemakers use the term *Brix* for the same type of measurement.

The second measure, original gravity, is the same as specific gravity, with the density expressed as a ratio relative to pure water; so a 1.040 wort is 1.040 times as dense as water. Sometimes the decimal point is omitted for convenience. It's important to know that when doing calculations with OG, the "1" and decimal point at the beginning are left out. Otherwise the arithmetic doesn't work. A very approximate rule of thumb is that the significant digit of an OG measurement often approximates alcohol content (1.050 = 5.0% alcohol/volume), although this is affected by many other factors.

Gravity is usually measured with a device called a hydrometer, normally a weighted glass tube with a scale inside that comes to rest at a certain level relative to the surface of the liquid being measured. The denser the liquid, the higher up the scale the hydrometer floats. A refractometer is sometimes used by more geeked-out homebrewers, as it is less messy and offers instant results. Because it measures original gravity by the refractive index of sugar, a refractometer is normally used to measure wort. In finished beer, alcohol distorts the reading, although correction spreadsheets are available.

PLATO TO OG CONVERSION

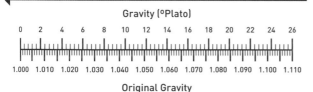

Plato (°P) and original gravity (OG) are two systems that measure the density of the wort, which is an early indicator of beer strength.

TERMINAL GRAVITY

This is expressed in the same units as original gravity but is a measurement of how much gravity is remaining at the end of fermentation, and from which the alcohol content of the finished beer can be calculated. This measurement is distorted by the presence of alcohol, which has a lower gravity than water (see Attenuation, page 34).

BEER COLOR

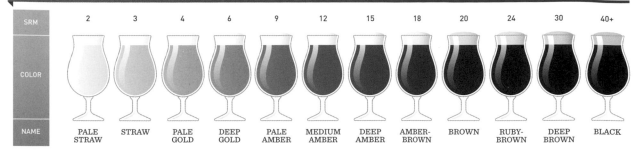

SRM	2	3	4	6	9	12	15	18	20	24	30	40+
COLOR												
NAME	PALE STRAW	STRAW	PALE GOLD	DEEP GOLD	PALE AMBER	MEDIUM AMBER	DEEP AMBER	AMBER-BROWN	BROWN	RUBY-BROWN	DEEP BROWN	BLACK

The range of beer colors and their corresponding Standard Reference Method (SRM) numbers. Note: Although the numbering system is standardized, there is no common agreement on color nomenclature.

ALCOHOL

This is the percentage of ethanol (ethyl alcohol) present in the finished beer. The current international and U.S. federal standard is percent by weight, and that's what we'll be using in this book, but many U.S. state laws are specified in percent by weight, a measurement adopted after Prohibition to make alcohol content look relatively low (4 percent by weight equals 5 percent by volume).

Alcohol content can be measured only by distilling it out of the beer and weighing it. So, most small-scale brewers make a rough calculation based on original versus terminal gravities that is relatively accurate. In order to do this, a "potential alcohol" scale is used. A reading is taken before fermentation and then again at the end. The latter is subtracted from the former, and the result is pretty close to the actual alcohol content of the beer.

POTENTIAL ALCOHOL AND ORIGINAL GRAVITY

Alcohol Potential (% by volume)

0 1 2 3 4 5 6 7 8 9 10 11 12 13

1.000 1.010 1.020 1.030 1.040 1.050 1.060 1.070 1.080 1.090 1.100

Original Gravity

Use this scale to estimate the potential alcohol percentage of your finished beer.

COLOR

This is a single value of lightness/darkness taken by putting a sample of beer into a spectrophotometer and reading the amount of absorption at a particular blue wavelength that is readily absorbed by beer. In the nineteenth century, Joseph Lovibond devised the first beer color scale using a series of colored glass disks. When the spectrophotometric method replaced the earlier method, it was found that the numbers matched up fairly closely with Lovibond's, so sometimes you still see beer and malt color described in degrees Lovibond. U.S. and European standards differ by the thickness of the cuvette used to hold the sample beer—$\frac{1}{2}$ inch in the U.S. Standard Reference Method (SRM), and 1 centimetre for the European Brewery Convention (EBC). Because of this, the same beer measured by the EBC method will have a number almost exactly twice as high as the SRM.

In addition to light and dark, beer may vary in its hue from reddish to yellowish. Methods using multiple colors, called *tristimulus*, can be used to measure beer in a way that matches more closely what the eye sees, but these are rarely used.

BITTERNESS

This is measured by a chemical assay test that requires some fairly scary chemicals and an ultraviolet spectrophotometer. The worldwide standard of Bitterness Units (BU) corresponds to parts-per-million (mg/L) of isomerized alpha acid in the finished beer, which corresponds to the perceived bitterness of the beer. There is a European version (EBU) of the measurement that gives very slightly different numbers, but for the most part these systems can be thought of as the same. Most homebrewers and small-scale brewers use a calculated BU number, which may vary considerably from measured numbers, depending on a large number of factors, especially at the higher end. For super-hoppy beers like double IPAs and their ilk (greater than 80 BU or so), there is some doubt as to the reliability of the standard assays.

ATTENUATION

This is a measure of how complete the fermentation is. It may be approximated by subtracting the final gravity from the original gravity, then dividing that number by the original gravity, and this gives a percentage. So if a 1.050 wort finishes at 1.010, then the 10 is subtracted from the 50, which gives 40, divided by 50, which equals 80 percent. This is called *apparent attenuation*, and it is inaccurate to some degree because the lower density of alcohol distorts the reading, making the beer appear more attenuated than it actually is. With super-dry beers, apparent attenuations of more than 100 percent are possible. To measure real attenuation, the alcohol needs to be distilled out of the beer and measured, then factored into the calculation. For obvious reasons, most small brewers use apparent attenuation, and it serves quite nicely.

The degree of attenuation is affected by a number of factors. Ingredients like sugar or honey are entirely fermentable, so they raise attenuation. Mashing technique also affects the fermentability of the wort, and is another tool the brewer can use to control the sweetness or dryness of the beer. Special techniques like fungus-derived enzymes are used to brew light, dry, and low-carb beers. Finally, yeast strain and fermentation conditions have an effect on attenuation that may be hard to predict.

ATTENUATION IN BEER

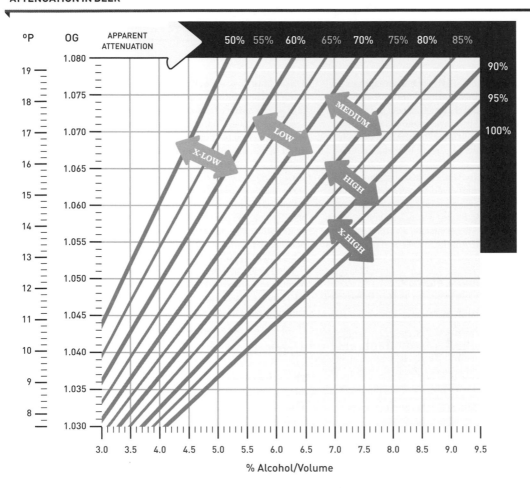

Apparent attenuation measures the completeness of fermentation. High apparent attenuation percentages indicate drier beers, while low apparent attenuation percentages indicate sweeter beers.

INTANGIBLES

We're done with numbers for now, but there are other qualities of beer that are difficult or impossible to measure. These may include more concrete attributes but describe some sensory qualities that can be just as important as the measurable metrics. Body and texture are important in beer, as is head retention, all of which may be affected by its colloidal, or protein, structure. *Balance* is a term used to describe the way different flavors and aromas interact, especially hops and malt, but it's not always just those two; other qualities that come into play include roastiness, acidity, fruitiness, and more. I prefer the term *contrast*, which better sums up the dynamic interaction of elements that add interest as you taste. *Drinkability* is the old warhorse term industrial brewers used as a sad excuse for how little they have to offer consumers. It is nonetheless an important quality to all brewers because few can make much of a business out of beers that are only sippable. *Complexity* is an obvious term encompassing a lot, and is always desirable, even in the palest and most refreshing beer. There will be a much more extended discussion of these qualities in chapter 7.

Beyond all that is something I just call *wonderfulness*. It's a summation of everything tasty, magical, and profound in a beer. It's a highly subjective and personal measure but one of the most important.

TASTING *and* EVALUATING BEER

Beer is a product that affects all our senses in complex and profound ways. Despite the common notion that beer is a rather simple product, it is in fact a good deal more complex than wine, with twice as many known flavor compounds. Learning to be a good beer taster means understanding your own sensory system and how it interacts with the huge range of tastes, aromas, and textures that every beer presents. It's a big challenge, but a worthy one, and as entertaining a pursuit as you can imagine.

OUR SENSES

Our eyes, lips, tongue, and nose are exquisitely attuned to appreciate beer's pleasures. Everything we do in the brewing process is centered around providing an amazing sensory experience. It's not just an important part of what beer is; beyond the alcohol, the sensory experience is the *only* thing that beer is.

It makes sense that brewers learn to be expert tasters, ideally at a far higher and more informed level than the people who drink their beer. Without good sensory chops, it is impossible to evaluate how the various ingredients interact in a recipe, how the brewing process has affected the flavor, what contribution the yeast has made, and to recognize off-flavors and problems with style. It's a serious discipline. Tasting is something that brewers have to work on with as much effort and determination as they do the actual brewing.

As a beer enthusiast and brewer, you already have some tasting experience, but becoming an expert taster involves attention and regular practice. It's also too complex to do much more than a brief overview of the subject in this book. The good news is that all this hard work actually involves putting some beer in your mouth.

The first step is to understand your sensory system. The senses of smell and taste have been shaped by hundreds of millions of years of evolution to inform us of good and bad things in the environment; they are the gate-keepers of what we consume. Smell and taste are processed in parts of our brains that are reactive and emotional rather than intellectual, which is one reason developing a good vocabulary of aromas is so difficult. It's a long journey from our lizard brain way up to where language is processed.

Sight can be problematic in beer tasting. Our visual sense is so overpowering that it can dominate other senses, forcing them to confirm what our eyes see even when they're getting it wrong. Wine judges presented with white wine colored red find all the expected fruit: cherries, bramble, mulberries, and so on. Beer people are not immune to this syndrome. If we are aware of it, we can use it like any perceptual reality harnessed to stoke the fires of art. Appearance matters. Proper presentation of beer is hugely important because it actually makes the beer taste better.

The tongue is a fairly straightforward chemical detector and the sense of taste is shared by other parts of the mouth, including the palate and inner surfaces of the cheeks and lips. Once in the mouth, chemicals in food and drink reach the taste buds, which are specialized cells living in the *papillae* (those bumps on your tongue) and elsewhere inside the mouth. These chemicals, which contain minerals, acidity, carbohydrates, and other substances we are sensitive to, fire off neural impulses that reach the parts of our brain that can make sense of them. Once believed to be limited to just sweet, sour, salty, and bitter sensations, we now know that we have many more, such as umami (a marker for protein), fat, carbonation, some forms of calcium like the flavor-enhancing kokumi, and metals such as iron and copper, and science will probably discover others. There is evidence to suggest that we are equipped to recognize all ten of the amino acids essential for life, but how we sense and interpret this is still a mystery. Sweet and fat tastes indicate high nutritional content, and our desire for them is innate. Bitterness is a warning from our friends in the plant world that whatever we're tasting might be poison, and for that reason we are averse to it as well as highly sensitive. Enjoyment of bitter tastes runs counter to millions of years of evolution, which is why it takes most people a while to acquire a taste for bitter beers.

There is very little truth to the old tongue map that located different tastes on specific parts of the tongue. In reality, the front half is equally sensitive to all tastes. At the back of the tongue there are areas on both sides that are somewhat more sensitive to sour, and across the very back is a row of taste buds that are more sensitive to bitterness and possibly other complex flavors like umami.

> *Probably the biggest mistake I see is a lack of objective tasting skills. Until that skill is developed, new brewers can't embark on the path of improving their brewing, as they have not yet recognized the off-flavor.*

HAROLD GULBRANSEN, award-winning brewer and QUAFF Homebrew Club organizer

Because of the way the chemical triggers are processed into nerve impulses, different tastes have different time constants. Sour and salty, for example, fire very rapidly to the brain, and register instantly. Because sweet, bitter, and umami are processed through intermediate proteins, they take a little longer to hit us and a little longer to leave. The result is that a taste is not just a single instant but a little movie that plays as different flavors come and go. One sip may last a minute or more.

Our sense of smell, known as olfaction, is much more complex than our sense of taste. A thousand different receptor types create about ten thousand different aromas by generating patterns of responses that are interpreted by the olfactory cortex, turned into "odor objects," and sent elsewhere in the the brain, including inner, ancient structures like the hippocampus and amygdala. These are the seats of emotion and memory, among other things, responsible for those vivid flashbacks that sometimes accompany a smell and send us back to a moment in our childhood. Research has shown that even aromas we are unaware of can affect our emotional state.

To further complicate things, we actually have two noses located in slightly different places. The first, the orthonasal, is right where you'd expect it to be, at the top of our nasal cavity. This is the sniffer we use to identify and evaluate and is somewhat more analytical than the other. The second center, the retronasal, is located just a bit farther back in our heads, and it responds to smells traveling up from the back of our mouths and throats. It is wired to parts of our brains that resonate with feelings of familiarity, preference, and dislike—it is the broccoli-hating, chocolate-loving part of your nose. Getting some aromas into both centers is important for a thorough evaluation of a beer's aroma. This is why in critical tasting, various techniques are used for letting the liquid warm in the mouth and release aromas that exit through the nose. It's also why swallowing beer, rather than spitting, is the norm during critical tasting or judging.

Flavor is a rather indefinite term. It is used casually to describe those sensations that come from aromas but present themselves in the mouth rather than the tongue. Science is coming around to the view that some of this is likely due to the way the retronasal center is wired; those "aromas" often come off more as flavors.

Mouthfeel is another important facet of beer. Nerves in our mouths respond to wetness, the prickle of carbonation, body, creaminess, astringency, and other stimuli. These characteristics add a lot to beer, and in certain styles they are very important. Some, like astringency, are not very pleasant and are definitely flaws in beer whenever they're encountered.

I always stress the significance of aroma. I have heard it argued that between 70 and 90 percent of total flavor perception is aroma. We always use the word taste. "This tastes like a strawberry." There are more than 360 contributing aromas in a strawberry, but only 5 (or 6) tastes. Nope. It's all in the nose, so you really gotta make the most of it. Swirl your glass; get those volatiles volatizing! Waft, short sniffs, longer sniff, and retronasal. But remember, this is it! Don't do it again. Don't fatigue, trust your first instincts—they are always right.

LAUREN SALAZAR, beer blending and sensory specialist, New Belgium Brewing Co.

THE TASTING ACT

There are a number of different types of situations where beer is critically tasted, from informal evaluations to competition judging to rigorous professional taste panel work. While the specifics may differ, the actual process of tasting is much the same for all situations, and once you learn how to do it, you'll find yourself approaching your first sip of every beer this way, no matter how bawdy the beerhall. I even find myself habitually sniffing my water glass these days.

To give every beer its best shot, try to keep distractions to a minimum, be sure the beer is in good condition, at an appropriate temperature, and served at the right fill level in an appropriate glass. White wine glasses with a slightly incurved rim are best for critical tasting. Never fill more than about a third of the way full.

First, smell. Many aroma compounds are extremely volatile and may vanish after a minute or two. Take small, short sniffs, not deep inhalations. When you overdo it, you saturate the receptors and they stop firing signals to the brain. If that happens, to reset take a short break or sniff something else, like the back of your hand.

Once you have an initial sense of the aroma, have a good look for color, clarity, and the staying power of the head. Then, take a sip. What are the tastes on your tongue? Any sweetness or acidity will register first. Pay attention to the bitterness as it builds and recedes. Let the liquid linger in your mouth. As it warms up, it will release more aroma. Breathe very gently in and out with your mouth partly closed, trying to get some of those aromas to go up and out through your nose. Finally, swallow, and breathe out slowly through your nose. At the very end, focus on the aftertaste. It should be clean and pleasant, in tune with the rest of the beer. If there are astringent or cardboardy, oxidized flavors, this is where you will find them.

Take notes on the experience. Writing things down helps you focus; and then you have a record of the experience. Pay special attention to those little aroma-triggered memory flashbacks. Bizarre as they seem, they can often put you in a place where you can name a very specific beer flavor chemical you encountered years ago in quite different circumstances. Unexpected memories of banana Runts, theater popcorn, or nail polish can point the way to quite specific beer aromas.

You have several goals. Number-one is to discover what's in the glass. Malt, hops, fermentation flavors, sweetness, bitterness, minerality, acidity—what do you get? Dig a little deeper. What's the malt base? What malt types are adding the color, the caramel, the toastiness, the creamy texture? Same goes for the hops. Can you identify the nation of origin? Some hop varieties are pretty distinctive and can be called out by name if you've had some practice.

How is the beer put together? Think about what recipe you might use to make this beer.

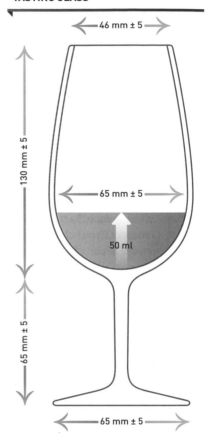

ISO (INTERNATIONAL ORGANIZATION FOR STANDARDIZATION) STANDARD TASTING GLASS

46 mm ± 5

130 mm ± 5

65 mm ± 5

50 ml

65 mm ± 5

65 mm ± 5

Although this glass is the gold standard for critical tasting, any similarly shaped vessel will do nicely. Note that the proper level for tasting is about one-third full.

Facing page: Aftermath of a commercial competition in Rimini, Italy in 2010.

Another important goal is to nitpick for flaws. A list of sensory defects is provided on the Atlas of Beer Flavor and Character on page 40. A critical evaluation will reveal that many beers have some small defect that affects flavor or aroma. If it's your beer, you sure want to know about it.

Another task, especially in competitions, is evaluating whether the beer fits a designated style. This is central to judging in the Beer Judge Certification Program (BJCP) and World Beer Cup/Great American Beer Festival (GABF) competitions, where every beer is compared to a published standard. Sometimes a small deviation—ester aromas in a lager, for example—will be enough to knock a beer from contention, no matter how good it tastes otherwise. To make this sort of evaluation, you really need a good working knowledge of the guidelines, plus a sort of internal calibration of color, bitterness, gravity, aroma, and the other parameters that define a style.

If you have the chance, it is really helpful to travel to the classic beer-producing regions to get on intimate terms with the different beer traditions. Beer that has crossed an ocean is often stale, changing a whole suite of subtle characteristics. The brands that are exported are not always the most representative examples of their home traditions and, for sure, a long voyage changes them noticeably. All beer tastes best and most characteristic when close to home.

Finally, step back and think about the intangibles. Is the beer balanced, lively, full of interesting tastes, textures, and aromas? Do they all work together, and if so, how? Are there two, three, or more different tastes that share the spotlight? Do they play nicely together? Does the beer feel like one thing all the way from the first whiff to that last lingering aftertaste? Sometimes, it does not. Would you drink a pint of this? Two? Would you pay for it? Lust after it? Will you be talking about this beer a year from now?

Beer-Tasting Checklist

 SMELL

Take short sniffs, and try to capture those first impressions. Pinpoint aromas as specifically as you can. Use those memory flashbacks!

 LOOK

Examine color, clarity, head retention.

 TASTE

Observe first flavors of sweetness, acidity, and pay attention as these drop away and bitterness builds. Are there any other flavors?

 RETRONASAL

As you swallow, breathe out slowly through your nose. This is your second shot at capturing the beer's aroma. The impressions may seem like flavor rather than aroma here.

 MOUTHFEEL

Note dryness, creaminess, body, etc. What about carbonation?

 AFTERTASTE/FINISH

What do you sense after swallowing? Is the finish clean, astringent, quick, long, yummy?

 STYLE

Is the beer what it purports to be? How does it stack up against other beers of its ilk?

 INTANGIBLES

Do you like it? Do all the parts work together to create a coherent idea? Does it have any magic?

AN ATLAS OF BEER FLAVOR AND CHARACTER

BREWING

PROCESS

Recipe
Water Chemistry
   Minerality
   Harshness
Brewhouse
   Mash
   Boiling
Fermentation
   Sanitation
   Yeast Selection
   Yeast Health
   Temperature
   Conditioning
Handling
   Freshness
   Oxidation/Stale Flavors
   Lightstruck
   Carbonation

INGREDIENTS

Malt
   Base
   Color/Flavor
Adjuncts
   Grains
   Sugar
Hops
   Bittering
   Aroma
Water
Yeast
Spices
Fruit/Vegetables

INTANGIBLE

AESTHETIC

Balance/Contrast
   Hop vs. Sweet Malt
   Roast Components
   Acidity
   Two-Way, Three-Way . . .
Drinkability
Fatiguing
Depth/Complexity
Subtlety
Coherence
Memorability
Originality
Deliciousness!

STYLISTIC

Gravity/Alcohol
Flavor Intensity
Drinkability
Color
Malt Character
Hop Aroma Intensity
Hop Character
Dry/Sweet
Body
Natural Character
Fermentation Character
   Yeast Strain
   Fermentation Temperature

SENSORY

VISUAL

Beer Color
   Light/Dark
   Hue (red/yellow)
Clarify/Haze
Head
   Color
   Density/Creaminess
   Longevity

TONGUE TASTES

Sweet
Sour
Bitter
Carbonation
Salty/Mineral
Metallic
Umami (aged beer)

AROMA

Pleasant/Unpleasant
Intensity
Complexity
Appropriateness

MOUTHFEEL

Carbonation
Body
Creamy
Oily
Astringent/Harsh
Tannic
Heat (chile)
Hot (alcoholic)

Beer is evaluated on a wide range of brewing, sensory, and aesthetic components. After some practice, a trained beer taster should be able to disassemble a beer into its component parts based on how the beer presents itself in the glass. This is a skill that may take years to master but is key to being able to brew world-class beers. This chart breaks the task into brewing, sensory, and intangible areas, all things a good taster should be thinking about when critically tasting a beer. The terms on these two pages will be discussed in detail in the next few chapters.

The right-hand side expands the aroma vocabulary of the wide range of beers brewed today. While some are negative in every situation, be aware that many of these are highly dependent on context and beer style—what is appropriate in one style may be completely out of character in another style.

AROMA VOCABULARY

FERMENTATION —POSITIVE

Yeasty
Alcohol/Ethanol
Fruity/Estery
 Apply/Ethyl Hexanoate
 Apricots
 Banana/Isoamyl Acetate
 Bubblegum
 Melon
 Peach
 Pear
 Strawberry
 Pineapple
Phenolic
 Black Pepper
 Clove/4-Vinyl Guaiacol
 Gumdrops/Allspice
Sulfur
 Burnt Match/Sulfite
 Rotten Eggs/Sulfide
Woody
Aged
 Leathery (aged beer)
 Sherry
Buttery (tiny amounts only)

FERMENTATION —NEGATIVE

Yeasty
Acetaldehyde
Acidic
 Sour/Tangy
 Acetic
 Lactic
Chemical
 Acetone
 Alcohol/Ethanol
 Rubbing Alcohol/Fuses
Fruity
 Estery (problem in lagers)
 Apple/Ethyl Hexanoate
 Banana/Isoamyl Acetate
 Bubblegum
 Overripe Pineapple
Sulfur
 Burnt Match/Sulfite/
  Sulfure Dioxide
Cooked Cabbage
 Cooked Corn/Dimethyl
  Sulfide (DMS)
 Rotten Eggs/Hydrogen Sulfide
Animal
 Buttery/Diacetyl
 Goaty/Caprylic, Caproic, etc.
 Barnyard/Horse Blanket

Phenolic
 Band-Aid/Chlorephenol
 Medicinal
 Plastic
 Bakelite
Aged
 Soapy/Autolyzed
 Soy Sauce/Umami
 Sherry
 Beeswax

MALTS AND ADJUNCTS —POSITIVE

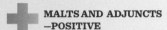

Grainy
Bread
Corn Grits
Cracker
Malt
Biscuit
Honey
Cookie
Caramel
Nuts
Toffee
Figs
Raisins
Prunes
Molasses
Spicy (Rye)
Rum
Toasted Marshmallow
Burnt Sugar
Toast
Roast
Coffee
Chocolate
Espresso

MALTS AND GRAINS —NEGATIVE

Worty
Cooked Corn/DMS
Cidery
Extracty/Ball-Point Pen
Grassy
Astringent
Oxidized
Papery/Cardboard
Husky/Phenolic/Smoky
Ashtray/Campfire
Bitter
Burnt

SPICED BEERS —POSITIVE

Coriander
Grains of Paradise
Star Anise
Licorice
Ginger
Cinnamon
Allspice
Lemongrass
Chile
Pumpkin Pie

SPICED BEERS —NEGATIVE

Hot-Dog Water
Vegetal
Overpowering

HOPS —POSITIVE

Grass
Spicy*
Herbal
 Sage
 Thyme
 Mint
 Dill
Fruity
 Apricot
 Passionfruit
 Vinous/Sauvignon
Citrus
 Grapefruit
 Lemon
 Lime
 Orange
Floral
 Rose
 Geranium
 Lavender
Resin
 Pine
 Sagebrush

*A rather indefinite term usu-
ally applied to hops, especially
varieties like Saaz and Styrian
Goldings types that are not easy
to describe in other terms.

HOPS —NEGATIVE

Catty (blackcurrant/*Ribes*)
Earth
Onion/Garlic
Astringent
Cheesy/Isovaleric Acid
Lightstruck
 Burnt Rubber
 Skunky

WILD AND WOOD-AGED —POSITIVE

Acid/Sour
 Vinegar/Acetic
 Lactic
Alcohol/Ethanol
Fruity/Estery
 Apple/Ethyl Hexanoate
 Apricots
 Banana/Isoamyl Acetate
 Pineapple
 Melon
 Peach
 Pear
 Strawberry
Phenolic
 Black Pepper
 Clove/4-Vinyl Guaiacol
Earthy
 Barnyard
 Horse Blanket
 Tobacco
Yeasty
 Vinous
Woody
 Oaky
 Vanilla
 Coconut
 Tannic
 Rosewood

WILD AND WOOD-AGED —NEGATIVE

Acid/Sour
 Vinegar/Acetic
Estery/Ethyl Acetate
Earthy
 Musty/Trichloroanisole

JUDGING, COMPETITIONS, and CERTIFICATIONS

Learning to be a great taster is something that you can do on your own, but it is far more productive in the company of others, especially those with more experience. The best way to put yourself in this position is to become a judge and stay active in homebrew competitions. You will taste a huge range of beers, often in the company of some very skilled judges, which is an incredible learning experience. In fact, even after evaluating beer seriously for more than twenty-five years, every time I sit down at a judging table, I learn something new.

The Beer Judge Certification Program (BJCP) is an all-volunteer nonprofit organization that certifies judges and sanctions competitions around the world. In order to become certified, you are required to take a test that covers a range of brewing and stylistic knowledge, as well as your ability to taste beers, rate them according to a style category, and identify some faults. A certain score gets you into the basic "recognized" judge category; higher scores and more experience points allow you to rise to higher levels of certification.

Competition organizers are always looking for people to help, so the best way to get started is to volunteer as a steward at your local competition. This job involves presenting judges with the proper beers in the right condition, and because you're hovering around the judging tables, it's a good way to get a feel for how the process goes. Some homebrew clubs regularly do practice judging; it's easy to accommodate a request for this, so don't feel shy about showing up at the club meeting and asking.

While there is no official preparatory course, many people preparing for the BJCP exam will form study groups and meet every week or two to taste and discuss the specifics of the twenty-eight styles of beer, mead, and cider that form the BJCP category list. You can download the BJCP guidelines in various forms along with other study material at www.bjcp.org.

Improving your ability as a beer taster is different from most learning we do. Tasting involves some very ancient and often hidden parts of our brains, and training them isn't as straightforward as memorizing some facts and figures. But if you do put the effort into it, your brain will respond and you will emerge a much more sensitive, capable, and maybe even self-aware person. Who knew beer could do *that*?

> *My training to become a beer judge was the most important factor for improvement of my brewing.*
>
> **JOE FORMANEK,** flavor chemist and winner of 2000 and 2006 Ninkasi Awards

Edward Bronson

Facing page; row by row from top left: Homebrew labels by Kim Theeson, Robert Alvord, Jim LaFleur, Steve Mastny, Grzegorz Zagłoba/Bartosz Wojtyra, Bogumil Rychlak, Randy LaCoille, Matteo Pellis/Alberto Bodritti, Szymon Tracz, Łukasz Szynkiewicz, Kim Theesen, Juleidy Peña, Tara Leigh Z, Marcin Lipiński, and Steve Mastny.

CHAPTER

3

Brewing INGREDIENTS

❧ It should be obvious that an understanding of the major ingredients is an important key to brewing great beer.

Malt and other grains provide the sugars that will be converted into alcohol by the yeast, as well as texture, mouthfeel, color, and a host of amazing aromas. Hops contribute a pleasing bitterness that brings the sweetness of malt into balance and adds complex perfumy aromas that resonate with their point of origin. Water blends into the background when used correctly, but can be a source of problems if one assumes all waters are the same. And yeast is no less important than any of these, but it's really a process more than an ingredient, so we'll cover it elsewhere.

Becoming personally familiar with the flavors of ingredients like malts and hops is a good first step for every brewer. Just like a chef, you have to get your hands dirty and stick your face in everything whenever you can. It is useful to do this both with ingredients in their raw form, and as they manifest themselves in that beer glass in your hand.

Just as important is an understanding of the underlying chemistry. Malts, for example, display a characteristic spectrum of aromas created when they are dried in the kiln or roasted afterward. Malt may be any shade between ivory and black, but color tells only part of the story. Knowing how the kilning process translates into malt aroma flavor helps you make better choices when making your beer.

> *The thing that inspires me the most might be the unbelievable possibilities in those four freakin' ingredients [malt, hops, water, yeast]. Humans have been making beer for thousands of years and there are still new beer flavors being revealed—and we can be part of that. New learning—yum.*

TONY MAGEE, founder and so much more, Lagunitas Brewing Company, Petaluma, CA

Barley has been the soul of beer for ten thousand years.

Hops add a spicy zip to beer and balance the sweetness of malt. All hops share the same bitter taste, but the amount of bitterness varies by a number of factors. It's a different story with aroma. Every hop variety has a certain personality, and the growing region puts a further stamp on it. I've tried to organize hops in a way that helps make sense of the challenging world of hop varieties and make it easier to find substitutes when necessary.

Water isn't nearly as inspiring an ingredient as malt and hops, but it is no less important. Mineral ions within it affect the brewing process in both positive and negative ways, depending on whether the beer is dark or pale, bitter or malty. It is worth taking the time to get to know your water and figure out what kind of treatment is needed to make the best possible beers from it. After some initial calculations, it becomes a matter of routine.

BARLEY, MALT, *and* GRAINS

With enough ingenuity, beer can be brewed from nearly any grain, but in Western culture barley is the heart of beer. In its malted form, barley normally contributes all the color and alcohol as well as much of the flavor of beer, although wheat, other grains, and sugars may contribute as well.

Barley is just perfect for making beer. It is a miraculous package of starch, proteins, enzymes, and other components. This simple grain contains a huge range of possibilities that we can transform into an astonishing range of different beers. A barley seed is a complex package of biochemistry, with specific characteristics, behaviors, and needs, all of which we must understand in order to get it to do what we want, as brewers have done since ancient times.

Barley is a grass of the genus *Hordeum*. Wheat is closely related, as is spelt— all have been used for brewing at various times and places. Barley was among the first grains domesticated in the Middle East at about 10,000 B.C.E. Early agricultural people carefully selected for desired qualities, replanting the choicest seeds, and ultimately creating strains perfectly suited to brewing beer: with low protein, lack of gluten (compared to wheat), and kernels that threshed with the husks intact. It's all pretty good evidence that ancient people were brewing beer, because barley with those characteristics is not all that great for bread or anything else but gruel, boring gruel.

Barley is classified according to the number of kernels at each position along the stalk: two-, four-, or six-row. The original wild form of barley is two-row, *Hordeum distichum*. Because of its clean flavor and low protein content, two-row is still the premium choice, especially for all-malt beers. Six-row forms have a greater proportion of husk and protein; neither is necessarily a good thing for brewing, and if used in large proportions, can add harsh astringent flavors and even haze in beers. Because of its high level of enzymes, six-row malt is best used for brewing beers with rice or corn adjuncts, which lack enzymes of their own. It is also used in traditional

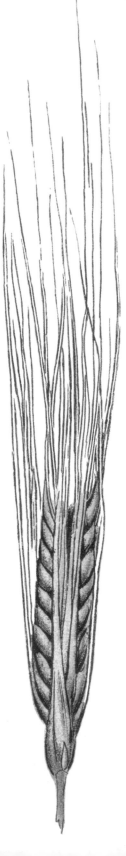

Belgian witbier, as the classic recipes contain as much as 50 percent unmalted wheat and oats, which also lack usable brewing enzymes. Four-row varieties (*Hordeum tetrastichum*) exist but are rarely cultivated.

Six-row barleys prefer hot climates such as those of North Africa, India, Mexico, and also do well in the Upper Midwest of the United States. Two-row barleys prefer more temperate climes such as the American Northwest and northern Europe. Within a particular type, the protein content—an important brewing parameter—tends to reflect the richness of the soil. American barley varieties, whether two- or six-rowed, have a higher protein content than their European cousins, while Australian and South American varieties tend to be low in protein due to the thin soil there.

While there are differences in specific strains and growing locations, they tend to be much less important than in a beverage like wine. A few barley types such as England's famous Maris Otter, do exhibit *terroir*, that unique expression of locality, but most strains are very much a commodity, chosen for yield, disease resistance, and other agricultural characteristics in addition to brewing value. It is the work of the maltster more than the soil or the weather to make the most important imprint on the malt.

MALTING

In its raw state, barley is almost flavorless and nearly impossible to brew with, but malting transforms it in profound ways, making it much more suitable for brewing. Simply put, malting is nothing more than a controlled sprouting followed by drying that may add varying amounts of color. Malting creates a product with a crumbly texture, a low gelatinization temperature, multiple enzyme systems essential for various brewing tasks, a readily available starch, plentiful proteins for yeast nutrition, and a neutral husk that makes a perfect filter with which to strain the sweet wort out at the end of the mash. When we're done, it also tastes great in the glass. It's a testament to the ingenuity and persistence of our ancient ancestors who shaped it from a scruffy wild grass to the noble thoroughbred it is today.

Only seed-grade barley is used for malting. A high level of germination (sprouting) is important for quality brewing because of efficiency, flavor, and other reasons. Only a small percentage of barley makes the cut; the rest goes for animal feed. Maltsters also look for other qualities that matter to brewers: uniform kernel size, protein content, and some very beer-specific things like glucans and SMM (S-Methylmethionine; the precursor to DMS, Dimethyl sulfides, a sulfur compound), which can be problematic in certain quantities.

After a good wash comes a steeping, which takes the grain from 12 percent moisture to more than 40 percent, waking it from a dormant state and readying it for growth. This usually takes 2 to 4 days. The grain is then held in a process called "couching," during which the grain starts to sprout.

Top to bottom: Barley is sprayed and soaked in water to bring up the moisture content; transferring the sprouting malt out of the steeping tanks; a mechanical turning device rests at the far end of the malting floor. Photos courtesy of Briess Industries, Inc.

Driven by hormonal signals sent by the germ, the grain begins to "chit," or show a rootlet at one end. Inside the husk, a shoot starts to develop. As malting proceeds, the shoot and roots continue to grow, and their length is an indication of the changes that are occurring inside the kernel. During this time the grain takes up oxygen. Sprouting produces so much heat that unless precautions are taken, the malt can actually set itself on fire. Traditional floor malting relies on a controlled turning of the grain, while more modern methods pump fresh air through the grain in deep beds to supply oxygen and remove heat.

BARLEY SEED ANATOMY

AWN (SPIKE) Thin, barbed spike at the end of the barley kernel when still attached to the seed head.

GLUME Thin, hairy spike on the kernels when on the seed head before threshing. Two per kernel.

BARLEY KERNEL AT THE END OF MALTING

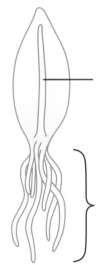

ACROSPIRE The small shoot that will eventually become the stem and leaves of the growing plant. In barley, it is protected under the husks until it reaches the far end of the kernel, when it will begin to protrude. The malting process is usually stopped just prior to this, when the acrospire reaches the full length of the kernel.

ROOTLETS As the name suggest, tiny nascent roots, typically seen in a fully developed barley sprout. These are of no brewing value and are removed after kilning.

Nodding heads of barley make a beautiful sight.

BARLEY KERNEL CROSS-SECTION

ALEURONE Thin protein-rich structure that surrounds the starchy endosperm. It is the source of about 30% of barley's proteins, and is especially rich in enzymes. Actively involved in malting the aleurone is the source of enzymes that break down the protein capsules containing the plant's starch reserve and the source of starch-degrading amylase enzymes. There is a sub-aleurone layer as well, that is intermediate in composition between the aleurone and the endosperm.

EPITHELIUM A layer of cells between the scutellum and the endosperm.

SCUTELLUM A shield-like structure that forms the boundary between the embryo and the endosperm.

These layers are involved in the transport of enzymes into the endosperm and of nutrients from the endosperm into the developing embryo.

PLUMULE Embryonic site from which the acrospire (shoot) will form.

RADICLE Embryonic site from which the root will form.

TESTA (SEED COAT) The outermost layer of the seed itself, often referred to as the bran, along with the pericarp. Mainly present as protection.

ENDOSPERM Starchy reserve that forms the bulk of the weight of the kernel, and from which the sugars used in brewing are liberated. Structure is of small balls or capsules of starch surrounded by protein shells. When these protein capsules are degraded during malting, the texture of the kernel changes from flinty to chalky.

PERICARP Inner membrane with photosynthetic activity, surrounding the barley kernel. A component of bran.

LEMMA, PALEA The husks of barley that are largely cellulose but form the filter bed in the mash, allowing the wort to run off.

EMPTY CELLS

EMBRYO The "brains" of the plant that controls germination and from which the acrospire and rootlets will emerge during sprouting (malting).

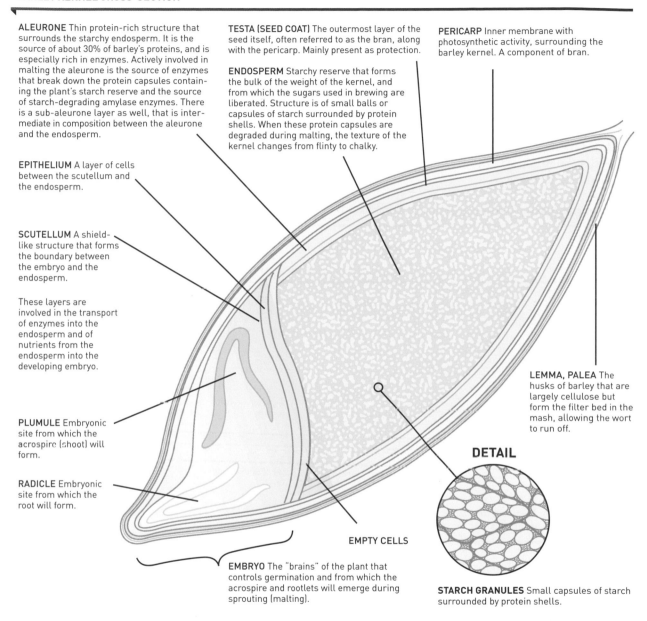

DETAIL

STARCH GRANULES Small capsules of starch surrounded by protein shells.

The anatomy of a barley seed reveals a complex structure that is perfect for beer brewing.

Meanwhile, enzymes are hydrating and folding into their working configurations. Proteolytic (protein-cutting) enzymes are chewing holes in the protein membranes that coat the little balls of starch that are the seed's food reserves. As a result, the kernel changes from a hard "flinty" texture—think unpopped popcorn—to a soft and chalky texture that will yield easily to the malt mill. The amount of this change, which proceeds from the germ end to the tip, is called modification. Some historical malts were only lightly modified, meaning there are some hard ends remaining; special mashes like decoctions were needed to deal with this. These malts are available nowadays as specialty items.

BARLEY SEED DURING MALTING

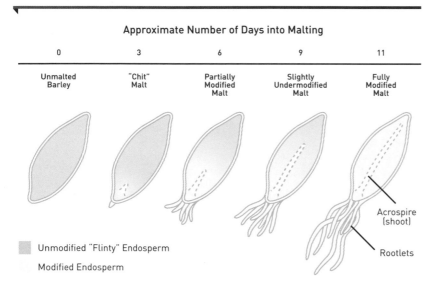

Approximate Number of Days into Malting

0	3	6	9	11
Unmalted Barley	"Chit" Malt	Partially Modified Malt	Slightly Undermodified Malt	Fully Modified Malt

Acrospire (shoot)

Rootlets

Unmodified "Flinty" Endosperm

Modified Endosperm

This barley seed has been fully modified during the malting process. Its kernel has changed from a hard "flinty" texture to a soft and chalky texture that will yield easily to the malt mill.

However, due to a quest for efficiency in the commercial brewhouse, fully modified malt is the norm these days. It responds beautifully to simple infusion mashes, during which the malt is steeped at a single temperature, without the step-ups common in the older recipes. Many of the old techniques like decoction work best with poorly modified malt, and using them with modern malt can actually cause problems with the body and head of the beer.

KILNING *and* ROASTING

When the malt has reached the desired degree of modification, it is kilned—a controlled heating that removes moisture, stopping further development of the plant, and stabilizing the malt for long-term storage.

The process of color and aromatic development during kilning is known as browning. Every time you pop a slice of bread into the toaster, you're doing it. Apply heat to some starchy or sugary foodstuff and, in time, color and flavors develop. Fresh-baked bread, toast, caramel, roasted meat, sautéed onions, chocolate, coffee, and many other foods share this chemistry. It would be a very bland world without it.

There are two types of browning: caramelization and Maillard browning. Both involve transforming carbohydrates, using heat, into color and aroma compounds. They differ by the presence or lack of nitrogen; simple caramel lacks it, but Maillard browning incorporates it. Each has its own personality, but in both, heat causes chemical reactions that transform sugars into two distinct sets of reaction products: melanoidins and small molecules known as heterocyclics.

Melanoidins are large, polymeric molecules with little aroma and varying amounts of bitterness, which may be important to consider in a recipe. They give beer its beautiful color. Science hasn't sorted out the specific chemistry of them, but it is known that lightly kilned malts tend to show more yellowish colors, while caramel and black malts often appear somewhat more reddish, an important detail if you're trying to nail a red beer.

Melanoidins are also important in redox reactions—the complex chemistry of oxidation so important to beer aging and flavor stability. Dark malts can act as oxidation scavengers, donating electrons to oxidizers (which is really what oxidation is all about) in one part of the brewing process, which is good, but then under certain conditions, releasing them again, which is bad. On balance, dark beers are less subject to oxidized flavors during aging, but melanoidins created in pale beer, say by direct-fired boiling, can be problematic.

Malt aroma comes from heterocyclic, or ring-shaped, molecules bearing one or more "foreign" atoms like oxygen, nitrogen, or sulfur somewhere on their ring. They have fire-related names like pyrrholes, pyrazines, furanones, and so on, and are amazingly potent aromatics; many have thresholds in the parts-per-trillion range. There are hundreds of them in malt and beer, and they create the full spectrum of malt aromatics: bread, crackers, cookies/cake, caramel, nuts, toast, roast, coffee, and chocolate.

Small variations in process create very different malt flavors. In fact, every different combination of carbohydrate, nitrogen, time, temperature, pH, and moisture level will give a different end product, a key fact to consider when choosing malts for a recipe.

There are many ways to put together a beer of a given color, which means that beers with identical color can have dramatically different flavors. A small amount of a dark malt will make a dramatically different beer than one brewed with a larger amount of not-so-dark malt. And further, even different malts with the same color can have dramatically different aromas, caused by different moisture levels or temperatures during kilning. Although color is important, it is also key to get the flavor right for the particular style or recipe idea.

Most malt flavor and aroma comes from Maillard browning, but in some malt types, non-Maillard caramelization dominates. With caramel malts, a good deal of malt starch has already been converted into sugars—you can tell by the glassy crunch—and much of this sugar will convert to caramel directly without incorporating nitrogen. Rather than the normal bread-to-roast spectrum of malt aromas, the aromas of caramel malt range from sweet caramel to toasted marshmallow to burnt sugar.

Maltsters use two different pieces of equipment to dry and color malt: a kiln and a roaster. Kilns do the bulk of the work, with lots of air movement and a lower range of temperatures. They drive off moisture and, as moisture drops and temperatures rise, begin to add color to the malt.

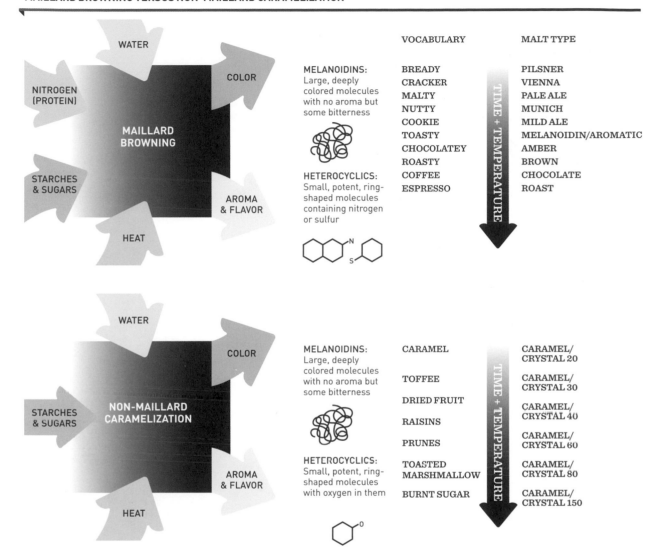

MELANOIDINS: Large, deeply colored molecules with no aroma but some bitterness

HETEROCYCLICS: Small, potent, ring-shaped molecules containing nitrogen or sulfur

MELANOIDINS: Large, deeply colored molecules with no aroma but some bitterness

HETEROCYCLICS: Small, potent, ring-shaped molecules with oxygen in them

VOCABULARY	MALT TYPE
BREADY	PILSNER
CRACKER	VIENNA
MALTY	PALE ALE
NUTTY	MUNICH
COOKIE	MILD ALE
TOASTY	MELANOIDIN/AROMATIC
CHOCOLATEY	AMBER
ROASTY	BROWN
COFFEE	CHOCOLATE
ESPRESSO	ROAST

TIME + TEMPERATURE

CARAMEL	CARAMEL/CRYSTAL 20
TOFFEE	CARAMEL/CRYSTAL 30
DRIED FRUIT	CARAMEL/CRYSTAL 40
RAISINS	CARAMEL/CRYSTAL 60
PRUNES	CARAMEL/CRYSTAL 80
TOASTED MARSHMALLOW	CARAMEL/CRYSTAL 150
BURNT SUGAR	

TIME + TEMPERATURE

Maillard browning and non-Maillard caramelization, which both use heat to transform carbohydrates into color and aroma compounds, differ only by the presence or lack of nitrogen.

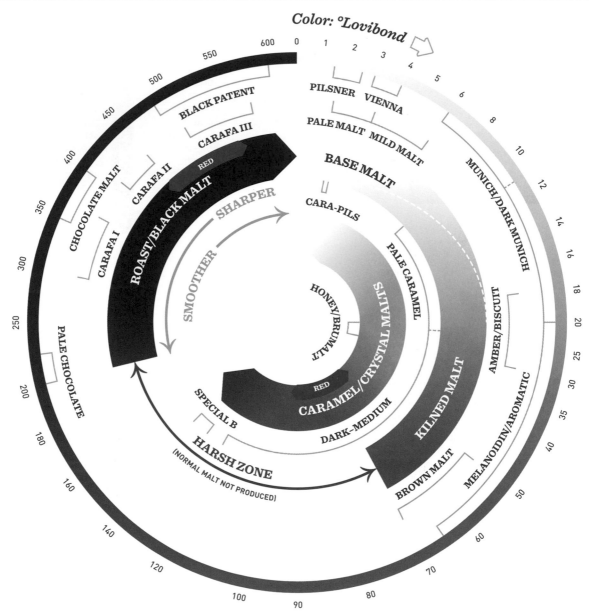

- Standard kilned and roasted malts around the outside
- Outermost malts kilned moist for more caramelly flavors
- Next inner types kilned dry for toasty flavors

- The gap indicates a harsh, ashy zone; no malt is made in this color range
- Inner ring is caramel malt types
- *Red* indicates the reddest shades of malt

The malt color wheel categorizes different types of malts according to the temperature at which they are kilned and the color that they produce.

MALT TYPES

Malts are divided into categories by the way they are kilned and how they are used in brewing. The groups proceed from light in color and enzyme-rich to deeply roasted and incapable of any enzyme activity. The terminology of malt can be confusing. There are often different terms for the same malt, and the same name can mean slightly different things in different places. Maltsters often have proprietary names for their malts and can be quite secretive about how their malts are produced, making it difficult to compare. The differences between malts can be quite dramatic, and there's no way you can have any success putting together a recipe until you have a personal sense of what different malts taste like. Get your hands on as many different malts as you can and do what good brewers always do—taste.

BASE MALTS

Lightly colored malts are collectively known as base malts, because they can form the bulk of a beer recipe, even in the darkest beers. Pilsner, pale, Vienna, mild, and Munich malts fall into this category. Base malts have sufficient enzymes to convert their starches into sugar, while darker malts often do not. Specific base malts are usually associated with either the continental or British brewing traditions. British malts tend to be kilned at lower moisture levels, which makes for more sharply toasty flavors, while continental malts, with higher moisture levels during kilning, display softer, more caramelly notes. English pale ale and German Oktoberfest are both pale amber beers brewed from similarly colored malt, but their malt flavors are very different, mainly due to different moisture levels during kilning. This dichotomy of toasty versus caramelly can be seen from the darker base malts, 5°L, right up to about the 30°L range, where the toasty biscuit/amber malt contrasts with the cookie-like melanoidin malt.

Even malts with moderate amounts of color can still have some enzyme activity. In modern malts, enzyme activity wanes above 25 to 30°L, but in the heyday of porter, malts such as brown and amber were reported to contain enough enzymes to convert themselves.

Grain Type and Alternative Names	Color (Lovibond)	Color (EBC)	Enzyme Activity	OG per lb in 5 gl	OG per kg in 20 L	Max %
SIX-ROW PILSNER MALT, Pils Malt, Lager Malt	1.4–2.2	3–5	Excellent	1.0068 (1.75°P)	1.0129 (3.30°P)	100

Origin and Notes: Pilsner malt bursts onto the beer scene in 1842 in Plzen, Bohemia, in connection with the first pale lager, Pilsner. Widely produced worldwide today, this malt forms the basis for most of the beer consumed on this planet. U.S. versions tend to be higher in protein content than European ones.

Production: A light and rapid kilning at 176 to 185°F/80 to 85°C, just enough to drive off moisture and much of the DMS precursor, leaves this malt with a very pale color.

Flavor and Aroma: Clean, malty aromas, showing white bread–like or soft cracker-like qualities. Flavor varies by maltster and especially by climate, soil, and grain origin.

Uses:
• As the primary malt in all kinds of pale beers from Pilsners and other lagers to blonde ales to Tripel
• Can lighten the color and reduce the toasty edge contributed by pale malt in IPA and golden/summer bitters
• Balance or thin out the rich, caramelly quality of Vienna or Munich malts in Märzen and Vienna lagers, as well as maibocks

Grain Type and Alternative Names	Color (Lovibond)	Color (EBC)	Enzyme Activity	OG per lb in 5 gl	OG per kg in 20 L	Max %
TWO-ROW PILSNER MALT, Pils Malt, Lager Malt	1.4–2.2	1.8–4.4	Very good to excellent	1.0070–73 (1.80 to 1.87°P)	1.0133–140 (3.40 to 3.57°P)	100

Origin and Notes: Pilsner malt bursts onto the beer scene in 1842 in Plzen, Bohemia, in connection with the first pale lager, Pilsner. Widely produced worldwide today, this malt forms the basis for most of the beer consumed on this planet. U.S. versions tend to be higher in protein content than European ones.

Production: A light and rapid kilning at 176 to 185°F/80 to 85°C, just enough to drive off moisture and DMS precursors, leaves this malt with a very pale color.

Flavor and Aroma: Clean, malty aromas, showing white bread–like or soft cracker-like qualities. Flavor varies by maltster and especially by grain origin, climate, and soil.

Uses:
• As the primary malt in all kinds of pale beers, from Pilsners and other lagers to blonde ales to Tripel
• Can lighten the color and reduce the toasty edge contributed by pale malt in IPA and golden/summer bitters
• Balance or thin out the rich, caramelly quality of Vienna or Munich malts in Märzen and Vienna lagers, as well as maibocks

Grain Type and Alternative Names	Color (Lovibond)	Color (EBC)	Enzyme Activity	OG per lb in 5 gl	OG per kg in 20 L	Max %
VIENNA MALT	3–4	6–8	Good	1.0071 (1.82°P)	1.0135 (3.45°P)	100

Origin and Notes: Vienna originated in its namesake city in the mid-nineteenth century, an intermediate between the darker Munich and paler Plzen types.

Production: Malt is processed like Pilsner malt, then kilned at 194 to 203°F/90 to 95°C for a few hours for color and flavor development.

Flavor and Aroma: A clean, caramelly character without toastiness.

Uses:
• Preferred malt for the Vienna style
• With its pale color, it can be used to lend complexity in blond ales and pale lagers (2 to 20%)
• Base malt when a caramel character without a toasty edge is desired

Grain Type and Alternative Names	Color (Lovibond)	Color (EBC)	Enzyme Activity	OG per lb in 5 gl	OG per kg in 20 L	Max %
MILD ALE MALT	3.5–5.5	7–11	Adequate for self-conversion	1.0070 (1.80°P)	1.0133 (3.40°P)	100

Origin and Notes: In Jolly Olde England, there was a definite pecking order to malt types and the beers made from them. At the top was pale ale malt and beers like October ale, the long-lived pale ales made in country-house breweries. Down from that a notch was this mild ale malt, made from slightly less plump barley and employed in dark beers intended for quicker consumption.
Production: Similar to pale ale malt, but with additional kilning for slightly higher color.
Flavor and Aroma: It is the British equivalent of Munich malt, with a dry, caramelly aroma.

Uses:
• Highly recommended as a base for all darker British ales, including mild ale, sweeter stouts, porter, and darker Scottish ales
• Adds depth and complexity to darker bitters and pale ales (5 to 25%)

Grain Type and Alternative Names	Color (Lovibond)	Color (EBC)	Enzyme Activity	OG per lb in 5 gl	OG per kg in 20 L	Max %
PALE ALE MALT	2–4	4–8	Very good	1.0073 (1.87°P)	1.0139 (3.55°P)	100

Origin and Notes: Becomes famous in connection with strong, extremely high-quality October and March beers brewed on English country estates, the beers that would go on to become pale and India pale ale. These malts had existed for a century or more before their popularity in the industry exploded around 1780, when brewers started measuring the gravity of their worts, as the pale malt yielded more extract than the brown and amber malts that had been the norm for dark beers up to that time.
Production: Historically, the very best, lowest-protein barleys were reserved for pale-malt production, as they gave the beers the ability to age well. Traditional (Tizard, 1850) pale ale malt kilning ramped temperatures up slowly from 80°F/27°C to 120°F/49°C over a period of four days. Modern kilning schedules for pale ale malt are shorter and hotter, with a drying at 104 to 113°F/40 to 45°C and a five-hour kilning of up to 203°F/95°C. Tizard also mentions a lower-kilned special pale malt for "India ales."
Flavor and Aroma: Clean, malty aromas, with very slight hints of toastiness. Certain heirloom strains like Maris Otter offer a more subtle and complex character.

Uses:
• As the primary malt in pale ale, India pale ale, and pale barley wines
• Can add a slight crisp edge to a blonde or a golden bitter ale made mainly from Pilsner malt
• Balances the richness of mild ale malt by blending into the base malts of darker beers such as stout, porter, and mild ale
• As a base or part of the base for amber- to brown-colored Belgian beers, especially in Belgian pale ales

A great homebrew shop may offer dozens of malty choices for unlimited recipe freedom.

COLOR MALTS

The next group, a little darker in color and with lower-to-no enzyme activity, is color malt, sometimes known as kilned or high-dried malt. These are created in the same kiln that's used for drying, but as soon as the moisture level reaches a certain point, the heat is increased and the malt takes on some additional color. The amount of moisture at this stage determines where the malt falls on a spectrum from crisp and toasty to smooth and caramelly. Time and temperature determine the depth of color and the flavors associated with the kilning. Kilning produces malt no darker than about 60 to 70°L.

There is no hard and fast line that separates base from color malts. Munich malt, for example, has sufficient enzymes to convert its own starch to sugar, and so can be used as a base malt in darker beers, but in paler beers may be used mainly for color and complexity.

Grain Type and Alternative Names	Color (Lovibond)	Color (EBC)	Enzyme Activity	OG per lb in 5 gl	OG per kg in 20 L	Max %
MUNICH MALT	6–12.5	12–25	Sufficient for self-conversion	1.0070 (1.80°P)	1.0133 (3.40°P)	100

Origin and Notes: In the old days, a city's malt determined the flavor and appearance of its beers. Munich was famous for a rich, reddish-brown lager brewed from a dark malt, but the modern version of Munich was created in the mid-nineteenth century.

Note that there are dark versions of Munich that go as high as 20°L/40°EBC in color, and these are essentially pale versions of melanoidin malts, with intermediate character: a little more toasty, but not the full-on, overbaked cookie flavor melanoidin malts exhibit.

Production: High-protein malt is first dried to 20% moisture, then kilned at 212 to 221°F/100 to 105°C for five hours for color and flavor development.

Flavor and Aroma: A profound caramelliness with a cookie-like toasty bite, which helps lend balance to the heavy, sweetish beers traditionally brewed from it.

Uses:
- Essential in dunkel lagers
- Often used in Märzen and altbier
- Common as base for darker Belgian ales
- Can give caramel underpinnings to porters and stouts
- Flavor enhancer on golden and amber beers (1 to 25%)

Grain Type and Alternative Names	Color (Lovibond)	Color (EBC)	Enzyme Activity	OG per lb in 5 gl	OG per kg in 20 L	Max %
AMBER MALT, Biscuit, Victory (Briess)	20–30	40–60	Poor to none	1.0066 (1.70°P)	1.039 (3.55°P)	30

Origin and Notes: Amber malt has been made in England a very long time, having a lineage that extends back to the days of unhopped ale 500 years ago, perhaps even longer.

Production: Basically a toasted pale ale malt, probably of great antiquity. Hough, Briggs, and Stevens (1971) say, "Amber malts are prepared by kiln-drying well-modified malt to 3 to 4% moisture and then 'ambering' in the kiln or a drum by heating rapidly to 200°F/93.3°C, in 15 to 20 minutes and then gradually to 280 to 300°F/138 to 149°C. The higher temperature is maintained until the correct colour, 35 to 100 EBC units is obtained." It is important to note that this malt is kilned in a dry state, which gives it quite a different aromatic profile from moist-kilned malts of similar color such as melanoidin. It is also one of the easiest malts to create at home, in that the starting point is simply dry pale malt.

Flavor and Aroma: Amber/biscuit has a sharply toasty, brown character, notably lacking in caramelly notes.

Uses:
- Signature malt in brown ale; in my experience, nothing tastes quite so "brown" as amber malt
- Adds depth and complexity to dry stouts, as it doesn't add sweetness that would be inappropriate for most versions of the style
- Dry, toasty accent (1 to 5%) in pale ales, barley wines
- Historic British brews, especially porter

Grain Type and Alternative Names	Color (Lovibond)	Color (EBC)	Enzyme Activity	OG per lb in 5 gl	OG per kg in 20 L	Max %
MELANOIDIN MALT, Dark Munich, Aromatic, Melano	15–33	30–66	Minimal to none	1.0070 (1.80°P)	1.0133 (3.40°P)	30

Origin and Notes: A spectrum of flavorful amber-colored malts most associated with Belgian and German brewing traditions with a range of different terms. Perhaps the most underappreciated malts. Beware of confusing nomenclature—check color and descriptions to make sure they match the characteristics you're seeking, and always taste before you buy.

Production: At the end of malting, high-moisture malt is artificially starved for air, which stops respiration but allows proteolytic and amylolytic enzymes to function. This creates a bounty of sugars and nitrogenous products to feed the Maillard activity that will occur during kilning. Dried like Munich malt, then cured at 239°F/115°C, although Gambrinus employs a hot stewing at the end of germination, before kilning for their Honey Malt.

Flavor and Aroma: A substantial yet soft cookie-like or cake-like maltiness very different from similarly colored amber/biscuit, which is kilned dry and is much more toasty. They also can provide some caramel aroma without the raisiny chewiness and unfermentable dextrin that caramel malt adds.

Uses:
• Showcase malt in dark Belgian ales, in which they can add richness and depth to amber or brown beers such as Belgian pale ales, Dubbel, or strong dark ale
• Complexity enhancers perfect for adding a little balance in many kinds of mid- to dark-colored beers from Oktoberfest to Scottish ales to bock to stout

Grain Type and Alternative Names	Color (Lovibond)	Color (EBC)	Enzyme Activity	OG per lb in 5 gl	OG per kg in 20 L	Max %
HONEY MALT (GAMBRINUS MALTING), Brumalt	20–30	40–60	Some to none, depending on manufacturer	1.0070 (1.80°P)	1.0133 (3.40°P)	15–25, depending on manufacturer

Origin and Notes: A sort of crystal/melanoidin hybrid malt mainly from German sources, although Hind, in 1948, describes a British malt called diamber that matches its profile quite closely. Some books describe brumalt and melanoidin as the same thing, but manufacturers sometimes make both types.

Production: A proprietary (read: secret) process is used to produce it, but Hough, Briggs, and Stevens (1971) describe a 122°F/50°C oxygen-starved rest of twenty-four hours at the end of malting, followed by a kilning at 212°F/100°C. Since this stewing and moist-kilning procedure is less intense than crystal, it contains sufficient enzymes to convert itself. For best results, honey malt/brumalt needs to be mashed with a base malt, but some flavor can be extracted with a steeping.

Flavor and Aroma: Despite the name, it tastes only a little like honey, but it is cleaner and less heavy than crystal of comparable color, with a more friable, less sugary texture, and some of Munich malt's deep caramelliness, with less of the heavy, dried-fruit character of caramel.

Uses:
• Alternate to heavier flavors and sweetness of crystal malts, especially in extract and steeped-grain brewing
• As a signature malt in French and Belgian mid-colored beers, such as bière de garde, Dubbel, and all manner of specialties
• Adds a firm supporting maltiness in dark beers such as schwarzbier, Baltic porter, or sweeter stouts like Imperial, London, or oatmeal stout
• Can add a bit of sweetness and depth to brown ales or dark lagers

Grain Type and Alternative Names	Color (Lovibond)	Color (EBC)	Enzyme Activity	OG per lb in 5 gl	OG per kg in 20 L	Max %
BROWN MALT	50–65	100–130	None	1.0066 (1.70°P)	1.0125 (3.20°P)	80

Origin and Notes: At first, the famous dark beer porter was based entirely on brown malt brought in from Hertfordshire, but as brewing scientists armed with hydrometers (Richardson, 1777) found out how much less extract was yielded from brown malt, things quickly changed, and this knowledge was, in fact, the impetus for the invention of black patent malt, which could be used in smaller quantities.

Production: As recently as the mid-twentieth century, brown malt was torrefied or puffed (in the old books, this was called blown malt) and roasted by heating rapidly over a roaring fire, traditionally of oak or even hornbeam logs. Hough, Briggs, and Stevens (1971) give a kilning profile of two and a half hours at 350°F/177°C and mention the "characteristic flavour derived from wood smoke." This "material" they noted in 1971, "is now only used rarely." Today, it gets a more conventional kilning, but brown malt still offers a unique flavor profile.

Flavor and Aroma: Deeply toasty, with mocha and chocolate overtones, sometimes with a bit of a campfire character, although contemporary versions are definitely not smoked.

Uses:
• Useful in all kinds of very dark beers like mild ales, stouts, and porter, especially when a bright, coffee-like touch is welcome
• Historic porter, where it can form the majority of the grist (with just enough pale malt added for conversion)
• Complexity addition in red ales, Scotch "ales," and old ales, or Belgian strong dark ales when a small quantity can add a bright roasty counterpoint to sweetness

ROASTED MALT

For darker types, dried malt is sent to a drum roaster, usually a modified coffee roaster. A rotating drum inside keeps the malt moving for uniform roasting. Rapid cooling is essential to stop the color development once a certain target is met. When the machinery to produce black malt was patented in 1819, the key breakthrough was not the roaster itself, but a water spray mechanism that instantly cooled the malt. Roasted malts include chocolate and the various shades of black malt, ranging from 300 to 600°L/600 to 1200°EBC.

You will notice on the malt color wheel (page 54) that there is a gap between mid- and dark-colored malts, between 70 and 200°L. In this gap, flavors are extremely harsh and ashtray-like, not at all suitable for beer brewing (the exception is dark crystal at 120 to 150°L). Above 200°L, the flavors mellow out to various types of roastiness, the unpleasant flavors having quite literally been burnt away. If you're roasting your own (see Roasting and Smoking Your Own Specialty Malts, page 71), this is an important phenomenon to be aware of.

While paler malts are kilned gently in specialized kilns, darker malts are roasted much like coffee, in similar equipment. Here, the roasting technician checks for color as roasting progresses. Photo courtesy of Briess Industries, Inc.

Grain Type and Alternative Names	Color (Lovibond)	Color (EBC)	Enzyme Activity	OG per lb in 5 gl	OG per kg in 20 L	Max %
CHOCOLATE MALT, Pale Chocolate, Coffee Malt	200–400	400–800	None	1.0061 (1.57°P)	1.0116 (3.00°P)	20

Origin and Notes: Paler version of black malt. Chocolate malts may also be made from rye and wheat, but these are actually darker, like black malt.
Production: Drum roasted just like black malt, but roasting is stopped at a lower color level.
Flavor and Aroma: Sharp, coffee-like roastiness, more piercing than black malt. Wheat and rye offer slightly different taste characteristics, normally darker, more chocolatey.

Uses:
• Adds complexity to dark ales, porters, and stouts
• Supporting malt for coffee-flavored beers

Grain Type and Alternative Names	Color (Lovibond)	Color (EBC)	Enzyme Activity	OG per lb in 5 gl	OG per kg in 20 L	Max %
RÖSTMALZ, Carafa (Weyermann)	300–600	600–1200	Minimal to none	1.0061 (1.57°P)	1.0116 (3.00°P)	20

Origin and Notes: These are the German take on black malt, most likely developed during the early nineteenth century as German brewers sought malts to create their own interpretations of porter, what was then the next big thing in the beer world. Since lagers have such smooth, clean flavors, it was logical that continental brewers would develop roast malts that worked with that aesthetic, and röstmalz was the result. It comes in a variety of colors, as shown by the Weyermann Carafa range: I at 337°L, II at 425°L, and III at 470°L, which is still a little less black than patent.
Production: Premoistened malt (10 to 15%) is heated in a drum roaster for sixty to ninety minutes at 350 to 425°F/177 to 208°C. Steam is applied to the malt, which carries away harsh, volatile Assamars, which would otherwise give the malt a harsh character—a process known as debittering. Dehusked versions offer even smoother flavors.
Flavor and Aroma: Deep, bittersweet-chocolate character. Noted for being exceptionally smooth and deliciously creamy, free from the kind of harsh bitterness that can accompany black patent malt.

Uses:
• Wherever a really smooth roastiness is desired, such as a schwarzbier or a Baltic porter; can temper harshness in oatmeal stouts and others where a smooth roastiness is desired
• A subtle, roasty kicker in dark bock and doppelbock, adding a gentle counterpart to the richness of Munich malt
• Röstmalz is also great for adding a redness and depth to red ales
• For black India pale ales and black witbiers in which a lot of color is needed without a huge amount of roasty character
• Unobtrusive as a coloring agent in any light- to medium-colored beer, even a pale lager

Grain Type and Alternative Names	Color (Lovibond)	Color (EBC)	Enzyme Activity	OG per lb in 5 gl	OG per kg in 20 L	Max %
BLACK MALT, Black Patent Malt	475–600	690–1250	None	1.0061 (1.57°P)	1.0116 (3.00°P)	10

Origin and Notes: Patented in England by Daniel Wheeler in 1817. Since that time, black malt, which finds wide usage in many other beer types, has been the workhorse malt in nearly all black beers. Roasted unmalted barley has the same specifications, but a sharper flavor.
Production: Roasted in drum kilns at high temperatures, typically two hours or so at 420 to 450°F/216 to 232°C.
Flavor and Aroma: A deep, bittersweet chocolate character, often with coffee or espresso notes. Ranges from smooth and mellow to a bit sharp depending on maltster. It is less strongly flavored than its color would suggest. Roasted unmalted barley has a drier, more acrid flavor.

Uses:
• Classic signature malt in all modern stouts and porters except Irish stout, which uses a roasted unmalted barley, and Baltic, which uses röstmalz
• A color booster, and can add a hint of deep roastiness in amber and brown beers such as Scotch "ales," old ales, mild ales, and dark barley wines
• With its reddish cast, black malt is also great for adding a redness and depth to red ales
• In small quantities (less than 2%), can be used as a coloring agent in any light- to medium-colored beer
• Irish stout (roasted unmalted barley)

CARAMEL AND CRYSTAL MALTS

Caramel or crystal malts are different names for the same family of malt. The processing is very different from other malt types. On the last day of malting, the maltster allows the temperature to rise to 113 to 122°F/45 to 50°C to begin the enzymatic breakdown of proteins and carbohydrates. A unique stewing process, that actually mashes the grain right inside the husk, converts the starches to sugars and gives it a characteristic glassy texture. The maltster "stews" this wet malt to saccharification temperature, about 150°F/66°C. When much of the starch has converted to sugars, the malt is dried and then kilned to various levels of color. Because there is a lot of simple sugar rather than starch, the caramelization is quite different from regular malts. Crystal malt presents a wide range of caramel, burnt sugar, and raisiny or dried fruit flavors. Each maltster's caramel/crystal malts are quite different—an important point when choosing them for your recipes.

This stewing process also creates a lot of short unfermentable starch chains called dextrins. They add some body and mouthfeel to a beer. Because of their unique chemistry, these dextrins resist further degradation during mashing, which means their body-building qualities will end up in the finished beer. In fact, the palest caramel/crystal malts are designed mainly for this purpose, to add body and richness to otherwise thin beers; extract brewers particularly value crystal malts because malt extract is often lacking in this aspect.

Although caramel/crystal malts have luscious flavors, they can be overbearing if used with abandon, creating heavy, sickly sweet beers. It's easy to get in the habit of using these malts, perhaps a bit too much, because they can be a good antidote to the thin blandness of extract beers. In my opinion, a light touch is best with crystals, unless you have a very specific reason for wanting them to dominate, as in a red ale.

Another group, called honey malt or brumalt, is intermediate between caramel and ordinary kilned malts. It has some of the rich flavors of caramel without the burnt sugar and heavy dextrins.

More than any other group of malts, the processes and materials used to make caramel malts by different maltsters results in a huge range of profoundly different flavors and aromas, even among caramels of the same color. It is especially important to taste any malt you are thinking about using to make sure it has a character that will lend the right flavor to your recipe.

Also, while I have separated them into groups, there is in reality an almost continuous range available from different maltsters, so my characterizations may be a bit limited—another reason for tasting every time you have the chance.

These intensely flavored specialty malts come in a wide range of colors. Every manufacturer's range has a unique signature, so taste often and get to know them.

Grain Type and Alternative Names	Color (Lovibond)	Color (EBC)	Enzyme Activity	OG per lb in 5 gl	OG per kg in 20 L	Max %
CARA-PILS, Carafoam (ultrapale caramel malt)	1.8–2.5	3.5–5	None	1.0067 (1.72°P)	1.0127 (3.25°P)	15

Origin and Notes: Became popular as an additive to high-adjunct lagers, where it helps compensate for the missing malt with some dextrins, body, and foam.
Production: Caramel malt process, but a light kilning only to reduce moisture content, resulting in a very pale color.
Flavor and Aroma: Very neutral; used mostly for body and foam.

Uses:
• Adds body and head benefits to paler beers
• Essential in high-adjunct beers (its most common commercial application)
• Useful in honey beers to add body and head

Grain Type and Alternative Names	Color (Lovibond)	Color (EBC)	Enzyme Activity	OG per lb in 5 gl	OG per kg in 20 L	Max %
PALE CARAMEL/CRYSTAL, 10–30°L Caramel/Crystal, Cara Hell, Cara Vienna	10–30	20–60	None	1.0066 (1.70°P)	1.0125 (3.20°P)	15

Origin and Notes: Pale amber-colored caramel-type malts.
Production: Caramel malt process, but kilned to 302 to 356°F/150 to 180°C for one to two hours.
Flavor and Aroma: Intense caramelly aromas, often with soft dried-fruit aromas—apricots, raisins, figs. Use caution, as caramel flavors can be quite assertive, and dextrins add to a beer's weight.

Uses:
• Body and flavor enhancer for pale-to-amber beers, especially pale ales and IPAs
• Not particularly useful in lagers, except in very small amounts to add complexity

Grain Type and Alternative Names	Color (Lovibond)	Color (EBC)	Enzyme Activity	OG per lb in 5 gl	OG per kg in 20 L	Max %
MEDIUM CARAMEL/CRYSTAL, 40 to 80°L Caramel/Crystal, Caramunich, Cara Red, Cara Wheat, Cara Rye	40–80	80–200	None	1.0066 (1.70°P)	1.0125 (3.20°P)	15

Origin and Notes: These malts often have a very reddish color.
Production: Caramel malt process, but kilned at 356 to 410°F/180 to 210°C for one to two hours. Wheat (Cara Wheat) and rye versions (Cara Rye) available.
Flavor and Aroma: Intense toasted caramelly and burnt sugar at the higher color range, or toasted-marshmallow aromas, often with strong dried-fruit aromas—caramelized raisins, figs, prunes. Use caution, as the burnt-sugar flavors in the darker ones can be quite assertive and often somewhat bitter as well. Wheat and rye versions have somewhat different flavor characteristics.

Uses:
• Body and flavor enhancer for darker beers like amber and stronger brown ales, porters, and stouts
• Adds toasted raisiny, fruity aromas in Belgian Dubbels and strong dark ales
• Not particularly useful in lagers, except in very small amounts to add complexity

Grain Type and Alternative Names	Color (Lovibond)	Color (EBC)	Enzyme Activity	OG per lb in 5 gl	OG per kg in 20 L	Max %
EXTRA DARK CARAMEL/ CRYSTAL, 100–140°L Caramel/Crystal, Special B, Cara Aroma	100–140	200–280	None	1.0057 (1.47°P)	1.0108 (2.77°P)	15

Origin and Notes: Super-dark versions of caramel malt, pioneered by DeWolf-Cosyns as Special B, now produced under that name by Castle Malting, other producers.
Production: Caramel malt process, but kilned above 400°F/204°C for two hours or more.
Flavor and Aroma: Unique, intense flavors of roasted sugar, toasted raisins, or Turkish coffee. Use sparingly, as this malt is quite assertive and often somewhat bitter as well.

Uses:
• Body and flavor enhancer for very dark beers like porters and stouts
• Adds unique toasted-sugar aromas in any dark ale or barley wine (1 to 5%)

WHEAT AND OTHER NON-BARLEY MALTS

Wheat has been a player in beer since the very beginning, way back in the Middle East. Because of the efforts of those early farmers in the ancient Middle East, wheat threshes "naked," that is, without the husk that clings to barley, so when wheat is used in high proportions in the mash it is often necessary to add rice hulls or other filtering material during brewing. Of the cereal grains, wheat requires the best soil, and because it is the preferred ingredient for baking bread, its use in brewing has often been restricted to make sure there's enough for bread baking.

Wheat brews a fine beer, a little more neutral in flavor and richer in texture than malted barley. It is classified into hard and soft varieties, with the low-protein "soft" varieties generally being the best for malting and brewing. Wheat malt is mostly available as a very lightly kilned product, although you can find kilned and caramel wheat malts.

Because of its protein structure, wheat contributes a lot of the mid-length protein desirable for beer's body and head. As a result, wheat malts have a long tradition in beers such as Kölsch and English bitter, where a bit more head is a good thing, and they should be in every brewer's kit for that purpose. Five to fifteen percent is a typical range as a head booster.

There are specific wheat beer styles, of course, including Bavarian hefe-weizen, Berliner weisse, and American wheat ales. The percentage of wheat varies by style, but 30 to 70 percent is the range for these styles. The Belgians use a lot of wheat in beers like witbier and lambic, but this is traditionally unmalted wheat, which takes special mashing techniques that are often difficult for the small-scale brewer to accomplish. Malted wheat can yield good results with step infusions; because it is not as intense in character as unmalted wheat, it is usually used in larger proportions, perhaps 60 to 70 percent as opposed to the usual 40 to 50 percent.

Wheat also has a reputation for making short-lived beers, and from my experience I have to agree. Because it doesn't have the profoundly malty flavors that barley malt does, very strong "wheat wines" tend to be a little on the bland side. Although there is no real historical precedent for them, I think wheat makes a fine addition to a porter or a stout, adding smooth, creamy textures that counterbalance the sharpness of the roast malts.

Grain Type and Alternative Names	Color (Lovibond)	Color (EBC)	Enzyme Activity	OG per lb in 5 gl	OG per kg in 20 L	Max %
MALTED WHEAT	1.5–2.0	3.0–4.0	Sufficient for self-conversion	1.0078 (2.00°P)	1.0146 (3.73°P)	100

Origin and Notes: Malted wheat has been used since the earliest days of brewing but has often been restricted so as not to limit the production of bread.
Production: A light and rapid kilning at 176°F/80°C leaves this malt with a very pale color. Dark (5.5 to 20°L), chocolate (300 to 450°L), and roasted versions are available, as well as caramel wheat.
Flavor and Aroma: Lacking much flavor of its own besides a clean graininess, but contributes a creamy mouthfeel and great foam.

Uses:
• Traditional wheat beers such as Bavarian hefeweizens, Berliner weisse, and American wheat ales
• Replacement (in larger proportion) for unmalted wheat in Belgian witbier and lambic recipes
• Head-improving grain for wide variety of beers, from bitter to Kölsch to saison

Grain Type and Alternative Names	Color (Lovibond)	Color (EBC)	Enzyme Activity	OG per lb in 5 gl	OG per kg in 20 L	Max %
OAT MALT	2	4	Moderate; high in beta-amylase	1.0050 (1.29°P)	1.0148 (3.87°P)	30

Origin and Notes: Because of their viscosity in the brewhouse and instability in the beer, oats have always been viewed as an inferior grain for brewing, but they do have their uses, especially in dark English ales and variants of Belgian witbiers.
Production: Malted and kilned to pale color in a similar manner to barley malt.
Flavor and Aroma: With little flavor, they mainly contribute a creamy texture and head-retention benefits. May be toasted at home to yield rich cookie aromas.

Uses:
• Any time a rich, creamy mouthfeel is desired
• In oatmeal stouts (10 to 20%)

OTHER SPECIALTY MALTS

ACID OR SOUR MALT

This is malt that has been allowed to stew in a *Lactobacillus* culture before kilning, developing 2 to 4 percent lactic acid, used as a Reinheitsgebot-legal method of acidifying a mash. (Reinheitsgebot is the German beer purity law that limits beer ingredients to malt, water, hops, and yeast.) It is useful as a convenient way of adding acidity to certain styles like Berliner weisse and witbier that traditionally employed lactic fermentations for sour flavors. At 1 percent of the grain bill, acidic flavors will be barely detectable; at 20 percent, the beer will be quite sour. Other parameters of gravity, color, etc., are like Pilsner malt.

SMOKED MALT

This is just a special finishing process in imitation of earlier days when kilns were fired by wood. Beechwood is traditional for the smoked beers of Bamberg, although oak is occasionally used; peat-smoked distiller's malt from Scotland is not traditional in beer, but can add some scotch whisky aromas. Briess malting makes a cherrywood-smoked malt that has a pungent spiciness.

Malt soaking up the mesquite on a home barbecue. Photo by Harold Gulbransen.

UNDERSTANDING *a* MALT ANALYSIS

Maltsters make various measurements of their malt for quality control purposes. When you buy a boxcar load at a time, you get measurements for that particular batch. Those of us who buy in smaller quantities have to settle for more general specifications, of the "not to exceed . . ." variety, which is plenty useful for us. Most malt makers have their specs posted on the Internet, so it's easy enough to look up whatever you may be using.

MOISTURE CONTENT (MC)

Given as a percentage. Lower is better, avoid malts with moisture content of 5% or more, as they have been poorly stored.

COLOR

Typically given in degrees Lovibond. European malts use European Brewing Convention (EBC) units. EBC = Lovibond × 2.

EXTRACT, DRY BASIS, COARSE GRIND (DBCG)

Extract yield, in percentage by weight, from the malt ground as a brewery would, adjusted to 0% moisture and mashed using the ASBC laboratory mash.

EXTRACT, DRY BASIS, FINE GRIND (DBFG)

Extract yield, in percentage by weight, from finely ground malt adjusted to 0% moisture and using American Society of Brewing Chemists (ASBC) laboratory mash. The higher the DBFG number, the better.

FG-CG DIFFERENCE

The difference between the fine grind and coarse grind extract indicates the degree of malt modification. Unless you are using a decoction mash, look for malt with an FG-CG difference of less than 2.0%.

DIASTATIC POWER (DP)

This measures combined alpha and beta amylase, the starch-converting power of the malt. Six-row lager malts have the highest diastatic power, followed by two-row Pilsner, lager, and pale ale malts. Darker kilned malts will have lower diastatic power. Malts above 25°L generally have no diastatic power.

PROTEIN

Expressed as a percentage. All-malt beers should not be brewed from malts that exceed 12% protein.

S/T (SOLUBLE NITROGEN/TOTAL NITROGEN RATIO)

An indicator of the degree of modification. Higher is better for most homebrewing purposes. Malts under 30% are undermodified and may need decoction.

MEALY/HALF-GLASSY/GLASSY

This is about texture, and is another indicator of modification. The more mealy a malt, the better it will mash. Glassy grains do not crush well. Look for malts with at least 92% mealy grains for step mashes or decoctions, and at least 95% mealy grains for single-step infusion mashes.

SIZE

Malt size is measured by running it through calibrated sieves. The plumper the malt, the better, though uniformity of size is also a factor to look for. *Thin* or *thru* means malt that is smaller than 2.2 mm. Look for malt that is 2% or less thin or thru.

VISCOSITY

This is a measure taken of the wort in a laboratory mash, and is an indicator of glucans or other gummy carbohydrates, which leads to slower lautering. Above 1.75 is considered high.

ODOR

This would indicate any good or bad odors detected in the mash. Most specialty malts will be *very aromatic*.

CLARITY

Most malts will be clear to slightly hazy. Highly kilned specialty malts will be noted as *dark*.

UNMALTED GRAINS

Unmalted grains have a very long history in beer, but malts have decided advantages: ease of use, readily available extract, and flavor. However, unmalted grains are useful in brewing for mouthfeel, head retention, flavor, or tradition. Ninety percent of the world's beer is adjunct-based mass-market lager made with corn or rice, which makes the beer easier to drink as well as cuts costs. But even the dreaded rice and corn can be used in creative and interesting ways. And unmalted oats, wheat, rye, and other grains have taste characteristics very different from barley malt, so they're a good tool to have in your bag of tricks.

In amounts up to 10 percent or so, adjunct grains in gelatinized forms like flakes can simply be added to the mash with good results. Brewers have long known that a dab of unmalted grain in a recipe can improve a beer's head, as the term "head corn" will attest. The proteins and complex sugars known as glucans and pentosans found in grains such as rye and oats can add a luxuriously creamy touch to everything from oatmeal stouts to witbier.

In larger quantities, unmalted grains are a little more difficult to use. Because their starches' gelatinization temperature is higher than that of malted barley, infusion or step mashes don't always do a great job of extracting the benefits from unmalted grain such as raw wheat. The gelatinization temperature of corn and rice starch is quite high, and these raw grains require a short boil to get much of anything out of them. The modified Adjunct mash procedure shown on page 138 should be used for any recipe with more than 10 percent of unmalted grain.

Unmalted grains in their natural, raw state may be available in a number of forms: whole, flaked, grits (pre-gelatinized or not), or torrefied (puffed). The best forms for brewing are generally pre-gelatinized. Such grains are like instant rice; they have gone through a cooking process that irreversibly changes the structure of the starch so they yield more easily in the mash. Small quantities—up to 10 percent—cause no problems.

Unmalted grains contain no active enzymes, so those must come from the rest of the grist. High-adjunct beers are usually based on six-row malt, which contains an abundance of enzymes. Adjuncts such as rice and corn lack nitrogen, so if used in large proportions, there may not be enough free amino nitrogen (FAN) for good yeast nutrition. This is especially true in lower-gravity beers, so yeast nutrient may need to be added if you're trying to copy a mass-market Pilsner or light beer.

Although oats can add a nice creaminess to beer, they have always been viewed as an inferior brewing ingredient better suited for adjunct duty.

Grain Type and Alternative Names	Color (Lovibond)	Color (EBC)	Enzyme Activity	OG per lb in 5 gl	OG per kg in 20 L	Max %
CORN, MAIZE	0.8	1.6	None	1.0078 (2.00°P)	1.0146 (3.73°P)	40

Origin and Notes: In the United States, this is the most common adjunct in mainstream beer, used by Miller, Pabst, and others.
Production: Minimal processing, although can be found flaked.
Flavor and Aroma: Nearly flavorless, but with a lingering, creamy corniness that can be tasted in many mainstream U.S. beers.

Uses:
• Pre-Prohibition U.S.-style Pilsners
• South American themes, as there is a long tradition and that region has some special breeds

Grain Type and Alternative Names	Color (Lovibond)	Color (EBC)	Enzyme Activity	OG per lb in 5 gl	OG per kg in 20 L	Max %
RICE	1	2	None	1.0078 (2°P)	1.0146 (3.73°P)	40

Origin and Notes: This is the adjunct of choice for Budweiser. In fact, most of the rice strains in the United States were bred for this very purpose. It is somewhat more expensive than corn.
Production: Minimal processing, although can be found flaked; rice-extract syrups are available and can be used in gluten-free beers.
Flavor and Aroma: It presents on the palate with a sharp, not quite astringent character that makes for a more refreshing beer—or so the marketers say. More interesting rice strains can be found all over Asia. Basmati rice has a nutty quality, and jasmine is a touch floral.

Uses:
• Pre-Prohibition U.S.-style Pilsners
• Asian themes; exotic strains with deep red and purple aleurone layers can add striking colors in otherwise pale beers
• Sake or sake-beer hybrids
• Gluten-free beers (available as extract syrup)

Grain Type and Alternative Names	Color (Lovibond)	Color (EBC)	Enzyme Activity	OG per lb in 5 gl	OG per kg in 20 L	Max %
UNMALTED WHEAT, Soft Red or White Wheat	1.4	2.8	None	1.0078 (2.00°P)	1.0146 (3.73°P)	50

Origin and Notes: Traditional in Belgian beers such as witbiers and lambics, due to a law that allowed a lower tax rate on unmalted grains. Low-protein, or soft, varieties are preferred. If in doubt as to soft or hard, check the nutritional statement. It should be somewhere below 11% protein. Red and white soft wheats seem to be identical in flavor. Unmalted wheat is best used with an American adjunct mash procedure (see Adjunct Mashing, page 137).
Production: Minimal processing, although can be found flaked and torrefied.
Flavor and Aroma: Light flavor, but adds a rich, creamy texture.

Uses:
• Witbier and lambic with classic turbid/slijm or American adjunct mashing procedures
• As adjunct to improve head in lighter beers such as English bitter and mild ale

Grain Type and Alternative Names	Color (Lovibond)	Color (EBC)	Enzyme Activity	OG per lb in 5 gl	OG per kg in 20 L	Max %
UNMALTED BARLEY, Flaked Barley	2–3	4–6	None	1.0078 (2°P)	1.0146 (3.73°P)	30

Origin and Notes: Sometimes used as a cheap adjunct in Britain, especially in Irish stout.
Production: Minimal processing; usually available in flaked form.
Flavor and Aroma: Light flavor, but adds a rich, creamy texture.

Uses:
• Adds creaminess to dry Irish stout (Guinness contains 30%)
• As adjunct to improve head in lighter beers such as English bitter and mild ale

Grain Type and Alternative Names	Color (Lovibond)	Color (EBC)	Enzyme Activity	OG per lb in 5 gl	OG per kg in 20 L	Max %
RYE	2–3	4–6	None	1.0078 (2°P)	1.0146 (3.73°P)	30

Origin and Notes: Hardy grain that grows well in northern regions.
Production: Minimal processing; usually available in flaked form. Rye malt is also sometimes available, some kilned to dark colors (chocolate rye). Due to high glucan content, rye is extremely sticky in the mash, and can cause stuck mashes above about 5%. A glucan rest at 95°F/35°C in the mash is recommended to help degrade these sticky carbohydrates.
Flavor and Aroma: Spicy, peppery aromas and flavor plus an oily/creamy texture.

Uses:
• Rye variants of Bavarian hefeweizens (*roggenbiers*)
• Northern brews such as Finnish sahti (about 10% rye) and Russian kvass, made from stale rye bread
• Hoppy, often strong red rye ales and Rye PAs are becoming popular in the United States these days

Grain Type and Alternative Names	Color (Lovibond)	Color (EBC)	Enzyme Activity	OG per lb in 5 gl	OG per kg in 20 L	Max %
OATS, Steel Cut Oatmeal, Oatmeal	2–3	4–6	None	1.005 (1.3°P)	1.0094 (2.4°P)	30

Origin and Notes: Historically, a cheap and inferior brewing grain compared to barley or wheat.
Production: Various types of oatmeal—old-fashioned, quick, and instant—differ only in their flake size, which affects cooking speed.
Flavor and Aroma: Light flavor, but adds an oily, super-creamy texture, often with a permanent haze as well.

Uses:
• Oatmeal stout
• Minor adjunct (5%) in classic Belgian witbier and many pre-1900 Belgian regional styles
• Creative uses such as oatmeal-cookie ale (toast them first), oatmeal-cream ale, oat India pale ale

EXOTIC ADJUNCT GRAINS

SPELT

Intermediate between wheat and barley, so follow the preceding usage instructions for either. May be malted, but rarely available. Some history in Belgian brewing, especially in Liège, and used today in some saisons (*épeautre*).

BUCKWHEAT

Not a grass, but a chenopod, related to rhubarb. Has intense, often pungent, flavors. Some history in Dutch and Belgian ales, especially Liège saison. Sold as "kasha" in Eastern European/Jewish groceries. Toasted versions are more pleasant.

WILD RICE

Aquatic grass that grows in the upper United States and southern Canada. Very hard and waxy starch requires long precooking—follow a regular culinary recipe for cooking. Lightens body and adds a pleasant, nutty flavor. Wild rice beers are a regional specialty in the upper Midwest of the United States, but make a great addition to English bitter.

QUINOA

Not a grass, but another chenopod like buckwheat, quinoa has a long brewing history in South America. It is high in protein (14%), but low in glucans and other gummy stuff. Can be malted, but not generally available that way, so needs a cereal cooking. Gluten-free beer is a common application. Delicate in flavor.

Left to right: Flaked maize, flaked wheat, flaked rye, oatmeal, spelt, basmati rice, heirloom rice, wild rice, quinoa, buckwheat.

MALT EXTRACT

For most beginning brewers, every batch begins with a few pounds of malt extract in dry or liquid form. This shortcut makes a lot of sense. Someone else has already done the hard work of converting malt starches into sugars, often blending in some color, even adding hops for bitterness—essentially instant wort. The happy homebrewer need only add water, boil to sanitize, add hops as needed, chill to fermentation temperature, and pitch the yeast. An extract batch takes just a couple of hours, and when done with care, can produce a wide range of great-tasting beers. Once they have the process dialed in, and with their friends and family lapping up every drop, many brewers feel no need to go beyond this.

There are, however, a few drawbacks. You pay for this convenience by handing control of your recipe to someone else, which you may find acceptable—or not. Fortunately, wheat malt extract and rice extract are available, so it's possible to make wheat beers and Grandpa's adjunct Pilsner.

Malt extracts differ greatly in their fermentability, making the beers sweeter or drier, and this information about specific brands may be hard to come by. There are also issues of freshness, especially with the syrup form.

Because malt extract is a highly concentrated mix of water, sugar, and protein, it has all the elements necessary for a Maillard browning reaction, even at room temperature, which can result in beer with an unpleasant lingering flavor that my colleagues in Chicago refer to as "ball-point pen" flavor. The term "cidery" is also sometimes used in this context. This browning reaction causes malt extract to darken as it ages, and also during manufacture, so it is often nigh impossible to brew an extremely pale beer, like a German-style Pilsner, with liquid extracts. Spray-dried extracts have a bit better track record for becoming stale and darkening, but they are not immune. Freshness matters, so find out which malt extract brands sell the fastest at your supplier, and stick to those.

Also, because extracts have been vacuum-concentrated, huge volumes of liquid have been forcibly removed from the wort to thicken it for packaging. And guess what? Along with the water, much of that beautiful malt aroma has been sucked out of the extract as well. As a result, beers made only from malt extract can taste rather lifeless and dull when it comes to the malt side.

The secret to good extract brewing is to get most of the flavor from specialty malts and hops. The malts in this type of brewing process are not mashed, so caramel malt or dark roasted malts are best because they give up their flavors and colors pretty easily. In extract recipes the malt is crushed, tossed into a mesh bag, and steeped in the heating wort until shortly before boiling when it is removed and discarded; this adds color, flavor, aroma, and body. Although you have a more limited range of malt choices in extract brewing, there is a still a wide range of flavors using caramel or roasted malts. Just be aware that caramel malts have fairly powerful flavors—not neutral or

particularly subtle; not every beer can tolerate their toasted caramel and burnt-sugar flavors. Use them with a light touch, and choose carefully to complement your recipe.

If you use extract syrups designed to make specific types of beer with no additional malts added, you give up quite a bit of control. There is great suspicion that the formulas used to make beer-specific extracts are not the same as recipes traditionally used to brew those beers. The manufacturers add other ingredients for color, bitterness, and hop aroma. Rather than brew authentic recipes, it's easier for the manufacturer to just add some caramel sugar or black malt syrup for an amber or a dark extract, so the flavors of those kits can be very different from what's in an authentic traditional brew. This goes double for hopped extracts: Tossing in a handful of hops is so simple and gratifying that I can't imagine a brewer finding the shortcut worthwhile. I say: Use real hops.

A mini-mash procedure is a step up in terms of control, but also requires a bit more time, attention, and equipment. To add flavor to the extract, you can do a short mash with malts such as pale, biscuit, Munich, or melanoidin that will not yield much in a simple steeping. Darker malts may not have the enzymes needed to convert themselves, so a bit of lager, Pilsner, or pale malt may need to be added to them to provide the necessary enzymes for conversion. After thirty minutes, the liquid is drained into the kettle.

Fortified with a pretty wide range of malts, the mini-mash technique can do a decent job with most beer styles. Grains like rye or oats can be used in quantities of 1 to 2 pounds/½ to 1 kg in a mini mash. Beers that need a large amount of a very specific malt may be difficult to duplicate with ordinary extract, although specialty extracts may sometimes be found. So for certain styles, flavors will have to be approximate: good beer, just not absolutely authentic.

ROASTING *and* SMOKING YOUR OWN SPECIALTY MALTS

Doing your own toasting and roasting of malt really is pretty easy, and allows you to create malts unavailable from commercial sources for unique flavors and aromas in your beers. Depending on what malts are normally available to you, this may or may not be worth the effort, but it's easy enough to try and requires no specialized equipment as long as you have access to an oven and a cookie sheet.

You are creating the conditions, more or less, in a commercial kiln or roaster. It is helpful to know your oven thermostat is accurate, but as long as you're always using the same oven, it really doesn't matter. Toaster ovens can be a bit more erratic, so keep a close eye on them for scorching as they sometimes heat up rather abruptly.

Not quite instant beer, but extract in liquid or dry form simplifies the brewing process.

For simple toasting, spread uncrushed Pilsner or pale malt on a cookie sheet, place into a preheated oven (use a 25°F/14°C lower setting with convection), and let 'er roast. Check every five minutes or so, paying special attention to the aroma. Break open the malt and check the color inside, as the husks toast more slowly than the insides. Use a spatula to turn the malt every ten minutes or so. Dump out onto a cool cake pan or cookie sheet to cool the malt fairly quickly so it doesn't get any darker. Remember the following:

- **MOISTURE LEVEL OF THE MALT IS IMPORTANT FOR FLAVOR.** Moist malts will toast with caramelly overtones, while dry malts will tend toward the toasty. So if you want more caramel, soak your malt from 4 to 8 hours in dechlorinated tap water before toasting.

- **TOAST BY AROMA, NOT BY COLOR.** Malt always brews a much darker beer than it looks like. If you cut it open and look inside, brown malt is barely a pinkish copper color, not actually brown.

- **TOASTED MALT NEEDS TO CURE BEFORE USING.** The kilning process creates lots of harsh, volatile chemicals that will give your beer an ashtray aroma if you don't give them time to leave. A couple of weeks in a paper bag should be adequate.

- **BEWARE THE HARSH ZONE.** If you look at the malt color wheel on page 54, you will see a gap between 75 and 200°L/150 and 400°EBC for noncaramel malts. Malts in this color range are quite pungent and unpleasant, so for the most part, confine your efforts to colors below 75°L/150°EBC, which means malts that are a pinkish-copper color inside. If you have a home-style coffee roaster, you can make dark malts as well, but these are difficult to achieve in an ordinary oven.

Smoking malt is just like the process of making barbecue, but without the meat—low and slow does it. A barbecue smoker, especially the electric type that can be operated at temperatures below 200°F/93°C, is ideal. Above that, you will get some toasting as well as smoke, which may or may not be what you want.

To smoke malt, you'll need to build simple screened frames from wood and bronze window screen to hold the malt in the smoker. Time is a big variable and will depend on many things, but you are likely to want to be in the range of 1 to 4 hours for most smoked malts. A huge variety of wood chips can be used, possibly with the addition of herbs and spices like rosemary or allspice, so you can create a lot of unique aromas for your smoked beer. Like toasting, the aroma will be a little smoother if you can allow a week or two between smoking and brewing.

TIME AND TEMPERATURE FOR HOME-ROASTED MALT

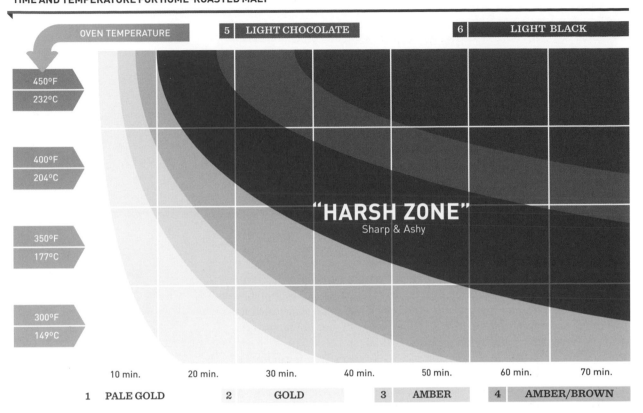

| OVEN TEMPERATURE | | 5 LIGHT CHOCOLATE | 6 LIGHT BLACK |

450°F / 232°C
400°F / 204°C
350°F / 177°C
300°F / 149°C

"HARSH ZONE"
Sharp & Ashy

10 min. 20 min. 30 min. 40 min. 50 min. 60 min. 70 min.

| 1 PALE GOLD | 2 GOLD | 3 AMBER | 4 AMBER/BROWN |

No.	COLOR	°LOVIBOND	FLAVOR/DESCRIPTION	INSIDE
1	PALE GOLD	7–12	Aromatic, nutty. Not toasted-tasting. Enzymes still active.	
2	GOLD	16–22	Malty, caramelly, rich. Not toasted-tasting. Limited enzyme activity.	
3	AMBER	28–35	Lightly toasted taste. Nutty, malty, caramelly. Enzymes pretty much inactive.	
4	AMBER/BROWN	55–70	Pronounced toasted taste. Nutty, toffeelike.	
X	HARSH ZONE	80–150	Very harsh and unpleasant roastiness. Don't go here.	
5	LIGHT CHOCOLATE	175	Sharply roasted flavor. Smooth, rich, lingering.	
6	LIGHT BLACK	250–350	Very rich, smooth, roasted taste.	

Achieve your desired beer color by determining the appropriate temperature and length of time needed to home-roast your malts.

BREWING SUGARS

For some of us who still recall the horrors of pre-enlightenment homebrew recipes containing a staggering amount of corn sugar (50 percent!), the notion of sugar in beer seems heretical. But quality sugar in appropriate quantities can make certain beer styles really shine. Belgian strong pale ales, abbey Dubbels, and Tripels all use sugar to lighten the palate, giving these strong beers an easy drinkability that has gotten many of us into trouble.

Some beers use caramel syrup to augment or substitute for colored malt. This technique dates back to the late eighteenth century, when English brewers colored their porters with a type of burnt sugar called *essentia binae*. In the nineteenth century, Flemish *oud bruins* were colored this way, and the everyday form of lambic, called *faro*, was sweetened and colored with caramel. Today caramel syrup remains a tool in the Belgian brewer's kit. Chouffe and Rochefort use no colored malts in their recipes; their delicious caramel flavors come from caramelized sugar.

The term *candi* as applied to Belgian brewers' sugar can be confusing, so I try to avoid it. There are two types of sugar that may be called *candi*: large rocks of crystallized beet sugar and caramelized sugar syrup. In general—and this is undoubtedly true historically—*sucre candi* (or *kandij zuiker* in Flemish) refers to caramelized sugar syrup. American craft- and homebrewers using the term are usually referring to the rock sugar.

No matter how exotic it may appear, pale rock sugar is nothing more than refined sucrose; even the darker varieties are only faintly flavorful. There's no magic about it. Rock sugar made from beets is used in Belgian beer because it's cheap there. If you want beet sugar for some weird reason, it's at your grocery store waiting for you in 5-pound/2.3-kg bags at a very attractive price. Just look for any sugar not called "cane."

Many partially refined sugars have interesting flavors that can make great additions to beer. Many plants have rich, sugary sap that can be boiled into a thick syrup or further condensed into solid sugars. Normal white sugar is made by carrying this process to the extreme; what is removed from the pure sugar ends up as molasses. Raw sugar can be quite elegant in flavor and can work in many beer styles; many have historical authenticity as well. Look for them at ethnic grocery stores, especially those with tropical connections.

Sugar can also simply be added to the boil kettle. To prevent scorching, be sure it is well dissolved before applying too much heat.

These global sugars offer a variety of rich, complex flavors that can make useful additions to many beers, especially strong ones in which sugar can help improve drinkability.

Top to bottom: Corn sugar, turbinado, Belgian brewers brown sugar, Thai palm, gula jawa, piloncillo.

Sugar	Plant	Origin	Form	OG per lb in 5 gl	OG per kg in 20 L
GULA JAWA	Sugar palm	Indonesia	Cylinders or blocks	1.0075 (1.93°P)	1.0143 (3.65°P)

Flavor and Use: Dark, rich, and fudgy sugar used as candy in Southeast Asia. Great for Dubbels and other dark Belgian-style ales.

Sugar	Plant	Origin	Form	OG per lb in 5 gl	OG per kg in 20 L
JAGGERY	Sugar palm	India	Large or small blunt cones	1.0075 (1.93°P)	1.0143 (3.65°P)

Flavor and Use: Pale, moderately flavorful sugar with rich, maple overtones and hints of something buttery. Historical use in IPA after 1847.

Sugar	Plant	Origin	Form	OG per lb in 5 gl	OG per kg in 20 L
PALM OR COCONUT	Sugar palm or coconut palm	Thailand, Indonesia	Disks, blocks, or semisolid in jars	1.0075–85 (1.93–2.18°P)	1.0143–62 (3.65–4.12°P)

Flavor and Use: Very pale, sometimes with a delicate coconut aroma and a haunting sweetness. Especially good in very strong pale beers like Tripels. Indian jaggery is generally more flavorful than the Thai or Indonesian types, often with a maple-like aroma.

Sugar	Plant	Origin	Form	OG per lb in 5 gl	OG per kg in 20 L
MAPLE SYRUP	Sugar maple	Northern United States or Canada	Thin syrup	1.0062 (1.59°P)	1.0117 (2.74°P)

Flavor and Use: Very lightly flavored syrup; difficult to get definite maple flavor imprinted on beer. Best used in fermenter, after primary is complete. Grade B is more flavorful than the paler Grade A. Maple sap can be used instead of brewing liquor with great results.

Sugar	Plant	Origin	Form	OG per lb in 5 gl	OG per kg in 20 L
MOLASSES	Sugarcane	Southern United States	Syrup	1.0052 (1.34°P)	1.0099 (2.54°P)

Flavor and Use: Cooked, slightly tarry flavors, more so in dark or blackstrap versions. Useful in Colonial (U.S.) dark ales. Adds nutty flavor in small (1 to 3%) quantities.

Sugar	Plant	Origin	Form	OG per lb in 5 gl	OG per kg in 20 L
PILONCILLO, Panela, Rapadura	Sugar	Colombia, elsewhere in Latin America, Brazil (rapadura)	Cones or disks	1.0094 (1.90°P)	1.0179 (4.55°P)

Flavor and Use: Varies widely in flavor intensity, but most have complex rum aromas with some minerality.

Sugar	Plant	Origin	Form	OG per lb in 5 gl	OG per kg in 20 L
SORGHUM	Sorghum (a type of millet)	Southern United States	Syrup	1.0074 (1.90°P)	1.0141 (3.60°P)

Flavor and Use: Tangy, minerally, slightly nutty.

Sugar	Plant	Origin	Form	OG per lb in 5 gl	OG per kg in 20 L
TURBINADO, Muscovado, Barbados, Sugar in the Raw, Others	Sugarcane	Caribbean and Southern United States	Small crystals	1.0094 (1.90°P)	1.0179 (4.55°P)

Flavor and Use: Fairly lightly flavored; little color added to beer despite tan appearance. Barbados sugar is especially delicious, with clean, rum-like aromas.

Left to right: Belgian caramel, maple, sorghum.

MAKING YOUR OWN CARAMEL

Caramelized sugar adds rich flavors that are a little different from any type of malt, and like all sugars, they thin out the body of a beer, an especially useful thing in strong beers. They are most associated with Belgian traditions and are used in many famous beers such as Rochefort and LaChouffe. It can be made at home without a lot of trouble.

Because of its chemical and electrical characteristics, caramel interacts strongly with the products it's used in. There are four types of sugar used in products with differing pH, alcohol, sulfites, and other ingredients. Class III is the one that is stable in beer.

This sounds pretty technical, but I can assure you the process is very simple. You first have to invert the sugar, splitting the sucrose into its glucose and fructose components. To do this, place 1 pound/454 g of cane sugar plus 2 cups/475 ml of water into a heavy saucepan, along with ¼ teaspoon/0.5 g of citric acid or cream of tartar. Heat on a medium-high flame, stirring gently to dissolve the added chemical and allow the mixture to warm. Boil for 20 minutes, which will invert the sugar. Then add 2 teaspoons/7 g of ammonium carbonate, which is sold as a leavening in Middle Eastern groceries. As a substitute, diammonium phosphate (sold as yeast nutrient) seems to work just fine. When the water boils away, the temperature will rise and the sugar will begin to darken. Don't turn your back on it; caramelization can be rapid once it starts. You can check the flavor as you go by putting small drops of it onto a sheet of aluminum foil, where they cool fairly rapidly. Judge your caramel by flavor as well as color.

When the caramel has progressed to your liking, turn off the heat and carefully (watch for steam and splattering) stir in a little water to bring it back to the consistency of thin honey. This makes it easier to use and relieves you of the need to rent a jackhammer to chisel it out of the pan. The caramel will keep for an extended time.

HONEY

The use of honey in fermented beverages undoubtedly predates beer. Rinsing the sugars off of honeycombs creates a dilute solution that ancient people would have been unable to avoid fermenting, and mead was born.

Chemically, honey is a solution of sugars in water, typically in the range of 18 percent water to 80 percent sugars (a mix of glucose and fructose), and the remaining 2 percent includes several enzymes and minerals, a tiny amount of amino acids and other compounds, plus a bit of bacteria and wild yeast.

One pound/454 g of honey added to a 5-gallon/19-L batch will contribute between 1.0070 and 1.0075 (1.7 to 1.8)°Plato. Because it is highly fermentable, honey beers can have very low finishing gravities and high attenuation, resulting in a beer that will be light on the palate. If you're simply looking for honey flavor, adjust the remainder of the beer recipe to be rather rich and underattenuated—by using more crystal malt than normal, for example—balancing the thinning effects of the honey.

With a little caution, good-quality caramel for brewing can be made in just minutes.

As with any sugar, honey can simply be added to the kettle, but because of its delicate aromatic nature, this isn't the best idea. Boiling dulls and drives off honey aromatics; the vigorous escape of CO_2 gas during fermentation carries more away, and you end up getting very little benefit from this expensive ingredient. Most mead experts feel that boiling, or even pasteurizing at lower temperatures, is unneeded. It's not exactly sterile, but the microorganisms in honey are highly specialized and rarely survive in beer.

In quantities of 20 percent or less, honey poses no special challenges, but at higher concentrations brewers need to be aware of a few things. First, honey contains very little of the free amino nitrogen needed for yeast health. It's hard to say exactly at what point adding some yeast nutrient is required, but when you get to the point where 30 percent or so of the fermentables are honey, you're definitely there. Honey also contains an enzyme called glucose oxidase that breaks up sugar molecules and continuously releases small amounts of hydrogen peroxide, which has antimicrobial properties that can be a challenge to fermentation.

The other thing to know about honey, as with any brewing sugar, is that yeast actually prefers honey's glucose to the maltose sugar that dominates the wort extracted from malt. It's a bit like giving a kid a large pile of candy before dinner. If yeast grows and develops in an environment where simple sugars abound, then it doesn't develop the enzymes needed to ferment maltose. Above 20 percent honey or sugar, you definitely can have a problem. The fix is to start the wort fermenting without honey, and then add it when the primary fermentation has calmed. This ensures adequate fermentation of the maltose and can avoid the stuck fermentation that can come from this problem. The aroma is better this way, anyway.

Honey's flavor reflects the flowers from which the bees draw the nectar, so there is a huge variation in the color, aroma, and price. Some can be quite exotic; others, like clover honey, are pretty mundane. Some, like orange blossom, carry the aromas of the flowers and plants into the honey, and on into the finished beer. Others bear little resemblance to what the bees started with. Some honeys are almost water-white and very clear, while others are dark or hazy. Flavors range from ethereal to earthy. The brewer needs to be match the honey to the recipe, using the honey in a way that contributes just the right character to the finished beer.

Notes on a Few Select Honeys

ACACIA
Made from the black locust, low acid, very pale

BUCKWHEAT
Dark, molasses-like, with spicy and woody notes

CHESTNUT
Dark, rich, high mineral content

CLOVER
Widely available, but coarse, harsh, and grassy

CRANBERRY
Bright, fruity flavors, slight perfume

FIREWEED
Delicate, fruity, pear-like, slightly buttery

HEATHER
Dark, jelly-like, with rich toffee flavors and smoky overtones

LEATHERWOOD
Strong and floral, with a distinctive piney flavor

MACADAMIA
Buttery, caramelly creaminess

ORANGE BLOSSOM
Made from mixed citrus; intensely floral, perfumy

THYME
Resinous, herbal, spicy/peppery

Honey is all about the terroir, and these exotic varieties reflect the huge range available Down Under.

HOPS: THE SPICE of BEER

Hops were known in ancient times, but there is no evidence that those first great brewing civilizations of the Middle East were ever tossing the sticky cones into their brews. The first solid evidence of hopped beer comes from pot scrapings dated to about 0 C.E. in the surprising location of northern Italy, a fact that must be extremely vexing to the Germans. I imagine Germanic archaeologists furiously digging holes in their countryside looking for potsherds to test, hoping to find evidence that predates those wine drinkers to their south.

Hops show up in medieval records about 800 C.E., with evidence of their use in beer about a century later. The smash hit phenomenon of hopped beers seems to have begun in northern Germany, probably in Bremen, and quickly spread to other Hansa trading league cities such as Hamburg. It took a century, but eventually the Dutch figured out how to make hopped beer, and a century or so later, the Flemish. By about 1420, hops jumped the channel to Kent, in southern England, which is still Britain's major hop cultivation region. By 1600, their clean bitterness, fragrant aroma, and preservative value made hops the primary herb of beer everywhere in Europe.

Early on, it was apparent that only certain regions produced good-quality hops. In the Old World, all the current hop-growing regions have been producing and exporting hops for centuries. Hops require a certain midsummer-day length to trigger cone production, so cultivation is restricted to certain latitudes. Moisture and drainage requirements are very specific, and hops are a tender plant, subject to many pests and diseases.

In the whole world, just a handful of places have just the right conditions to produce truly delicious hops. The flaming orange soil of the Goldbach Valley in western Bohemia, near the town of Saaz, and the Mittelfrüh subregion of the Hallertau are the most famous. Wine people use the term *terroir* to refer to that special combination of climate, soil, and everything else that makes a wine from one particular place unique from all others. Beer isn't so terroir-soaked as wine, but hops surely demonstrate it in full measure.

Few areas had more than one hop type growing, and turnover in varieties was measured in centuries, so hops tended to develop spontaneously and were named after the areas where they were grown. Many of these treasured old breeds still give stellar service. In the modern era, the breeding of new varieties has accelerated at a crazy pace, which means we have lots of new flavor possibilities for our beers. I used to feel I had a pretty good handle on hop varieties, but lately it seems that I find a new one every time I turn around.

These hops in Germany's Hallertau region will be picked within days.

HOPS' FORM *and* FUNCTION

Hop cones, once harvested and dried, are either packed "whole," without further processing, or formed into pellets. Dried hops are finely ground and extruded through a circular die, forming small pellets held together by the resins present. Although pellets are by far the more common form, some feel that whole hops have cleaner flavors because their cellular membranes haven't been torn apart in the pelletizing process. But "whole" hops aren't very compact, they don't store well, and only a few varieties are available to homebrewers.

Further processing results in separate aromatic oils and bittering compounds, but these processed components are not commonly used in homebrewing.

Hops contribute several things to beer. In addition to the bitterness and pleasant aromas, hops provide some antibiotic effect against gram-positive (a broad category of bacteria including beer-spoilage organisms *Lactobacillus* and *Pediococcus*) bacteria, which makes beer more stable, in theory at least. Hops also contain tannins (polyphenols) that are attracted to proteins in the boil, helping to clear the wort of unwanted, long-chain proteins. The result is a clearer beer in the end.

Bitterness comes from the alpha acids, and to a lesser extent, the related beta acids. Each hop crop is assayed and sold with an alpha acid percentage—ranging from 2 to nearly 20—that indicates its bittering power. Hops, of course, have greatly differing aromas, but the quality of the bitterness is always the same, even though the percentage varies. Aroma oils vary as well, but there is no generally available assay for this, which is one reason brewers often personally evaluate hops before purchasing.

Alpha acid is not stable; time and temperature take their toll on bittering power, which is why hops are best stored cold or frozen, and with limited access to oxygen. Some varieties are more unstable than others. While the specifics may vary, even well-stored hops can lose a third or more of their bittering power over the course of a year. If you're into fine-tuning, you'll want to adjust your hop quantities upward if you're using hops more than a few months old.

HOPS *in the* BREW

In its raw state, alpha acid is not very bitter or particularly soluble. A vigorous boil is needed to make a chemical change called isomerization, during which some parts of a molecule get rearranged, without adding or losing any atoms. The extent of alpha acid isomerization increases with boil time. Most of it will occur in the first hour, but small increases happen for about another two hours. After that, the wort actually becomes less bitter as the alpha acids break down. The amount of bitterness extracted from the hops is called utilization, and is expressed as a simple percentage, usually somewhere between 5 and 30 percent for homebrewers, depending on a large number of variables,

Hops are available as whole cones (top), pellets (middle), and isomerized alpha acid for bittering and aroma oil (bottom). Most homebrewers use pellets exclusively.

including time, pH, wort gravity, boil temperature and vigor, and others. Bitterness levels vary considerably from beer to beer, and are an important parameter of any style. The range is from under 10 BU (Bitterness Units) for lightly hopped beers such as American adjunct lagers and German wheat ales to upward of 70 BUs for double IPAs. The arms race of bitterness has stalled out due to solubility limits at about 100 BUs; despite this, there are efforts to climb even higher.

Boiling drives off a lot of aromatics, so for aroma, hops will need to be added later in the boil. Aroma hopping can be done in several ways: during the last 5 or 10 minutes, at the end of the boil in the kettle at flameout, flowing the hot wort through hops in a device called a hop back, or later during conditioning, or even in the serving cask, as is traditional for real ales. This technique of adding hops to conditioning beer is called "dry hopping." It is widely used for IPA and other hop-centric beers.

Another technique called "first wort hopping" is used to add hop character. Aroma hops are added to the kettle as the fresh wort is run off the mash, resulting in a richer hop aroma and flavor. This does contribute some bitterness, perhaps a third of what would be expected from a full 60-minute boil. Although the mechanism is still somewhat debatable, it is believed to involve something called hop glycosides, compounds in which various hop aroma components are bound to sugar or other carbohydrates. As long as the aroma components stay bound to the sugars, they aren't volatile, and so survive the boiling and fermentation process. These chemicals are always important for good hop flavor. The compounds are quite different from the aromatic hop oils, adding a lot of fruity and spicy notes.

Beer is normally brewed using hops that have been dried; but a frequent harvest specialty these days is "fresh hopping," using fresh, undried hops right off the vine. Because undried hops are not available commercially, many homebrewers and small breweries are harvesting hops grown locally for this purpose. Fresh hopped beers are supposed to have fresher, "greener" aromas and a certain just-picked briskness. I love the close-to-nature aspect, but just between you and me, I am not sure these beers offer better flavors in the glass.

HOP VARIETIES *and* PERSONALITY GROUPS

Every hop variety has its own aroma profile, reflecting its unique blend of dozens of aromatic oils. This also depends on where the hops are grown, and varies a bit from year to year as well. Getting a grip on the complex aroma profiles of the different varieties is a real challenge for all brewers, compounded by the fact that our vocabulary for hops is rudimentary and incomplete.

Brewers and breeders divide hops into three categories: those used for bittering and bought on the basis of the quantity of alpha acid; premium low-alpha hops used exclusively for aroma; and hops that are considered dual-use, with pleasant aromas and moderate alpha levels. This scheme tells us nothing about their aromatic personalities, of course. With the large number of hop varieties available, it is helpful to separate them into groups of similar characteristics. National origin is one possibility for an organizing principle, but this doesn't work so well considering that hop varieties may be bred in one place specifically to taste like hops from another country. So a flavor-based classification is more useful.

The specific ratios between the many aromatic oils offer a precise, if highly complex, measure of aromatic character, but with well over 100 different oils, it gets confusing very fast. One oil, cohumulone, is a convenient marker for a pungent character that is considered the antithesis of noble, and indeed low-cohumulone hops are clean and mellow in aroma, but recent studies indicate that the "low-co" measurement may be overrated.

I've divided the world of hops into neat, clear categories. But be aware that this sort of exercise is fraught with danger and skims over some fine points of individual hop personalities. I've picked unique names for these categories to emphasize that these are my own groups and are flavor-based rather than origin-related. These groups should be viewed as a helpful tool, and not the final word.

Within each category there is a progression from top to bottom from one flavor characteristic to another. Behind each hop name is a bar graph showing relative bitterness in alpha acid percentage; the faded area indicates the extent of the minimum and maximum levels.

There are relationships between the groups as well. In some ways, Styriacs are just a continuation of some English characteristics, or perhaps even a bridge to Continental "spicy" Saaz aromas, but I think of them quite separately. Bittering hops can all be lumped together, because for bittering, you're not getting all that much character out of them unless you're a hop freak that gets perverse pleasure out of beating the system and using bittering hops for aroma—nothing wrong with that. Normally, with bittering hops you're trying to make sure they support, or at least stay out of the way of, your aroma hops.

Hops with similar aromas are near to one another on the list. When trying to find a substitute, just look for hops near the hop you're trying to replace. Be aware of the direction. Do you want to go cleaner or more classic? Or racy, spicy, and more eccentric? Move up or down the list accordingly, and, of course, be aware of the differences in bitterness and adjust quantities accordingly.

Top to bottom: Hops ready for the harvest in Germany's Hallertau region; Communist-era glory for proletariat hop workers; Saaz bines on their way from the field to the picking shed; a stationary picker in Zatec, Czech Republic.

NOBLESSE

This group represents the continuum of Germanic hops, from the dry herbaceous, almost minty aromas of the classic Hallertau Mittelfrüh and its related varieties, through spicy varieties like Hersbrucker and Spalt and their variations to more modern, and even somewhat bent versions of the basic idea. They all tend to be low- to mid-alpha content, bred specifically for aroma.

SAAZY

This is a family of hops with Saaz as its spiritual homeland. The Saaz family is generally described with that vague word "spicy," but once you smell them, you know that word isn't quite right. The aroma is unique and delicious, yet delicate and subtle at the same time. Saaz resists efforts to reproduce its Czech character in other locations, but its close relatives thrive in far-flung places like Poland, the United States, and Asia. As you move to the bottom of the list, the aromas get less pure and Saazy, picking up notes of fruit, lemongrass, and other complex aromas.

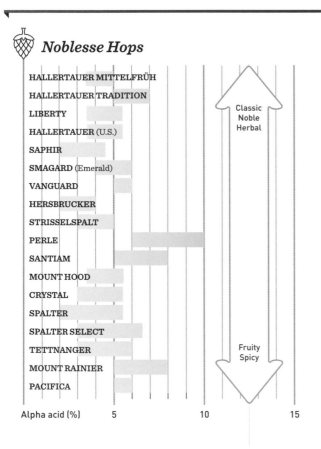

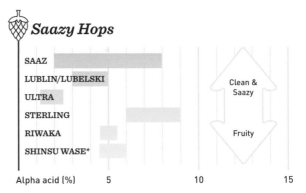

*Declining in acreage and may be difficult to find. Shown for substitution purposes

Hops have long been an international product because of their high value and expression of specific terroir, as shown by this label.

BRITANNIC

Classic English hop aromas are difficult to describe, but are often characterized as green, tangy, and a bit grassy, perhaps with some spiciness as well. This uniquely English character is crucial for pale ales and IPAs. East Kent emerged as *the* English hop-growing region during the eighteenth century, and Goldings from that area were the hop of choice for the strong, pale, and very highly hopped October beers that would eventually morph into IPAs a century later. Experimental breeding, especially with dwarf varieties, has produced useful results. Efforts to produce hops with this distinct character outside of England have only been partly successful. As you move down the list, the hops get more fruity and sometimes even edgy, with varying degrees of earthiness. Toward the bottom, they mellow out into a cool woodsiness that I find especially appropriate for dark beers.

Britannic Hops

KENT GOLDING
FIRST GOLD
GOLDING
WGV (Whitbread Golding Variety)

Clean
&
Classic

PIONEER
PHOENIX
PILGRIM
CHALLENGER
PROGRESS
FUGGLE
WILLAMETTE

Tangy
&
Earthy

PALISADE
BRAMLING CROSS
NORTHDOWN
NORTHERN BREWER

Woody
&
Neutral

Alpha acid (%)   5   10   15

Seasoned professional John J. Hall engaging in a hop evaluation "rubdown," where hops are rubbed vigorously against the heels of the hands and the cupped hands are smelled.

STYRIAC

Styria is a region in Slovenia where a form of Fuggles has been grown for a century or more under the name Styrian Goldings. In that location, Fuggles are more ethereal and less earthy than in their homeland, and are elegant enough to stand alone in pale beers, and are especially popular in Belgium for that purpose. On this list, the classic variety is in the middle; above it, the hops get even more bright and elegant; below it, a bit more earthy and spicy. All the hops in this category have very nice aromatic characteristics.

CASCADIAN

In the 1970s, classic Old World varieties crossed with New World wild hops created new strains with pungent, floral, piney, and citrusy characters. These became the heart and soul of the new American pale ales that emerged around 1980 with beers like Anchor Liberty Ale and Sierra Nevada Pale Ale.

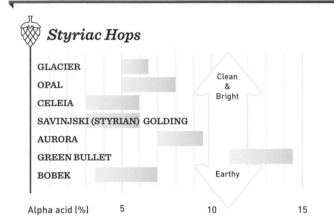

Styriac Hops

GLACIER
OPAL
CELEIA
SAVINJSKI (STYRIAN) GOLDING
AURORA
GREEN BULLET
BOBEK

Clean & Bright

Earthy

Alpha acid (%)   5   10   15

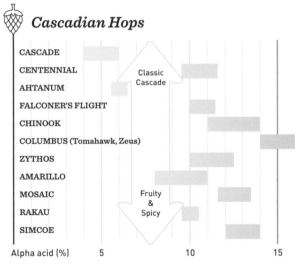

Cascadian Hops

CASCADE
CENTENNIAL
AHTANUM
FALCONER'S FLIGHT
CHINOOK
COLUMBUS (Tomahawk, Zeus)
ZYTHOS
AMARILLO
MOSAIC
RAKAU
SIMCOE

Classic Cascade

Fruity & Spicy

Alpha acid (%)   5   10   15

The purple paper is traditional and helps evaluate the color of the cones. Every lot is different.

PACIFICAL

This is a slightly unruly group of newer hops with fairly distinct personalities, showing aromas of apricot, passionfruit, wine grapes, and other fruits.

FOR BITTERING ONLY

For the most part, these hops are really only good for bittering. Many of the older varieties were bred as utilitarian workhorses without much thought of refinement, so some of them can be pretty pungent, but as purely bittering hops, that doesn't matter too much. While brewers may choose to get some aroma out of them for historical or sentimental reasons, most of these hops are best used early in the boil, leaving aroma duties up to more sophisticated varieties.

At the top of the chart are hops with neutral or subtle aromatic character that won't get in the way of elegant aromas from noble varieties like Hallertau. Moving toward the bottom, the character becomes more resiny, citrusy, and earthy.

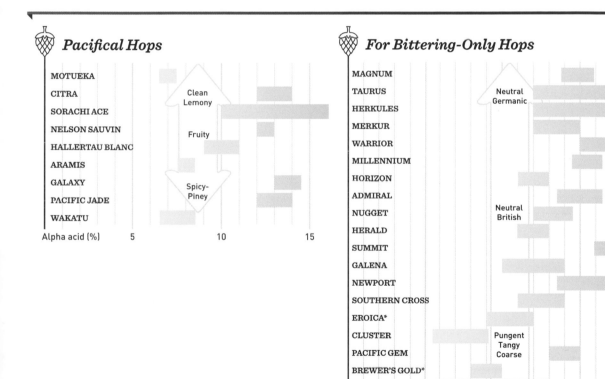

*Declining in acreage and may be difficult to find. Shown for substitution purposes.

HOP VARIETIES *in* DETAIL

The following is a list of most of the varieties of hops available in the world market. No single supplier will carry them all. Some boutique varieties can be scarce, so you may have to be flexible. Still, there are always lots of choices for making great beers, and by the time the ink is dry on this book there will be new ones to look for. This list is alphabetical; for substitutions and closely related varieties, refer to the preceding charts.

The vocabulary used to describe hops is particularly poor, as the dozens of different aromatic oils and other flavors do not correspond precisely to our sensory memories. Think about the smell of a Saaz. It is quite distinctive and really wonderful, but we end up using the deeply inadequate word "spicy" to describe its aroma. In the context of hops, *spicy* takes on a special meaning, so even though there isn't anything really spicy about Saaz, we accept the mismatch, because it's the best we can do. Terms like "fruity" and "floral" aren't much better. When we get to "pine" and "citrus," the words actually start to make sense.

In general, it's best if you develop your own sense of what each hop variety smells like and what it can do for a beer. Be aware that a variety may be very different in character and bittering power depending on where it's grown.

Variety	Origin	Type	Alpha Acid (%)	Group
ADMIRAL	England	Bittering	13.5–16.5	Britannic

History and Notes: English character high-alpha hop bred in 1998.
Aroma: Subtle, English, relatively neutral.

Uses:
• Bittering for a wide variety of English- and American-style ales

Variety	Origin	Type	Alpha Acid (%)	Group
AHTANUM	United States	Dual	5.7–6.3	Cascadian

History and Notes: Named for early hop area near Yakima, Washington.
Aroma: Floral and citrus; a bit more English and also more grapefruity than Cascade. Similar to Willamette, but a bit more racy.

Uses:
• Wide variety of aromatic American ales
• American versions of English bitters

Variety	Origin	Type	Alpha Acid (%)	Group
AMARILLO	United States	Dual	8–11	Cascadian

History and Notes: Privately developed in the late 1990s, this hop has found a home in sophisticated hoppy beers in the American craft tradition.
Aroma: A lightly floral and intensely citrusy character with a hint of the tropical.

Uses:
• American pale ales and IPAs; Belgian IPAs
• American wheat ales
• Single-hop ales

Variety	Origin	Type	Alpha Acid (%)	Group
ARAMIS	France (Alsace)	Aroma	7.5–8.5	Styriac

History and Notes: Strisselspalt parentage, released in 2013.
Aroma: Clean, unique, and fruity with hints of apricot, pear, citrus, and herbs.

Uses:
• Adventurous pale lagers
• Euro/Belgo pale and golden ales

Variety	Origin	Type	Alpha Acid (%)	Group
AURORA	Slovenia	Dual	7–9.5	Styriac

History and Notes: Northern Brewer parentage super-Styrian type created in the 1970s.
Aroma: Mix of spicy and bright grassy aromas.

Uses:
• Belgian pale-colored beers
• Bittering for lagers

Variety	Origin	Type	Alpha Acid (%)	Group
BOBEK	Czech Republic	Dual	3.5–7	Styriac

History and Notes: Northern Brewer + Yugoslavian male cross, created in the 1970s.
Aroma: Tangy as well as earthy.

Uses:
• Bittering for lagers
• A clean bittering choice for Belgian ales, light or dark

Variety	Origin	Type	Alpha Acid (%)	Group
BRAMLING CROSS	England	Aroma	5–7	Britannic

History and Notes: Golding + wild Manitoba hop cross.
Aroma: Spicy, leaning to blackcurrant (cat pee), in the best possible way.

Uses:
• Aroma for a dark hoppy English ale, should you want to make one
• Adds aromatic complexity to English-style pale ales, old ales, and barley wines

Variety	Origin	Type	Alpha Acid (%)	Group
CASCADE	United States, Argentina, New Zealand	Dual	4.5–7	Cascadian

History and Notes: Developed in 1972, from an open-pollinated seed discovered in 1956. Grown elsewhere with varying results.
Aroma: Unique American floral/spice character, defines U.S. pale ale style. Argentine versions quite pungent and earthy.

Uses:
• American pale ale
• Argentine-grown for Dorada Pampeana (Pampas gold)

Variety	Origin	Type	Alpha Acid (%)	Group
CELEIA	Slovenia	Aroma	3–6	Styriac

History and Notes: Cross between Styrian Goldings, Aurora, and a wild Slovenian hop.
Aroma: High quality, somewhere between Saaz and Styrian Goldings.

Uses:
• Belgian strong golden ales
• Suitable for lager bittering

Variety	Origin	Type	Alpha Acid (%)	Group
CENTENNIAL	United States	Dual	9.5–11.5	Cascadian

History and Notes: Sort of a super-Cascade, with similar character but higher alpha, created in 1990. Formerly called CFJ 90. Highly versatile.
Aroma: Intense floral-fruity aroma, very similar to Cascade.

Uses:
• Bittering and aroma in a wide variety of American-style bitter beers such as IPAs

Variety	Origin	Type	Alpha Acid (%)	Group
CHALLENGER	England	Dual	5–9	Britannic

History and Notes: Highly versatile English hop.
Aroma: A bit of a continental spicy-fruity aroma.

Uses:
• English golden/summer bitters and wheat ales
• Pleasant in a wide range of English ales

Variety	Origin	Type	Alpha Acid (%)	Group
CHINOOK	United States	Dual	11–14	Cascadian

History and Notes: Golding ancestry; released in 1985, one of the first big, resiny high-alpha hops to find favor for aroma.
Aroma: Resiny, piney, grapefruity punch.

Uses:
• Big, grapefruity IPAs and Double IPAs

Variety	Origin	Type	Alpha Acid (%)	Group
CITRA	United States	Aroma	11–13	Pacifical

History and Notes: Created in 2007 as exotic flavor variety.
Aroma: A fruit bowl of exotic aromas: lime, lemon, grapefruit, passionfruit, and litchi, but sometimes with a touch of oniony character.

Uses:
• Wacky wheat ales and fruit ales
• Showcase hop for IPAs and other hop-centric styles

Variety	Origin	Type	Alpha Acid (%)	Group
CLUSTER	United States	Bittering	5.5–8.5	Bittering Only

History and Notes: The original American hop, used since the nineteenth century for mainstream lager production.
Aroma: Pretty coarse, with floral and spicy notes, plus cattiness.

Uses:
• Pre-Prohibition and other American Pilsner, cream ale, historic steam beer

Variety	Origin	Type	Alpha Acid (%)	Group
COLUMBUS (a.k.a. Tomahawk, a.k.a. Zeus)	United States	Dual	14–16	Cascadian

History and Notes: A real hop blast, introduced in 2000. Has become a darling of the double IPA brewers.
Aroma: Unique, pepper, pine, and citrus with licorice notes as well.

Uses:
• Double IPAs
• Great for Belgian IPAs, saisons

Variety	Origin	Type	Alpha Acid (%)	Group
CRYSTAL	United States	Aroma	3–5.5	Noblesse

History and Notes: Triploid hybrid (1993) with Hallertauer parentage.
Aroma: Most spicy and tangy of the recent U.S. Hallertau types.

Uses:
• Aroma for variations of German-style Pils
• Great for Kölsch and cream ale

EMERALD (*see* Smagard)

Variety	Origin	Type	Alpha Acid (%)	Group
FALCONER'S FLIGHT	United States	Dual	10–12	Cascadian

History and Notes: A blend of "C" hops plus experimental varieties.
Aroma: Floral, lemon, grapefruit, and a ton of American character.

Uses:
• Developed with American pale and India pale ales
• Works in other beers where citrusy American character feels right

Variety	Origin	Type	Alpha Acid (%)	Group
FIRST GOLD	England	Dual	6.5–8.5	Britannic

History and Notes: Dwarf hop with WGV heritage, introduced in the 1990s.
Aroma: Fine English Golding character.

Uses:
• Classic for English-syle pale ales and bitters

Variety	Origin	Type	Alpha Acid (%)	Group
FUGGLE	England, United States	Dual	3–6	Britannic

History and Notes: Discovered in 1861. Always considered a lesser hop than the Goldings type.
Aroma: Less refined aroma than Goldings, a little more earthy and woody.

Uses:
• Traditional hop for darker English beers

Variety	Origin	Type	Alpha Acid (%)	Group
GALAXY	Australia	Dual	11–16	Bittering Only

History and Notes: Perle parentage, bred in 1994.
Aroma: Interesting citrus and passionfruit notes.

Uses:
• Creative interpretations of pale lagers
• Interesting topnotes on IPAs and other hoppy ales

Variety	Origin	Type	Alpha Acid (%)	Group
GALENA	United States	Bittering	12–14	Bittering Only

History and Notes: Created in 1978 from Brewer's Gold ancestry, and grown in large amounts.
Aroma: Intense English flavor with some citrus, but generally one of the less pungent of the U.S. high-alpha types.

Uses:
• Clean bittering for a wide variety of Anglo-American craft beers

Variety	Origin	Type	Alpha Acid (%)	Group
GLACIER	United States	Dual	5–6.5	Styriac

History and Notes: Introduced in 2000, it is broadly in the Fuggle family, but I'd call it more of a super Styrian; low cohumulone.
Aroma: Somewhat indistinct in character, but very clean and elegant.

Uses:
• Pale Belgian sles and saisons
• Super-clean aroma in blonde ales and international lagers

Variety	Origin	Type	Alpha Acid (%)	Group
GOLDING	United States, Canada	Aroma	4–6	Britannic

History and Notes: American-grown version of the English classic.
Aroma: Mild, pleasant, and very English.

Uses:
- Aroma in English-style ales
- Adds a spot of English flavor to American pale ales, IPAs

Variety	Origin	Type	Alpha Acid (%)	Group
GREEN BULLET	New Zealand	Bittering	11–14	Styriac

History and Notes: Clean, neutral bittering.
Aroma: Some floral and fruity/raisiny aromas; some Styrian character.

Uses:
- Bittering for Southern Hemisphere lagers and ales
- Bittering for many different Belgian-style ales

Variety	Origin	Type	Alpha Acid (%)	Group
HALLERTAU BLANC	Germany	Aroma	9–11	Pacifical

History and Notes: Released in 2013; developed from Hallertau parentage.
Aroma: Floral, lemon, grapefruit, and a ton of American character.

Uses:
- Distinctive aroma notes in delicate beers
- Great in fruit beers

Variety	Origin	Type	Alpha Acid (%)	Group
HALLERTAUER MITTELFRÜH	Germany	Aroma	5–7	Noblesse

History and Notes: Original noble aroma hop of northern Bavaria; was being replaced with newer varieties until interest from U.S. brewers, notably Boston Beer Co., created some demand.
Aroma: Very cool, herbal, with a bit of woodiness and hints of mint.

Uses:
- *The* classic for German Pilsners

Variety	Origin	Type	Alpha Acid (%)	Group
HALLERTAUER (U.S.)	United States	Aroma	3.5–5.5	Noblesse

History and Notes: American-grown version of German noble aroma hop.
Aroma: A bit coarser and more spicy than the classic Mittelfrüh.

Uses:
- American-style lagers
- Wherever a dry, herbaceous character is desired

Variety	Origin	Type	Alpha Acid (%)	Group
HALLERTAUER TRADITION	Germany	Aroma	5–7	Noblesse

History and Notes: Disease-resistant variety based on Hallertau introduced in 1993.
Aroma: Clean, reasonably noble; a little less refined than Hallertau Mittelfrüh.

Uses:
- Aroma in a wide variety of lagers, especially German-style ones

Variety	Origin	Type	Alpha Acid (%)	Group
HERALD	England	Bittering	11–13	Bittering Only

History and Notes: New high-alpha dwarf, a sister of Pioneer.
Aroma: Described as having an "acceptable flavor" in the English vein.

Uses:
- Bittering for a wide variety of English-inflected ales

Variety	Origin	Type	Alpha Acid (%)	Group
HERKULES	Germany	Bittering	12–17	Bittering Only

History and Notes: Newer high-alpha hop developed in northern Bavaria.
Aroma: Vague, but clean and delicate aromas.

Uses:
- Bittering for a wide variety of lagers and continental ales

Variety	Origin	Type	Alpha Acid (%)	Group
HERSBRUCKER	Germany	Aroma	2–5	Noblesse

History and Notes: Traditional German variety not designated as noble, but with a fine aroma nonetheless.
Aroma: Spicier and a bit more fruity than Hallertauer and perhaps a bit less complex.

Uses:
- Aroma for a variety of lagers and continental ales

Variety	Origin	Type	Alpha Acid (%)	Group
HORIZON	United States	Bittering	11–13	Bittering Only

History and Notes: High-alpha hop created in 1970 and related to Nugget.
Aroma: Floral and spicy, with low cohumulone.

Uses:
• Bittering for a wide variety of American-style ales

Variety	Origin	Type	Alpha Acid (%)	Group
KENT GOLDING	England	Aroma	4–7	Britannic

History and Notes: For centuries, known as the finest traditional English aroma hop.
Aroma: Tangy, spicy, and somewhat grassy, yet refined in character.

Uses:
• Historically reserved for pale ales
• Amazing in strong ales and barley wines

Variety	Origin	Type	Alpha Acid (%)	Group
LIBERTY	United States	Aroma	3.5–5	Noblesse

History and Notes: American Hallertauer clone.
Aroma: The most Hallertau-like of the American Hallertau types, but somewhat floral and fruity, often with a pronounced pineapple character.

Uses:
• Suitable for aroma in most lager styles

Variety	Origin	Type	Alpha Acid (%)	Group
LUBLIN/LUBELSKI	Poland	Aroma	3–5	Saazy

History and Notes: Classic Polish hop with Saaz origins.
Aroma: A refined spicy flavor, not quite as elegant as Saaz.

Uses:
• Eastern European lagers
• Belgian blonde and strong golden ales

Variety	Origin	Type	Alpha Acid (%)	Group
MAGNUM	Germany, United States	Bittering	11–16	Bittering Only

History and Notes: High-alpha variety with some German taste characteristics. German and American versions very similar in use.
Aroma: Super-clean and neutral in character, with little aroma.

Uses:
• Bittering for lagers
• Any beer where a super-clean bitterness is needed

Variety	Origin	Type	Alpha Acid (%)	Group
MERKUR	Germany	Dual	12–15	Bittering Only

History and Notes: Newer hop with Magnum parentage, low-cohumulone.
Aroma: Vibrant spicy/floral, with some earthiness.

Uses:
• Bittering for all lagers
• Radical versions of Germanic beers. German IPA, anybody?

Variety	Origin	Type	Alpha Acid (%)	Group
MILLENNIUM	United States	Bittering	14.5–16.5	Bittering Only

History and Notes: A descendant of Nugget, created in 2000.
Aroma: Described as mild and neutral, great for a bittering hop.

Uses:
• Wide variety of bittering duties

Variety	Origin	Type	Alpha Acid (%)	Group
MOSAIC	United States	Aroma	11.5–13.5	Cascadian

History and Notes: A daughter of Simcoe, released in 2012.
Aroma: Complex, with tropical fruits, citrus, berries, pine, and earth.

Uses:
• Showcase hop for modern IPAs, pale ales
• Hop-forward wheat ales

Variety	Origin	Type	Alpha Acid (%)	Group
MOTUEKA	New Zealand	Aroma	6.5–8.5	Pacifical

History and Notes: Newer hop bred in New Zealand from Saaz parentage.
Aroma: Super-clean lemon-lime citrus; blends well with Saaz.

Uses:
• Saison, witbier, and other non-German wheat beers
• Fantastic in fruit ales

Variety	Origin	Type	Alpha Acid (%)	Group
MOUNT HOOD	United States	Aroma	4–8	Noblesse

History and Notes: An American Hallertauer clone with similarities to Hersbrucker. Developed with Liberty, Crystal, and Ultra.
Aroma: Seminoble, mild, a bit pungent.

Uses:
• Aroma in a wide variety of blonde ales and lagers where super-tradtional aroma isn't needed

Variety	Origin	Type	Alpha Acid (%)	Group
MOUNT RAINIER	United States	Dual	5–8	Noblesse

History and Notes: Newer variety with German and English parentage.
Aroma: Described as noble with a touch of citrus and licorice.

Uses:
• Characterful lagers
• Dark Belgian ales and American brown ales

Variety	Origin	Type	Alpha Acid (%)	Group
NELSON SAUVIN	New Zealand	Dual	11–13	Pacifical

History and Notes: Created in 2000.
Aroma: Super-fruity, a bit like sauvignon blanc wine, with gooseberry accents; a love-it-or- hate-it hop.

Uses:
• Single-hop beers
• A twist on strong goldens and saisons

Variety	Origin	Type	Alpha Acid (%)	Group
NEWPORT	United States	Bittering	13.5–17	Bittering Only

History and Notes: Created in 2002, a high-alpha variety with the focus on bitterness.
Aroma: Pungent and somewhat resiny.

Uses:
• Bittering for American ales
• Anywhere a sharp, resiny character is desired

Variety	Origin	Type	Alpha Acid (%)	Group
NORTHDOWN	England	Dual	7–10	Britannic

History and Notes: Bred in England in the 1970s, and a relative of Challenger and Target. One of the best of the English dual-use hops.
Aroma: Mellow, a bit dark; more like Northern Brewer than Goldings.

Uses:
• Great in dark beers
• Steam beer

Variety	Origin	Type	Alpha Acid (%)	Group
NORTHERN BREWER	United States, Germany, England	Dual	7.5–10	Britannic

History and Notes: Neutral-tasting multipurpose hop, bred in England from Golding parent in 1934.
Aroma: Subtle, woody, evergreen notes, with chocolatey bitterness.

Uses:
• California common (Anchor Steam facsimiles)
• Dark Belgian ales

Variety	Origin	Type	Alpha Acid (%)	Group
NUGGET	United States, Germany	Bittering	12–14.5	Bittering Only

History and Notes: High-alpha hop with Brewers Gold + Golding parentage, released in 1983.
Aroma: Delicate but pleasant.

Uses:
• Workhorse bittering hop for American-style ales

Variety	Origin	Type	Alpha Acid (%)	Group
OPAL	Germany	Dual	5–8	Styriac

History and Notes: Low-cohumulone; spicy/grassy with a nearly English character.
Aroma: A mix of fruity, flowery, citrus, and herbs.

Uses:
• Belgian ales
• Bent versions of German classics

Variety	Origin	Type	Alpha Acid (%)	Group
PACIFIC GEM	New Zealand	Bittering	13–15	Bittering Only

History and Notes: Newer bittering variety.
Aroma: Rather coarse mix of fruit and a slight oakiness.

Uses:
• Great for bittering dark beers
• Try it for a wood-aged beer

Variety	Origin	Type	Alpha Acid (%)	Group
PACIFIC JADE	New Zealand	Dual	12–14	Pacifical

History and Notes: Versatile hop released in 2004.
Aroma: Described as "black pepper and citrus."

Uses:
• Southern Hemisphere lagers and golden ales
• Should work great in a saison or a reinterpreted hefeweizen

Variety	Origin	Type	Alpha Acid (%)	Group
PACIFICA	New Zealand	Dual	5–6	Noblesse

History and Notes: Hallertau parentage.
Aroma: Noble hop with a New World edge of citrus and flowers, plus a touch of orange Creamsicle.

Uses:
• Lager, golden ale, saison, strong golden
• Southern Hemisphere IPAs

Variety	Origin	Type	Alpha Acid (%)	Group
PALISADE	United States	Dual	5.5–9.5	Britannic

History and Notes: High-alpha variety with versatile character.
Aroma: Floral and fruity, with a mix of English and German character with some earthiness.

Uses:
• All-purpose bittering
• Aroma for creative versions of lagers or European ales

Variety	Origin	Type	Alpha Acid (%)	Group
PERLE	Germany, United States	Dual	6–10	Noblesse

History and Notes: German-bred Hallertau type, released in 1978.
Aroma: Spicier than Hallertau, with delicate floral and fruity notes.

Uses:
• Noble hop substitute in lagers and elsewhere
• Nice in weiss!

Variety	Origin	Type	Alpha Acid (%)	Group
PHOENIX	England	Dual	8.5–11.5	Britannic

History and Notes: Newer variety.
Aroma: Described as having a bright and pleasantly attractive English character.

Uses:
• Bittering for English pale ales, IPA, golden bitter
• Adds English notes to New World ales

Variety	Origin	Type	Alpha Acid (%)	Group
PILGRIM	England	Dual	7–11	Britannic

History and Notes: Newer variety developed at Wye and released in 2000.
Aroma: Citrus notes with dark cedar and honey character; earthy.

Uses:
• English wheat or summer ales
• Saison and witbier

Variety	Origin	Type	Alpha Acid (%)	Group
PIONEER	England	Dual	8–10	Britannic

History and Notes: New dwarf variety released in 1990s.
Aroma: Pleasant, clean bitterness and mild English aroma, with hints of citrus.

Uses:
• Adds complexity in English pale and golden ales
• Non-German wheat ales

Variety	Origin	Type	Alpha Acid (%)	Group
PRIDE OF RINGWOOD	Australia	Dual	8.5–10	Bittering Only

History and Notes: Tasmanian wild/English cross.
Aroma: Rough and spicy English-character hop.

Uses:
• Bittering for darker ales

Variety	Origin	Type	Alpha Acid (%)	Group
PROGRESS	England	Aroma	4–7	Britannic

History and Notes: WGV and American parentage, bred in the 1960s.
Aroma: Intense English character, like Fuggle, but a little sweeter.

Uses:
• Aroma in wide variety of English-style ales

Variety	Origin	Type	Alpha Acid (%)	Group
RAKAU	New Zealand	Dual	10–11	Cascadian

History and Notes: Developed as a pleasant bittering variety from Saaz parentage.
Aroma: Fruity, with tropical aroma highlights of passionfruit, mango, and peach, but also a bit peppery and spicy; low cohumulone.

Uses:
- Southern Hemisphere lagers and ales, especially Australian golden bitters and sparkling ales
- Any beer where a tropical fruity character is desirable

Variety	Origin	Type	Alpha Acid (%)	Group
RIWAKA	New Zealand	Aroma	4.5–6.5	Saazy

History and Notes: Saaz parentage, created in 1997.
Aroma: Saazy spiciness, twisted up with lots of grapefruit and other citrus; high oil content.

Uses:
- Sounds like a wild Southern Hemisphere IPA to me

Variety	Origin	Type	Alpha Acid (%)	Group
SAAZ	Czech Republic, United States	Aroma	2–8	Saazy

History and Notes: The classic Pilsner hop from Bohemia; Saaz grown elsewhere has a less distinct and not as refined a varietal character.
Aroma: Usually described as spicy, but that's just code for "Saazy."

Uses:
- The classic spicy/herbal hop of Pilsner beers
- Belgian strong golden ales and Tripels, especially mixed with Styrians.

Variety	Origin	Type	Alpha Acid (%)	Group
SANTIAM	United States	Dual	5–7	Noblesse

History and Notes: Introduced in 1997, with Tettnang + Halletau parentage and character.
Aroma: Clean, noble hop character.

Uses:
- Apropriate bittering and aroma for any Germanic beer
- Adds unique character to hoppy ales

Variety	Origin	Type	Alpha Acid (%)	Group
SAPHIR	Germany	Aroma	2–4.5	Noblesse

History and Notes: Low cohumulone aroma hop developed in 2002.
Aroma: Distinctive flowery and fruity character.

Uses:
- Oddball Germanic beers or Euro-pale ales, wheat ales, Kölsch
- Single-hop beers

Variety	Origin	Type	Alpha Acid (%)	Group
SAVINJSKI (STYRIAN) GOLDING	Slovenia	Aroma	3–6	Styriac

History and Notes: Formerly known as Styrian Goldings. English Fuggles transplanted to Slovenia in the last century.
Aroma: A Fuggle, but with a rich Golding character.

Uses:
- Classic in pale-colored Belgian ales
- Slavic ales

Variety	Origin	Type	Alpha Acid (%)	Group
SIMCOE	United States	Dual	12–14	Cascadian

History and Notes: Recently developed as a bittering hop with unique and pleasant aromatic character.
Aroma: Unique apricot aroma with piney and citrusy overtones.

Uses:
- Single-hop ales
- Belgian, American IPAs

Variety	Origin	Type	Alpha Acid (%)	Group
SMAGARD (a.k.a. Emerald)	Germany	Dual	4–6	Noblesse

History and Notes: Part of a series of gemstone-named hops developed in Bavaria since 2000.
Aroma: Fruity and flowery.

Uses:
- Recommended for altbier and Kölsch
- Many creative lager uses possible

Variety	Origin	Type	Alpha Acid (%)	Group
SORACHI ACE	United States	Dual	10–16	Pacifical

History and Notes: Newer hop with complex parentage of noble Euro-hops plus Japanese varieties.
Aroma: Unique citrusy punch, said to have a touch of dill aroma.

Uses:
• Popular in single-hop beers
• Saison and other pale Belgian styles

Variety	Origin	Type	Alpha Acid (%)	Group
SOUTHERN CROSS	New Zealand	Bittering	11–14	Bittering Only

History and Notes: Bittering hop released in 1994.
Aroma: Lemon peel, pine/resin, and a bit of spice.

Uses:
• Southern Hemisphere lager bittering, or unique IPAs
• Bittering in hoppy red, brown, and rye ales

Variety	Origin	Type	Alpha Acid (%)	Group
SPALTER	Germany	Aroma	2–5.5	Noblesse

History and Notes: Highly valued traditional German noble hop.
Aroma: Less herbal than Hallertau, but not as spicy as Saaz.

Uses:
• Classic in altbier and Kölsch

Variety	Origin	Type	Alpha Acid (%)	Group
SPALTER SELECT	Germany	Aroma	3–6.5	Noblesse

History and Notes: Disease-resistant cultivar of Spalt, created in 1991.
Aroma: A bit more like Tettnang or Hersbrucker than Spalt.

Uses:
• Euro-lagers and wheat beers

Variety	Origin	Type	Alpha Acid (%)	Group
STERLING	United States	Aroma	6–9	Saazy

History and Notes: Introduced in 1998, bred from complex European ancestry.
Aroma: Pleasant mix of herbs and spices, with hints of flowers and citrus; reasonably Saaz-like.

Uses:
• American Pilsners, wheat ales

Variety	Origin	Type	Alpha Acid (%)	Group
STRISSELSPALT	France	Aroma	2–3	Noblesse

History and Notes: Classic French/Alsatian variety, probably related to Hallertauer.
Aroma: Clean, slightly spicy.

Uses:
• All manner of French and Belgian beers, especially bière de garde

Variety	Origin	Type	Alpha Acid (%)	Group
SUMMIT	United States	Bittering	16–19	Bittering Only

History and Notes: Dwarf hop related to Nugget, released in 2003.
Aroma: Described as having a touch of onion and garlic along with citrus and spice.

Uses:
• Bittering for a wide variety of ales

Variety	Origin	Type	Alpha Acid (%)	Group
TARGET	England	Bittering	8–13	Bittering Only

History and Notes: Early high-alpha variety from Kent Golding parentage; mostly goes into extract products.
Aroma: Intense, not well regarded.

Uses:
• Bittering for English-style beers

Variety	Origin	Type	Alpha Acid (%)	Group
TAURUS	Germany	Bittering	12–17	Bittering Only

History and Notes: Hallertau parentage, bred at the German Hops Research Institute.
Aroma: Ultra-high-alpha hop with some German character.

Uses:
• Clean bitterness for lagers and other beers where a neutral character is desired

Variety	Origin	Type	Alpha Acid (%)	Group
TETTNANGER	Germany, United States	Aroma	3–6	Noblesse

History and Notes: Traditional Bavarian aroma hop related to Saaz.
Aroma: Bright, clean, with a soft spiciness.

Uses:
- Great in weissbier!
- A classic component of many American lagers

TOMAHAWK (*see* Columbus)

Variety	Origin	Type	Alpha Acid (%)	Group
ULTRA	United States	Aroma	2.2–3.5	Saazy

History and Notes: Newer high quality aroma variety.
Aroma: Very nice Saaz character.

Uses:
- Czech-style Pilsners, Belgian-style golden

Variety	Origin	Type	Alpha Acid (%)	Group
VANGUARD	United States	Dual	5–6	Noblesse

History and Notes: Created in 1997 from Hallertau parentage.
Aroma: Gentle, somewhat noble character with a touch of spice.

Uses:
- Aroma for a variety of continental lagers and ales

Variety	Origin	Type	Alpha Acid (%)	Group
WAKATU	New Zealand	Bittering	6.5–8.5	Pacifical

History and Notes: Hallertau + New Zealand parentage.
Aroma: Bold pine and orange, plus floral notes.

Uses:
- Distinctive in IPAs and similar styles
- Great for hoppy dark beers

Variety	Origin	Type	Alpha Acid (%)	Group
WARRIOR	United States	Bittering	15–17	Bittering Only

History and Notes: Newer high-alpha variety with little aromatic use.
Aroma: Mild and relatively indistinct. Very clean bittering hop.

Uses:
- Versatile Bittering Only hop

Variety	Origin	Type	Alpha Acid (%)	Group
WGV (Whitbread Golding Variety)	England	Dual	5–8	Britannic

History and Notes: Traditional English hop that came to prominence in the nineteenth century.
Aroma: A sweet, fruity aroma; a little coarse.

Uses:
- Bittering and aroma for a wide variety of English-style ales

Variety	Origin	Type	Alpha Acid (%)	Group
WILLAMETTE	United States	4–6	Dual	Britannic

History and Notes: American-grown version of Fuggle.
Aroma: English character very similar to Fuggle, but a bit softer.

Uses:
- American versions of English-style ales
- Adds English character to any beer

ZEUS (*see* Columbus)

Variety	Origin	Type	Alpha Acid (%)	Group
ZYTHOS	United States	10–12.5	Aroma	Cascadian

History and Notes: A proprietary blend of newer hop varieties.
Aroma: Pineapple + citrus and a bit piney.

Uses:
- Pale ales, IPAs, and any other hop-forward American style ales

WATCH FOR THESE NEW OR LESSER-KNOWN VARIETIES:

Agnus, Amethyst, Apollo, Archer, Baron, Beata, Belma, Bishop, Bodaceia, Bouclier, Bravo, Calypso, Dana, Delta, Dr. Rudi, Duchess, El Dorado, Ella, Endeavor, Flyer, Harmonie, Huell Melon, Jester, Junga, Kazbek, Kohatu, Landlady, Lemondrop, Mandarina Bavaria, Marynka, Minstrel, Multihead, Pilot, Polaris, Premiant, Sladek, Sonnet, Sovereign, Summer, Super Galena, Super Pride, Sussex, Sybilla, Sylva, Topaz, Triskel, Vital, Wai-Iti, Waimea

WATER WITHOUT TEARS

Brewing water isn't about the romance of mountain springs or glacier-fed northern lakes. It's pure chemistry, which for many of us can be a dry topic, and maybe even a bit intimidating. Hopefully, I can lay it out so even an artistic brain can understand it. As chemistry goes, this is pretty simple stuff.

Water is often described as the universal solvent. This is because its component atoms—two hydrogen and one oxygen—balance each other and leave the molecule with a positive charge on one end and a negative one on the other. These charges are important because the things we might want to dissolve in water have charges, too. When ionic compounds like mineral salts go into solution, they temporarily break apart, gravitating toward one or the other end of the water molecules. These detached molecule parts are called ions, and they are of prime importance in brewing. We'll be looking at adding or removing these in order to get the perfect water to make any given beer.

The minerals are there because water falling as rain interacts with the rocks that are under our feet. In areas with limestone geology, the water picks up calcium carbonate and forms hard, alkaline water, which is very common. In areas with volcanic rock, the minerals tend to be relatively insoluble, so the water remains soft. In the relatively rare places where limestone has been altered by volcanic activity to make gypsum, that mineral causes an acidic hardness.

Minerals dissolved in water may have some flavors of their own but, more important, they affect the chemistry and pH of the mash, and also affect the flavor of hops in specific ways. Prior to about 1880, brewers didn't really understand water chemistry, so they had to make do with what they had, brewing beers that worked with the local water. Most of the world's great beer styles originated this way. Today, of course, we have the luxury of brewing any beer style wherever we want, because we can treat the water to create any profile we want.

There are two extremes to water treatment. You can dive in deeply and re-create classic brewing waters down to the last molecule, measure every batch minute-by-minute with a pH meter, and generally geek out over water. I would say that if this is your idea of fun, by all means, go for it. And if you're a million-barrel-a-year brewery, such attention to details would probably be wise. But for most of us, just a little consideration of your water chemistry will yield great results. Fortunately, once you do the calculations for a few different beer types, you're set. It's usually not necessary to fine-tune every batch.

So what's in your water? This varies, but we can think of water minerals in a few distinct categories.

THE BIG SIX WATER MINERALS

There are just a few ions in common in water that play the major roles in mash chemistry, pH, and beer flavor. The cations (positive ions) include calcium (the most important one), magnesium, and sodium. Anions (negative ions) include bicarbonate, sulfate, and chloride. These all have different effects in mash chemistry and beer flavor. Calcium or magnesium bicarbonate contributes temporary hardness that can easily be removed by a number of methods. Calcium or (less commonly) magnesium sulfate is much more difficult to remove and so is considered permanent hardness.

Positive and negative ions combine to form mineral molecules in specific proportions, which means there is a specific ratio of calcium to carbonate, for example, or sodium to chloride. This has to be taken into account when adding or removing minerals. When we remove carbonate, we can remove only as much of it as there is calcium to pair with, which of course removes calcium. Because calcium is crucial for good mash functioning, we have to add it back, but that in turn brings other minerals like sulfate or chloride with it, and these have specific effects of their own.

MINERAL IONS IN BREWING WATER

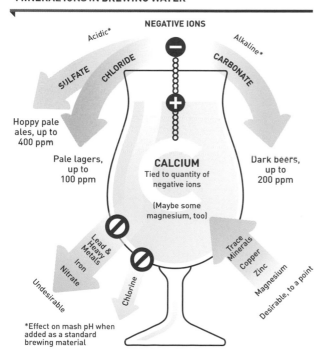

Ratios of negative and positive hardness minerals in brewing water play a role in mash pH and other chemistry, and also affect the flavor of hops.

TRACE MINERALS

While they have little or no effect on mash chemistry, they are important for yeast nutrition—especially copper, zinc, and magnesium. However, in large quantities these can cause problems such as off-flavors and haze formation. All but the softest (or distilled) water has a reasonably good mix of trace minerals, although yeast experts believe that most fermentations can benefit by the addition of small amounts of zinc, which is removed during the mash, and which is why that element is usually included in yeast nutrient.

HEAVY METALS AND OTHER CONTAMINANTS

Brewing water must be of good drinking quality, and municipalities have to meet EPA standards for metals, pesticides, nitrates (a marker for organic pollution), and others. Lead and iron can be picked up from pipes, especially with soft or acidic water, and the same is true for brewing equipment. Brass fittings generally contain lead in the mix, which makes them easier to drill and machine. Well water should be tested, especially in mountainous regions or areas where mining for metals is common, as things like arsenic and other dangerous heavy metals may be present. These are generally difficult to filter out, so in those cases, starting with distilled or reverse osmosis (RO) water is probably best.

CHLORINE

This is added as an antimicrobial to municipal water supplies, either as free chlorine or a chemical called chloramine. While not harmful, free chlorine is highly reactive and can combine with phenolic compounds in malt and hops to create chlorophenols, a group of persistent and nasty-smelling chemicals that reek of bandages and electrical fires. Boiling or standing overnight will remove free chlorine, but not chloramines. Carbon filters will remove both, but vary in their success with chloramines, which also generally require a slow flow through the filter for best results.

Potassium metabisulfite (Campden tablets) can be used to remove either form of chlorine. One 0.5-gram tablet, crushed and dissolved, is capable of dechlorinating (or dechloraminating) 20 gallons/76 L of water. The process is pretty much instantaneous.

BREWING WATER MINERALS *in* DETAIL

The following is a list of the ions that are most commonly encountered in water. Some of these have important effects on the mash, while others just come along for the ride.

Ion	Symbol	Charge	Typical ppm	Water Soluble?	ppm = Millival
CALCIUM	Ca	++	25–90	Yes	0.050

Effect on Mash and Beer: Acidifies. Precipitates phosphates. Enhances enzyme action. Improves runoff. Speeds proteolysis. Enhances stability of finished beer. Improves clarification. Principal component of hardness.

Ion	Symbol	Charge	Typical ppm	Water Soluble?	ppm = Millival
MAGNESIUM	Mg	++	1–10	Yes	0.0833

Effect on Mash and Beer: Acidifies. Precipitates phosphates. In excess, may contribute to unpleasant bitter flavor.

Ion	Symbol	Charge	Typical ppm	Water Soluble?	ppm = Millival
SODIUM	Na	+	2–12	Highly	0.0435

Effect on Mash and Beer: Not really important in the mash. Disagreeable in excess. In moderation, adds a fullness, especially to darker beers. Enhances sweetness.

Ion	Symbol	Charge	Typical ppm	Water Soluble?	ppm = Millival
POTASSIUM	K	+	0.5–2	Highly	0.0256

Effect on Mash and Beer: Similar to sodium, but needed for yeast nutrition. Not really important in the mash.

Ion	Symbol	Charge	Typical ppm	Water Soluble?	ppm = Millival
CHLORIDE	Cl	–	5–16	Highly	0.02817

Effect on Mash and Beer: No effect on mash in normal quantities. Increases hop bitterness. In limited amounts, gives fullness.

Ion	Symbol	Charge	Typical ppm	Water Soluble?	ppm = Millival
SULFATE	SO_4	––	5–70	Yes	0.02083

Effect on Mash and Beer: Best for pale, dry beers, especially pale ales. Enhances clean hop flavor. Accentuates/sharpens hop bitterness. Lightens color. Sulfate is usually in the form of calcium sulfate ($CaSO_4$), or gypsum.

Ion	Symbol	Charge	Typical ppm	Water Soluble?	ppm = Millival
BICARBONATE	HCO_3	–	10–300	Yes	0.01639

Effect on Mash and Beer: Strongly alkaline; resists acidification of the mash. Hinders alpha amylase. Reddens pale beers. Impedes cold break. Emphasizes bitterness, but harshly. Best for lightly hopped and dark beers. May be removed by boiling, which drives off CO_2 and changes bicarbonate into insoluble carbonate.

Ion	Symbol	Charge	Typical ppm	Water Soluble?	ppm = Millival
CARBONATE	CO_3	––	—	No	0.03333

Effect on Mash and Beer: As an insoluble mineral, carbonate has no effect on brewing in this form.

WATER MINERALS *and* BREWING

The first thing you need to do is find out what kind of water you have. Regions vary according to the underlying rock formations from where the water is drawn, and in some regions, such as New York City and much of California, the source may be quite a distance away from the tap. To further complicate things, there may be seasonal variations that range from chlorination level (usually higher in the summer) to frequent changes in water sources (sometimes weekly as is the case for much of Southern California). Municipal water supplies are required by law to provide their customers with an analysis, so these should be easy to get hold of to sort out what kind of water you have and what kind of beer it wants to make. Well water is more variable, and if you're drinking it, you should be testing it. If you're in a hard water area (most of the Midwest, for example), well water is likely to be twice as hard or even more than the ground water, and often contains contaminants such as sulfur and iron, so be cautious.

MINERAL IONS IN BREWING WATER

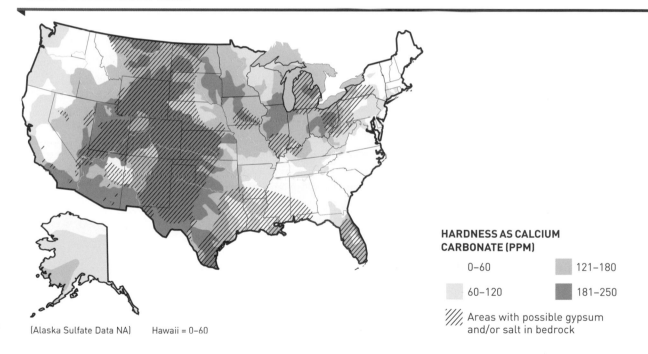

HARDNESS AS CALCIUM CARBONATE (PPM)

0–60   121–180

60–120   181–250

/// Areas with possible gypsum and/or salt in bedrock

(Alaska Sulfate Data NA)   Hawaii = 0–60

Ratios of negative and positive hardness minerals in brewing water play a role in mash pH and other chemistry, and also affect the flavor of hops. Water supplies drawn from large lakes and rivers will generally have lower mineral content than shown on this map. Well water may be harder. Southern California and some other locations draw water from multiple sources, and water makeup may change rapidly when sources are switched. This is just a general guide. Most areas have small-scale local variation. Consult your local water utility for more accurate information.

In most places, water will be somewhere on the spectrum between very soft and very hard and alkaline (temporary hardness) water. Sulfate water is rarer, so we'll deal with it later. "Soft," for brewing purposes, is anything under 60 to 70 ppm of bicarbonate. At these levels, alkaline minerals are unlikely to have much influence on mash chemistry or hop flavor.

Now, we need to think about what kind of beer we're brewing and what we might need to do to the water to make a delicious beer. We'll start the easy way, by looking at tradition and overlooking the complicated calculations that allow you to precisely target your mash chemistry and pH levels. How precisely you need to twiddle is a matter of debate. Certainly, it is possible to brew excellent beer by just observing some general principles, and to be honest, the great majority of craft breweries in the United States do very little in the way of water treatment unless they have extreme water, either hard or soft.

For sure, you want to remove the chlorine added to city water supplies as an antimicrobial. Free chlorine is easily removed by all carbon drinking-water filters, although for best results, limit the flow to something like $\frac{1}{2}$ gallon/ 2 L per minute. Many water utilities now use a different chemical, chloramine (NH_2Cl) that is more difficult to remove. Better-quality carbon filters will take it out, but a slow flow rate is recommended. Alternatively, Campden tablets (potassium metabisulfite), found in the winemaking section of your homebrew shop, can be used by simply dissolving one-fourth of a 0.5-gram tablet per 5 gallons/19 L of brewing water, then letting it stand for a minute or two.

You need to consider two things about your beer recipe: the color and the bitterness level. Color affects mash pH because colored malts are much more acidic than pale ones. So they can counteract the affects of alkaline water, and indeed the great centers of dark beer production (Munich, London, Dublin) all have hard, alkaline water. Bitterness is important because pH has a great effect on the way hop-bittering compounds are incorporated into beer. At higher pH (more alkaline), hop bitterness becomes astringent, harsh, and unpleasant.

In other words, dark beers and paler beers without a great deal of bitterness can tolerate some alkalinity in the brewing water. Munich water, at just under 170 ppm of bicarbonate, is a good reference here. Famous for dark beer, they also produce a pale lager called *helles* with their hard water, but the BU is some-where around 20 or so, low enough not to fight the alkalinity. That amount of carbonate (200) is about the upper limit; if your water is higher than that, you'll need to treat it for any beer you brew.

If your water is in the sub-200 ppm of carbonate range, you're in good shape for dark or non-hoppy beers. The facing chart sums it up. But with pale *and* hoppy beers, you must take action. The most obvious thing might be to add some acidity to balance the alkaline carbonate, and this is sometimes done, either with sour malt or food-grade lactic or phosphoric acid. However, carbonate is a fine buffer and can soak up a lot of acidity while still remaining in solution to cause problems, and at a certain level too much acidity can be tasted.

It is better if the carbonate is removed. The usual method for homebrewers is to boil the water, driving off the dissolved CO_2 gas, turning soluble bicarbonate into insoluble carbonate that then sinks like a stone—which it is, actually—to the bottom of the vessel. This is the familiar lime crust that forms on teakettles. When it precipitates, the carbonate takes a precise amount of calcium with it. In fact, the amount of calcium is a limiting factor, because carbonate can precipitate only to the extent that there is calcium in the water for it to combine with. So usually calcium sulfate or calcium chloride is added to replace the calcium removed.

The following chart shows color and bitterness, the two main factors that determine the type of minerals needed for good brewing water chemistry. At the bottom left are pale, hoppy beers, which need to be brewed from water with a carbonate content below 70 ppm. At the top and right, dark and non-hoppy beers can be brewed from water with up to about 220 ppm of carbonate. All beers, regardless of color, need at least 50 ppm of calcium for good mash chemistry.

WATER MINERALS, COLOR, AND BITTERNESS

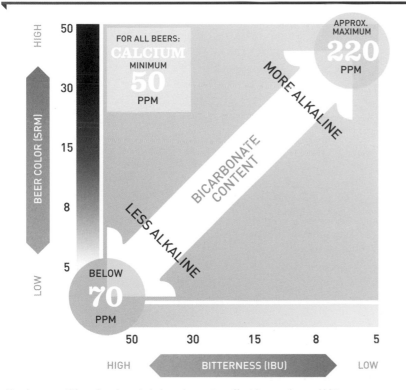

Varying quantities of carbonate in brewing water affect beer color and bitterness.

Normally, some gypsum or calcium chloride is added before boiling to remove carbonate. After a brief boil, the water should be drawn off, leaving the calcium carbonate behind. How much to add will depend on your water's mineral content, but 2.5 grams of calcium sulfate (gypsum) or 5 grams of calcium chloride per 5 gallons/19 L is a good start, and should, for most water in the 100 to 200 ppm of carbonate range, leave you with enough calcium for decent mash performance.

An easier alternative to boiling is simply to dilute your carbonate tap water with distilled or RO water to drop the carbonate content down to 70 or below. Breweries often decarbonate using slaked lime (calcium oxide), which removes CO_2 without the need to heat the water, but this requires precise calculation.

WATER MINERAL ADDITIONS *and* ION CONTENT

Mineral/Common Name	Chem Symbol	1 g/gl = ppm		1 g/L = ppm	
CALCIUM SULFATE/GYPSUM	$CaSO_4$	Ca 62	SO_4 147	Ca 233	SO_4 556
MAGNESIUM SULFATE/EPSOM SALTS	$MgSO_4$	Mg 37	SO_4 145	Mg 140	SO_4 549
SODIUM CHLORIDE/TABLE SALT	NaCl	Na 104	Cl 160	Na 394	Cl 606
CALCIUM CHLORIDE (DIHYDRATE)	$CaCl_2H_4O_2$	Ca 72	Cl 128	Ca 273	Cl 784

Water with a lot of calcium sulfate is termed "permanently hard," and guess what that means? There is no easy way to remove it. Sulfate isn't as negative for brewing as carbonate, but it does have a particular character that may be out of place in anything but a hoppy, not-too-dark beer.

Those of you with very soft water have the opposite problem, plus a new one. Anything you brew is going to need calcium, which needs to be in the 50 ppm range or above. For pale lagers, the softer taste of calcium chloride works best. For the crisp bite of a Burton-style IPA, you will want to add 5 to 120 grams per 5 gallons/19 L of calcium sulfate to reach the 150 to 250 ppm range of sulfate. It's not a highly soluble mineral, so stir it well and give it some time to dissolve. Although people sometimes do it, I don't see much of a point in adding huge amounts of calcium and magnesium sulfates to emulate the super-minerally Burton well water.

For darker beers, calcium chloride works, but if you want to replicate a more alkaline water, calcium carbonate, while not particularly soluble in water, will dissolve in the mash with the acidity provided by dark malts; 120 to 150 ppm is probably a good range to shoot for.

Soft water is deficient in trace minerals. For healthy yeast, zinc and copper are critical, as well as small amounts of potassium, magnesium, and others. Copper can be added by dropping pennies or other pieces of the metal into the kettle, but for a balanced spectrum, it is probably best to use either a zinc-enhanced yeast nutrient like Servomyces or to add a portion of bottled mineral water with a high mineral content—Evian comes to mind—to get some trace elements in the brew.

All the above is a simplification, but in general, such an approach will result in great beer, as evidenced by most of the craft beer on the shelves out there. It is possible to do much more precise manipulations, including estimating and compensating for residual alkalinity, which will allow you to predict your mash pH. While these kinds of calculations are fun for engineers, they give artists a headache, so you have to decide how much precision *you* really need. If you want to pursue this further, I can recommend John Palmer's excellent *How to Brew*, which gives the rocket scientist's perspective along with some very clever tools for manipulating water chemistry. Many of the brewing calculation software packages deal with water chemistry as well.

Clean and chemically correct water is key to brewing great beer and should never be overlooked.

WATER TRACE MINERALS in DETAIL

Below is a list of ions that may be present in brewing water. Some are essential for yeast nutrition in small quantities and may be harmful above a certain amount. Others are contaminants and are always undesirable. In city water, these are mandated by law to be below harmful levels, but well water may pick up problematic amounts of various things. This varies by region. Iron, for example, may be found in some limestone-derived water, while heavy metals can sometimes be found in mountainous areas.

Ion	Max ppm
ALUMINUM	1.0

Notes: Can be involved in haze formation. Experiments have shown it unlikely to leach from cooking vessels into wort during normal brewing operations.

Ion	Max ppm
CHLORINE (free)	0.1

Notes: Added to municipal water supplies as an antiseptic agent, typically at 2 ppm or less. Highly toxic to yeast. Carbon filtration removes; reduced by boiling or allowing water to stand uncovered a few days.

Ion	Max ppm
COPPER	0.05–0.1

Notes: Important yeast nutrient, but may inhibit yeast growth in large quantities. Important in reducing sulfur compounds during fermentation. To add, drop a couple of pennies in the boil kettle.

Ion	Max ppm
IRON	0.3

Notes: Causes yeast degeneration and haze formation, and can cause bloody or metallic tastes in the finished beer. Often a real problem with Midwestern well water, and also can be picked up from iron or steel in equipment. Can be removed in various ways, including sand filtration, oxygenation, and chemical treatment.

Ion	Max ppm
LEAD	0.1

Notes: Toxic to yeast as well as humans, and causes haze. May have leached from brass faucets and solder joints in pipes and equipment. Some specialized drinking-water filters are designed to remove lead and other heavy metals.

Ion	Max ppm
MANGANESE	0.05

Notes: Similar to iron. Often a problem in groundwater.

Ion	Max ppm
NITRATE	1.0

Notes: Over 10 ppm indicates polluted water. Degrades to toxic nitrite during fermentation. Highly undesirable.

Ion	Max ppm
NITRITE	0.1

Notes: Found only in highly polluted water. So toxic to microorganisms such as yeast, it is used as a preservative in meats.

Ion	Max ppm
TIN	1.0

Notes: Not very toxic, but a powerful haze former. May have leached out of solder joints in equipment.

Ion	Max ppm
ZINC	1.0

Notes: Needed in very small amounts for yeast nutrition, but harmful to yeast in larger amounts.

Ion	Max ppm
CADMIUM, MERCURY, SILVER, ARSENIC, BERYLLIUM, NICKEL	0.001 to 0.1

Notes: Dangerous human toxins and extremely powerful yeast growth inhibitors. Not normally present in problem-causing quantities.

ALTERNATE INGREDIENTS

Brewers today are looking to make the widest possible range of delicious, interesting, and meaningful beers. By themselves, hops and malt can make an incredible range of beers, but there are many more tools available to the creative brewer. For most of beer's long history, people used whatever was at hand to add some unique quality to beer. This didn't end until the major modern beer styles emerged in Europe a couple of hundred years ago when industrialization took hold.

If you think about beer as cuisine, the restrictions on brewing ingredients seem strange. Would we be happy if our food choices were limited to meat and potatoes? This is what we've come to with beer—that is, before home-brewing started widening the possibilities. Of course, Belgium never got the message to give up on the wacky stuff.

Until recently, there was still something a bit daring about using ingredients beyond the big four: malt, hops, water, and yeast. But in a few short years, things have really changed. There has never been a bigger variety of flavors, ingredients, techniques, and great beers out there to taste.

This section covers all the nonstandard ingredients: spices, fruits, and vegetables. Many have associations with beer that go back thousands of years. Others are more recent discoveries made by modern brewers seeking to incorporate the world they see around them into their beers. Either way, it's an exciting bunch.

Left to right: Chiles, cacao, and coffee are specialty ingredients that offer a range of flavors that go far beyond malt and hops traditionalism.

HERBS and SPICES

Get your nose in them and you'll find the astonishing range of spices is nothing short of miraculous, and hopefully your thirsty friends will, too. It's no wonder people used to trade their weight in gold for them. Herbs and spices may be just another tool in your kit, but they're a valuable one. Used with the right touch, they can add a world of amazing possibilities to your beers, and *that's* the spice of life.

Different herbs and spices vary hugely in their strength, from no more potent than hops to very powerful. Some of the old English books give quantities of grains of paradise as small as a few grams per barrel. Spices can also vary widely by quality, origin, and freshness—some spices, like coriander, are incredibly different from region to region in intensity and character, even more so than hops. And, of course, what the seasoning is doing in a recipe varies as well, so there's no easy recommendation for quantities except it's better to be conservative until you have some experience with a particular spice.

It pays to know your spices, and to seek out something other than the grocery-store varieties. High-grade Saigon cassia cinnamon, for example, may contain four times as much aromatic oil as the standard store variety. Korintje is actually a separate species with a somewhat different aroma and neither one is the same as true cinnamon, which comes from Ceylon. Spice specialty stores can offer better culinary grades, usually with cleaner and more intense flavors. Ethnic markets of all kinds carry spices, often very fresh and typically less expensive.

Spices have varying shelf lives, from very short in the case of flowers like elder, heather, and chamomile to very long for things like black pepper and grains of paradise. Storing in the freezer may prolong the useful life of more delicate herbs. Grinding exposes the spice to air, causing the aromas to fade. Whenever possible, start with freshly ground spices.

Always add the spices to the kettle in the last five minutes of the boil. Otherwise, it is just for the neighbors, eh?

PIERRE CELIS, witbier legend and founder, Hoegaarden brewery, Hoegaarden, Belgium

Clockwise from left: Pink peppercorns, black peppercorns, nutmeg, star anise, coriander seeds, saffron, sour orange peel, and Ceylon cinnamon represent many spices that were commonplace in beer just a couple of centuries ago.

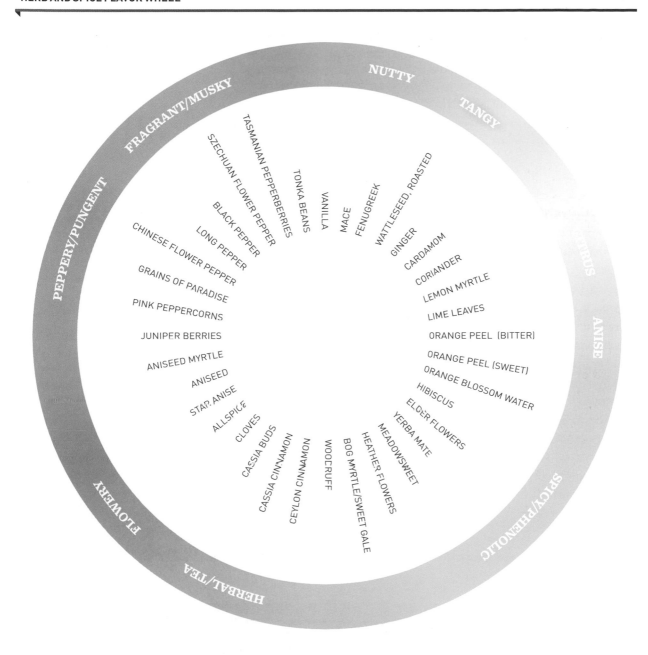

This is an attempt to place similar spices next to one another to make it easier to find compatible flavors. It isn't perfect; some transitions from one flavor to another are more abrupt than others, and of course there are dozens more herbs that are suitable for use in beer. Note that one herb, wormwood, has been omitted because it defies attempts to group it with others, as it is primarily bitter and has very little aroma.

HERBS AND SPICES FOR BREWING

The following table shows typical usage rates for some of the most useful herbs and spices for beer. Pay attention to the source. Just like hops, most herbs and spices show a great variation in flavor, intensity, and terroir that requires the brewer to go beyond just the name and get familiar with the source country and suppliers.

Ingredient	Scientific Name	Key Flavor	g per 5 gl/19 L
ALLSPICE	*Pimenta dioica*	Gumdrops	1–5
ANISE, STAR	*Illicium verum*	Anise/complex	0.5–8
ANISEED	*Pimpinella anisum*	Anise taste	0.5–5
ANISEED MYRTLE	*Backhousia anisata*	Soft anise	2–10
BOG MYRTLE	*Myrica gale*	Resiny	5–20
CARDAMOM	*Elettaria cardamomum*	Exotic	2–8
CASSIA	*Cinnamomum cassia*	Cinnamon	1–10
CHAMOMILE	*Anthemis nobilis*	Fruity/floral	5–15
CINNAMON	*Cinnamomum zeylanicum*	Cinnamon/woody	1–10
CLOVES	*Eugenia aromatica*	Clovey	1–8
CORIANDER	*Coriandrum sativum*	Citrus/piney	5–50
ELDER FLOWERS	*Sambucus canadensis*	Fruity/floral	10–30
FENUGREEK	*Trigonellum foenum-graecum*	Maple	1–8
GINGER	*Zingiber officinale*	Spicy/woody	5–45
GRAINS OF PARADISE	*Aframonium melegueta*	Spicy/sprucy	1–8
HEATHER (flowers)	*Calluna* species	Floral/honeyish	10–30
HIBISCUS (flowers), **FLOR DE JAMAICA**	*Hibiscus sabdariffa*	Winey, tannic	20–100
JUNIPER BERRIES	*Juniperus communis*	Gin	15–6
LEMON MYRTLE	*Backhousia citriodora*	Lemondrops	3–10
LICORICE, LIQUORICE	*Glycerrhiza glabra*	Sweet/licorice	10–30
LIME LEAVES	*Citrus hystrix*	Lime oil	1–5
MACE	*Myristica fragrans*	Sweet/spicy	0.5–5

Ingredient	Scientific Name	Key Flavor	g per 5 gl/19 L
MEADOWSWEET	*Filipendula ulmaria*	Sweet tea	3–15
NUTMEG	*Myristica fragrans*	Pungent/spicy	0.5–5
ORANGE BLOSSOM (water)	*Citrus sinensis*	Orangey/perfumy	2–15
ORANGE PEEL (bitter)	*Citrus aurantia*	Marmalade	3–30
ORANGE PEEL (sweet)	*Citrus sinensis*	Sweet orange, orange juice	5–45
PEPPER, BLACK	*Piper nigrum*	Peppery/piney	2–15
PEPPER, INDIAN LONG	*Piper longum*	Peppery/enhancing	2–10
PEPPER, PINK	*Schinus molle*	Spicy/fruity	3–15
PEPPER, SICHUAN FLOWER OR SANSHO	*Xanthoxylum piperitum*	Complex	2–10
PUMPKIN PIE SPICE	(mixed)	Pie-like	5–15
TASMANIAN PEPPERBERRY	*Tasmannia lanceolata*	Spicy, complex	0.5–5
TONKA BEANS *(potentially toxic; see cautions on page 328)*	*Dipteryx odorata*	Almond, Vanilla	0.5–1
VANILLA	*Vanilla planifolia*	Vanilla	1–8
WATTLESEED, ROASTED	*Acacia* species	Peanutty	5–30
WOODRUFF	*Asperula odorata*	Sassafras/spicy	1–10
WORMWOOD	*Artemesia absinthum*	Bitter!	0.2–15
YERBA MATÉ	*Ilex paraguaiensis*	Herby, tea-like	5–30

Left to right: Allspice, aniseed, bog myrtle, cardamom, Indian coriander, elder flowers, chipped dried ginger, grains of paradise, hibiscus flowers, Tasmanian pepper-berries, licorice root slices, long pepper.

FRUITS

Wine likely dates back about as far as beer, but from what we can tell, early people didn't draw such a distinction as today and were happy to mix their fermentable materials into many different types of beverages. Chemical evidence for beer with grapes or other fruit in it (honey, too) dates back to at least the tenth millennium B.C.E., at the very beginning of beer. Anthropologist Patrick McGovern calls these mixed concoctions "neolithic grog."

Although they're ancient, it's not clear if there has ever been a time and place where fruit beers were the dominant brew; certainly not in the last thousand years or so, at least. There are probably a number of reasons for this. First, fruit is a perishable product and so, to a certain extent, is beer. Making wine once a year preserves the harvest. Beer needs to be brewed more than once a year, so fruit is not always available. I think fruit beer was always a special treat. In fruit growing regions, whatever fruit was handy often got added, making a special batch of beer with a very different flavor.

In the ancient Middle East, dates were probably used in addition to grapes. Northern people used cranberries in their meads and beers. Sources going back at least 400 years mention sloe (a type of plum), elderberries, raspberries, and others. We don't know how ancient the cherry lambic, kriek, is, but the raspberry version was created as recently as the 1970s, and flavors like peach and blackcurrant even more recently.

The earliest brewers probably used whole fruit, and then when pressing technology arrived, just the juice. Today, these are still the best ways of adding fruit flavor and aroma to beer. If you know anything about wine, you know that the strain, season, weather, soil, and orientation play a huge role in the quality and flavor of the grapes used for wine. The same is true about any fruit we might want to put in beer. A lot of fruit on the market is beautiful to look at, but tastes little better than the plastic it's packaged in. Fresh fruit from the supermarket is pretty much useless for beer, but there is often good fruit to be had from farmers' markets.

The flavor of frozen fruit is usually pretty good. It is picked ripe and frozen near the fields, often using varieties that actually have some flavor. For tropical fruits, whole or puréed may be the only forms available. Freezing is actually beneficial to brewing, in that it reduces the microbial load a bit but, more important, ruptures the cell walls, allowing juices to flow more freely into our beer. In addition, many frozen purées have been pasteurized before freezing. If you are using frozen fruit, be sure to let it warm to fermenting temperature before adding, as a sudden chill can irreparably shock the yeast and halt fermentation.

Winemakers' concentrates are available in many flavors other than grapes, and these offer the advantage of being pure slurry, without skins that can float to the top of the fermenter and form a safe harbor for mold. They are not cheap, but we're talking about a pretty special beverage.

For whole, puréed, or concentrated fruit, the best time to add it is at the end of the primary, as this helps to preserve aromas. One note of caution with whole fruit is to make sure the pieces can't possibly block the hole in the stopper. If they do, even a small amount of pressure can easily burst the carboy, making for a dangerous and very messy accident. Plenty of headspace is a good policy, but if you have to use a mostly full carboy, cover the top with clean aluminum foil rather than a stopper and airlock.

Some other more highly refined products may be useful in brewing. Fruit syrups may have nice—if sometimes one-dimensonal—flavors. Sour cherry, blackcurrant, strawberry, and blackberry syrups can be found in Eastern European markets. From Asia come passionfruit, mangosteen, litchi, and others. These syrups usually contain some sugar in addition to the fruit; your recipe will have to accommodate this. Aromatic extracts are also an option; they are water-clear, just pure aromas, pulled from the fruit by vacuum distillation. Use them in very small amounts to augment or replace whole character that may be missing from an ingredient like syrup or fruit aroma lost during fermentation. Some fruits, especially peaches and apricots, are vulnerable to this, so adding peach extract on top of real peaches is often the only way to make a peachy-tasting peach beer. Extracts are best added after fermentation, at packaging.

Winemakers' concentrates or frozen purées are an easy way to get real fruit flavor in your beer. Extracts are best used to enhance and augment real fruit.

FRUIT BY THE NUMBERS

All fruit is assumed to be unsweetened

Fruit	Form	Typical Quantity Used		Typical Sugar Content	OG/lb	°P/kg	Acidity
		lb/g	g/L)	(%) g/L			
APPLE JUICE	Frozen Concentrate	0.5–2.0	60–240	39	1.0035	0.90	Med.
APRICOT	Fresh/Frozen	1–4.0	120–500	6–9	1.0007	0.18	Med.
BLACKBERRIES	Frozen	1–3.0	120–350	7.0	1.0006	0.15	Low
BLACKCURRANT	Concentrate	0.5–1.5	60–180	30	1.0028	0.73	Med.
BLUEBERRIES	Frozen	1–3.0	120–350	9–10	1.0009	0.22	Low
CHERRY, SOUR	Frozen	1–4.0	120–500	12	1.0011	0.33	High
CHERRY, SWEET	Frozen	1–4.0	120–500	13.8	1.0012	0.30	Med.
DATE	Syrup	0.2–0.7	24–85	70	1.0064	1.65	None
GRAPE	Wine Concentrate	0.5–2.0	60–240	45–68	1.0040–61	1.0–1.6	Med.
GUAVA	Frozen Purée	0.5–1.5	60–180	50	1.0045	1.6	Low
MANGO	Frozen Purée	0.5–1.5	60–180	50	1.0045	1.6	Med.
PASSIONFRUIT	Frozen Purée	0.5–1.5	60–180	50	1.0045	1.6	High
PEACHES	Frozen	1.5–5.0	180–600	7.5–8.5	1.0007	0.18	Med.
PEAR JUICE	Concentrate	0.5–2.0	60–240	50	1.0045	1.6	Low
PINEAPPLE	Frozen Purée	0.5–2.0	60–240	50	1.0045	1.6	High
POMEGRANATE	Juice Concentrate	0.2–0.7	24–85	38	1.0035	0.90	High
RASPBERRIES	Frozen	0.5–3.0	60–350	4.3	1.0004	0.11	High
STRAWBERRIES	Frozen	1–5	120–600	4.5–5.5	1.0004	0.11	Low

VEGETABLES *and* BEYOND *in* YOUR BEER

In the past, vegetables were rarely anybody's first choice as a brewing ingredient. I have an old recipe that claims to make an absolutely delicious ale by boiling a bushel of pea shells, which would otherwise have gone to waste, of course. The early U.S. colonists used dried pumpkin to make beer, although they didn't seem all that thrilled about it, and eventually switched to rum and other spirits. During the two World Wars, the Belgians took to tossing sliced sugar beets into the kettle, just to get something that would ferment. Sounds a lot like prison hooch.

Things have changed, at least a little. Pumpkin beer is one of the liveliest seasonal beers, with an eager demand every fall. Beers with chocolate, coffee, chile, and nuts can be found pretty regularly. Many of these products offer wonderfully delicious flavors in beer, and are well worth considering for use in special beers.

If you're having trouble with the whole concept of vegetables in beer, it might help to consider that many "vegetables" like squash, tomatoes, and others, are actually fruit in botanical terms. Chocolate, chile, and coffee act more like spices, and have some special cautions and techniques to make sure you get the best out of these expensive ingredients.

While it might not be an obvious choice at first, the ethereal peachiness of chanterelle mushrooms harmonizes beautifully with subtle beers.

CHILE

There are many varieties, available in fresh and dried form. Flavors range from bright savory like jalapeño and New Mexico (Hatch) to the spicy fruitiness of habañero to the leathery toastiness of dark, dried chiles like ancho and mulato. In general, chiles are best used as a subtle flavoring, added to the end of the boil, like a spice. Quantity is a huge variable, depending on chile, beer concept, and heat level. Two teaspoons per batch of freshly ground ancho will give a pleasant chile flavor and the barest tickle of heat.

Chile beers range from habañero screamers to beers that use ancho to augment the toasted malt character. Really hot beers are just for totally chile-addled individuals, although I know there are plenty of you out there. It's easy to make a chile beer that is a spicy novelty. The best chile beers to me are those that use the chile character as a subtle aromatic that blends with the rest of the beer, with the heat at the end as a tangy counterpoint to the richness of malt, like hops. Be aware that hops accentuate the heat of capsicum, and their aroma can mask the sometimes-elusive chile aroma.

Smoke can be a useful accompaniment to chile beers, and some varieties, like chipotle and Spanish smoked paprika, come with smoke as part of the deal. In a beer, it is as if the smoke gives permission for the heat to be there, which isn't surprising, given how many hot foods also have a smoke component—our brains expect the combination.

CHOCOLATE

The Aztecs used to brew all kinds of beverages from chocolate, which was so precious it was often reserved for royalty. They also made a fermented beverage from the fruity pulp that surrounds the cocoa beans. For beer, roasted cocoa nibs that have not yet been ground into chocolate give the most luxurious and complete chocolate flavor. Sam Adams reportedly uses $1/2$ pound/227 g per barrel, steeped in the secondary for their Chocolate Bock. This works out to $1\frac{1}{2}$ ounces per 5 gallons (43 grams per 19 liters) per batch, but this could easily be higher. Also important for chocolate is to make it taste as much like chocolate as you can, using various dark malts, so that when you add the chocolate, its true character can shine. Avoid using too much dark caramel malt, whose burnt-sugar flavor can cover up some chocolatey aromas. And don't be misled by its name; I find chocolate malt to have more of a sharp coffee-like roastiness rather than something truly chocolatey.

COFFEE

Never heat or boil coffee used for beer, or it will become harsh, like old diner coffee. A cold-water extraction gives the smoothest taste. Steep coarsely ground coffee in cold water (8 ounces/240 ml water for every 1 ounce/28 g of coffee) for 12 hours, drain through a screen filter, and then add the liquid to the secondary. Recipes vary from $3/4$ to $1\frac{1}{2}$ ounces/20 to 40 g coffee per 5-gallon/19-L batch. The notion of building a very coffee-like beer before the coffee is added applies here as well. Lighter dark malts like chocolate and Carafa have the sharpest, most coffee-like aromas, while darker malts are more chocolatey.

MUSHROOMS

I am notorious for making a chanterelle mushroom ale, based on the idea that the Germans made a schnapps out of this subtly perfumed mushroom. Use ½ to 1 pound/227 to 454 g fresh chanterelles or 1 to 3 ounces/28 to 85 g dried chanterelles soaked in vodka for a few days, then add the filtered liquid at kegging or bottling. It's a pretty unique mushroom with a peachy fruitiness, and works best in a strong golden ale or other subtly flavored beer. The earthy, heavy flavors of most other mushrooms make them difficult to work with as a brewing ingredient.

NUTS AND CHESTNUTS

These flavors can harmonize extremely well with beer, but care needs to be taken to get the right amount of nutty character, and build the beer so it's not just a silly novelty that you'll only want to drink a swallow at a time. It's best to toast the nuts first and add them either directly to the boil or to the fermenter after the primary has slowed down. Quantity depends on the recipe, but ½ to 2 pounds/227 to 907 g per batch seems to be the workable range. Most nuts contain oils that can theoretically interfere with a beer's head, but for some reason this is not generally a problem in practice. Extracts of nut flavors like hazelnut and pecan are available, although these can be a bit one-dimensional.

Chestnuts are an entirely different animal, with nearly 80 percent carbohydrate content and very little (1 to 2 percent) oil. Chestnuts definitely benefit from being added to the mash. You can use roasted and mashed fresh chestnuts, and I've had good results with toasting the dried variety found in Asian markets. When raw, chestnuts can be a little astringent and otherwise flavorless, so toasting/roasting is definitely recommended.

PUMPKIN

Although pumpkin beer goes back a couple of hundred years, it wasn't until about 1995 that pumpkin beers started to become a popular craft beer specialty. Now there are so many that Seattle's Elysian Brewing has a pumpkin beer festival with several dozen beers in many different styles.

Any winter squash can work just as well as pumpkin; I like kabocha and hubbard, but there are many others. Fresh pumpkin can be used by cutting in half or in large chunks, and roasting, flesh-side down, on a cookie sheet at 350°F/177°C until soft and starting to caramelize on the bottom. Let cool and scoop out the flesh. Lots of brewers, especially commercial ones, use canned pumpkin, which is actually a selection of squashes chosen for best flavor and texture. Pumpkin can be mashed, but most brewers say they get better flavor with less trouble by simply adding it to the boil. There are not a lot of starches that need to be converted, so a mash doesn't add anything in terms of extract. Fresh or canned pumpkin can be treated this way.

That said, pumpkin beer is all about the spice, so unless you want a very subtle experience, think about adding some of the classic pumpkin spices to your brew.

SPRUCE AND TREE EXTRACTS

Native Americans used sugar-rich spruce tips to make a spring tonic, and it remains a sought-after seasonal product today. Surprisingly, it tastes nothing like spruce, but has a rich, deep fruit flavor perhaps a little reminiscent of black cherries. A similar substance made from *Pinus sylvestris* tips harvested from Bulgaria's Rhodope Mountains is sometimes available in Eastern European markets in the United States. It has 74 percent sugar content (some of which is added), is similar to honey, and has a pleasant herby/piney aroma.

Tree sap can yield flavorful sugars. Maple is the most common. Birch yields a very weak, but highly flavorful sap that is processed into syrup in Alaska. It is a very expensive product.

SWEET POTATO

Not too many of these beers are out there, but The Bruery in Southern California cooks up a fine Autumn Maple beer out of sweet potatoes. They can be peeled, roasted, and treated just like pumpkin. Canned versions are available as well. Sugar-preserved, dried sweet potato can be found in Latin markets.

AND BEYOND . . .

There is a whole kingdom to explore here, although not too many are really well suited for flavoring beer. I had a beet beer at a recent AHA National Homebrewers Conference, and it was beautifully magenta and a very nice expression of that sweet and earthy beet character that people either love or hate. Parsnips and carrots can be cooked like pumpkin and added to beer. A good friend brewed a parsnip wine almost forty years ago, and it still tastes like nectar. I've tasted guacamole saison, pizza beer, and bloody Mary ale; all were less horrible than they sound. Tomatoes, especially dried ones, offer some promise I've yet to explore. And tamarind's sour zip will sure make for a refreshing wheat beer when I get around to it.

THE BREWING PROCESS

CHAPTER 4

➼ Brewing is unique among fermented beverages.

It is dependent on a number of complex processes that allow the starch stored in grain to be broken down and ultimately converted into sugar that will ferment to make beer. While the agricultural aspects are important, the conscious choices made by maltsters and brewers have a much more noticeable affect. Wine is a direct expression of the soil on which the grapes are grown. The winemaker coaxes: refining, pushing, prodding a little, but mostly trying to stay out of the way of nature. The brewer, on the other hand, *creates*: picking and choosing from a world full of ingredients to do his or her will. Gaze into a glass of wine and you may see the sun and the soil, but in every beer you experience the soul of the brewer.

Ready to jump right in and start brewing? Turn the page and you'll find my all-in-one get-brewing recipe in a graphic.

Head of Foodways at Colonial Williamsburg, Frank Clark re-creates early American beers with tools quite similar to those used by modern homebrewers. Photo: courtesy of Colonial Williamsburg.

The AMAZING SHAPE-SHIFTING BEER RECIPE

QTY: 5 gallons/19 L
GRAVITY: 1.053–4
ALCOHOL APPROX: 5.0–5.5
BITTERNESS: 18–70

➨ FILTERED TAP WATER

Should be good tap water, carbon filtered to remove chlorine, if necessary. Ideally, calcium content should be a least 50 ppm, and for pale and bitter beers, carbonate content should be below 150 ppm. For now, don't sweat it.

4 gl/15 L

+ PALE MALT EXTRACT

DRY PALE MALT EXTRACT
5.3 lb/2.4 kg

OR

PALE MALT EXTRACT SYRUP
6.1 lb/2.8 kg

Put water and malt extract in your brew kettle and start to heat.

Stir well to make sure malt extract is dissolved.

+ONE OF THESE
or a similar combination

SMOOTHLY GOLD
4 SRM / 1.053 OG (13.1ºP)

0.75 lb/340 g
20ºL Caramel/Crystal Malt
+
0.25 lb/113 g
Honey Malt

CRISP & NUTTY
9 SRM / 1.054 OG (13.3ºP)

1.0 lb/454 g
Honey Malt
+
0.25 lb/113 g
120ºL Caramel/Crystal Malt

TOASTY/RAISINY
16 SRM / 1.054 OG (13.3ºP)

0.5 lb/227 g
60ºL Caramel/Crystal Malt
+
0.5 lb/227 g
120ºL Caramel/Crystal Malt
+
2 oz/57 g
Chocolate Malt

BLACK & ROASTY
40 SRM / 1.053 OG (13.1ºP)

0.75 lb/340 g
Black Malt (your choice)
+
0.5 lb/227 g
120ºL Caramel/Crystal Malt

OPTIONAL ADJUNCTS

1 lb/454 g
Exotic Sugar
thins body

OR

1 lb/454 g
Wheat Extract
adds creaminess

Either adds 1.0092 (2.4ºP)

Place crushed grain in grain bag—not too tight.

Add to wort in brew kettle.

Bring to 180ºF/82ºC over 30 minutes or so.

Remove and drain all liquid from grain bag.

Bring wort to a boil. Watch for boilovers.

When stable rolling boil is achieved, add first hops, set timer for 55 minutes.

"You don't really need me to tell you what you like, do you?"

+ ONE OF THESE HOP ADDITIONS

figured for pellets

Hop quantities can be varied a lot to achieve different bitterness and aroma levels. Feel free to experiment. Also, there are plenty of different varieties out there to play with.

	BITTERING 60-minute boil	AROMA 5-minute boil
SOFT & NOBLE		
18 BU	0.7 oz/20 g U.S. Tettnang/ Hallertau	1.8 oz/50 g Saaz, Ultra, or Hallertau
BRITTASTIC		
38 BU	1.3 oz/37 g U.S. Fuggle	4 oz/113 g U.K. Goldins
GONZO LUPULO		
70 BU	1.5 oz/42 g Chinook or Centennial	3 oz/85 g Cascade, Simcoe, or...

+ KETTLE FININGS

1 tbsp IRISH MOSS	**OR**	OTHER PRODUCT *follow manufacturer's instructions*

Hops should be placed in fine-mesh bags unless you have some means of screening them out at the end of the boil

Continue to boil for 55 minutes, then add the second hop addition plus the kettle finings.

Set the timer for 5 minutes.

At 0 minutes, turn off the heat. Chill as quickly as you can.

Transfer to carboy. See number 7, page 119.

Add enough just-boiled tap water to total 5.5 gl/20 L.

+ LIQUID *or* DRY YEAST

NOTE: *Lager yeast is not recommended for beginners. For lager-like beer, use German ale yeast at 60–63°F/16–17°C*

BRITISH/U.S. ALE

Fruity with some complexity

GERMAN ALE

Fruity, but clean and neutral

BELGIAN ALE

Fruity, spicy, highly characterful

For fermentation procedures, see page 217. See manufacturer's recommendations for fermentation temperatures. At high end of range, expect yeast character (especially fruity/spicy aromas) to be more pronounced. Be sure not to drop below recommended temperature range, or yeast could go dormant.

YOUR FIRST BEER: GETTING STARTED *with* EXTRACT BREWING

While it's possible to jump right into more advanced methods, the vast majority of homebrewers start with malt extract plus some steeped grains. It's simpler, less time-consuming, and lets you get a few batches under your belt (literally!) before moving on to more complex techniques. Your start-up gear will be usable as your techniques advance as long as you have a good size brew kettle. The small pot recommended here (5 gallons/20 L or slightly less) is not really adequate for mashed beers where the full volume of the wort must be boiled. So you either need to come up with a smaller pot to tide you through or step up and buy a 7- to 10-gallon/25- to 40-L pot and be covered when you make the jump to full mashing.

As far as what to brew, that is up to you. I'd suggest you start with the Amazing Shape-Shifting Recipe that precedes this section. By making a few choices, it will allow you to create a customized recipe to suit your own taste. If you'd rather, you can choose one of the other recipes in the book as long as it has an extract plus steeped-grain formula.

MAKE SURE YOU HAVE THE FOLLOWING PIECES OF EQUIPMENT AVAILABLE, ALONG WITH A STOVE TO HEAT THE KETTLE:

- A large stainless-steel cooking pot or enameled canning kettle. 3.5 gallon/ 13 L is the absolute minimum; 5 gallon/ 19 L is better.
- A 6-gallon/25-L glass carboy. Note: This is larger than the type usually sold with a startup kit. It is helpful to add 5 gallons/19 L of liquid to it as a way of determining volume so you can make a mark or place a piece of tape at the 5-gallon/19-L mark.
- A long metal or plastic spoon.
- A racking cane and 3 feet/1 m length of food-grade vinyl hose with shutoff clip.
- Three nylon or cheesecloth grain/hop boiling bags.
- Cleaning and sanitizing products—non-caustic alkaline cleaner and an acid sanitizer (PBW and Star San, or similar products).
- Aluminum foil or an airlock and stopper to fit the carboy neck.

- A 1-gallon/4-L food-grade plastic bucket or tub for soaking hose and small parts. When brewing, fill it with water and the recommended amount of sanitizer.
- A hydrometer to measure the beer's original and finishing gravity and to check progress, if needed.

OPTIONAL, BUT NOT ABSOLUTELY NECESSARY:

- Wort chiller.
- Some kind of temperature control, depending on where you live and what season it is. This batch should be fermented somewhere between 58°F/14°C and 72°F/22°C for best results.

AS FAR AS INGREDIENTS FOR THE BREW, YOU WILL NEED:

- 7 gallons/25 L of carbon-filtered/ dechlorinated tap water (does not have to be all in one place at one time). If you live in an area with very hard water (over 150 ppm of alkalinity/carbonate), it will probably be worth diluting your tap water with distilled or reverse osmosis water.

- Choose your fermentables. Start with the Amazing Shape-Shifting Recipe on page 116, and choose the kind of ingredients to make the beer you prefer, or make something up. You will definitely need some dry pale malt extract or pale liquid malt extract, which should be unhopped and as fresh as possible—if your shop sells bulk extract, that will be the freshest option available. You will also need some specialty grains according to the grist types shown.
- In the same way, choose your hops. If you decide to make substitutions, try to end up with hops that have similar alpha acid content or use more or less to compensate. For example, if your chosen hop has half the alpha of the one in the recipe, use twice as much.
- One package of ale yeast, your choice. Liquid types are best, but dry yeast, if fresh and fermented below 70°F/21°C, can produce acceptable results. If it is a Wyeast "smack pack," be sure to smack it one to two days in advance.

I know I'm turning you loose without a specific recipe, but I want people to get in the habit of thinking for themselves and making beer using their own ideas. I promise you can't screw this up as long as you keep things clean. If you need some inspiration, there are dozens of recipes in this book that are suitable for this first brew (they're marked "SE," which stands for either "Steeped Extract" or "Super Easy").

FOR BOTTLING, YOU WILL NEED:

- Enough bottle caps for a little more than two cases.
- Bottle-filler attachment for hose.
- A 5-gallon/19-L food-grade plastic bucket, preferably with a spigot near the bottom.
- Clean, capable, non-twist-off bottles or swingtops (be sure the gaskets are flexible and not compressed). It takes fifty-three 12-oz/thirty-eight 0.5-L for 5 gallons/19 L.
- Bottle capper.

EXTRACT PLUS STEEPED-GRAIN PROCEDURE

This is the standard version of this procedure, which should be followed when making extract versions of the recipes in this book.

1

Put the crushed crystal malt in one of the sacks and tie it off. Allow some room to expand, if possible. Add the bittering hops to another sack, and the aroma hops to the third.

2

Put 3 gallons/11 L of filtered water in the brewpot, then turn on the heat. When the water is warm, pour in malt extract syrup, using hot water to rinse remaining extract from can. Stir gently until all the syrup is dissolved; syrup on bottom can scorch easily.

3

Add the grain sack, turn up the heat, and bring to a boil in no particular hurry. When it gets close to boiling, watch closely so it doesn't boil over.

4

When the wort begins to boil, remove the grain bag while allowing any excess liquid to drain back into the kettle. Add the bittering hops bag, but watch for boilovers when you do. Note the time at the beginning of the boil. 60 minutes to go.

5

Sanitize carboy according to sanitizer directions and fill partway with water, so that when the boiled wort is added, the total amount will be 5 gallons/19 L.

6

After 55 minutes, add the bag of aroma hops. Boil 5 minutes longer, then turn off the heat. Do not cover pot. Let stand 5 minutes to settle.

7

Siphon with a sterilized siphon hose or carefully pour hot wort through sterilized filter funnel (or cheesecloth) into carboy. If you end up a bit short, add a little water to make sure you have at least 5 gallons/ 19 L of wort in the carboy.

Note: There are a million ways to start a siphon, but this is how I do it. After sterilizing the racking tube and hose, fit them together and fill with cold tap water (hold both ends up at the same level). Use a hose clamp to pinch the tube shut. Quickly insert the racking tube into the full vessel, then place the hose into a dump bucket of some kind. Release the clamp and dump the water, then re-clamp, move the end of the hose into the receiving vessel, and let the beer flow.

8

Cover carboy and let stand until wort cools to 75°F/24°C.

9

Sanitize hydrometer and measure the specific gravity. Note the temperature and make corrections, if needed (see Hydro-meter chart, page 185). Make a note of the original gravity.

10

Pitch the yeast. If you're using dry yeast, rehydrate it in 110°F/43°C dechlorinated water for 10 minutes before using.

11

Fit with sanitized fermentation lock (I like to fill mine with vodka), and put fermenter where the temperature will remain steady: 58 to 72°F/14 to 22°C. Keep away from bright light. Note temperature on log sheet.

12

In 2 to 24 hours you should see fermen-tation as patches or gobs of frothy stuff on the surface. Once it starts, the beer will go through a few days of very active fermentation, which may cause foam to ooze out of fermentation lock. Clean up the mess and replace with a clean lock, if necessary. This is the primary stage.

13

Allow beer to sit in carboy for about 2 weeks. The bubbling will slow down and stop, the foam will dissipate, and the beer will appear to darken as it clears. When this happens, it is ready to bottle.

14

Check gravity with sterilized hydrometer. For an extract beer of this strength, gravity should be at or under 1.012 (3°P) for bottling. If not, wait another week or two.

15

To bottle, put 3½ ounces/100 g (about ½ cup/120 ml) of corn sugar (dextrose), or refer to the chart on page 225, into a clean saucepan with 1 to 2 cups/250 to 500 ml of water. Stir to dissolve well, boil for 10 minutes, cover, and cool.

16

Without splashing, siphon enough beer into the saucepan to fill it halfway. Gently transfer the rest into your sanitized plastic bucket.

17

Gently pour the beer-syrup from the saucepan to the beer that is now in the bottling bucket. Stir well, but don't splash.

18

Clean the bottles thoroughly, sanitize, rinse if necessary, and drain. A turkey baster is useful for squirting sterilizer into the bottles.

19

Using the special bottle-filling tube on the end of the siphon, fill each bottle to within 1 inch/2.5 cm of the top; top-up by pouring from a bottle if needed. Don't splash if you can help it.

20

Cap with sanitized caps, then rinse or sponge off bottles.

21

With a permanent marker, label the caps with a number 1 for the batch and, if you like, some sort of code for the type of beer it is, for example, "PA" for pale ale.

22

Store the bottles where you kept the fermenting beer. After a couple of weeks, carbonation should be complete, but the beer will continue to clear and improve for several weeks. I sometimes find it handy to fill one PET (polyethylene terophthalate) plastic soda bottle (don't use a root beer bottle!), which allows you to squeeze the plastic and tell how carbonated the beer is getting.

Ingredients are hugely important and of course the varieties, locations, cultivation methods, and processing all have a role to play. But in beer, the choice of ingredients and the way they are put together matter more than the agricultural aspects. Every drop of beer depends on a series of complex chemical reactions that the brewer must understand and control in order to coax soul-satisfying beer from dormant grain and herbs. The process affects the flavor and character just as much as the list of ingredients does.

Brewing consists of a number of specific steps, each of which has its own requirements.

CRUSHING

Breaking up the kernels of malt as thoroughly as possible while preserving the husks relatively intact. Huskless grain can be finely ground.

MASHING

Cooking the malt in a porridge-like mash, during which various enzyme processes are active. Most important is the breaking down of starch to sugar that happens at about 150°F/66°C.

WORT RECOVERY OR LAUTERING

Draining, and then rinsing (sparging) the mash to remove as much extract-rich liquid as possible.

WORT BOILING

Sanitizes the wort, ends enzyme activity, removes unpleasant DMS aromas, and coagulates excess protein, plus the ever-important job of isomerizing and dissolving hop alpha acids for a bitter counterpoint to malt's sweetness. A typical boil is 60 minutes long.

CLARIFYING

Removing spent hops as well as proteins coagulated in the boil (hot break) and possibly in the cold break created by chilling.

CHILLING

Rapid cooling gets the wort ready for fermentation, and precipitates some additional protein and lipids.

GRAIN CRUSHING

Malt needs to be crushed so that its starches can be accessed by enzymes in the mash. Preground malt is available, but it has a short shelf life. Most homebrew shops have a mill that their customers can use, so if you don't want to invest in your own mill, this is the best option.

In theory, malt crushing is pretty simple. A set of rollers crushes the kernels gently, breaking up the starch in the chalky endosperm, while preserving the husks intact to serve as filtering material during the sparge. This is brewing, however, and there are some devils in the details.

Malt mills are discussed in chapter 5, but in general, homebrew mills use a pair of textured or knurled rollers that draw in the malt and squeeze it until it breaks apart. Most do an adequate job of crushing the malt, but some of the more deeply knurled rollers can pierce the hulls and leave them vulnerable to breaking.

Before crushing the whole batch, run a handful through and see what the crush looks like. Break the kernels open with your fingers, because sometimes kernels that look whole are actually broken and are just waiting to fall apart. If there are whole kernels coming thorough, tighten the gap between rollers. If the malt seems too finely chopped, try opening the gap. Try another handful and check again. When you get it as good as you can, do the whole batch. Usually slower is better, as too much speed can rip the husks a bit.

If you grind your color malts first, the pale base malt that follows will clean the mill nicely for the next batch.

For most two-row malts, the same gap should work for all. Six-row malt is narrower and will require you to reset the gap a little tighter, so mill it separately. The same is true for oat malt. Wheat, rye, and other naked grains can be ground nearly to flour, as there are no husks that need to be protected. I have found that malt mills sometime struggle with wheat, and may have a very hard time with any unmalted grains. For that reason, I recommend a feed mill or an old coffee grinder if you're planning on using a lot of unmalted grains in your beers. Flaked grains do not need to be ground before using.

MASHING

Mashing turns grain into fermentable sugars—the heart of the brewing process. There are a number of schemes for this, but at the core is a holding period, or as brewers say, a rest, at about 150°F/66°C, for approximately an hour, during which the enzymes present in the malt chop up the starches in the malt into simple sugars. The mashing process can be as easy as that, or can include a number of other rests for specific brewing purposes, plus sideshows like mash boiling, cereal cooking, and more. The good news is that for most brews the process is quite uncomplicated, and good results can be had from even the simplest procedures.

Malt not quite crushed enough. Whole pieces won't yield much extract, leading to low efficiency.

A good malt crush. The endosperm is broken into small pieces; the husks are in relatively large chunks.

Overcrushed grain. The endosperm is broken up nicely, but so are the husks; these small pieces won't create an effective, free-flowing filter bed, which means a high likelihood of a slow or stuck mash.

THE MASH: MAGIC PORRIDGE

The barley kernel is built to have everything it needs to sit quietly waiting for the right weather, then quickly spring to life, converting its proteins and starch reserves into a new living plant. We co-opt that machinery and turn it into beer instead of growing new barley plants.

To do that we need to understand enzymes, the specialized proteins that assist with chemical reactions in very specific ways. Because of their chemical, electrical, and physical configurations, enzymes are capable of lowering the energy needed to cause a chemical reaction, such as the breaking of a molecular bond. Without an enzyme assisting, the required energy would be much higher, sometimes by a factor of a million or more. Without enzymes in brewing, there would be no beer.

Each enzyme has a specific reaction it assists, and specific chemicals that undergo the reaction. The convention is to name enzymes after their target molecule, plus the suffix *ase*. So, starch-chopping enzymes are *amylase*, named for amylose and amylopectin, the two forms of starch they attack. Proteinase, beta glucanase, and others follow this same pattern. Conditions such as temperature, water concentration, pH, and others also have an effect on enzyme activity. It is the job of the brewer to create the right conditions for the enzymes in malt to make wort with the qualities needed for a given beer.

Each of the mashing enzymes works best under a different set of conditions, so brewers perform the mash as a series of steps or rests. Each temperature rest is optimized for one or more enzymes to do their thing to the wort. If you look at the ideal temperature and pH ranges in the tables, you realize that no single set of conditions is ideal, so mashing is always a bit of a compromise.

What are we trying to accomplish in the mash? No matter what else is going on, we *always* need to break those bonds in the starch molecules and release fermentable sugars. This is called *saccharification*, and without it, there is no beer. With some beer styles and certain ingredients, mashes can sometimes be very complex with six or more steps, but the vast majority of beers are brewed with just one or two. Modern barley has been designed to work best with a simple mash, so when it's used with complex methods and multiple steps, it may not perform very well.

As we add hot water to the malt, the starch granules swell and eventually burst. This change, called gelatinization, also involves a phase transition (like ice melting) of the crystalline starches in grains. Locked up in their crystalline form, starches are relatively inaccessible to the enzymes in the mash. Every type of grain has a different gelatinization temperature, and there is even considerable variation within the same grain based on agricultural conditions. Barley malt starch begins to gelatinize at 138 to 149°F/59 to 65°C, fortunately lower than saccharification temperatures. Other grains, especially corn and rice, have much higher gelatinization temperatures—up to 185°F/85°C, which is why they require precooking when used as adjuncts in brewing.

For saccharification, we're lucky to have two enzymes to work with: alpha and beta amylase. Because they work best at slightly different temperatures, we can favor one or the other and get a wort that is higher or lower in fermentability, creating beers that are crisp and dry, rich and sweet, or anywhere in between. Beta amylase is more active at lower temperatures, and actually starts to be denatured at higher temperatures where the alpha amylase is working best. The neutral point between high and low fermentability is usually designated as 150°F/66°C. Mash warmer, and you get less fermentable wort for a richer, heavier beer. Mash at lower temperatures and the result is a more fermentable wort and a drier, leaner beer.

Temperature isn't the only factor; pH is also important, but usually manipulated as a part of overall water chemistry, not to achieve a particular mashing aim. Dilution has a small effect; mashes for highly fermentable beers tend to be thin, while less fermentable worts tend to be mashed thicker. A common ratio of water to grist, or the grain part of the recipe, is around 1.5 quarts per 1 pound/1.4 L per 1 kg. This effect amounts to just a few percent, and so mash thickness is often decided by other factors.

It's also important to understand that the two enzymes work together. At the beginning, there are relatively few molecular chain ends for the beta amylase to work on, and maltose liberation proceeds slowly. If left at low temperatures, beta amylase eventually will get a lot of conversion done, but it can take hours. When alpha amylase is active, it breaks the starch chains randomly, which means every time it breaks a chain, there is one more place for beta amylase to start working.

Because saccharification is the centerpiece of the mash, and by far its most important step, conditions like pH and dilution are usually designed to optimize that stage. Fortunately, outside of temperature, the other enzyme systems in the mash are perfectly happy under the same conditions as the two amylase enzymes.

There are other things besides sugar liberation we may want to achieve in the mash. Malt contains a spectrum of different lengths of proteins. We want to make sure that at the end of mashing we have the right mix. We want few of the large proteins that can cause haze and instability, a generous helping of mid-length proteins for body and head retention, plus fragments like amino acids that are critical for yeast nutrition.

Historic mashing processes were developed to create this perfect mix, but the malt was different then, and needed a protein rest in the mash. With modern malt, not only are protein rests usually unnecessary, but they can be harmful to beer, breaking up the mid-length proteins the maltster worked so hard to obtain. Historical mashes like decoctions may be desirable for flavor reasons, but they need to be changed to skip the protein rest when used with modern malts.

A hot water infusion initiates a complex cascade of biochemical reactions resulting in rich, sugary wort.

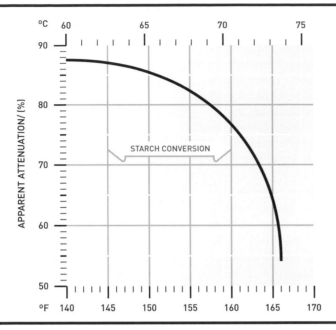

Potential attenuation, and therefore fermentability, can be very different at different mash temperatures; 50°F/66°C is considered the middle of the range, producing beers that are neither dry nor sweet. Note that this is a very general guide only; many other things affect mash outcomes.

Malted wheat is different. If its long proteins are not broken up in the mash, they clump together and fall out of the beer rather than staying and providing an attractive haze. So, it is beneficial to use a protein rest in any beer with more than about 15 percent wheat in the grist.

Many raw grains such as oats and rye, as well as unmalted barley and wheat, contain large amounts of a gummy carbohydrate called beta glucan. This sticky stuff can cause a mash to become gelatinous and resist efforts to drain it off. A low-temperature rest around 100 to 110°F/38 to 43°C for 30 minutes at the start of mashing, or mash-in, can help.

One more mash step that is sometimes used is a ferulic acid rest. This liberates a phenolic acid that is a precursor to 4-vinyl guiacol, the clove-tinged compound so important for proper hefeweizen aroma. The rest takes place around 110°F/43°C, and lasts 30 minutes or less. Your mileage may vary: some people report great results and others find it not worth the bother. Still, if you're a hefeweizen fanatic who feels as if there's never enough clove, it might be worth a try.

Before we leave the mash, we need to do one more thing. Even though the enzymes are partially degraded, they will continue converting starches into sugars, making the wort more and more fermentable. If we wish to lock in a certain mix of sugars for a certain fermentability, we need to raise the mash temperature to a point high enough to deactivate the enzymes—usually around 170°F/77°C, a step called a mash-out. This means the end of the mash, so hot water may be added without fear of overly diluting the mash. An added benefit is a temperature boost; a nice hot mash is necessary to keep the gelatinized starches liquefied and the wort flowing freely during sparging.

Amylopectin* (Starch) Prior to Mashing

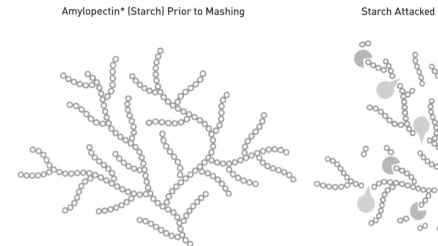

Starch Attacked by Enzymes During Mashing

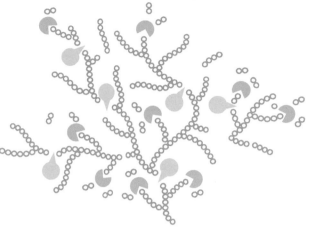

*Note that amylose, another form of starch composed of unbranched straight chains, is also present in the malt. It has been omitted for clarity.

Sugars After Mashing

Amylolytic Enzymes

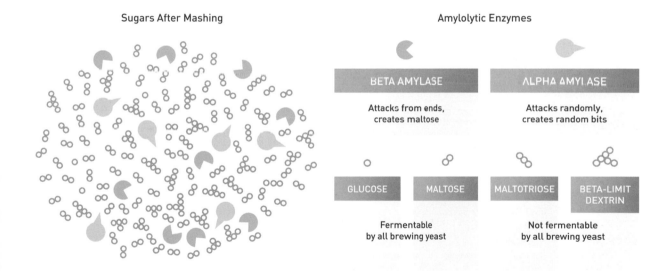

Starches are broken down by beta and alpha amylase enzymes during mashing in order to liberate dextrin and fermentable sugars.

ENEMYZES *in* DETAIL

Enzyme	Target Molecule	End Product	Optimum Temperature Range	pH	Destroyed Above
PHYTASE	Phytic acid	Calcium and magnesium phosphates = lowered pH	86–126°F/30–52°C	5–5.5	131°F/55°C

Notes: Phytase breaks up phytic acid, which then releases calcium phosphate, which then lowers the mash pH. This happens slowly over several hours, which explains the long, warmish initial soaks that were once a common feature of historic mashes but, due to good water chemistry and a need for speed, are no longer used.

BETA GLUCANASE	Beta glucans, pentosan	Various dextrins, small amounts of glucose	93–113°F/37–45°C	4.5–5.0	122°F/50°C

Notes: Beta glucan is a sticky carbohydrate; think about the gummy nature of oatmeal, which is loaded with it. It can be a major problem in beers made from high-dried malts, such as Munich, or adjuncts such as oats, rye, and raw barley or wheat, as mash can turn into a thick, jelly-like mess. Use low-temperature dough-in for a beta glucanase rest when brewing such beers.

PROTEINASE	Proteins	Smaller proteins, peptides, amino acids	122°F/50°C	4.6–5	150°F/66°C; unstable over 140°F/60°C

Notes: In malting as well as mashing, proteinase randomly attacks long-chain proteins and cuts them into intermediate-length chunks that are good for beer's head and body, as well as amino acids (free-amino nitrogen), important for yeast nutrition. Depending on the malt, this may have been done at a sufficient level when the malt is manufactured, and it may not be helpful to encourage it in the mash. Don't do a mash with this rest if you're not sure you need it.

PEPTIDASE	Proteins	Peptides, amino acids	122°F/50°C	5–6	160°F/72°C

Notes: This enzyme is a specialized proteinase that breaks the intermediate protein products above into smaller, soluble units—amino acids, which are important for yeast nutrition. Peptidase is normally destroyed by the heat of malt kilning and is thus inactive in the mash.

FERULOYL ESTERASE	Complexes of cellulose and feruloyl, a phenolic acid	Ferulic acid	104–113°F/40–45°C	5.7–5.8	149°F/65°C

Notes: Mashing in at a low temperature creates ferulic acid, which is important because it is a precursor to 4-vinyl guaiacol, which gives hefeweizen much of its clovey, phenolic aroma. Practical experiments do not always affirm the benefit of the ferulic acid rest.

BETA AMYLASE	Amylose and amylopectin (starch)	Maltose	140–149°F/60–65°C	5.4–5.6	160°F/72°C

Notes: Beta amylase chomps two-glucose-unit maltose molecules from one end of starch chains, leaving behind only beta-limit dextrins—small Y-shaped branches of carbohydrate. When mash temperature is optimized for this enzyme, the wort is highly fermentable, making a dry-tasting beer.

ALPHA AMYLASE	Amylose and amylopectin (starch)	Maltose, maltotriose, and longer sugars, dextrins, and starches	162–167 °F/72-75°C	5.6–5.8	175°F/79°C

Notes: Alpha amylase attacks starch molecules in random locations, rapidly lowering mash viscosity and providing many new ends for beta amylase to work on. Mash conditions optimized for this enzyme result in wort with a high percentage of unfermentable dextrins for a rich, filling beer.

LIMIT DEXTRINASE	Branching bonds of amylopectin starch	Maltose and longer sugars	133–140°F/55–60°C	5.1	140°F/60°C

Notes: Limit dextrinase breaks the branching bonds of the amylopectin starch that can't be broken by alpha or beta amylase, thereby creating a more fermentable wort. However, because of its low temperature range, limit dextrinase is inactive in most single-step mashes, but plays a part in the two-step lager mashes and is useful for creating very attenuated beers.

THE MINI-MASH METHOD

Once you've brewed a batch or two and are starting to work with different malts as well as extract, it's time to think about getting control over more of your brewing process. You have two choices: jumping in with both feet and going to full-mash beers; or dipping your toes in the water by doing some mini mashes that use the same process as a full mash, but scaled back to a smaller volume, just large enough to incorporate the full range of specialty malts into your brew. The advantage of a halfway approach is that the equipment is smaller and less expensive, and it takes a little less time than a full mash. If you're boiling less than the full volume of the recipe, you can stay with this method.

The mini-mash method is a pretty flexible option that allows you to make most beer styles. The disadvantage is that you're tied to malt extract, which means you're not fully in control of your base malt. Not a problem for many beers, but if you want to use a large proportion of mild or Vienna malts, or a particular cultivar like Maris Otter pale malt, be aware that these specialty malts may be difficult to find.

A small, insulated cooler (coolbox) of 1 to 2 gallons/3.5 to 7 L can serve as a mash tun, as long as some arrangement is made to provide filtering. There are various products sold for this purpose, ranging from plastic or metal false bottoms to tubular draining devices made from screen mesh or braided hose. If you're fairly handy, you can rig something up rather than buy it. For a small mash tun, the simplest build is to just drop one of those flappy fold-up vegetable strainers into the center of a small round cooler. It's important to remember that the screen won't do the actual filtering; that task will be handled by the malt husks. So, the screen needs to be just fine enough to block the larger malt particles: 1/8 inch/2 mm should be good.

The particular enzyme chemistry, conversion, and runoff of mini mashing are pretty much the same as with full batches, so the information that follows applies equally well to these little side batches. You probably will get a somewhat lower efficiency with this process, so be generous with your quantities. Recipes for mini mashes in this book are calculated at 50 percent efficient, but your efficiency may vary. After a batch or two, you can calculate predicted yield versus actual, and make adjustments to nail the OG for the next time. A mini mash takes about 45 minutes before you're ready to add its runoff to the rest of your brew. Time the extract portion so it's close to a boil when your mini mash is ready, then add the new wort and continue.

This small-scale mash is the midway step between extract and full-grain brewing methods and offers many flavor possibilities for your brews. A folding vegetable steamer insert makes an easy and effective false bottom.

EXTRACT PLUS STEEPED-GRAIN PROCEDURE

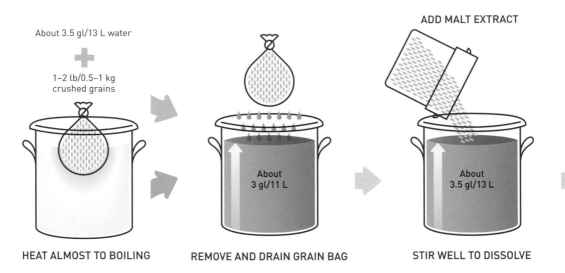

About 3.5 gl/13 L water

+

1–2 lb/0.5–1 kg
crushed grains

ADD MALT EXTRACT

About
3 gl/11 L

About
3.5 gl/13 L

HEAT ALMOST TO BOILING   **REMOVE AND DRAIN GRAIN BAG**   **STIR WELL TO DISSOLVE**

The extract plus steeped-grain procedure includes steeping the grains, boiling the hops, transferring the liquid to a carboy, and adding sterile water.

MINI-MASH PROCEDURE

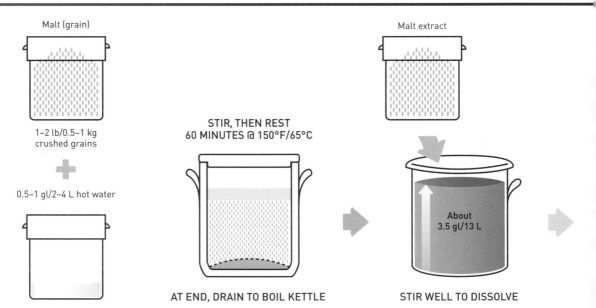

Malt (grain)

1–2 lb/0.5–1 kg
crushed grains

+

0.5–1 gl/2–4 L hot water

**STIR, THEN REST
60 MINUTES @ 150°F/65°C**

Malt extract

About
3.5 gl/13 L

AT END, DRAIN TO BOIL KETTLE   **STIR WELL TO DISSOLVE**

This is the standard procedure to follow when brewing mini-mash versions of the recipes in this book. Use the times and temperatures given here unless instructed otherwise in the recipe.

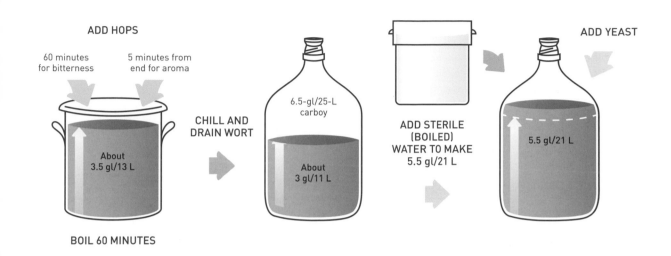

ADD HOPS

60 minutes for bitterness

5 minutes from end for aroma

About 3.5 gl/13 L

BOIL 60 MINUTES

CHILL AND DRAIN WORT

6.5-gl/25-L carboy

About 3 gl/11 L

ADD STERILE (BOILED) WATER TO MAKE 5.5 gl/21 L

ADD YEAST

5.5 gl/21 L

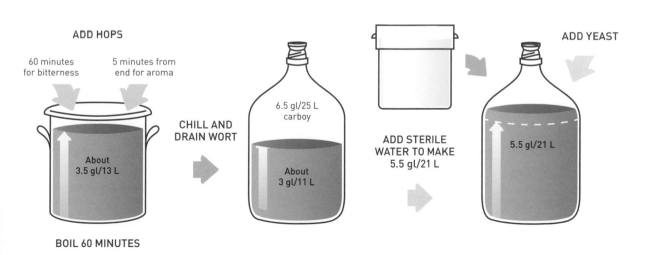

ADD HOPS

60 minutes for bitterness

5 minutes from end for aroma

About 3.5 gl/13 L

BOIL 60 MINUTES

CHILL AND DRAIN WORT

6.5 gl/25 L carboy

About 3 gl/11 L

ADD STERILE WATER TO MAKE 5.5 gl/21 L

ADD YEAST

5.5 gl/21 L

INFUSION MASHING *for* ALL-GRAIN BREWING

Most beers can be brewed just fine with a simple infusion mash, which means only one rest, at saccharification temperatures, and no other step except for a mash-out at the end.

The procedure to some degree will follow your equipment, but the basics remain the same. Brewing water, called *liquor*, is prepared according to the style of the beer. Total weight of the grain is noted, and based on the target mash dilution a quantity of water is heated, plus a little more to adjust the final temperature, if necessary. This is called the strike water. Use the following chart to choose an appropriate strike water temperature that will get your mash to the desired temperature.

STRIKE-WATER TEMPERATURE-DIFFERENCE

STRIKE TEMPERATURE	MASH DILUTION					TEMPERATURE	
						MASH REST	AMBIENT
180°F / 82°C	145°F / 62.8°C	150°F / 65.3°C	154°F / 67.8°C	158.5°F / 70.3°C	160°F / 71°C		
170°F / 76.7°C	139°F / 59.4°C	144°F / 62.2°C	148°F / 64.4°C	151.5°F / 50.4°C	154°F / 67.7°C		
160°F / 71°C	134°F / 56.7°C	138°F / 58.8°C	142°F / 61°C	145.5°F / 63°C	148°F / 64.4°C		
150°F / 65.6°C	129°F / 54°C	133°F / 56°C	136°F / 57.8°C	139°F / 59.4°C	140.5°F / 60.3°C		
140°F / 60°C	125°F / 51.5°C	128°F / 53.2°C	131°F / 55°C	132°F / 55.6°C	133°F / 56°C		
130°F / 54.4°C	120°F / 48.7°C	123°F / 50.5°C	124.5°F / 51.4°C	125.5°F / 52°C	126°F / 52.2°C		
	0.5 qt/lb / 1.01 L/kg	0.75 qt/lb / 1.5 L/kg	1.0 qt/lb / 2.1 L/kg	1.25 qt/lb / 2.6 L/kg	1.5 qt/lb / 3.1 L/kg	RECORD YOUR RESULTS HERE	

This chart was created based on using a plastic mash tun at a cool room temperature. Depending on your vessel construction and ambient temperature, your results will probably differ. Use the empty boxes at right to record your results and the ambient temperature.

Add about two-thirds of the strike water to the tun, and then dump the malt on top. Stir gently until hydrated, checking for balls of unmoistened malt. Give the temperature a couple of minutes to equalize, then check. If it's low, add some more hot water, stir, and recheck. Repeat if needed to get to your desired mash temperature. In the unlikely event that you've overshot the temperature, cold water can cool it down. Now, you're mashing.

Once the mash has been set, close the lid. Cooler-style mash tuns are often used because they make this easy, but with bucket mash tuns a blanket or Styrofoam jacket can help hold in the heat. A thermometer with a probe that can be read without opening the lid is helpful, because honestly, there's not much to look at. Check the mash about halfway through. Taste for sweetness to see if it's converting (it will be, but it's always a thrill). If the temperature has dropped by more than 3 or 4 degrees, it might be worthwhile adding some 170 to 180°F/77 to 82°C water to bring the temperature back up.

Contact between hot mash or wort and oxygen has been implicated in reactions that can create stale, cardboard flavors in the finished product. Do what you can to prevent splashing or extended contact of the mash with air. Some obsessive types have gone so far as to purge the mash tun with CO_2, but this seems like a lot of work. Don't worry about aluminum pickup or flavor in the beer—this has been shown not to happen.

Proper temperature control is key to getting the desired results from your mash.

While you are mashing, start heating your sparge water to a temperature of about 170°F/77°C. Treat it exactly like the rest of your brewing water, with filtration and minerals if needed. The total quantity needs to account for the water lost by soaking into the grain, trapped in dead space under the false bottom, evaporated during the boil, and stuck in the hops and trub (coagulated protein and hop sludge), in the kettle and the yeast in the beer. As a basic rule, you need 20 to 25 percent more brewing water than your batch size, plus about 2.5 fluid ounces per 1 pound/163 ml per 1 kg of grain in the recipe. Of course, because of the many variables, every system will be different, so for your first few brews it may be very helpful to have a little extra water available on brew day. Take good notes and you can dial it in for future brews.

TIME AND TEMPERATURE FOR BASIC INFUSION MASH

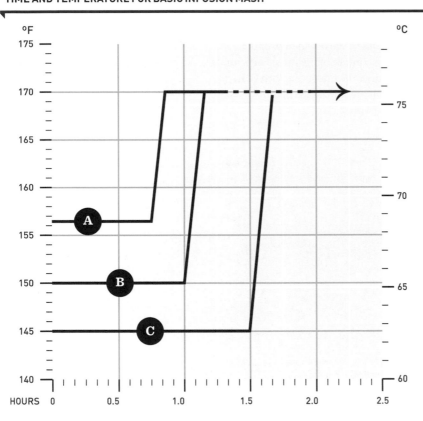

A: High-temperature mash used to brew a dense, poorly attenuated brew such as a Scotch ale. High enzyme activity means a shorter mash is possible.

B: A standard mash that will give a nice balance of fermentable and unfermentable wort.

C: A low-temperature mash used to make a dry, well-attenuated beer. Lower temperatures require more time for conversion.

The basic infusion mash results in three possible extremes: a high-temperature mash, a standard mash, and a low-temperature mash. The dark lines show the time and temperature curves for the three extremes possible with the basic infusion mash. All show a mash-out at the end of mashing, a rise to 170°F/77°C normally accomplished by adding hot water. The dotted line indicates sparging. In reality, most setups will show temperature drops of a few degrees per hour because of imperfect insulation. Many variations are possible between these extremes.

One more simple mashing procedure is commonly used, especially for lagers. It is a two-step mash that starts out in the beta amylase range, typically about 143°F/62°C, then, after a 30-minute rest, is raised to an alpha amylase range (160°F/71°C) to complete saccharification. There is nothing specifically lager-like about this, except that it will produce a wort that will attenuate well, and therefore suits a fairly dry beer such as a Pilsner. This mashing schedule is a bit more efficient than a single-step infusion. There are similar two-step infusions in the British tradition, like the dark beer mash shown on the following chart.

MASH SCHEDULE FOR LAGER BREWING

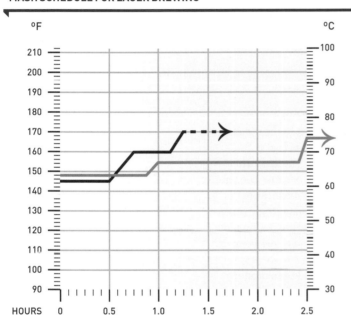

Black line indicates a modern lager mash. Step-ups are usually accomplished by steam in commercial breweries. Brown line shows a historical English mash for mild, brown ale and stout. Longer rests may have been used to compensate for poorer malt quality and imperfect crush.

Lager brewing typically incorporates a two-step infusion process, producing a well-attenuating wort.

The mash-out is the final step for any mash. In basic systems, an addition of hot water at up to 200°F/93°C is added to the mash with the aim of raising the temperature up to around 170°F/77°C. In addition to deactivating the enzymes, the additional water acts as a sort of pre-sparge, diluting the mash and helping to carry away sugars when drained. Brewing systems such as RIMS, HERMS, and direct-heated tuns that are capable of heating the mash can mash-out without adding any water.

DOING IT *the* HARD WAY

Sure, today, we like brewing to be nice and easy, but it wasn't always so simple. The old books are loaded with mashing schemes so complex that they must have been just an excuse for the brewers to stay at the brewery all night with their pals and brew (and drink!). Some of the old methods are just curiosities now, but there are some techniques that are worth the extra effort for certain beer styles, producing rewards of flavor and texture as well as historical authenticity.

Decoction mashing originated in Germany, especially Bavaria. It involves removing and boiling a portion of the mash before returning it to the mash, creating an upward temperature step. Belgium had some truly zany schemes that worked well with unmalted grain, particularly wheat. These were modernized in the early nineteenth century and laid the groundwork for adjunct mashing procedures that are still in use by mega-brewers all over the world brewing lager with rice or corn adjuncts.

DECOCTION MASHING

Decoctions work by removing a portion of the mash from the tun, raising it through some steps on its way to a short boil, then returning it to the mash, which raises the temperature to the next step. The advantage is that in any given place, a fixed volume of boiling mash will raise the mash temperature by a specific amount—without needing a thermometer. Also, because the volume of the decoction is usually one-third or less of the whole mash, a small kettle can be used and the mash conducted in a wooden tun, meaningful in the days when metal vessels were very expensive. Because of their extended cooking processes, decoctions are very efficient in terms of yield, less so in terms of energy and time.

Historically, malts for decoctions were much less modified than modern ones and required boiling to gelatinize the hard, steely ends typical of such malt. In terms of taste, decocted beers show a nice layer of caramelized flavors, picked up during the short boil(s) that is part of the process. However, modern malt doesn't benefit from decoctions. The multiple mash steps in the classic decoctions negatively affect the protein structure of the wort, stripping away body and foam stability.

For those interested in pursuing the classic three-mash Pilsner decoction, less well-modified Moravian malt is available. This is a test of skill and commitment, the brewer's equivalent of an Iron Man race, with twenty-two separate actions required and lasting over five hours—*before* beginning the sparge. Start early.

There are two reasonable uses for a decoction. The first is to add those caramelized nuances to dark lagers like doppelbock and Munich dunkel. This can be done without a lot of fuss simply by using the decoction to raise the temperature for a mash-out. Once the mashing is complete, remove a thick one-third portion of the mash, put it into a heavy-bottomed cooking pot, and set it on a medium burner. Stir gently, making sure nothing is sticking to the bottom of the pot. Do not use a thin stainless-steel pot or converted keg for this! You *must* have a layer of copper or aluminum in the pot, or use a piece of metal as a heat diffuser. Raising the decoction to a boil will take 10 to 20 minutes depending on the quantity of the mash relative to the burner. When it comes to a boil, maintain for 10 to 15 minutes, stirring gently and scraping the bottom as necessary to keep from scorching, then transfer back to the main mash, where it should raise the temperature into the mash-out range.

MINI DECOCTION TIME AND TEMPERATURE

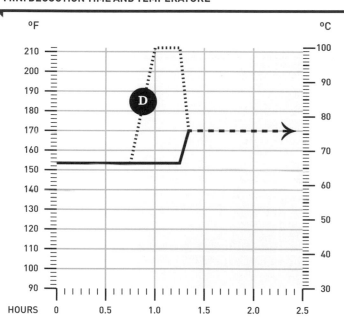

This is a simplified decoction that gives good results with beers like Czech-style Pilsners that benefit from a simple decoction. The dotted line is the decoction, a thick one-third of the mash that is removed and given a short boil in a heavy-bottomed pot before being returned to raise the temperature of the rest of the mash.

The other good use of a decoction is for wheat beer. A lot of hefeweizen fanatics believe that a decoction makes a real improvement in flavor and texture and boosts the efficiency as well. Because wheat benefits from a protein rest, this decoction procedure can incorporate that step so it looks more like a traditional decoction mash schedule. Mash is started at 122°F/50°C, and allowed to rest for 15 minutes; a thick one-third of the mash is removed, brought to saccharification temperature, and held for 15 minutes before continuing up to a boil of 10 to 15 minutes. Then it's added back, raising the temperature to bring the whole mash into saccharification range. As with any rise involving hot liquid, don't add the decoction all at once; make sure you're not overshooting your desired temperature with the first two-thirds, then add the rest. It's helpful to have some hot (180°F/82°C) water ready in case the temperature needs to be raised a bit once the whole batch is reunited. For dark wheat beers, a second decoction can add a little caramelized flavor if used to make the step up to mash-out, as shown by the pale dotted line in the following chart.

WHEAT-BEER DECOCTION TIME AND TEMPERATURE

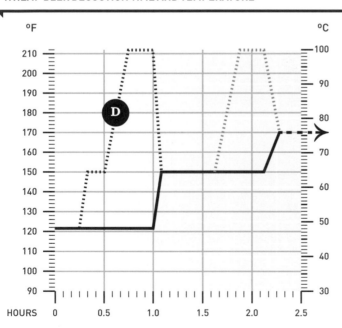

The dark dotted line (D) is the decoction, a thick one-third of the mash that is removed and given a short boil before being returned to raise the temperature of the rest of the mash. The pale line represents a second decoction that can be added to dark wheat beers for additional caramelly flavors.

ADJUNCT MASHING

Unmalted grains can be used in small quantities of 10 or 15 percent, especially if they're flaked, torrefied, or otherwise pre-gelatinized. But for those who wish to make truly authentic versions of Belgian witbiers or American pre-Prohibition adjunct lagers, larger percentages must be used. Most raw grain really benefits in terms of extract and character from some intensive cooking. Whether it needs a short boil or just a high-temperature rest depends on the grain's gelatinization temperature. Unmalted wheat, with a relatively low gelatinization temperature, can be boiled but responds about as well from a short rest at 185°F/85°C yielding far more of its silky texture than in a normal infusion mash. Corn and especially rice have much higher gelatinization temperatures and other characteristics that demand an actual boil as part of their mashing.

Because raw grains and even naked malts, like wheat and rye, lack husks, it is a good idea to add some rice hulls to the mash along with them. They are quite inert and add no flavors to the beer. I usually add them at a ratio of 1 pound/455 g of hulls per 5 pounds/2.3 kg of huskless malt or raw grain. Cheap insurance against a stuck mash, I think.

For this procedure, the adjunct mash is started first. This contains all the raw grain plus about 20 percent of the malt to help with conversion. This adjunct mash is rested twice on its way to a boil: first to digest some proteins and second to get as much sugar conversion as possible to thin the mash before boiling. After 10 minutes of boiling (or resting), mash in your malt mash with the remaining 80 percent of the malt, resting at 122°F/50°C, right about the time the adjunct mash boil is finished. Then combine the adjunct decoction with the main mash, rest at saccharification temperature for an hour, then mash-out and sparge as with any other brew.

Maize, which became an important ingredient in American lager brewing in the late nineteenth century, needs a specific mashing process for best results.

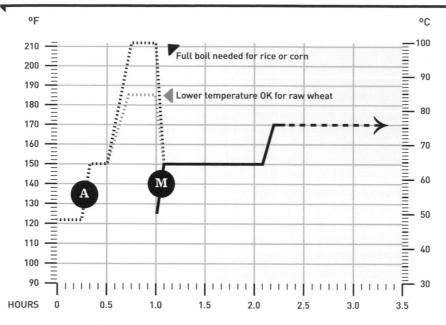

The dark dotted line (A) indicates decoction for rice or corn, plus 20 percent of the malt. Note that because of wheat's lower gelatinization temperature, the rest, at about 185°F/85°C, shown by the pale dotted line, is about as effective as a boil. The solid line (M) indicates malt mash, then the combined malt and adjunct mash.

EXTREME MASHING

Beyond these basic techniques, history offers up a bounty of crazy schemes, some of which can be useful to small-scale brewers.

PARTI-GYLE

The word *gyle* roughly means batch, and applies to the runoff from the mash. In the old days of English and Belgian beer, most beers were *parti-gyle*, meaning that first, second, third, and sometimes even fourth runnings were either fermented separately or blended together in specific ways to create strong, middling, and weak beers from every batch. The first third of the wort is approximately twice as high in gravity as the second two-thirds. For example, 7.5 gallons/28 L of wort can yield 2.5 gallons/ 9.5 L of 1.090 (21.5°P) wort plus 5 gallons/19 L of wort at 1.045 (11.2°P). For a brewer, this offers the convenience of making several beers from one batch, but it adds a degree of difficulty as

well, as it's tricky to formulate a recipe that will work well at all strengths, and there is a fixed ratio between the quantities of the different beers, consumer demand be damned.

For modern small-scale brewers, a parti-gyle is often a necessary side effect of brewing strong beers. All systems have a limit to the amount of malt they can handle, so for strong batches it's sometimes best to make a smaller batch and use only the first runnings. This leaves a considerable amount of extract behind, so sometimes a second, small beer is brewed using the old English technique of throwing some additional dark or caramel malt on top of the grain before sparging the goods, adding some flavor, body, and color.

DOUBLE BREWING

This is another method used to turn out very strong worts, and shows up in the record as early as Elizabethan England. Two batches of malt are used to make one beer. The first is mashed and run off, then that rich wort is added to the second batch of malt instead of water. This "doubles" the malt and allows a brewer to produce worts of 1.120 (29°P) or even higher. Unless a small beer is made from what's left (see parti-gyle in previous entry), it is pretty wasteful.

SLIJM (BELGIAN TURBID MASH) MASHING

Slijm means "silt" in Dutch and refers to the cloudy, gritty first wort created by this process. Historically used for both witbier and lambic wort production, slijm mashing is a result of a couple of factors. One is the Dutch law instituted in Belgium in 1822 that taxed brewers on the volume of their mash tuns, so they sought ways to brew beer with their tuns stuffed full and using a minimum of liquid. The second was a demand for very low gravity beers prior to the mid-twentieth century. Turbid mashing is an effective—if time-consuming—way to brew a weak beer with a lot of flavor and texture; it produces a highly dextrinous wort that leaves some substance in the finished beer, which gives some weight on the palate to an otherwise weak beer. In lambic brewing, these dextrins are essential to proper souring, as they are food for the lactic acid bacteria that will create the essential acidity in that wild, sour style.

While the specifics are often horrifyingly complex, the basic idea is that the grist is mashed-in somewhat warm and very thick; as soon as it is hydrated, the cloudy wort is removed and immediately boiled in a kettle called a "chain copper," featuring a rotating bar with loops of chain dragging along the bottom to keep the starchy matter from scorching. This boiling destroys any enzymes present in the wort. The mash is rehydrated with near-boiling water, allowed to rest at saccharification temperature, then run off to a second kettle. The boiled, cloudy wort is reinfused into the mash, rested, run off, and added, then the whole batch boiled. Often a very small beer would be brewed with the extract remaining in the grist. Sometimes wheat and malt mashes were processed completely separately all the way through the boil before being recombined, taking as long as seven or eight hours to perform.

OVERNIGHT MASHING

Some brewers who are pressed for time will do an overnight mash, waking up the next day to reheat to mash-out temperatures. This shortens the brew day, taking up part of the previous evening, which for many is a fine trade-off. The procedure is exactly the same as for any other mash. As always, the initial strike temperature is most important. The obvious concern that such long mashing will create a too-fermentable wort are unfounded, as beta amylase is degraded within an hour at normal mash temperatures around 150°F/66°C. The other potential problem is acidification and unpleasant aromas from *Lactobacillus* present on the malt, but mash temperatures kill a lot of these, and those bacteria are very slow to grow. Mash souring usually becomes barely noticeable at six to eight hours. It takes perhaps twice as long for weird aromas to develop.

Having a well-insulated mash tun is helpful. Standard picnic coolers usually leak too much around the lid. You can either seal the lid with duct tape and/or put a heavy blanket over it, or get one of the super-insulated coolers with better insulating power.

SOUR MASHING

Malt is loaded with *Lactobacillus*, which under the right conditions will feast on the sugars and starches in malt, creating some acidity. Some older brewing methods use long, warmish pre-soaks to encourage the activity of the phytase enzymes, which lowers the mash pH. These long mashes may develop some lactic acid bacteria growth as well. Small-scale brewers have experimented with sour mashing to emulate the process used in bourbon making, or to add lactic flavors and acidity without the danger of exposing the fermentation vessels to *Lactobacillus* and *Pediococcus* bacteria. A couple of things are helpful to know. Some bacteria in the mix can produce a lot of butyric acid, which has rancid butter or "barf" aromas, obviously unsuited to fine beer. They seem to need oxygen and are somewhat sensitive to high temperatures, so if you're trying this method, keep the temperature at or above 120°F/49°C, and exclude air as much as possible. A sheet of aluminum foil right on top of the mash should be helpful.

As an easy alternative to sour mashing, some maltsters offer acidulated malt, which has already undergone this process and then been kilned to sterilize. It's quite sour, so for most purposes, between 1 and 5 percent is the norm, or perhaps more if you're aiming for a seriously sour style like Berliner weisse.

LAUTERING *and* SPARGING

Sparging is nothing more than the act of rinsing the mash with hot water to recover as much extract as is reasonable. There's nothing much chemical going on; it's mostly a mechanical process. How well the bed drains off depends on a number of factors: grain or malt types, especially the gluten content, the way it was ground, the bed temperature, and the specific geometry of the tun, including bed depth, strainer/false-bottom specifics, hydrostatics, and more.

If a hot water infusion has been used to raise the goods up to a mash-out, then some of the water needed for rinsing is already there. Most homebrewers mash and sparge in the same vessel, but if the mash is transferred from a mash kettle to a lauter tun, it needs a period of time to settle before runoff can begin.

Start the runoff slow by opening the valve partway, and letting some of the cloudy wort trickle out. This will be gently recycled through the grain bed to clarify, a process known as *vorlaufing*. Usually after 1 gallon/3.8 L (or less) of cloudiness, the wort begins to run clear. When the wort flow has been established, open the mash tun valve more fully to increase the flow rate. If the valve is opened fully at the beginning, rapid wort runoff can create a vacuum under the false bottom that sucks the mash down and compresses it, making further runoff slow and annoying.

When moving wort around, take special care not to splash it or otherwise expose it to air any more than absolutely necessary. Oxygen picked up here can linger around all the way through the process and come out in unpleasant ways after the beer is packaged, a process known as "hot-side aeration," that inspires much dread among obsessive brewers. Older systems featured revolving spray arms that sprinkled water over the mash as they rotated; but for a small vessel in a homebrew setup, this is unnecessary and may be problematic, as sprinkling introduces oxygen into the sparge water and at the surface when it splashes. The best system is to put a perforated plate or piece of screen on top of the mash and using a piece of hose from your hot liquor tank, let the water flow out at a rate about equal to the flow rate of wort out the bottom. The perforated plate keeps the flow from digging holes in the grain bed, and may or may not be needed.

The wort should be flowing out in a heavy trickle, and it typically takes about an hour to collect the full volume of wort. Sometimes the sparge becomes stuck, and the flow slows down to near zero, most commonly with raw grains or naked malts like wheat or rye. If this happens, the best you can do is stir it up nearly to the bottom, and if you have 1 pound/454 g of rice hulls on hand, stir them in with the mash. Restart your runoff slowly, to avoid sucking the grains down onto the false bottom.

If this happens a lot, you need to go through your system and sparging procedure and find the problem. A proper grain grind is hugely important, and can be difficult to achieve or even verify. Try grinding your next batch with somebody else's mill, or try the rice hulls added to the mash for more filtering material. Make sure your false bottom or pickup manifold is correctly constructed. Remember, the mash filters itself. The perforations are only there to hold it up and keep the chunks out. If the screen you're using as a false bottom is too fine, this can be a problem.

Grain depth should be 12 inches/30 cm or less, ideally, although deeper grain beds are common, especially with bigger beers. Tubular screen pickups usually work fine, but they do present a small surface area, and if that becomes clogged, there's nowhere else for the wort to go. And above everything else, make sure your mash being sparged is always above 145°F/63°C, because below that, barley starch begins to gelatinize, and you can't sparge Jell-O.

If you have a seriously stuck mash, add some hot water through the bottom, if possible, and then cut through the surface of the mash by dragging your spoon through it. If that doesn't do the job, then re-stir the whole batch and allow it to settle for a while before slowly running off. It's not a bad idea to have a bag of rice hulls handy for just such emergencies, as sometimes they can help.

Pay attention to the liquid level in your mash tun. Until you get to the end of runoff, the top of the mash should still be underwater. This is important both to exclude oxygen and to keep the mash floating, which keeps it light and fluffy. When the supporting liquid is removed, the mash tends to collapse under its own weight, and in the early stages of runoff this can make a good flow difficult to achieve. Toward the end of the mash the liquid level can be allowed to drop as the last of the sparge water finds its way out of the tun.

Brewers should be concerned about taking too much very thin wort out of the goods, as these impoverished last runnings have a higher pH and can leach unpleasant tannic substances out of the grain and husks. In general, the best practice is to calculate the total volume of water needed and when you get wort filling your kettle to an appropriate level, stop the sparge and call it a day.

As the wort is removed, it can be added to the kettle and heated. Ideally the whole batch will be ready to come to a boil just as the last of the wort is going in. This saves time, of course, but as a general rule it's a bad idea to let hot wort sit around doing nothing. I find that the little details of timing can add up to a large difference in the time it takes to brew. Having things ready, getting ready for the next step, and generally avoiding any waiting is the secret to a short brew session.

For many brewers, the phrase stuck mash *conjures up images of late nights in the brewhouse, dinners gone cold, and attempts of Zen-like calm in the face of great frustration.*

GARRETT OLIVER, brewmaster, Brooklyn Brewery, and author of *The Brewmaster's Table* and *The Oxford Companion to Beer*

Welded together from pieces of wire with a V-shaped profile, this is the type of lauter tun false bottom many professional breweries use. Open area is about 10 percent.

ADDITIONAL SPARGING TECHNIQUES

The described sparging technique is just a scaled-down version of what happens in commercial breweries. Clever homebrewers, in search of simplicity or speed, have thrown out the rule book and found a number of alternate methods of separating the wort from the spent grain. These can work well and may suit your needs. Just be aware that the quicker and easier the method, the less efficient it is—a trade-off that many homebrewers are quite happy to make.

BATCH SPARGING

Batch sparging involves draining out the first runnings until the mash is nearly dry, then reinfusing with the rest of the sparge water, allowing the mash to re-settle, then draining again. This is perhaps a little less fussy than the continuous method described, but it doesn't really save you much time, either. Plus, it may expose the wort to more oxygen. Unless you really have an attention span problem, I'd do the more conventional sparge.

"NO-SPARGE" BREWING

This technique is just what it sounds like. A thin mash is made containing a mixture that when drained off contains the right liquid and extract to hit the recipe's target gravity. This shaves off about a half hour from the process, which for many people will be worth the slightly increased expense that is the price paid for lower efficiency. The main additional benefit is a more stable pH during the brew, meaning less chance of extracting harsh tannins during the later stages of the sparge. Devotees report smoother-tasting beers. Grain bill quantities need to be 20 to 25 percent larger; but more important, no-sparge brewing requires a mash tun at least double the size of your brew, because the vessel has to hold the grain and the liquid for the entire volume of the batch.

BREW-IN-A-BAG

These systems are one variation on "no-sparge." This method replaces a stainless mash basket with a cloth one, sort of like taking the false bottom out of the mash tun, and making it the bottom of a cloth sack, with a large, looped basket-style handle across the top. A mash is made as usual, and after mash-out, the bag is lifted by its handle so it's free of the wort, allowed to drain for a time, maybe squeezed and prodded a bit, then the mash is discarded. This cuts a half hour of mash draining down to just a few minutes, and for sure is the simplest way to do a full-mash batch. Efficiencies are similar to the no-sparge method, so follow similar recipe modifications. It has become quite popular in Australia, and based on the beers I tasted there, seems to work quite nicely.

These easy-to-use systems speed the sparging process at a slight loss in efficiency. After mashing, the bag is simply lifted and drained, while boiling commences in the same pot. Photos courtesy of Brew-in-a-Bag.

SPARGING TECHNIQUES

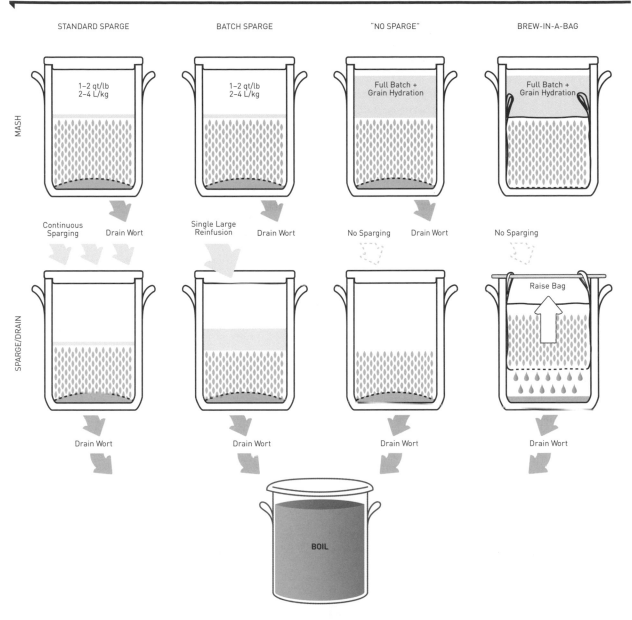

Various mechanical methods can be employed to separate the wort from the spent grain.

SPARGING *with* RECIRCULATING MASH SYSTEMS

Homebrewers looking for more control and automation often turn to recirculating mash systems that constantly move the wort through a heater, allowing mash temperatures to be held or ramped up very precisely. Commercially made versions can be fairly basic or can come with all the bells and whistles, including computerized control systems. The two forms, HERMS and RIMS, are discussed in chapter 5. Both systems operate by immediately going into a sort of sparge mode, with the runoff being pumped through some heating arrangement before being returned to heat the mash in the tun. Temperature is maintained or increased by turning on a pump that moves the wort through the heater and back to the wort until the desired rest temperature has been reached. If the temperature drops, the pump cycles on again and brings the heat back up a degree or two.

HERMS (heat-exchange recirculating mash system) units work by constantly recirculating wort through a heat-exchange coil immersed in hot water. While they can be run manually, a temperature probe and a controller are commonly used to cycle the pump on and off, moving the wort through the exchanger, thereby maintaining or raising its temperature. In sparge mode, hoses are reconfigured to pump hot sparge liquor over the bed, while the wort is drained to the boil kettle.

RIMS (recirculating infusion mash system) units use a dedicated heater unit instead of the heat exchanger.

Because the wort is constantly moving around in these systems, actually doing the sparge is just a matter of changing over the hose so it fills the boil kettle rather than recirculating. There is no need for vorlaufing, as the wort should be crystal clear long before it's ready for the kettle.

Recirculating mash systems heat the mash by pumping the wort through a heating device, in this case a small external heater. While the Sabco Brew Magic shown here is a commercial unit, many homebrewers have made their own recirculating mash systems from scratch.

HEAT-EXCHANGE RECIRCULATING MASH SYSTEM (HERMS)

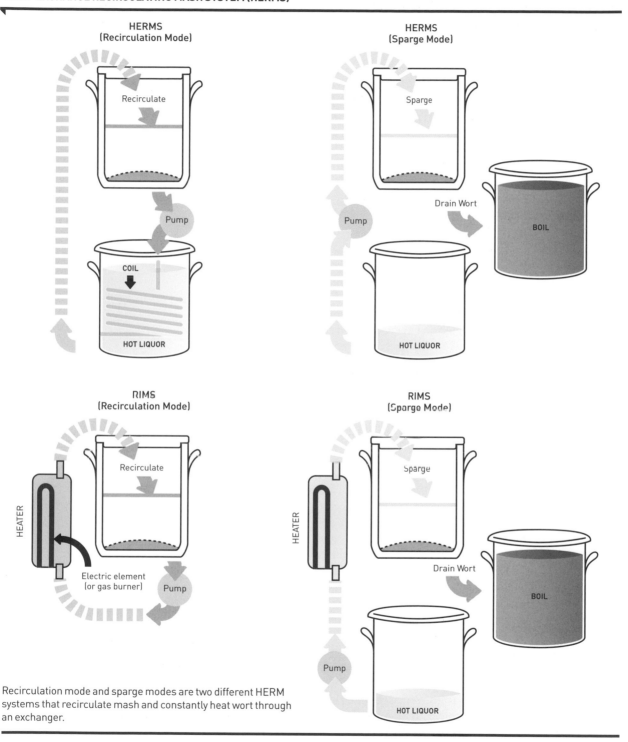

Recirculation mode and sparge modes are two different HERM systems that recirculate mash and constantly heat wort through an exchanger.

THE BOIL

With a few exceptions, like old-school Berliner weisse, beer wort is always boiled. In most cases this lasts about an hour, during which a number of important changes take place.

WHAT HAPPENS in the KETTLE

Several important things happen in the kettle in the course of an hour or so of vigorous boiling:

- Pasteurization of the wort
- Cessation of any remaining enzyme activity
- Isomerization and dissolving of hop bittering compounds
- The removal of unwanted aromatic compounds, especially DMS, but also some unpleasant hop and roasted malt volatiles
- Coagulation of excess long-chain proteins, aided by hop tannins
- Incorporation of hop aromas through different mechanisms

Sanitizing the wort is of obvious benefit, as malt is filthy with things that can take your beer in some pretty unpleasant directions. This pasteurization happens quickly, as does complete inactivation of the enzymes.

Hop bitterness and aroma are both extracted in the brew kettle. When hops are boiled, a chemical change happens that creates hop bitterness. The alpha acids present in hops are *isomerized*, a chemical term for the rearrangement of a molecule whereby its constituent atoms change places without gaining or losing anything, which makes them both more bitter as well as much more soluble. Transformed, hop substances dissolve readily, imparting the desired bitterness to the brew. This transformation takes a vigorous boiling and some time to accomplish. The degree to which hop bitterness is isomerized and dissolved in the wort is called *utilization*, and this varies by time, boil temperature (altitude) and vigor, pH, wort gravity, and more. This vigorous activity has the negative effect of driving off hop aroma, so we'll need to add more hops later in the boil if we want a noticeable hop aroma in the beer.

Some undesirable volatiles are removed during the boil. The most important one is DMS (dimethyl sulfide) a sulfur compound that reeks of creamed corn. It is created in the kettle from a precursor, SMM (S-methyl methionine), found in malt, especially Pilsner/lager types, at temperatures above 185°F/85°C. Because it is a light molecule with a low boiling point, a good rolling boil will expel it pretty effectively. Some of the precursor molecules are also destroyed in the boil, but usually enough remain to continue DMS production after boiling stops and before the wort is chilled—not a good situation. Like I said, it's never a good thing when hot wort is allowed to sit around doing nothing.

There are some other unpleasant aromas removed by boiling. Dark malts contain some burnt, ashtray aromas, and hops may contain some pretty harsh volatile oils. All of which is a good reason to never, *ever*, boil with a lid on. This just allows the evaporated substances to recondense and drip back into the wort, defeating the purpose. It's okay to have the lid on before the wort comes to a boil if you want to save a little energy.

Other unwanted materials are removed by coagulation. Haze-forming long-chain proteins are electrically attracted to tannic material from the hops, combining to form large flakes that fall out of solution and drop to the bottom to be filtered out with the hops. This is called the "hot break" and it looks like egg drop soup (because chemically it's similar—coagulated protein). This happens within 10 minutes or so of the start of the boil, and is pretty dramatic to see. A kettle coagulant like Irish moss is typically added to help remove more than would otherwise drop out. It's cheap, harmless, and even vegan; just get in the habit of adding it when you measure out your last charge of hops. If you're using a yeast nutrient, this is a good time to add that as well.

Hop aroma oils dissolve in the boil, although many of these will be expelled by the boil or lost in the tremendous off-gassing during fermentation. There is some evidence that what we experience as hop aroma (and normally attribute to dissolved oils) is actually due to chemicals called hop glycosides, sugars with hop compounds bound to them. These hoppy hitchhikers have aromas from fruity to floral to vanilla to honey-like, but as long as they remain bound to the sugars, they have no flavor or aroma. When they separate, the water-soluble aromatic molecules are free to follow their destiny of floating up into your nose and latching on to an olfactory receptor.

MANAGING *the* BOIL

In practical terms, there are just a few things to watch out for. One is to get the right amount of heat for a full rolling boil. The second revolves around dealing with the excess heat. In general, a good boil will seriously roil about half the surface of the wort. If you can, it's good to have the flame somewhat off-center, as this encourages a circular flow—up one side and down the other. Obviously, a sensitive-enough control valve to let you throttle the heat precisely is a must. A large-enough capacity is also very helpful. While you can theoretically boil 5 gallons/19 L in a 6-gallon/23-L pot (I've done it!), in practice it's pretty tough and you get more of a feeble simmer. At least 25 percent extra capacity is required; 50 percent or more is better and makes a boilover less likely.

Your first test of heat control will come early. Wort fresh from the tun has a relatively high surface tension. This allows wort to foam easily, leading to boilovers. Nucleation sites from hops added to the boil only make the situation worse, so it's a general rule to let the wort come to a boil and stabilize before adding any hops. As the wort comes to a boil, it will become very twitchy—calm one moment, flailing wildly the next. It's best to throttle back and let it go through its gyrations until its ready to behave, perhaps 5 minutes or so. Once the boil is steady, turn the heat down or off, and add the first charge of

hops. Give them a minute to hydrate, then turn the heat back on. As the boil progresses, the surface tension drops pretty rapidly, and you generally don't need to use this same level of caution with your other hop additions.

The other heat problem is less visible. Modern brewing science has come to the realization that the intense heating of wort that you get from a flame under a thin vessel of stainless steel is bad for beer. The problem is the formation of *reductones*, certain chemicals that can latch on to and then release oxygen. So, most homebrewers have a problem because of our direct-fired stainless-steel kettles. The problem isn't the metal itself; it's the fact that stainless steel is a very poor heat conductor, so heat applied to one area tends to stay there and become quite hot, rather than spreading out at a more moderate temperature. In fact, the heat at this boundary layer may be far higher than desirable. If you can see the pattern of the burner after you've emptied your kettle, it's too hot. If you have black char, you really have big trouble. For flat-bottomed pots, it's easy enough to make a heat diffuser that more than covers the size of the burner and evens out the heat. Pots with slugs of aluminum on the bottom will solve the problem and are available for very reasonable prices.

How long should you boil? The old wisdom said, "The darker the beer, the longer the boil," but that has changed. The same cautions about overheating wort also apply to boil length; for most beers, 1 hour should be sufficient. The one exception is for worts of mostly Pils or lager malts. These contain more DMS precursor, and so may benefit from 90 minutes of boiling rather than 60 minutes. In those cases, be sure the cautions about heat intensity mentioned previously are addressed, because they are most problematic in very pale beers.

Typically homebrewers boil bittering hops for 60 minutes and add aroma hops at the end of the boil or a few minutes before. Many brewers also add hops in between, at 20 or 30 minutes. This adds a mix of bitterness and aroma. In practice, I have found that this doesn't do much that can't be accomplished with the first and final additions, but it certainly can't hurt. It is good practice to boil hops no longer than 90 minutes or they will start to break down into some nasty-flavored chemicals.

Finally, be sure to turn off the boil when you planned to. One distracting little phone call, and you've got more bitterness and less aroma than you planned, with no easy way to fix it. Ask me how I know.

COOLING

Our goal in this almost final brewing step is simple: get the hot wort to fermentation temperature as quickly as possible. If you have a snowbank handy, this works well, but most of us will need to use a chiller of some sort to cool the wort. Immersion coolers are the simplest: just 30 feet/10 m or so of copper tubing with hose fittings on the ends. The tubing is connected to tap water and a drain; the cool water flows through, pulling heat out of the wort. It's a relatively slow process, but immersion chillers are cheap, effective, and easy to clean. They work best if the wort is moving, so some gentle stirring with a sanitized spoon will reduce your chill time. RIMS/HERMS often have a tangential fitting to develop a circular flow, or whirlpool, so the wort can be drained off, leaving a pile of spent hops and trub behind.

Besides the hops and coagulated hot break, some additional coagulated material called *cold break* may drop out of suspension during chilling. In addition to protein, the cold break also contains some lipids. Whether these should be removed or not is a matter of debate. There is some potential for increased haze from the proteins and also a possibility of soapy flavors from the lipids present; on the other hand, the yeast experts say the lipids are a valuable nutritional supplement for the yeast. I usually do what the yeast guys say. Either way, the beer will be fine.

Chilling obviously requires cold, or at least cool, tap water. In hotter regions a second chiller is often used to pre-chill the cooling water by immersing it in a bucket filled with ice water. It's a little cumbersome but effective. Your goal is to get the temperature right where you want it for fermentation. Don't overchill or you may cold-shock the yeast. If you do, fermentation may be very difficult to restart.

In the most common coil-type counterflow chillers, wort flows through a tube surrounded by a larger tube, with water flowing the opposite direction in the space between. There are also brazed-plate chillers that look like small metal bricks, but the principle is the same. Cooling water and hot wort flow in opposite directions so the hottest wort meets the coldest water. Chilling is nearly instantaneous, although it will take several minutes to get the whole batch through the device. Many come with a small *T* fitting at the end where the chilled wort exits, into which a thermometer can be attached. The cold water can be throttled back to a speed that gets the temperature where you want it.

Counterflow chillers usually work best with a pump, as flow can be pretty slow using only gravity. Their biggest drawback is that you can't see or scrub the inside. You must employ a rigorous cleaning regimen, especially with the brick chillers, which can trap hop particles that may be difficult to dislodge. I back-flush mine, then pump non-caustic alkaline cleaner like PBW through it for 10 minutes or so to remove any protein film, flush with water, then run another 10 minutes with a dilute phosphoric acid, then another rinse with water, and a good draining before storage.

Due to its simplicity and ease of use, an immersion wort chiller is the most common chiller type used by homebrewers, although most are made of copper rather than stainless steel.

CLEANING UP

I often bang my head against the wall for having chosen a hobby that involves so much plumbing and cleaning, but at least there's the drinking to make up for it. Keeping things clean is not in any way fun or glamorous but it is absolutely crucial to making good beer. Although it requires serious attention to detail, with modern cleaning products and methods, it's not too burdensome a chore.

On the hot side of the brewery, we are mainly concerned with cleaning rather than sanitizing. There is no point in sanitizing a vessel like the mash tun that will be holding malt loaded up with bacteria, or a vessel that is going to be filled with boiling wort. Some basic cleaning materials and a good scrubbing are all that's needed. But once the beer leaves the kettle, everything changes. From this point on, your wort is extremely vulnerable to contamination from microorganisms in the environment.

CLEANING and SANITIZING CHEMICALS for the HOME BREWERY

Cleaning and sanitizing chemicals are really quite different today than when I started brewing. We now can get pretty much the same chemicals used at larger breweries. Not only are these chemicals safer and better for the environment than the old ones, they are highly effective as long as you understand what their capabilities are and how they need to be used.

Sanitizers can have negative flavor consequences. Some, like chlorine bleach, need to be rinsed quite thoroughly, while others, like acids and chlorine dioxide, are what are called "post rinse," meaning they can be used and drained without having to rinse away the residue.

ELECTRON MICROGRAPH OF BIOFILM

This stuff will haunt you, as this pile of microbes glued together by carbohydrates and other residue can't be seen by the naked eye. Photo used with permission from Sterilex Corporation, Hunt Valley, MD.

WARNING: HANDLING CLEANING CHEMICALS

You should be aware that even modern brewery cleaning products are powerful chemicals that carry some risks. Be sure to observe safe handling procedures.

- Keep all cleaning chemicals out of the reach of children.
- Always follow manufacturers' recommendations about concentration, handling, and compatibilities.
- Wear eye protection and rubber gloves when handling corrosive or irritating chemicals.
- Never mix different cleaning chemicals unless recommended by manufacturer.

Anything that touches the beer must be sanitized before using it. Here are some definitions that will probably help.

CLEANING

The late, brilliant homebrewing scientist George Fix liked to say, "You can't sanitize dirt," and this is a crucial truth. Films or particles of dirt offer refuge to microorganisms from sanitizers, and this is obviously a problem. The first line of defense is a product that is specially formulated to remove brewery dirt, especially stubborn protein films that cling to every surface that has been in extended contact with beer or wort. Everything in the brewery, from brewhouse to packaging, should be clean.

SANITIZING

This is the level of disinfection required in the cold side of the brewery, meaning vessels, hoses, and other equipment that will come in contract with wort once it is chilled. While sanitization kills wild yeast and bacteria to a government-approved 99.999 percent level, it does not kill spores, which are the very tough encapsulated forms of bacteria that allow the tiny creatures to survive harsh conditions temporarily. Spores are not a huge bother in brewing—they are much more significant in health care—which is why sanitization is adequate for everything in the brewery except for yeast cultivation, where contamination from spores can cause problems.

STERILIZING

This means the death of all living things on the sterilized objects, including yeast, bacteria and their spores, and viruses. It requires either very high levels of heat or other processes like chlorine dioxide gas or radiation. In the brewery, it is needed only in yeast-propagation procedures like plating and slants, and is usually accomplished in the brewery lab by the use of an autoclave, a specialized pressure cooker used for the purpose.

Brewery dirt comes in a number of different forms.

BIOFILM

This is a thin, often invisible layer of bacteria glued together with carbohydrates and other goop stuck onto glass, plastic, and metal surfaces. Techniques that remove beerstone and protein films will also remove biofilm.

CARBOHYDRATES

Usually comprises a baked-on layer of sugars mixed with some minerals and proteins that occurs at or just above the liquid line on a boiling kettle. Water and scrubbing should get most of it, and an alkaline cleaner should remove any remaining residue. If for some reason you get scorched, carbonized crud on the bottom of a vessel, I have found Dawn Power Dissolver particularly effective at removing it, but scorching is a very bad sign that you are doing something seriously wrong, and you should make some changes so this doesn't happen again.

GREASE

This is seldom a problem with brewing equipment, but if you make chocolate or coconut beers or use your brewpot for an occasional batch of chili, then you'll need to remove the fat so it won't interfere with your beer's head retention. Standard liquid dishwashing detergents are highly effective on greasy films. Be sure to rinse well, as detergent itself can wreck a beer's head.

PROTEIN RESIDUE

This is a thin, nearly invisible film deposited from beer or wort onto glass, plastic, and metal surfaces. While it might not look like much microscopically, it is rough enough to harbor bacteria and other critters, and so needs to be removed. Alkaline cleaners are best for this.

SCALE

This includes beerstone, calcium (lime), and other minerals on brewery surfaces, especially ones that have undergone boiling. Simple minerals come off or dissolve in mild acids, but beerstone is a pernicious mix of minerals like calcium oxylate, plus proteins. The most effective procedure is an acid cleaner first, followed by a non-caustic alkaline cleaner, with no rinse in between.

CLEANING CHEMICALS

These are the cleaning chemicals commonly encountered by the homebrewer. It should be noted that these are for cleaning only, and won't sanitize anything.

ACID CLEANERS

These come in different formulations, usually with phosphoric acid as a major constituent, sometimes with nitric acid as well, and often with wetting and/or foaming agents. These are effective at removing scale, and at the correct concentrations are highly effective as sanitizers (see facing page). Some chemicals are formulated specifically for brewers, but I have found that phosphoric acid dairy rinse, available at farm supply stores, and even household anti-scale products, like CLR (lactic and gluconic acids with a wetting agent), are effective for most home brewery-acid cleaning needs.
COMPATIBILITY: Stainless steel, glass, plastic, aluminum. Mildly corrosive on copper and brass; highly corrosive to steel and iron.
CAUTIONS: Skin and eye irritant.

ALKALINE NON-CAUSTIC CLEANER

These are alkaline detergents similar to household dishwasher detergent or oxygen bleaches, but specially formulated for brewery dirt. They are especially effective at removing protein films. Work okay at room temperatures, but definitely better hot; the manufacturer of one such product, Five Star PBW, recommends 130 to 180°F/54 to 82°C. Liquid beverage-line cleaners are also available to clean hoses, but your general-purpose brewery cleaner should work just as well.
COMPATIBILITY: Glass, stainless steel, plastic. Mildly corrosive to copper and brass.
CAUTIONS: Mild skin and eye irritant.

CAUSTIC/SODIUM HYDROXIDE/LYE

Powerful caustic cleaner used by breweries but not generally recommended for homebrewing use. Must be used very hot to be effective, is difficult to rinse, and causes calcium deposits when used with hard water, which need to be removed by an acid rinse. Non-caustic cleaners are just as effective on brewery dirt, are better for the environment, and are much safer and easier to use.
COMPATIBILITY: Glass, stainless steel, plastic. Highly corrosive to aluminum, copper, brass, fabric.
CAUTIONS: Very strong skin and eye irritant.

Cleaning and sanitizing are very different processes; both are best done with specialized chemicals rather than household products.

SANITIZING CHEMICALS

The following chemicals are used for sanitizing brewery surfaces that will come in contact with cooled wort or beer. These are not cleaners and will not provide adequate sanitization unless used on surfaces that have been properly cleaned beforehand.

ACID SANITIZERS

Generally effective after a few minutes of contact, and does not need to be rinsed after use. The same chemicals can also function as cleaners, especially on scale and beerstone. A very powerful sanitizer called peracetic acid, a blend of acetic acid and hydrogen peroxide, is sometimes used as the sanitizer of last resort in breweries, but it's generally considered too hazardous and unnecessary for home use.
COMPATIBILITY: Stainless steel, glass, plastic, aluminum. Mildly corrosive on copper and brass; highly corrosive to steel and iron.
CAUTIONS: Skin and eye irritant.

CHLORINE BLEACH (SODIUM HYPOCHLORITE)

Household bleach is sodium hypochlorite (NaOCl) at 5.25 percent. Two ounces/60 ml of bleach per 5 gallons/19 L of water gets you 163 ppm, in the middle of the 100 to 200 ppm recommended range. It is effective for sanitizing, but has a few drawbacks: It must be thoroughly rinsed, or residue will combine with compounds in beer to form unpleasant, adhesive bandage–like aromas. Not environmentally friendly, either, so not generally recommended.
COMPATIBILITY: Glass, plastic. Corrosive to most metals, including stainless steel (short contact time okay). Dangerously reactive with some other cleaning chemicals.
CAUTIONS: Eye and skin irritant, damages clothing.

CHLORINE DIOXIDE

This is a very potent sanitizer that does not require rinsing and has minimal environmental issues. It disrupts cellular chemistry, killing a very wide spectrum of microorganisms as well as mold and spores. Once spent, the residue is mainly table salt. A product called Oxine is available from some homebrew suppliers and online. Most products require mixing an acid such as citric acid with the chlorine-containing chemical (do *not* try this with bleach!), and the resulting mix has a short shelf life. Always follow manufacturer's directions, as the acid activator needs to be measured carefully, and higher-than-recommended concentrations may be harmful.
COMPATIBILITY: All brewery materials and surfaces.
CAUTIONS: Eye irritant.

IODOPHOR

This has similar properties to chlorine, but is not as corrosive. Normal use is around 12.5 ppm of iodine, typically a 1000:1 dilution, but check manufacturer's directions. For a 1.75 percent iodine concentrate, use 1 ounce/30 ml per 5 gallons/19 L of water to achieve 25 ppm active, the maximum that should be used. At this concentration, iodophor does not require rinsing. Some people react negatively to iodine.
COMPATIBILITY: Glass, plastic, metal. Will stain plastic.
CAUTIONS: Eye and skin irritant, stains clothing.

ISOPROPYL ALCOHOL

This is the familiar rubbing alcohol, and is best used in a spray bottle where it can be used to clean valves, carboy tops, and other external surfaces in the brewery.
COMPATIBILITY: All brewery materials and surfaces, but don't get it in the beer.
CAUTIONS: Eye irritant.

SODIUM METABISULFITE (CAMPDEN TABLETS)

This is a chemical that will release free sulfite when used. It is not a sanitizer, but rather an inhibitor of wild yeast. Not generally used in the brewing hobby, it may be useful when working with wine barrels or any situation where the inhibition of wild yeast is desired, such as cider making or brewing with fruit.
COMPATIBILITITY: Everything.
CAUTIONS: None.

VODKA (40 PERCENT ETHANOL)

I buy the cheapest stuff I can find and use it to fill airlocks and store my aeration stone in it. I like it because it really doesn't matter if a little of it gets in the beer.
COMPATIBILITY: Everything.
CAUTIONS: Flammable if heated.

CLEANING YOUR EQUIPMENT

It's good to get into a routine of cleaning all equipment after every use to prevent film buildup and more difficult cleaning later. Here's what I recommend:

CARBOYS

I remember the first time I used an alkaline cleaner on the filmy crud in my carboys. Big floppy scraps of stuff came off; it looked like there were bats flying around in there. It is best to clean carboys after use, as the gunk on there hardens into an epoxy-like substance if it dries out and then becomes much more difficult to remove. The easiest way I've found to clean them is to rinse out all the old yeast, then put some alkaline cleaner in the bottom, fill to the brim with very hot water, and allow to stand a few minutes. Usually, the ring of dark goop from the yeast will need a little hand scrubbing with a bottle brush or carboy brush, then perhaps a little more soaking time before siphoning out the cleaning solution and giving it a rinse.

When clean, I usually put 1 to 2 ounces/30 to 60 ml of acid sanitizer in the clean carboy, swirl it around over all surfaces, and cover the top with plastic wrap (or the screw cap on 25-liter ones) and store them this way. Then just add a little water to the acid, re-swirl, and drain before the next use.

HOSES

Always make sure to rinse and clean immediately after use, because if anything dries in there, kiss that hose good-bye. I find the alkaline cleaners great for hoses. Just put the hose into your little cleaner bucket, and use a turkey baster to squirt in cleaning solution. Always hang up to dry so the hose can drain completely.

KETTLES

Just get in there and scrub first to get a lot of the loose stuff. Follow with an alkaline cleaner, which should remove most of the film. If there are some stubborn deposits of beerstone, an acid cleaner should remove it. A toilet brush is a pretty good-shaped implement for pot cleaning, and a non-scratch scrub pad will remove dirt but not scratch the metal. For stubborn dirt and scorch marks, a brass-bristled brush or a copper scrubber can be very effective.

SMALL STUFF

When I'm brewing, I usually keep two small plastic tubs handy, one filled with alkaline cleaner and the other with a sanitizer. When things like airlocks and Corny keg parts come off, I can just drop them in the cleaner, let them sit a while, rinse them off, and drop into the sanitizer bucket.

Passivation and Stainless Steel

Stainless steel is a complex mix of iron, nickel, chromium, and sometimes other metals. Chromium in the alloy forms an inert oxide layer that protects it from attack from oxygen and other corrosive chemicals. When stainless is ground, welded, attacked by certain chemicals, or otherwise assaulted, the oxide layer can become damaged, and it is possible for stainless to, well, stain. Passivation uses acids to replenish the chromium oxide layer. It's not necessary at home; regular use of an acid cleaner/sanitizer is sufficient to maintain stainless steel—another good reason to use such products.

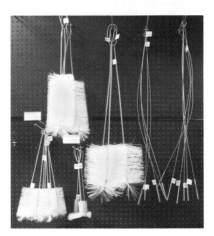

A selection of brushes from my local brew shop.

Facing page, row by row from top left: homebrew labels by Dave Gallagher, Daniele Rocchi, Bogumil Rychlak, Kevin Bastian, Tara Leigh Z, Robert Alvord, Kevin Bastian, Kim Theesen, Łukasz Szynkiewicz, Kim Leshinski, Fantastic Mykel, and Szymon Tracz/Jim LaFleur.

Verbosity

QUIET PLEASE

DOMINE'S Pizza

HIGH WATER BREWERY

DAL DAL'S BEER

WAITANGI
"SOUTH PACIFIC" IPA

BIERRA VIVA ARTIGIANALE AD ALTA FERMENTAZIONE NON PASTORIZZATA, NON FILTRATA E SENZA USO DI CONSERVANTI

CONSERVARE IN LUOGO FRESCO E ASCIUTTO, AL RIPARO DALLA LUCE E IN POSIZIONE VERTICALE

PRODUZIONE PERSONALE NON DESTINATA ALLA VENDITA

RIVISITAZIONE PERSONALE DELLO STILE INDIA PALE ALE. PRODOTTA CON SOLI LUPPOLI NEOZELANDESI SU CLASSICA BASE MALTATA.

RIFERMENTATA IN BOTTIGLIA PRESENTA UN LIEVE DEPOSITO DI LIEVITO SUL FONDO A CAUSA DEL PROCESSO NATURALE DI LAVORAZIONE.

INGREDIENTI: ACQUA, ORZO, LUPPOLO, LIEVITO E ZUCCHERO

IMBOTTIGLIATA:

PRODUZIONE N°:

REALIZZATA PRESSO

DAL'S CORNER BREWING

ALC. 6.4% 50 CL.

"TO ALCOHOL! THE CAUSE OF ...AND SOLUTION TO... ALL OF LIFE'S PROBLEMS"

GDZIEŚ DALEKO NA KRAŃCACH GALAKTYKI NAJSŁYNNIEJSZY I NAJBARDZIEJ SKUTECZNY ŁOWCA NAGRÓD, LOBO, TEŻ SZUKA CHWILI WYTCHNIENIA OD ZAPUSZCZANIA SONDY W JELITA ZŁOCZYŃCÓW...

STWORZYLIŚMY SPECJALNIE DLA NIEGO PIWO ANI MĘTNE, ANI CAŁKIEM KLAROWNE, ANI MOCNE, ALE NIE SŁABE, ANI AIPA, ANI LAGER, PEŁNE SPRZECZNOŚCI JAK ON SAM

SKŁAD: CHMIEL ZIEM SŁODY KOSMICZNE

WODA ZE ŹRÓDEŁ CZARNII

EKSTRAKT NIEZNAN ALKOHOL DOBRZE UKRYTY

STINGO
ENGLISH BARLEYWINE ♥ 9% ABV ♥ BOTTLED 12.09.13 ♥ ⊘DROOD ONE ⊘TATARCHY

---

bob's chicago style home brew

Standard Bitter

OD MORNING, GOOD MORNING
TOUT WITH CHOCOLATE & RIVER CITY ROASTERS COFFEE

Lisle, Illinois | 12 fl oz | 6.5 vol% | Bottled on

BLACKBIRD BREWING

MASHING DEBUT
Single Malt & Single Hop Pale Ale

This job first knocked down on [...], soil in 1961...

BLACKBIRD BREWING
EST. 2010 | Lisle, Illinois | 12 fl oz | 6.2 vol% | Bottled on

---

Kim Brough

CRACKALICIOUS
EVIL FINNISH JUNIPER BERRY
GRUIT
BEER QUEST 10:10:10

With rye, mugwort, sweet gale, coriander, pepper and juniper.
Base Beer: Saison-Sahti
Yeast: Wyeast Belgian Saison

Piwo w stylu Special Bitter warzone na II połfinał Piwowar Battle w ogdańskiej Degustałoni 07.12.2013r.

Warka nr 20
Uwarzone: Butelkowane:
29.09.2013r. 12.10.2013r.

Ekstrakt: 11,6° BLG
Alkohol 4,2% ABV
Goryczka: 35 IBU

Browar domoun

OBSZYMJFANI

Kot Schrödingera

Żywy & Martwy

Special Bitter

Skład: Woda, słody Pale Ale, Karmelo. Płatki Jęczmie biscuit. Częstałowy C chmiele: Challen Target, EKG omchłyte Mangrove Jaci M79 Burton Uni

Temperatura: $r
12°c
14°C

LEAPING WILDEBEAST

OLD ALE
500 ML
6.0% ABV

BREWED BY RILEY'S
CRAFTED BY HANE

JAPANESE IPA
SORACHI ACE SINGLE HOP
14° Blg
5,5% alk.

browar rzemieslnicz

MAKAK

LAFLEURILLUSTRATION.COM
TWITTER: DOODLEMATT
773-218-9680

LAFLEUR BREWING COMPANY
EVANSTON, ILLINOIS

Not Your Honey

THE Brewery

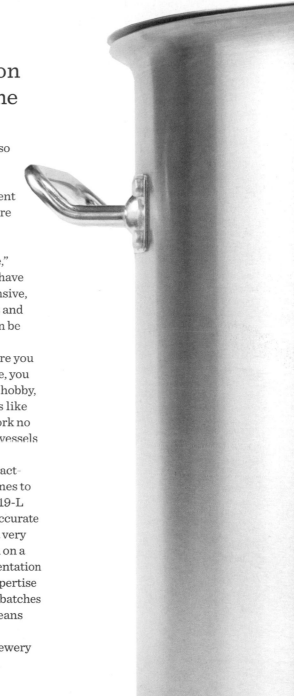

◆◆ Every detail of your beer depends on your ability to control the variables of the brewing process.

This, in turn, is dependent on your skills, experience, and focus, but also on your equipment. Each piece of gear, from your brew kettle to your thermometer, determines what is possible and affects the quality of your beer in some way. The difference between good and bad equipment can show up not only in the quality of your beer, but also in the pleasure you get from the hobby. There's nothing worse than a brew day spent cursing, fixing, and generally managing problem equipment.

Get good stuff. My welding instructor is fond of saying, "Buy for life," meaning that if you get the best-quality tools available, you'll seldom have to worry about them. As hobbies go, the equipment isn't all that expensive, so it's not difficult to afford good-quality stuff. If you want all the bells and whistles, it will cost you; but it's amazing how sophisticated a beer can be made from very simple equipment.

Ideally you want to buy your starter setup with an eye toward where you might like to go. But this isn't completely possible because as a newbie, you really don't know where this thing will take you. As you grow into the hobby, it will start to be apparent to you what your end game is. The basics like fermenters, instrumentation, wort chillers, and other tools should work no matter what size home brewery you're running. Mashing and boiling vessels need to be sized for the batch.

Almost everybody starts out making 5 gallons/20 L at a time of extract-based beer. (Numbers in this book are for 5-gallon recipes, which comes to 19 L rather than 20. If you're brewing metric, you can either stick to a 19-L batch size or increase quantities of all ingredients by 5 percent to get accurate results with a 20-L batch.) And unless you have the jones real bad or a very large circle of thirsty friends, you should, too. This allows you to learn on a smaller scale and manage important things like sanitization and fermentation before moving on to advanced techniques like mashing. Experts on expertise say it takes ten years to master a subject. I will say that after just a few batches your beers will be pretty damn good; but at ten years, you are by no means through with learning. Brewing is the hobby that keeps on giving.

A complete list of necessary and optional equipment for a home brewery startup is on page 118, with the instructions for malt extract brewing.

SAFETY *in the* BREWERY

There are a lot of potential dangers in even the smallest brewhouse—from simple burns and cuts from broken glass to a few freak accidents like a bourbon barrel exploding when a burning sulfur wick was inserted. In general, use common sense: If something seems dangerous, it probably is. Always keep children, and other bystanders like your drinking pals, out of harm's way. Remember: Don't overdo it on brew day. However wonderful it is to drink your own delicious homebrew, be sure you are fully in command of your faculties until the wort is safely in the carboy. What follows is a list of possible hazards in all their gory detail.

ELECTRICITY

In a wet, well-grounded location like a brewery, this is a potential hazard. A GFCI circuit breaker should be your first line of defense, and is code for wet locations. However, older houses may not have them. Install one if it's not there; plug-in versions are available.

Never defeat the grounding pin of an electrical plug. If you're building equipment, do so in a safe and professional manner by proper wiring and grounding techniques, using watertight electrical boxes, cables, and so on. Switching with float switches and thermostats should always be done at low voltage (6 to 24 VDC) through a water-resistant relay housing that switches the line voltage. If you are unsure of proper technique, get some help. It's a rare homebrew club that doesn't have an electrician or electrical engineer (or three) in its midst.

GAS CYLINDERS AND PRESSURE

Carbon dioxide and oxygen cylinders are constructed exactly like bombs. The compressed gas inside represents a huge amount of potential energy that can wreak havoc when unintentionally released. Shearing off the valve of a CO_2 cylinder turns it into a rocket that can easily punch its way through a concrete-block wall. It's true. I've seen it on TV. Treat them with respect, and make sure they are secured with a chain or a strap so they can't fall over. Be especially careful when moving them around and make sure not to defeat the protective rupture disk in the gas regulator.

GFCI circuits are mandatory for working in wet locations, and are available in plug-in form (left). CO_2 regulators (above) need to be kept in good condition.

GLASS CARBOYS

Hands down, these are the most dangerous things in the brewery. They're large, slippery, heavy, and fragile—not a great combination. Broken, they unleash a rain of glass scimitars that will just about slice off a foot. Be super-cautious and look into the various devices like slings for handling them safely—milk crates work for some sizes. Be aware that the handles that clamp on the necks won't support the weight of a full carboy and can cause the neck to snap off. Also make sure there is nothing sitting above a carboy that can fall onto it and break it. And finally, when fermenting fruit in a carboy, use a piece of foil or plastic over the neck, as the small hole in a stopper used with a fermentation lock can clog, and even a small amount of pressure can blow the whole thing to bits.

HEAT AND HOT WATER

Any liquid above 140°F/60°C has the potential to cause burns, so this means anything at mash temperature or above. Make sure all vessels holding hot materials are stable and not easily tipped over. Are your hose clamps tight? Heat softens vinyl hoses and can cause them to loosen and slip off, spraying hot wort or water around, so check them every time you brew.

Brewery burners can create a huge amount of heat, so it's a good idea for safety as well as efficiency to rig up some kind of heat shield that helps keep the heat directed toward the kettle. Also, be aware that heat rises, so valves, thermometers, and other devices attached to the kettle may get fairly hot and may need to be heat-resistant or require some additional heat shielding. If there are electrical cords near the heat source, be especially careful with them, as electrical insulation melts pretty quickly and that can create an electrical hazard.

MOTORS

Anything powerful enough to crush grain or stir a mash can also break a finger. Be aware of a motor's malevolent potential and keep hands, hair, and loose clothing well out of the way. Better yet, install a guard on the moving parts that makes it hard to get too close to the danger.

PROPANE AND NATURAL GAS

Ever wonder why the propane tanks are always outside the hardware store? Propane is considered a hazard indoors, and here's why. Unlike natural gas, propane is heavier than air, so if there's a leak, it will flow all through the bottom of a space, find its way to the pilot lights and explode. So, no propane indoors, ever! With all gas connections, confirm that equipment is approved and professionally installed according to code. Be sure your burner is not making any orange, sooty flames, as this can mean incomplete combustion and very likely some carbon monoxide. With any large burner in an interior space, a carbon monoxide detector is a very good idea, as is a smoke detector.

Smoke detectors and carbon monoxide detectors should be first on any indoor brewer's list.

YOUR SYSTEM, YOUR GOALS

Most of us end up cobbling together systems chunk by chunk and eventually get something suitable to our needs. Hobbies like this move forward one bright idea after another. Throw in the random nature of salvage and surplus acquisitions, and the Frankenstein approach often dominates. There is a certain pleasure in reanimating industrial castoffs even if they add a certain funkiness to our systems, or maybe especially because they do.

But a little forethought ought to help make a system that does what you ask it to. No matter where you are in your journey as a brewer, it is always helpful to take stock of your wants and needs for your system. The most obvious question is, how big? The standard batch size is 5 gallons/19 L, which is fine for most brewers. All-grain brewers can double that quantity for maybe a half-hour extra brewing time, and many feel this is well worth doing. Larger homebrew systems exist, but are fairly rare. The next question is, how much can you drink or give away? One brewer I know brewed 10 gallons/40 L a week just to keep the band coming to his house for practice.

Ten-gallon/40-L systems are too big for the kitchen and they need a high-capacity heat source of 50,000 BTU or so, which means they need to go outdoors or to an appropriately set-up garage or basement. Height can be an issue because a gravity-driven system probably needs 6 feet/2 m at minimum for the three vessels to drain into one another. Without gravity, you are dependent on a pump. Consider your system size carefully, as you will be locked into it unless you change a lot of equipment. With big burners, make sure you know where that heat will go; if allowed to build up near flammable surfaces, the heat can cause problems. For enclosed spaces, ventilation and makeup air are also important; consult a professional if you need to.

It is important to consider what kind of brewing techniques and procedures you would like to use. For most brewers, even commercial ones, single-infusion mashing is all they ever want or need. This system is quick and energy efficient; for modern malts it's perfect for most beers. It also requires the simplest equipment, because an infusion mash tun needs only insulation and not a heat source. Mash-out can be attained by an addition of hot water to raise the temperature. If you're looking at doing decoctions or American-style adjunct mashes, an infusion system can work fine with the addition of a heavy-bottomed pot of approximately half the batch size.

Another good question to ask yourself is, what's your philosophical approach? Are you a minimalist who wants to keep things streamlined or do you really want to have all the trimmings? Are you willing to work with a system limited to simple mashing techniques, or do you want to be able to tackle the most complex antique mash schedule just for fun? How important is a shorter brew day? Do you want something really cool looking? Historically authentic?

Finally, it's always good to take a good, hard look at one's limitations. What do you have in the way of skills, tools, access to salvaged stuff, and money? Don't forget spouse tolerance. Like any hobby, this one can rage out of control, and it takes a pretty tolerant partner to put up with endless tinkering in the brewery, unless he or she really likes beer.

There are some very fine manufactured homebrewing systems out there, but if you're the right kind of person, building your own system can be an incredible learning experience, and the journey is every bit as much fun as brewing beer on it when you're done—which of course you never are.

DESIGN CONSIDERATIONS

Modularity is something that helps make sure all the parts fit together well, and can eliminate the need for multiple copies of expensive items like pumps. Start with hoses and the fittings used to connect them. I began with a mishmash of different types, which meant each hose was different and only fit in one location. When I switched to identical valves, fittings, and hoses, I spent a lot less time trying to figure out where the damned (technical term) hose was for the next task. It seems like such a stupid, simple thing, but it made a big difference. Everything fits everything. That's the goal.

Pumps, float switches, and other devices can be moved around as needed, so you don't have to buy multiple copies. At this point, my pump is built into a little wheeled cart that can be rolled around the brewery floor to put it where it's needed. My float switches have brackets that allow them to be attached to any location they're needed with just a thumbscrew.

Calibration is another important concept, something that's worth taking the time to do. Hitting your brewing targets efficiently requires knowing exactly how much material is involved. Solids are weighed, so it's important to have confidence that your scales are reasonably accurate. Liquids are best kept track of by calibrating all the equipment where it will spend any time. While the vessels themselves can be marked in various ways, it is often easier to use what is called a gauge stick, something as simple as a slat of wood or piece of plastic that is marked off in quarts, gallons, or liters, depending on your needs. It is just placed in the vessel, and the liquid will come to a level that has previously been marked. It should be obvious that a different gauge marking will be needed for each vessel, but two or more sets of markings can share a single stick.

Mechanization can affect all areas of the brewing process. A system can be entirely manual, from hand cranking the malt mill to siphoning the wort into the fermenter, but machines are available to help with the chores. For small batches, cranking the mill by hand isn't a big deal, but it gets pretty tiring with a big batch like 40 pounds/18 kg.

Pumps are the next most common machine in the brewery. For brewing rigs like HERMS and RIMS, they're mandatory. Pumps may seem simple, but they are a mysterious and often recalcitrant partner in the brewery. It is helpful to have a good understanding of the specific model you have, what it can and cannot do, and how to set things up to keep it happily humming away, pumping liquid around your brewery.

Automation is the next level up. This involves using some kind of a control system to manage a particular task, turning a heater, valve, motor, or anything on or off. The gold standard is automated commercial brewing systems such as those manufactured by Kaspar Schultz in Germany, which will brew pretty much unattended, and even call your cell phone to tell you it's time to add the yeast. I haven't seen a homebrew system like this, but I'm betting some clever engineer with a pile of Arduino components is working on it right now.

Most brewery automation is simpler than this and can really make the brew day easier, allowing you to focus on other brewery tasks rather than having to spend an hour with your hand on the valve or switch while sparging takes place. The machine can do it with greater precision than you can, anyway, minimizing batch-to-batch variations.

Here are the simplest ways to use automation in the home brewery.

FLOW CONTROL

While opening or closing a valve isn't a big deal, doing so at exactly the right moment under the proper conditions isn't always so easy; it requires a watchfulness that can be hard to maintain in the multitasking environment of the brew day. Very simple control systems can be made from solenoid valves turned on or off with float switches. One good use for this is a fill level control for a hot liquor tank or kettle. As long as the float switch is not immersed in water, the valve remains open and fills the tank. When the water hits the float, it bobs up, changing its signal and telling the valve to close, which means your tank won't overflow and require a lot of annoying mopping.

In a non-gravity-fed system, another good use is to control the pumping of sparge water from the receiving vessel below the lauter tun (known as a grant) to the boil kettle. When a float switch inside the grant detects liquid, the pump turns on and wort moves to the kettle. Similarly, a float switch can be used to maintain the liquid level in the mash tun, by opening a valve or turning on a pump to let sparge water flow in.

TEMPERATURE

This can be useful in a number of brewery areas, and is often very simple to do. Basic mechanical thermostats can be used to regulate heaters for sparge water, yeast starters on hot plates, and the fermenters themselves, as long as they need heating rather than cooling. Electronic controllers called PIDs are widely used in the industry and so are readily available as surplus. These offer more sophisticated methods of regulating temperature precisely; usually they take an external probe such as a thermocouple.

Jim Hodge, an engineer by trade, put together the sweetest little automated 5-gallon brewery I ever saw. He's not bored; he's plotting world domination.

GEAR

There are a lot of equipment choices for today's homebrewer. For the beginning brewer, equipment is pretty basic. Suggestions for a starter kit are in the Your First Beer section on page 118. As your interest in the hobby grows, it will make sense to add pieces of equipment: wort chiller, grain grinder, flasks for yeast starters, and more. At the high end are manufactured systems or your own hand-built one, depending on your needs, skills, and available cash. Every piece of equipment has its own set of features, capacity, and capabilities. To help you choose, here are some thoughts on the most common pieces of homebrewing gear.

GRAIN MILLS

The object of malt milling is to crush the starchy endosperm of the grain while leaving the outer husks untouched. It is a goal seldom perfectly accomplished. Large breweries use multiple rollers and screening systems to sort out the chunks that need re-crushing from everything else, and the resulting mills are as large as minivans, obviously problematic for the homebrewer.

Most models designed for small-scale brewing use two rollers. If set up properly, these mills can do an adequate job and shouldn't cause problems. Be sure to get one that adjusts on both ends of the rollers. The gap setting should be marked or indexed so you know what setting it's on, and if you change the gap for a specialty grain, you can change it back to normal without a lot of fiddling.

Corn grinders like Corona mills aren't really suitable for malt, as they tend to tear up the husks, but serve well as a secondary grinder for wheat and unmalted grains where the husk is not a concern. Antique grocery-store type coffee mills work really well for this task.

Most hand mills can be motorized, but check with the manufacturer. The simplest way is to just take off the crank handle and attach a variable speed electric drill and grind away. With a little ingenuity, a small surplus gear motor such as those that drive copy machines at 60 to 200 rpm can be hooked up with a shaft coupler. Check to make sure motor and mill direction are compatible before buying. Larger motors and belt/pulley drives are also an option, but be sure to get that speed down to under 200 rpm, or you may damage the grain.

Most purpose-built homebrew mills follow this basic pattern, and most are easy to motorize with an electric drill or gear motor. Here, a Barley Crusher model. Inset shows textured rollers.

MALT MILL

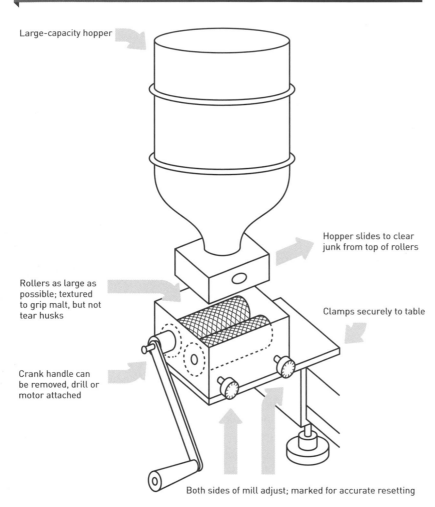

Large-capacity hopper

Hopper slides to clear junk from top of rollers

Rollers as large as possible; textured to grip malt, but not tear husks

Clamps securely to table

Crank handle can be removed, drill or motor attached

Both sides of mill adjust; marked for accurate resetting

Mills made with large rollers and adjustments on both sides are recommended to effectively crush the endosperm of the malt grains while keeping the husks intact.

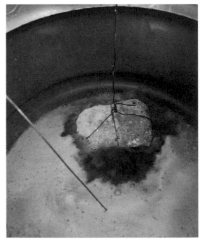

If you want to try brewing the *really* old-fashioned way, beer can be boiled using nothing but red-hot rocks and a lot of caution. Proper safety gear required!

SCALES/BALANCES

You can, of course, meter out your ingredients by eyeballing fractions of grain or hop packs as they come from the homebrew shop, but this is pretty crude, and makes it hard to hit specific targets of gravity, color, and bitterness. Far better to weigh things yourself. We're dealing with a couple of ranges here, from 0 to maybe 20 pounds/9 kg for grain and from 0 to about ½ pound/227 g for hops. For the latter, a small lab balance or postage scale can be used. I prefer the greater precision of grams to ounces. A larger package-weighing scale can be used for grain. These are pretty common at flea markets and everywhere else that old junk is sold.

With any scale, be sure it has a "tare" feature, so that the weight of a container can be deducted. For modern electronic scales, it usually is a matter of placing your empty container on the platform and pressing "zero," which will reset the scale and ignore the weight of the vessel. On older balance scales, a turn of a knob will zero out the weight.

BURNERS, FLAMES, and HEATERS

Heat plays a big part in brewing, and sometimes a lot of it is required. Standard 5-gallon/19-L batches can be made on kitchen stoves with burners in the 15,000 to 20,000 BTU range, but larger batches need commercial-size burners. For 10- or 15-gallon/38- to 57-L batches, homebrewers mostly use propane turkey fryer–type burners outdoors, usually in the 35,000 to 60,000 BTU range. Jet-style burners, either the noisy single jets or the multiple jet wok burners, are not that desirable for brewing because they are meant to be run at their max and when throttled back by more than half, start to produce orange flame, which means soot, and that's a sign of carbon monoxide, a deadly toxic gas. The banjo-style burners are generally best, and if you can find one with dual burner rings that can be adjusted separately, this is the best arrangement, because sometimes you want a low flame to simply maintain temperature—for sparge water, for example. Single-burner restaurant stoves sometimes have this arrangement, although they will most likely be set up for natural gas.

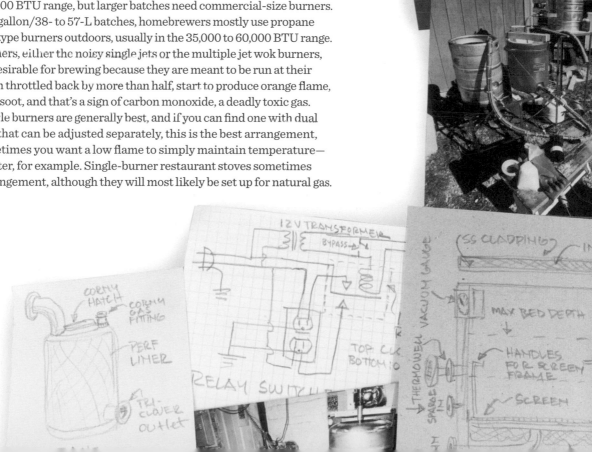

Homebrew burners typically run on propane, but some can be converted to natural gas with special parts. Here, a Banjo brand burner.

While propane is normally the fuel of choice for U.S. homebrewers, these large burners can often be set up to run just as well on natural gas. Usually, a different orifice is needed to account for the different pressure and energy density between the two fuels. Make sure any burner conversion is done professionally, with manufacturer-approved parts.

Another consideration is stability. A 10-gallon/38-L pot of wort weighs 100 pounds/45 kg or so, and if that thing tips over, there's going to be bad trouble. If it's hot wort, an accident may land you in the hospital. So, a nice, wide base and sturdy, level pot-support arms are a must. If your surface is not level, be sure to chock it up to level, and make sure nothing's wobbly. If you're building a burner stand or a tiered rig of some kind, it's a good idea to install leveling feet and maybe a cheap bubble level to make it easier to ensure a solid footing.

MASH/LAUTER TUNS

For a simple device, boy, are there a lot of choices out there! All are designed to contain the grist for the duration of the mash and facilitate draining the sweet wort and rinsing with hot water to recover the sugars left behind in the grain.

The most common mash/lauter tun is a plastic cooler of either the vertical beverage type or the rectangular all-purpose variety. It should be fitted with some sort of pickup system or manifold that allows the wort to drain while retaining the grain in the bed. Coolers are a good choice because they're insulated, inexpensive, and inert enough for our purposes. As a general rule, a mash tun the same size as the batch size will work for all but the strongest or most malt-heavy beers. However, if you're making a lot of big beers or doing no-sparge mashes, a tun that's double the batch size is a good idea.

Due to their simplicity, low cost, and good insulation, plastic coolers are among the most popular mash/lauter vessels. Vertical versions work equally well in most cases.

MASH TUN

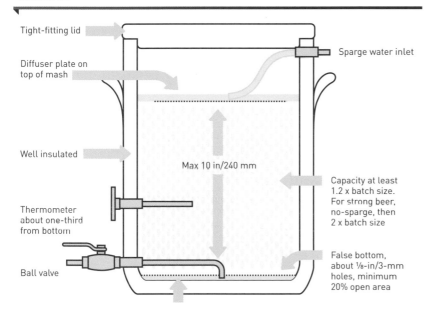

Tight-fitting lid

Diffuser plate on top of mash

Sparge water inlet

Well insulated

Max 10 in/240 mm

Capacity at least 1.2 x batch size. For strong beer, no-sparge, then 2 x batch size

Thermometer about one-third from bottom

Ball valve

False bottom, about ⅛-in/3-mm holes, minimum 20% open area

Minimal space below false bottom

An effective mash tun will have a false bottom, a diffuser plate, a ball valve, a thermometer, a tight-fitting lid, and a straining device that drains the grains from the wort.

It's easy enough to convert a standard cooler, but most homebrew suppliers sell modified cooler mash tuns ready to go. To make a good mash tun, a strainer device must be added to allow the wort to drain while holding the grain in place above it. In a round, vertical drinks cooler, this is often a traditional false-bottom configuration—a plastic or metal screen that covers most or all of the cooler bottom, with some provision for conveying the wort to the valve so the wort can drain. With an all-purpose rectangular cooler, a different approach is usually employed, such as a manifold of copper pipes with slots about every 1 inch/2.5 cm or less (typically oriented on the bottom half of the pipe) that lets the wort drain out. Another common approach is a tube made of stainless screen mesh or hose braid that accomplishes more or less the same thing. With these types of strainers it's important to get one that covers a fair amount of the area of the tun, as a single tube extending halfway or less into the cooler may well leave a good deal of extract behind in the areas it's not near, not an ideal situation.

PICNIC-COOLER MASH TUN (exploded view)

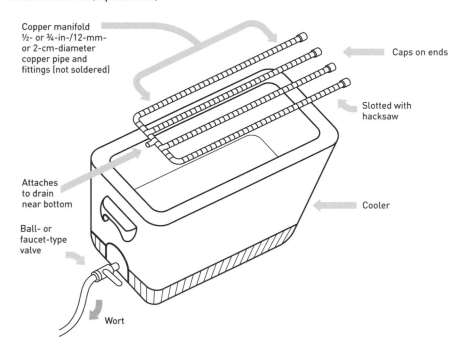

Copper manifold
½- or ¾-in-/12-mm-
or 2-cm-diameter
copper pipe and
fittings (not soldered)

Caps on ends

Slotted with
hacksaw

Attaches
to drain
near bottom

Cooler

Ball- or
faucet-type
valve

Wort

The picnic-cooler mash lauter is a simple and inexpensive mash tun that uses a slotted copper manifold to drain the wort.

The second modification is the valve. The little flip-up stoppers or push-button valves that come standard with coolers are obviously not good choices here. Generally, all that plastic stuff is removed and a metal ball valve is tightened in place using rubber gaskets to make it watertight.

Sometimes, mashing and lautering are carried out separately, in different, specialized vessels. Although it requires a separate piece of equipment, each can be designed to do its job without compromises inherent in a combined vessel. The advantage of a dedicated lauter is that the mash, when completed, can be transferred into it on a bed of water that covers the false bottom, and the mash bed will arrange itself so that sparging is pretty efficient. With a combo mash/lauter, the mash needs to be mixed up, and the act of stirring does a pretty good job of jamming the false-bottom holes with bits of malt husks, which can make for a sluggish runoff.

Without a false bottom that blocks heat transfer to the mash, a metal mash tun may be heated directly, but this requires gentle, even heat on the bottom of the vessel; naked stainless steel is not recommended. Pots with aluminum or copper slabs in the bottom are preferred, but as long as the bottom is flat, a slab of aluminum or other metal can be used as a flame tamer to diffuse the heat from the burner. Dedicated mash tuns can be manually stirred, but are much more convenient to operate with a mechanical stirring paddle, although this gets complicated pretty fast. Many people who want to heat their mashes use a HERMS- or RIMS-type system.

HERMS, RIMS, *and* DIRECT-HEATED SYSTEMS

These are the big dogs of the homebrewing world, and offer degrees of automation and control difficult to attain in other ways. HERMS and RIMS are both systems in which the wort is constantly circulating through a heater, and then returned to the mash where it creates a temperature rise. The difference is mainly in the heating apparatus. HERMS setups use the hot liquor tank as a source of heat. The wort flows through a coil submerged in the tank, and this transfers some heat to the wort. Usually a thermo-controller switches the pump on and off to maintain or raise the mash temperature, although this can be done manually. In a RIMS unit, a dedicated heater assembly heats the wort flowing through it. Electric elements are typically used, although it is possible to use some alternate method. The high temperatures of electric elements can caramelize the wort in ways that create the potential for oxidation, or in the worst-case scenario can burn the wort, depositing crusty charred bits on the element and imparting an ashy taste to the beer. In well-engineered commercial systems, this shouldn't be a problem. In general, HERMS units provide for gentler wort heating without scorching than RIMS.

DOUBLE BUCKET MASH/LAUTER

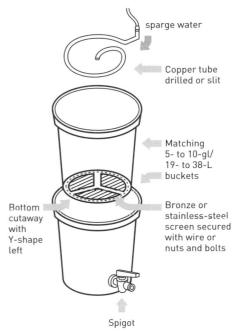

sparge water

Copper tube drilled or slit

Matching 5- to 10-gl/ 19- to 38-L buckets

Bottom cutaway with Y-shape left

Bronze or stainless-steel screen secured with wire or nuts and bolts

Spigot

= cut out

BOTTOM VIEW

It's super-cheap and low-tech, but a double-bucket mash tun can make fine beer as long as a little insulation is added. It completes the mashing and lautering processes in one vessel. These can be purchased readymade.

Another variation, charmingly called FART (fire actuated recirculating tun) by some of the Alabama rocket scientists using it, employs a direct-fired heater vessel through which the wort can flow. This can also be a bit problematic, but depends highly on the quality of the wort-heating vessel; using a copper or aluminum heat diffuser is in order here.

In theory, it is possible to do recirculation heating in a mash kettle with a false bottom atop a burner: The flame is turned on, the wort below the false bottom is withdrawn and pumped back to the top of the grain bed, raising the mash temperature. The big problem here is that unless the bottom of the pot has a nice thick layer of a heat-conductive material, there will be scorching. Chunks of malt inevitably make it through the false bottom, and it is quite impossible to get in there and stir things up with the whole mash on top of the false bottom.

In all these recirculating systems, the runoff begins almost immediately. This means that particular attention needs to be paid to the factors affecting runoff, especially getting a good quality of crush. If the mash doesn't run off freely, these systems can't operate as they should and then you have big trouble. It's also important to pay attention to pump speed: too high an outflow rate, especially early in the process, can draw the mash down into a thick brick that will discourage further runoff, and will need to be stirred up and resettled before continuing.

GRANT (WORT RECEIVER)

A grant is a small vessel to collect wort as it runs off from the lauter tun, holding it for transfer to the boil kettle. In a full gravity system, a grant is not needed, as the wort dumps directly into the kettle below. In a very manual system, a grant can be a simple plastic bucket just below the mash tun, and you can use a scoop or big ladle to transfer wort to the kettle. In larger and more elaborate systems, the grant has a valve near the bottom connected to a pump, which is controlled by a flat switch. When the wort level reaches a certain point, the pump kicks on and transfers it to the boil kettle. This obviously adds complications, but allows this process to go on more or less automatically, a trade-off I find worthwhile.

This nearly indestructible stainless-steel racking cane is a worthwhile upgrade from basic kit gear.

MOVING WORT

One of the important tasks in the brewery is racking, which is moving wort and beer from one stage to the next. A racking cane is a piece of rigid tubing long enough to reach the bottom of a carboy, with a crook at one end and usually a little plastic tip that fits on the other to help prevent too much yeast pickup when racking. The racking cane is typically ⅜ inch/10 mm in diameter and is used to transfer beer or wort from vessels that do not have a drain valve at the bottom. It's definitely worth paying to upgrade from plastic to stainless steel for the cane, as the plastic ones get soggy in hot wort.

HOSES

Hoses are necessary for obvious reasons. Attention should be paid to the material. Most are vinyl (Tygon is a popular brand), and it's important that it always be food grade, as vinyl hose sometimes contains toxic plasticizers—that "new car" smell. Braided reinforcement is not necessary for wort or beer transfer. Silicone tubing is also used sometimes, especially on the hot side of the brewery, as it is more heat-resistant than vinyl.

Hoses need to be attached to various pieces of equipment, and this requires some sort of fitting. NPT are the threaded pipe fittings standard in the United States, and they work well for permanent installations such as kettle valves and the like, but are not great for this kind of use. I like an industrial compression fitting called a Swagelok (trade name), a robust and widespread fitting with a tapered ring that when first installed tightens as a nut is turned around the tubing, then serves as a seal when reconnected. After the first installation, just finger tighten, then a little bump with a wrench is all that's needed. For 10- to 20-gallon/38- to 76-L systems, ⅜ or ½ inch/10 or 12 mm are appropriate. A friend of mine has a 5-gallon/19-L HERMS unit plumbed with ¼-inch/6-mm Swageloks—the most adorable little brew system you ever saw.

Top to bottom: General purpose food grade vinyl; heat-resistant silicone; and dual wall beverage tubing for CO_2 and beer under pressure.

PIPE *and* TUBING FITTINGS

Tri-clamp–type sanitary fittings are great because they have no nooks or crannies where bugs can hide, and some advanced homebreweries are fitted with them. Generally, it will be impractical to use them for your hose connections, but they are useful for attaching thermometer wells and valves to kettles and other vessels, allowing for easy removal for cleaning.

Quick-disconnect fittings lock into place with a mechanical device like a locking ring or tab. The fittings used on Corny kegs for draft beer are a common example. They come in a bewildering array of types and sizes. Some, like the keg fittings, seal off the flow of liquid when disconnected, but these are not the best type for the hot side of the brewery, as they have to be disassembled to be cleaned. The open-flow types are more useful. Plastic disconnects are cheap, but they're more fragile and not heat-resistant.

Don't forget about quick disconnects for your hot and cold water hose(s), used for cleaning and wort chilling. Brass disconnects for this purpose can be found in the garden section of the local hardware store.

Use the same type for *all* your connections on the system or expect to spend a lot of time searching for the right hose as the brew day moves from task to task.

USEFUL FITTINGS FOR THE HOME BREWERY

A Swagelok-type compression fitting is like the hardware store variety, but heavier and more reliable.

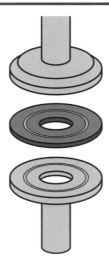

A sanitary (tri-clover) type, in which two flanges with a concentric groove mate with a rubber washer between and are held in place by an external clamp (not shown).

Brass garden-hose connectors are for hooking up your washdown hoses, chiller, bottle washer, etc.

PUMPS

Pumps are definitely a double-edged sword. When they work, they're great, but it seems there's always some issue: cavitation, priming, problems with hot liquids, things wearing out, and so on. To avoid problems, it's helpful to know what's out there and what to expect, so you can keep their little gremlins at bay. There are four pump types seen in home breweries.

CENTRIFUGAL PUMP

The most common homebrew pump is of the centrifugal type, which works by flinging wort from the inside of a set of spinning blades to the outside. They work great, but there are a couple of things you need to know. First, when they're dry, they create no suction, so they need to be pre-filled with liquid to start pumping, an action known as priming. When a pump is in-line, it can be difficult to get the priming water in there if the pump is full of air. Often a pump is plumbed so there is a three-way valve on the "out" side that can be opened so water can displace the air and flow into the pump housing, then closed to start pumping. Most pumps are not designed to run dry, and doing so for more than a few seconds can damage them severely.

Centrifugal pumps can suffer from something called cavitation. The faster the blades of the pump turn, the greater the chance they will create a vacuum, effectively "boiling" the liquid and introducing vapor into the pump, which makes it not pump very well. At room temperatures and pressures, this isn't a problem; but as water heats, the amount of vacuum needed to boil it becomes less. As a result, centrifugal pumps have a temperature maximum, so make sure your pump can work with hot wort. The materials the pump is made of will also affect the working temperature range, so check the manufacturer's specifications.

Look for a pump that is magnetically coupled. The advantages to this are the shaft can't fail and leak liquid into the motor, a potential hazard; and when the pumping resistance becomes too great, the pump automatically decouples from the motor, to avoid burning it out.

GEAR PUMP

This pump uses small spinning gears that mesh closely and pump water through them as they do. These are generally "positive displacement" pumps that do create some suction and so do not require priming. Micropump is a common brand and, while hideously expensive when new, aren't prohibitively rare in the surplus market.

CENTRIFUGAL PUMP

Inlet

Outlet

The most common type in all breweries.

GEAR PUMP

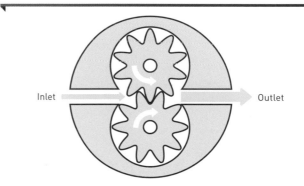

Inlet

Outlet

Typically made by Micropump.

ROTARY-VANE PUMP

This pump uses an eccentric drum with spring-loaded vanes that slide in and out as the drum rotates in its housing, drawing the liquid in, pushing it around, then expelling it before beginning the next revolution. Procon is a common brand (used as a pump in soda carbonators). Generally, these are pretty powerful pumps, as they're coupled to a ¼-horsepower or larger motor. These are great for cleaning units to spray hot cleaning solution. They are not positive displacement, so they need to be plumbed for easy priming.

PERISTALTIC PUMP

In this pump, rollers squeeze a specially engineered tube, forcing liquid through without it touching any parts of the pump. For that reason, they are common in medical devices like heart-lung machines, and also make great beer-transfer pumps. Cole Parmer's Masterflex pumps are widespread and available in sizes appropriate for homebrewing, but double-check the flow rates, because some of them are designed for very small volumes.

ROTARY VANE PUMP

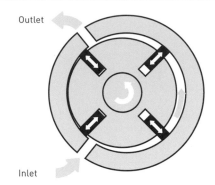

Outlet

Inlet

Procon is the common manufacturer.

PERISTALTIC PUMP

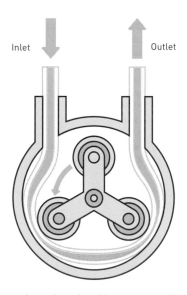

Inlet   Outlet

Squeezes wort through a tube with no contact with the pump mechanism.

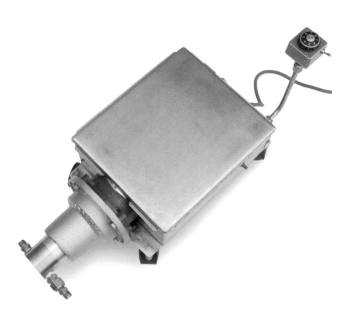

A ⅓ hp variable-speed DC-driven positive displacement Micropump.

BREW KETTLES

This vessel is where the wort will be boiled with the hops. Stainless steel is generally the best choice, but it has its drawbacks. Although corrosion-resistant, stainless is a very poor heat conductor. With a flame as a heat source, heat goes through the metal with no problem, but it doesn't spread across the metal, meaning the heat tends to stay concentrated right at the flames; the result is temperatures that actually cause steam pockets, impeding the transfer of heat, overheating the wort, and creating the potential for oxidation further downstream. Beerstone deposits that match the shape of the burner are a telltale sign and an indication of too-high boundary temperatures. A brew kettle is much better with a layer of aluminum or other good heat conductor either built into the bottom, or placed between the kettle and the flame, like a giant flame-tamer. A 1/8-inch-/3-mm-thick piece of copper, aluminum, or even steel will improve this considerably, although the flame-tamer approach is obviously suited only for flat-bottomed pots.

A stainless-steel brewpot with a heavy heat-conducting bottom is the heart of most homebrewers' systems. It should be at least 25 percent larger than the batch size, and a little bigger is better.

IDEAL FEATURES FOR BREW KETTLES

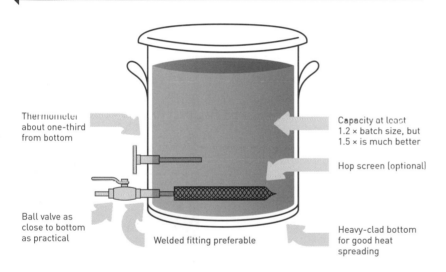

Thermometer about one-third from bottom

Capacity at least 1.2 × batch size, but 1.5 × is much better

Hop screen (optional)

Ball valve as close to bottom as practical

Welded fitting preferable

Heavy-clad bottom for good heat spreading

An ideal brew kettle will feature a drain valve near the bottom, a thermometer, a lid, and a heavy-clad bottom.

A drain valve near the bottom of the kettle is just about mandatory, especially in larger pots. Ball valves are best because they can be opened and closed quickly. "No-weld" fittings are available, but obviously with a weld there is far less likelihood of leaks. Thermometers aren't really needed for a boil kettle, but if you, like most of us, also use your kettle for a hot-liquor tank, then it's really helpful. Generally, the thermometer coupling is best placed about one-third of the way up the side, on the front.

A lid is helpful on a liquor tank, but should not be used when boiling wort, as this will let the escaping DMS and other undesirable compounds condense on the lid and drip back into the wort, defeating the purpose of the boil.

Some provision may be added to help remove hops. A tubular screen can be attached to the inside of the valve fitting, which will serve as a hop strainer. The alternative, often used in larger systems that incorporate a pump, is to create a whirlpool. By spinning the wort, centrifugal force piles the hops and other solids in a heap on the bottom. Typically, this is achieved with a piece of bent tubing hung over the edge of the kettle or attached to the immersion wort chiller to direct the wort along the wall of the kettle, setting the wort spinning in motion. Often a small barrier is tack-welded to the bottom, in front of the valve, to prevent hops from sliding off the pile and into the drain.

In theory, a whirlpool can be created by gently rotating a spoon in the wort, but be aware that in a small kettle, it is unlikely to create a neat pile, and there are more effective ways of separating the hops and other solids from the wort.

BREW KETTLE FITTED FOR A WHIRLPOOL

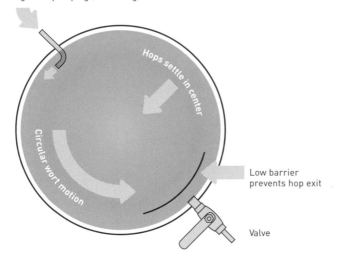

Tangential pumping (or stirring)

Hops settle in center

Circular wort motion

Low barrier prevents hop exit

Valve

In this top view of a kettle whirlpool, a circular flow is set up by either tangential pumping or gentle stirring, and as the liquid circles, the hops' inertia causes them to settle in the center. This may be done as wort is chilling with an immersion chiller. A short metal barrier welded near the valve helps prevent hops from sliding out the valve.

HOP BACK

Built to deal with large amounts of aroma hops, the hop back is a luxury item in a small brewery. It is essentially a simple filter that attaches to the out-flow valve on the brew kettle, and usually comprises a small vessel, maybe one-tenth of the batch size, that can be sealed up watertight, with in and out connections for wort and some screen material inside that either holds the kettle hops back, preventing them from entering the fermenter, or can be charged with hops through which the wort will flow. There are commercial versions available, but I have also seen them made from small pressure cookers or flip-seal type stainless canisters. A piece of stainless-steel screen is all that's needed. To make the conversion, see the image that follows.

HOMEBREW HOP BACK

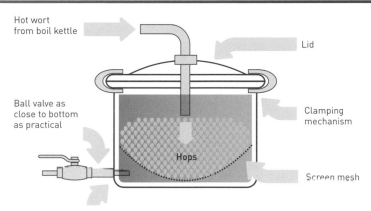

Hot wort from boil kettle

Lid

Ball valve as close to bottom as practical

Clamping mechanism

Hops

Screen mesh

Welded fittings preferable

This is a simple design for an external hop back, a filter that can either be used to filter out the hops from your brew or can be charged with fresh hops and have hot wort run through them. A circle of fine-mesh screen a bit larger than the vessel diameter is bent into a dish that keeps the hops from the drain valve. Versions can be made from small stainless-steel pressure cookers, canisters, or other sealable vessels.

My home-built 15-gallon (57-L) homebrew system. Mash kettle with motorized stirring paddle and copper bottom (opposite, top), lauter tun with vacuum gauge to check vacuum pressure under the false bottom to avoid a compacted mash (opposite, bottom), boiling kettle with copper bottom on custom stove (right, top), hop back, lined with fine perf screen, with corny keg hatch for access/cleanout (right, bottom).

WORT CHILLER

A wort chiller is designed to rapidly cool the wort so yeast can be pitched (added to start fermentation). There are two configurations available for homebrewers: immersion and counterflow. An immersion chiller is nothing more than a length of copper tubing formed into a spiral or a coil, with hose fittings on either end. As the name suggests, it is simply immersed in the hot wort while cold tap water is flowed through, cooling the wort over a period of some minutes (depending on variables like tube geometry and cold water temperature). Gently stirring or whirlpooling the wort speeds up the cooling. In locations with tepid tap water, a second chiller may be inserted into an ice bath to pre-chill the water before it can effectively cool the beer.

IMMERSION CHILLER IN USE

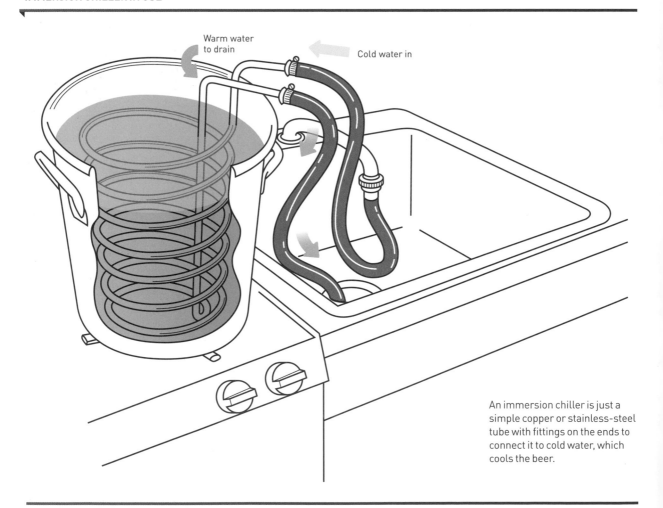

Warm water to drain

Cold water in

An immersion chiller is just a simple copper or stainless-steel tube with fittings on the ends to connect it to cold water, which cools the beer.

Counterflow chillers add a jacket around the tube, and wort flows through the inner tubing, while cold water flows the opposite direction through the jacket, hence the name. They chill the wort more quickly, but may end up taking about the same amount of time as an immersion chiller by the time all the wort goes through. As you can imagine, they can be a little difficult to clean and sanitize, a task made easier by incorporating a pump into the system. "Brick," or brazed plate, chillers are available that flow the wort and water through interleaved small plates. These offer a bit better efficiency, but must be scrupulously cleaned to avoid building up crud and bits of hops inside.

Brazed plate brick-style heat exchangers are made from super-thin stainless-steel and offer very high efficiency, but can be fussy to clean.

COUNTERFLOW CHILLER IN USE

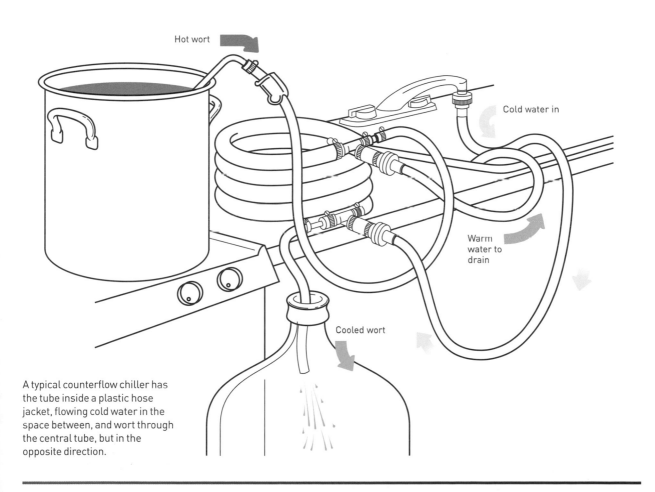

Hot wort

Cold water in

Warm water to drain

Cooled wort

A typical counterflow chiller has the tube inside a plastic hose jacket, flowing cold water in the space between, and wort through the central tube, but in the opposite direction.

WORT AERATION

Yeast needs oxygen in order to make lipids, which are needed to make more yeast. Because more yeast equals better beer in most cases, it makes sense to help the yeast out. Traditional techniques for doing this include splashing with a sanitized spoon, shaking the carboy, or using a simple piece of tubing cut and drilled with small holes to aerate the liquid that flows through it (like a venturi) on the way to the fermenter. Success can be evaluated by how much dense foam is created after the aeration efforts. An ideal oxygen level in wort is about 8 ppm for normal-strength ales and somewhat higher, about 12 ppm, for lagers and strong ales. For wheat beers, lower rates may be desirable. These oxygen rates are difficult to reach with these simple methods; but the good news is that yeast is a lot happier at 2 to 3 ppm than it is at 0, so anything you do will be better than nothing.

VENTURI-STYLE WORT AERATOR

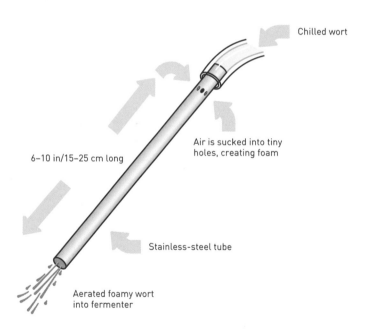

Chilled wort

Air is sucked into tiny holes, creating foam

6–10 in/15–25 cm long

Stainless-steel tube

Aerated foamy wort into fermenter

A venturi-style wort aerator supplies air to the chilled wort as it travels to the fermenter, providing the yeast with oxygen.

While this carboy (and keg) washer is a bit more elaborate than most, plans are out there for easier-to-build devices that function just as well.

A more effective method is to use an aeration "stone," a small tubular device usually made of finely sintered beads of stainless steel, essentially a more high-tech version of an aquarium stone. Gas shoots through the spaces between the sintered beads, releasing super-fine bubbles. The finer the bubbles, the more surface area there is for any given volume of gas, and therefore the more gas gets dissolved in the wort. This stone can be hooked up to an aquarium air pump fitted with a 0.2-micron filter, small enough to block all wild yeast and bacteria. Inserted into the wort and allowed to bubble for 15 to 30 minutes, it will get a fair amount of oxygen dissolved, but because air is only about 21 percent oxygen, the limit is about 7 to 8 ppm.

Pure oxygen does better. White Labs found that a good, 0.5-micron air stone, at a flow rate of 1 liter per minute of pure oxygen for 30 seconds, gets the wort to about 5 ppm; a full minute reaches 9 ppm, and 2 minutes gets to 14 ppm. Be aware that it is possible to over-oxygenate, so don't exceed 8 to 9 ppm unless you have good reason to do so. Small disposable tanks meant for hobbyist oxy-gas welding torches can be found from homebrew suppliers or hardware stores, and usually have enough gas for half a dozen batches. Larger tanks can be obtained from welding supply stores. Welding and medical oxygen are identical, but for some reason it is illegal to refill medical tanks without a prescription, so get a small welding tank and a regulator or adaptor that fits it.

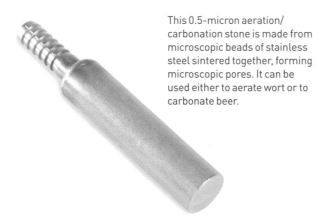

This 0.5-micron aeration/carbonation stone is made from microscopic beads of stainless steel sintered together, forming microscopic pores. It can be used either to aerate wort or to carbonate beer.

FERMENTERS

At the high-tech end of the fermenting-gear spectrum are mini versions of the cylindro-conical tanks that large breweries use. Yeast collects in the cone from where it can be dumped, leaving the beer clear and ready to condition. Because they are typically made of stainless and fabricated with good sanitary techniques, they tend to be quite expensive and beyond the reach of most homebrewers.

At the other end are the plastic buckets that often come with inexpensive starter kits. These are fine for a few quick batches, but plastic has some disadvantages. It is soft and quickly gets covered in small scratches that harbor bacteria beyond the reach of cleaners and sanitizers; and the second, less obvious, issue is that many plastics are quite transparent to oxygen. If the beer remains in the bucket for more than a couple of weeks, oxidation can intensify and aerobic bacteria like acetobacteria can take hold.

By far the most popular choice for homebrew fermentations are glass carboys. They are cheap, available, easy to clean, and have the definite advantage of allowing you to see what's going on during fermentation. Although the more common size is 5 gallons/19 L, 6.5-gallon/25-L versions are readily available, and these are big enough to hold a 5-gallon/19-L batch and still have some room for the kräusen (foamy head), although they may overflow if the fermentation is really vigorous.

The biggest problem with glass carboys is their fragility; when they break, razor-sharp shards of glass can cause serious accidents. Always exercise extreme care when moving them around, and wear closed-top shoes. Many people keep their carboys in milk-crate type containers, which offer some handholds, a little cushion on the bottom, and some protection from a break. Another problem with a glass carboy is a clogged stopper hole, typically from a piece of fruit or other solid, that blocks the CO_2 escape and causes the carboy to burst.

There is a new generation of carboys made from PET plastic that have an oxygen barrier and a super-smooth interior, plus handy features like drain spouts and custom-fit fermentation locks and blow-offs. BetterBottle is one such product line.

High-tech PET plastic bottles have some advantages over glass. Glass carboys can be dangerous and have caused severe injuries.

The fermenting beer will release a lot of gas. It is standard laboratory procedure to cover a starter or fermenter with a piece of sanitized aluminum foil, and this will do the job, the yeast experts tell me. The standard procedure in the hobby is either a rubber stopper or a plastic cap, either of which will be fitted with a hole to accommodate a fermentation lock, a small plastic or glass device that uses a liquid (I like to fill mine with vodka) as a barrier to keep dust and microbes from entering, but allows the exit of the CO_2 gas. Replace the stoppers and caps periodically, as the materials break down and can become difficult to clean and sanitize.

Another method is to use a blow-off, typically a large-diameter tube jammed into the neck of the carboy, with the exit end submerged in some bleach water in a small bucket. It is also possible to make a closed blow-off, in which the secondary container has a lid and a lock, to keep anything from contaminating it.

OPEN AND CLOSED BLOW-OFF SYSTEMS

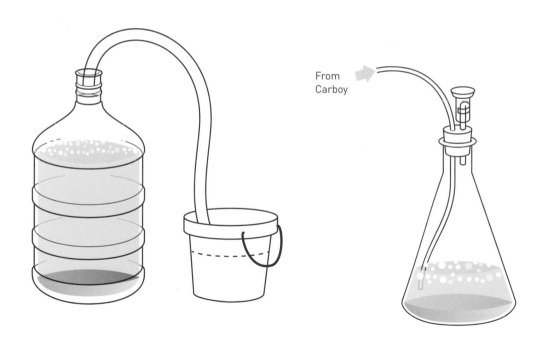

From Carboy

A blow-off system allows the exit of CO_2 gas while preventing foreign matter from contaminating the contents of the fermenter.

MEASUREMENTS *and* INSTRUMENTATION

Brewers made quite delicious beer for millennia before the advent of devices to measure the physical and chemical aspects of brewing. Instrumentation for homebrewing doesn't have to be complicated, but a few simple devices will take the guesswork out of the process and allow you more control, which means better beer in the end.

HYDROMETER

Measures original gravity of wort and beer. Most homebrewing versions cover a wide range and are marked with both OG and Plato scales. Most also include a potential-alcohol scale, which allows you to calculate the amount of alcohol in a finished beer.

REFRACTOMETER

Using the differences between the refractive index of sugar and water, this device measures the original gravity of the wort. Usually marked in the Plato or Brix (same thing, more or less) scales, a refractometer cannot be used to measure the finished gravity, because alcohol has a high refractive index, and thus distorts the readings. These are convenient and easy to use, but their high price tag does not make them truly necessary—nice toy, though.

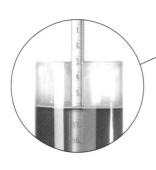

The reading is taken at the intersection of the tube and the meniscus, or curved part of the water, where it joins the glass.

A brewing hydrometer is commonly a weighted glass tube with one or more scales at the top. Hydrometers are calibrated for one specific temperature. This model has a built-in thermometer and correction scales.

HYDROMETER CORRECTION

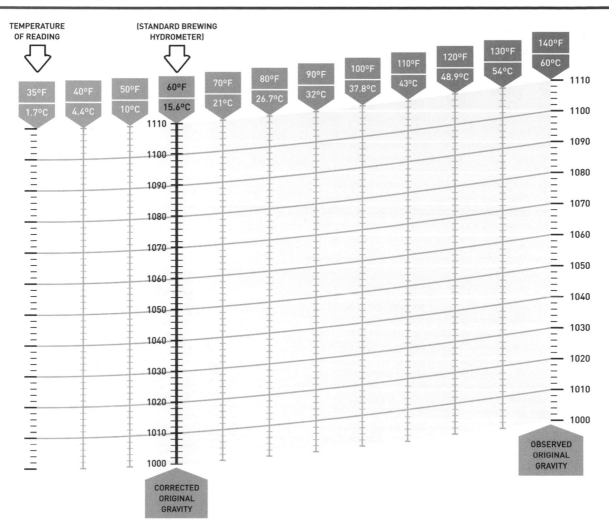

TEMPERATURE OF READING

(STANDARD BREWING HYDROMETER)

| 35°F | 40°F | 50°F | 60°F | 70°F | 80°F | 90°F | 100°F | 110°F | 120°F | 130°F | 140°F |
| 1.7°C | 4.4°C | 10°C | 15.6°C | 21°C | 26.7°C | 32°C | 37.8°C | 43°C | 48.9°C | 54°C | 60°C |

CORRECTED ORIGINAL GRAVITY

OBSERVED ORIGINAL GRAVITY

This chart is designed to compensate for the fact that the density of liquids changes with temperature, causing errors in readings taken at temperatures other than those for which the instrument is calibrated. At elevated temperatures the liquid expands, lowering its density and causing low readings. At low temperatures, the liquid becomes denser and shows readings that are erroneously high.

HOW TO USE THIS CHART

If you're taking a gravity reading at any temperature other than the calibrated temperature written on your hydrometer (usually 60°F/15.6°C), you'll need this chart. Take the gravity and jot it down. Next, take the temperature of the wort or beer tested. Find the vertical line on the chart closest to the temperature recorded.

Reading on the right-hand side of the chart, find the gravity you observed. Following the curved line, trace across to where your vertical (temperature) line is. Then, trace across horizontally (ignore the curves now) to the scale with the dark line at 60°F/15.6°C. The white lines serve as a guide. The number on the left-hand scale is your actual gravity, corrected for temperature errors.

This chart is for hydrometers calibrated at 60°F/15.6°C, the most common type. With others, you must make some changes. Write in the new calibration temperature under the heavy vertical line at 60°F/15.6°C. Then, renumber the other vertical lines to be 10°F apart, starting with your calibration temperature. If your hydrometer's stated temperature is 68°F, the heavy vertical line becomes 68°F. The line immediately to its right becomes 78°F, the next 88°F, and so on. To the left, subtract 10°F: 58°F, 48°F, etc.

pH METER

This is an electronic device that measures the concentration of hydrogen ions in a solution, which is a measure of its acidity or alkalinity. It is used in brewing to check water and mash pH levels. Typically a brewer will use one for a few brews, get a handle on what works and what doesn't, and retire the pH meter after that. This makes them a good candidate for a shared or club purchase. If you pay attention to water chemistry, and make sure that you have the correct mix of minerals appropriate for a given beer (see Water without Tears, page 96), there really isn't much point in measuring pH. For those people who want to control every little thing, a pH meter can add one more level of comfort in the brewing process. Units that measure to 0.1 pH are sufficient for brewing purposes. Be aware that all pH meters require frequent calibration, the sensing elements have a limited lifespan, and they must be stored in very particular ways to maintain their usefulness.

Not an absolute necessity, but a pH meter can give you insight into the unseen workings of your mash.

THERMOMETER

This device is optional for extract beer, but absolutely crucial for mashing, because the chemistry acts in different ways at specific temperatures. There are tons of choices, from pretty basic to very high-end. You want something that is accurate to within 1°F/0.5°C. Bimetallic dial types are pretty reliable, and are typically inserted into kettle and mash tun fittings to give an instant readout. Glass thermometers can be highly accurate, but they're a pain to use and, of course, they're highly fragile; mercury-filled ones can be hazardous, so are generally not recommended.

There are several types of electronic thermometers. The least expensive type uses a thermistor, which changes resistance at different temperatures. Because these are semiconductors, they are most accurate and stable below the boiling point, but repeated heating will cause them to degrade over time, so check them every so often. Thermocouple thermometers use a junction of two dissimilar metals that generate a very small voltage that can be amplified and sent to a digital display. They are highly stable and accurate, great for brewing. Thermocouples come in several flavors, designated with letters; types K and J are the most common. Meters generally accept only one type. Versions with two or three feet of cable from the probe to the meter are most useful. Platinum RTD thermometers use microthin platinum wire that changes resistance with temperature. They are super-stable and superbly accurate, but because they're made from platinum, they are expensive—overkill for most brewing purposes.

A typical handheld thermocouple thermometer with a detachable probe.

A foldable Thermapen thermocouple thermometer that does great double duty as an accurate culinary thermometer.

PACKAGING BEER

Once the beer is fully fermented, it needs to be transferred to its serving vessel. For beginning brewers, this means bottles. They're cheap, portable, and do not require a lot of equipment to do well. Bottles also allow you to build up an inventory of different beers and allow you to age strong brews for extended periods of time.

Draft systems are easy to put together, but their cost usually puts them into the advanced category. Because of their ease of use, most of those who use them feel they are well worth the extra expense.

BOTTLING GEAR

The equipment for this is pretty simple stuff. A racking cane, some food-grade transfer hose, a bottling wand, a capper, and a food-grade bucket with a valve near the bottom are all that's needed for basic bottling. Just prior to bottling, a measured amount of priming sugar is added, restarting fermentation and carbonating the beer inside the bottles. The priming sugar is dissolved in a small amount of water heated in a small saucepan.

Let's not forget the bottles themselves. You can use any size beer bottle you like, but it is best not to use twist-off caps, as they don't seal as securely with home cappers. You can buy new bottles at the homebrew shop, but there's no reason that discarded commercial beer bottles can't be used as long as they're cleaned well. For decency's sake, scrape off the old labels. Some TSP (trisodium phosphate) in very hot water may be helpful in soaking paper labels off. Larger formats like 750-ml champagne bottles or swingtop bottles make a nice presentation for parties or gifts.

When the bottles are filled, a capper is used to crimp the star-shaped flares around the cap edge, making the seal. There are lever-type as well as bench-type affairs. In general the lever types are more fussy about the bottle geometry, and need a particular type of bulge a certain distance below the bottle rim to grip onto and squeeze against when seating the cap. They're fine for standard longnecks, but may be problematic with oddball bottles. Bench cappers generally put their leverage against the whole height of the bottle, so they don't care at all what kind of ridges are on the bottle. Make sure you get one that's easily adjustable and tall enough to do champagne bottles. There are plenty of beautiful old cast-iron ones at flea markets just aching to help make beer again; so give one of these noble old beasts a new home and maybe a fresh coat of paint if you can.

There are two sizes of cap. The standard beer bottle cap is 26 mm. European champagne-style caps are larger at 29 mm. They take a different capper, but some models can swap out crowning dies to fit either size.

Whether prim and proper or edge-of-madness avant-garde, like this self-portrait by artist and filmmaker Jonathan Levin, homebrew makes a bigger impression when labeled.

A common lever-type capper is great for standard beer bottles but may be a struggle with other types.

Antique precursors of this modern bench-style capper are easy to find at flea markets.

CO$_2$ tanks contain hundreds of pounds of pressure and must be handled with respect. In the United States, tanks must be pressure tested and recertified every five years.

KEG *and* DRAFT SYSTEMS

Sooner or later (usually sooner!), people get tired of the tedium of bottling and move to a keg system. It's a lot easier to clean and fill one big container than fifty or so small ones.

HOMEBREW CORNY-KEG DRAFT SETUP WITH CO₂ TANK AND REGULATOR

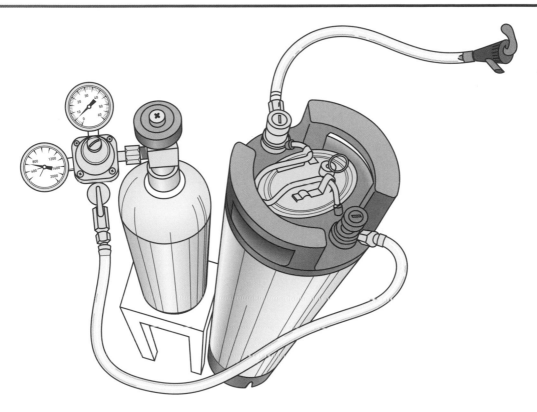

Simple, sturdy, and easy to clean, "Corny" tanks are perfect for storing homebrews and relatively easy to find in used or reconditioned states.

Pioneered by Dogfish Head Craft Ales, these filter setups known as "Randalls" infuse the beer with whatever you load into the cartridges.

Draft homebrew owes its existence to the soda business—specifically a type of 5-gallon/19-L keg called a "Corny" tank, after one of its manufacturers, Cornelius. These held pre-mixed soft drinks, but the industry has moved to a different system, resulting in the availability of mountains of used Corny tanks over the past twenty years. They're perfect for our purposes: simple, sturdy, pressure-rated at 130 psi/8.89 bar, with gas and liquid quick disconnects and an arm-wide hatch that allows access and easy cleaning. And though the supply is starting to dry up, they're still pretty cheap, at least in the United States.

Cornys come with two different styles of quick disconnect: pin-lock, favored by Coca-Cola bottlers, and ball-lock, used by Pepsi and everyone else. They are not interchangeable. The pin-lock kegs are a little wider and a bit shorter; parts are available to convert them to ball-lock. It's best to standardize on one system or the other, because it's a mess having two different systems.

To use these kegs, you will need a CO_2 system consisting of a tank and a regulator, plus the appropriate hoses and keg fittings. A regulator attaches to the gas cylinder and drops the pressure from 800 psi/55.16 bar or so down to normal draft serving pressure, 10 to 12 psi/0.69 to 0.83 bar. A screw in the center of the regulator adjusts the pressure, which is displayed on a pressure gauge. A second gauge indicates the gas cylinder pressure. Most regulators have a shutoff valve for the low-pressure gas, and some have Y splitters or manifolds that allow one regulator to serve several kegs. Low-pressure dropping regulators can be inserted in between that allow the pressure of each beer to be adjusted separately.

The valves on the gas cylinders themselves are designed to seal when open as well as closed, so when you open them, do so fully and tighten them upward, which will help prevent leaks around the stem. Please note that all gas cylinders are potentially quite dangerous and require special handling. Be sure to read and follow the cautions at the beginning of this chapter.

Used Corny tanks are absolutely fine as long as they're not damaged or leaking. Strongly flavored soda like root beer permanently taints the rubber gaskets, so it's a good idea to replace them all. The spring-loaded poppets in the quick disconnects and pressure relief valves may fail and can also pick up flavors, so should be replaced as well. Many homebrew suppliers sell reconditioned Cornys that have had these small parts replaced.

This tap handle shows you never know what you might be able to make out of stuff from the junk drawer.

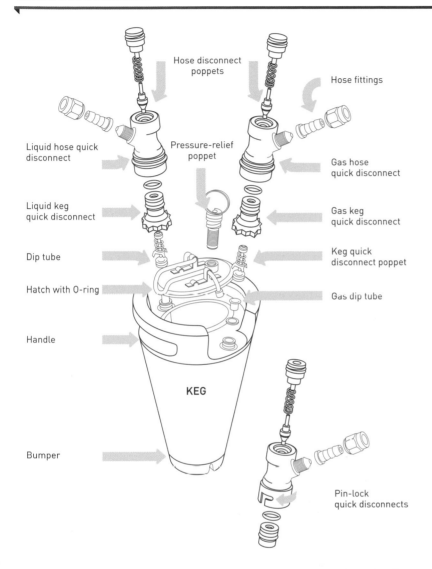

Hose disconnect poppets

Hose fittings

Liquid hose quick disconnect

Pressure-relief poppet

Gas hose quick disconnect

Liquid keg quick disconnect

Gas keg quick disconnect

Dip tube

Keg quick disconnect poppet

Hatch with O-ring

Gas dip tube

Handle

KEG

Bumper

Pin-lock quick disconnects

A Corny keg is made of numerous components, including a tank pressured at 130 psi/ 8.89 bar, a hatch, quick disconnects, poppets, dip tubes, bumpers, and handles.

CORNY KEG FEATURES

TANK
Pressure-rated to 130 psi/8.89 bar, and sanitary in construction, made of 304 stainless steel.

HATCH
Large enough to fit a medium-size hand for scrubbing and inspection. Lever handle clips the lid in place, but the large O-ring seals well only when gas pressure is applied. Usually with pressure-relief valve with manual release.

QUICK DISCONNECTS
Ball-lock fittings work by lifting a retaining ring and pushing on or pulling off; pin-lock has a locking ring that must be twisted. Gas and liquid fittings have *slightly* different threads and disconnect geometry. Gas fittings have a cut or a star-shaped grip for the wrench, but if you're not paying attention, it's easy to mix them up. If it feels either too tight or too loose, it's probably the wrong fitting.

POPPETS
There are three: one in each quick disconnect that stops the flow when the hose fitting is removed and a third that serves as a pressure-relief valve.

DIP TUBES
The liquid fitting has a dip tube that goes all the way to the bottom, sometimes into an indentation. The gas dip tube is short. They're interchangeable, so be sure to remember to put them in their proper holes. Each has an O-ring that helps it seal against the shoulder of the hole in the keg.

Hoses for gas are typically ¼ inch/6 mm I.D. (inside diameter), and should be braided food-grade vinyl or polyethylene. Do not use silicone hose, as it is porous to CO_2 and will let your gas leak out. Plastic or metal quick disconnects are available, and should be attached to the hoses using hose clamps to prevent leakage.

Note that the gas and liquid disconnects are slightly different—the gas fitting is usually either star-shaped or has a groove cut into its hex faces. If a fitting doesn't want to tighten easily, double-check which type you have, because forcing it can cause problems like stripped threads. Same with the hose fittings: don't force them onto the Corny quick disconnect or they may get stuck and become damaged.

On the serving end, either a conventional metal beer tap is used or, more typically, a small plastic "cobra" tap that dispenses beer when a lever is pressed. The most important draft system concept is system balancing. This means that the pressure applied to the beer in the keg must match the resistance created by the tubing and valves of the dispense system. Unbalanced, the beer comes out foamy, and by the time it settles, has lost a lot of its sparkle. Use ³⁄₁₆-inch/5-mm I.D. tubing for draft beer lines, as the small diameter offers a lot more resistance than larger tubing; plan on somewhere between 5 to 8 feet/1.5 to 2.5 m of tubing for adequate balancing. There is more information on system balancing on page 230 (Serving Draft Beer).

Once you start kegging beers, it becomes obvious that storing them in the family fridge is a threat to domestic harmony, so most of us invest in a garage refrigerator or keg cooler of some type. Chest freezers are popular because they're cheap and sized to hold Corny tanks pretty well. They can be fitted with a setback thermostat to drop the temperature to an appropriate range for serving beer.

A rack of casks (set up for a tasting event) with cooling coils, insulating jackets, and hand pumps. Note the ones on the top are being served by gravity, as is typical for festivals. Photo by Edward Bronson.

FIRKINS, PUMPS, *and* REAL ALE

Real ale is an English tradition of top-fermented beer that is unfiltered, unpasteurized, and carbonated in its serving vessel, whether it's a bottle or a cask. While real ale can be carbonated and served in a Corny keg, the traditional vessel is a barrel-shaped cask. The standard commercial size is a firkin, which holds 10.8 gallons/41 L, but for homebrewers, a smaller cask called a *pin*, at 5.4 gallons/20.5 L, is a much better size. To use a cask, some wooden or plastic bits are needed: a shive to fit the hole on top of the cask; hard and soft spiles to place into the hole in the shive; a keystone, which is a bung with a knockout plug in the center into which the tap is pounded for serving. An outsized wooden mallet is a comical but necessary accessory.

A beer engine, which is designed for pumping beer from a cellar up to the pub level and into the glass, is among the coolest pieces of brewing hardware on the planet; but it is almost useless to the average homebrewer, except as decoration. So unless you're a show-offy anglo-aleo-phile (I know you're out there), stop lusting for one and use the less glamorous plastic gravity tap. When broached, a cask left to its own devices will last in decent condition for only a couple of days. There are devices called cask breathers that apply a bit of blanket CO_2 pressure to prevent the entry of air. These are not particularly traditional, but will keep the beer drinking well for many days, if not weeks.

A REAL ALE CASK AND ITS PARTS

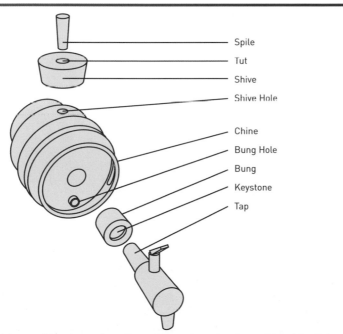

Spile
Tut
Shive
Shive Hole
Chine
Bung Hole
Bung
Keystone
Tap

A real ale cask is a traditional vessel used in making and serving the traditional English top-fermented beer.

CHAPTER

6

YEAST

and

Fermentation

→→ So amazing is the transformation of sugary wort by yeast into a delicious and lightly intoxicating product that medieval brewers could only marvel and call it "Godisgood."

Today, with our knowledge of biochemistry that reveals the inner workings of the yeast cell, it is no less amazing. However complicated the following explanation may seem, it is still a grotesque oversimplification of yeast's true complexity.

Brewer's yeast, *Saccharomyces cerevesiae*, is a single-celled fungus. It is one member of a large family of yeasts, a few of which are useful in brewing, many of which can be problematic. Its natural habitat is any niche that holds the promise of a meal of sugar, so it especially likes fruit. That waxy sheen on grapes and other fruit is actually brewer's yeast.

YEAST in BREWING

Like many domesticated plants and animals, yeast has found it convenient to hitch a ride with human beings, who care for it and feed it the sugar and other nutrients it loves. Brewing, baking, winemaking, distillation, and even fuel ethanol all depend on yeast. The diversity of strains attests to its great age and versatility. It is believed that the ale yeasts we brew with today are direct descendants of yeast first brought into the domestic sphere about ten thousand years ago. Brew by brew, jugs of slurry have been handed off from brewer to brewer, treasured like the ember of a fire too precious to be allowed to go cold.

Sometime around 1500, a new hybrid yeast appeared that was happy in much colder conditions than ale yeast. This yeast, *Saccharomyces pastorianus*, developed along with a new type of cold-fermented beer, lager. It is now known that this yeast came from hybridization of an ale yeast with a cold-tolerant yeast called *Saccharomyces eubayanus*, which was recently found living in Patagonia. How this happened is a bit of a mystery, as the timing of lager and New World voyages don't quite match.

Lager yeast stayed in Bavaria until the mid-nineteenth century, when the lager explosion took the world by storm. Viewed as a more modern type of beer, lager was subject to an enormous amount of research to improve its production. Lager yeast was purified, reduced to a single-cell culture by Emil Christian Hansen at Carlsberg in Denmark, who also isolated the Tuborg strain a little later. Today's lager yeasts descend from these original purified strains, and as a result, there is very little genetic variation among lager strains. While there are some differences, they tend to be minor, perhaps more related to behavior in the brewery than any obvious effect on beer flavor.

Ale yeast remains vastly more complex. Some strains, like those used for altbier and Kölsch, are neutral and clean, and will tolerate some cold conditioning. Strains from Britain show a wide range of personality: spicy, fruity, woody, malty, and more. You will probably not be surprised to learn that it is Belgium that has the greatest variety of yeast. The beer there was never nationalized; separate languages and other regional differences have preserved many different beer styles, although much has been lost as well. Even in Belgium, one reads accounts from the early twentieth century that the beers were more complex before they went to single-cell cultures.

Belgian yeast strains are so distinctive that they will turn any kind of wort into a Belgian beer. Their flavors range from fruity and gently aromatic to a big complex esteriness to spice-tinged strains to those like saison that are dryly phenolic, and for which the common descriptor is "peppery." And that's just the brewer's yeast. Several Belgian beer types use wild yeast and even bacteria like *Pediococcus* to ferment beer. A broad range of microorganisms in your beer is an almost inevitable consequence of fermenting in wood, but as breweries have modernized, specific yeasts like various *Brettanomyces* species have been cultured and added to the stainless tanks, and this is becoming popular elsewhere, too.

Convenient and shelf stable, dry yeast is available in a number of styles, including lager and even saison.

Wild critters are not limited to Belgium. Scratch the surface of lager-mad Germany and you will find survivors like Berliner weisse, made briskly sour by a *Lactobacillus* fermentation. Right in the very heart of Reinheitsgebot country, the popular Bavarian specialty, hefeweizen, uses a unique yeast, *Torulaspora delbrueckii,* to add a complex banana/bubblegum/clove aroma that is key to the style.

Although wild-fermented beers like lambics may be quite challenging, working with wild yeasts is not beyond the reach of the average homebrewer, and can be a useful addition to your bag of tricks.

BRETTANOMYCES

This genus includes several species used in brewing, mostly in the Belgian tradition. *Brett* will ferment wort by itself, but it's slowgoing, so it is best used pitched after a conventional fermentation and allowed to add its unique spicy, fruity, and barnyard aromas over an extended aging period.

SACCHAROMYCES CEREVISIAE

This is the familiar ale yeast, in all its variation. It is usually referred to as a top-fermenting yeast, because it prefers to work at or near the top of the fermenting vessel. Most strains prefer temperatures above 55°F/13°C, but the Rhine Valley strains will tolerate cold conditioning. There are hundreds of ale-brewing strains, with a wide variety of flavor and performance characteristics.

SACCHAROMYCES PASTORIANUS

This is the current scientific name of lager yeast (it was formerly called *S. carlsbergensis* or *S. uvarum*). Lager yeast is referred to as bottom-fermenting yeast because it normally sinks to the bottom of the fermenter and does its work there. It is cold-tolerant down to about 40°F/4.4°C, although it may be used at higher temperatures, producing beers with ale-like characteristics, such as fruity aromas, that are absent when fermented cold. Several closely related strains are available.

TORULASPORA DELBRUECKII
a.k.a. SACCHAROMYCES DELBRUECKII

This is the phenolic yeast used to give Bavarian hefeweizen its characteristic spicy, clovey aroma, as well as bubblegum and banana fruitiness. There are limited strains available. Outside of the phenolic aromas produced, its behavior is very similar to that of ale yeast.

White Labs and Wyeast pioneered the use of pure liquid yeast for homebrewing and small-scale commercial brewing. Both offer dozens of pedigreed brewing strains. Photo at far left courtesy of White Labs.

YEAST BIOLOGY

Yeast is a fungus, which is the kingdom intermediate between animals and plants. While we think of mushrooms and other fungi more like vegetables, fungal biology is actually more similar to animals than to plants. And although yeast is single-celled, it has a nucleus, which is a giant step above bacteria in evolutionary terms.

Though yeast might look like a simple little thing under the microscope, it is magnificently complex. Yeast is a complete living thing, capable of eating, ridding itself of toxins, reacting to its environment, and, finally reproducing. Yeast even has the ability to communicate with its neighbors, sending out messenger chemicals like heat shock proteins that warn of troublesome living conditions. Some yeasts can even kill other microbes.

INSIDE THE YEAST CELL

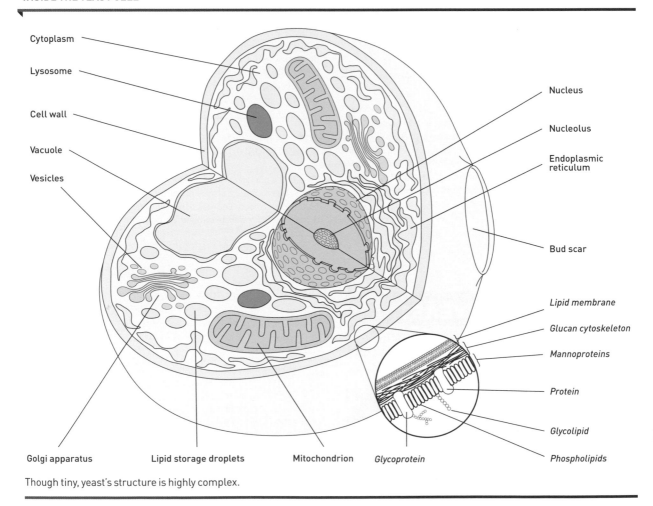

Though tiny, yeast's structure is highly complex.

CYTOPLASM

The jelly-like liquid that fills the cell, and in which everything else is suspended. It is not inert. Plenty of cellular processes take place within it.

NUCLEUS

The brain of the cell, which directs activities and contains the genetic material needed for reproduction.

NUCLEOLUS

A structure contained within the the nucleus, with specialized functions to create ribosomes, cellular structures where proteins are synthesized, and to produce ribonucleic acid (RNA).

ENDOPLASMIC RETICULUM (ER)

An extensive network of wobbly sheetlike structures throughout the cell but especially clustered near the nucleus. One type of ER temporarily shelters ribosomes, the cell's protein manufacturers. Another type of ER has a complex function including lipid synthesis and metabolism of certain substances, and a variant of this regulates calcium levels within the cell. Both are connected to the nucleus by tubular structures.

BUD SCAR

The mark left after a daughter cell buds off of the mother.

MITOCHONDRION

A specialized organelle where energy production takes place. In yeast, sugars are broken down and converted to adenosine triphosphate (ATP), which can power various processes in the cell.

LIPID STORAGE DROPLETS

Lipids (fats) form an energy storage mechanism for cells.

GOLGI APPARATUS

Sort of a packaging department for cellular proteins that will be secreted from the cell. It is formed by a stack of cisternae, blobby disks with unique capabilities. The proteins arrive and depart in vesicles, and are processed by moving through the stack of disks.

VESICLES

Encapsulated droplets containing substances that need to be transported without being diluted in the cell's cytoplasm.

VACUOLE

Essentially a reservoir, both for chemicals the cell may need to keep handy for certain functions and also to sequester toxins such as heavy metals. It also manages the internal pressure of the cell, adapting it to different densities of liquids in which it is immersed.

CELL WALL

This is composed of a lipid membrane supported by a cytoskeleton made from fibers of a glucan carbohydrate. While some small molecules can pass through without assistance, larger molecules require the aid of specialized proteins that act as gatekeepers.

LYSOSOME

These organelles digest worn-out cellular parts and food particles and attack bacteria and viruses. They disgorge their contents into the vacuole.

YEAST *and* THE BIOCHEMISTRY *of* BEER FLAVOR

All this yeast activity turns wort into beer for our benefit: As sugar is metabolized into energy for the cell, the yeast's waste products—carbon dioxide and alcohol—are excreted. Lucky for us, these are two of beer's most enjoyable qualities. Other by-products of these vital tasks are responsible for the aromatic complexity yeast brings to beer. But in large amounts, these chemicals can create inappropriate or even unpleasant aromas in our beer.

I find it useful to think about yeast as a leaky bag of goo. It has a skin formed from a plasma membrane composed of two layers of specialized lipids, backed by a complex structure of proteins and carbohydrates, mostly glucans, loosely woven together into a sort of molecular felt and anchored into the cell's inner structure. Small molecules like oxygen, esters, and alcohol can pass through easily. Embedded in this membrane are some proteins and enzymes that serve as gatekeepers for larger molecules such as sugars.

Every function, like extracting energy from sugar molecules, has many steps, typically aided by enzymes. Certain of these processes take place in specialized organelles like mitochondria, but many take place right in the cell's protoplasm, just sort of floating around in the jelly-like goop.

Each pathway has a huge number of intermediate chemicals that are just a means to an end for the yeast. Some of them have potent aromas.

Despite all its hard work, yeast is a bit sloppy, so some of the intermediate chemicals that play roles in metabolism, protein synthesis, and other functions ooze out of the cell and into the surrounding beer. One group of these is known as *congeners*; in beer, these include higher alcohols that may add subtle spicy flavors and warming sensations, but in large quantities can smell like rubbing alcohol (which they are) and give you a crackin' hangover. Another group, esters, can add delightful fruity aromas or, in excess, smell like banana candy or nail polish remover.

All of this is temperature driven. At the cool temperatures of a lager fermentation, the yeast is fairly well-mannered, taking its time and cleaning its plate, producing relatively little in the way of congeners. This is why lagers tend to taste of their ingredients more; they don't have the layer of fruity and spicy flavors to complicate things. The higher the temperature, the more copious the congeners; but this is very much strain dependent and also affected by things like yeast stress, pitching rate, pressure, and more.

Esters and higher alcohols aren't the only flavor compounds inadvertently created by yeast. Many chemicals created during the flurry of activity in the initial stages of fermentation are reabsorbed during conditioning, an important transformation that happens in that stage. The grassy/apple-like aromas of acetaldehyde and buttery notes of diacetyl are symptomatic of green, or incompletely matured beer. Given the proper time and conditions, these will go away.

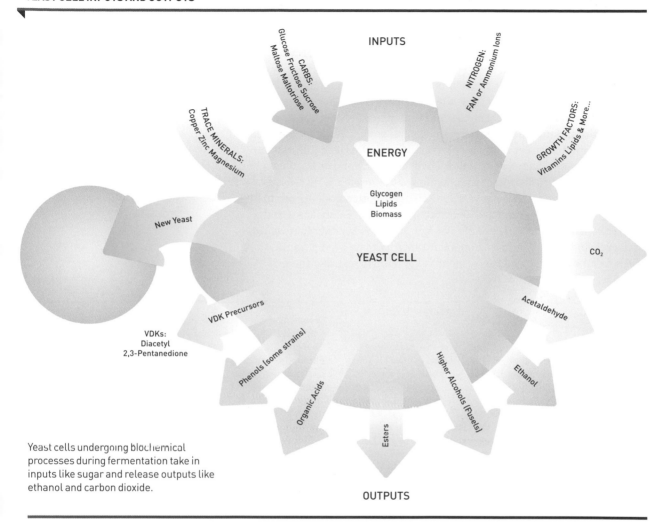

Yeast cells undergoing biochemical processes during fermentation take in inputs like sugar and release outputs like ethanol and carbon dioxide.

Each family of yeast-derived flavor chemicals can be produced in greater or lesser quantities depending on the many variables of the fermentation process. Temperature, pitching rate, alcohol level, wort oxygenation, nutrients like copper and zinc, fermentation pressure, and others have effects that depend on specific biochemical processes. What lowers one flavor may increase another, so there may be some compromises. And, every yeast reacts a little differently.

Fortunately, using good fresh yeast with known characteristics, pitching at an appropriate rate, employing good yeast-handling practices, aerating well, and fermenting at a temperature range appropriate for the yeast as well as the beer should minimize the chances of poor results or an unpleasant imbalance of yeast flavors.

YEAST FLAVOR CHEMICALS in BEER

The following list includes the most important secondary products of yeast, which add many different flavors to beer. These chemicals vary in their appropriateness in beer. Some are always unwanted, if they can be perceived. Others may be pleasing or not, depending on their concentration and what style of beer they're present in. Following each flavor description is a bar chart that shows the relationship between fermentation conditions and production of the flavor compound being discussed above it. Upward arrows indicate that increasing the variable (like temperature, for example) increases production of the flavor compound. Downward arrows show a decrease in production as the variable is increased. Double arrows means that the variable may act in both ways, and may indicate a sweet spot for maximum or minimum effect. "NA" means that the particular variable has a negligible effect. In some cases, either increasing or decreasing a variable, like temperature, may increase production of a given flavor chemical, and this is indicated by both up and down arrows.

ALDEHYDES

The most important aldehyde of many, relative to fermentation, is acetaldehyde. It has a somewhat nasty aroma of lawn clippings and old apple peels that is never desirable in beer. It is the main precursor to making alcohol inside the cell, so there is plenty of it, and some inevitably leaks into the surrounding beer. Because it is useful to the yeast, it is easily reabsorbed and converted to alcohol, but this takes time. Acetaldehyde reduction is one of the most important changes that happens during maturation. Like other yeast-generated aromatics, it is strain dependent. Aldehydes also play an important role in oxidized or stale flavors, but yeast's role in that is far from clear.

FERMENTATION VARIABLES AND ACETALDEHYDE

Temperature ↑/↓   OG ↑   Pitching Rate ↓   Wort O₂ ↓   Low Zn/Cu ↑

ESTERS

These are responsible for the characteristic fruitiness of ale. It is a broad class of chemicals that are closely related to alcohols. Small chemical changes can convert alcohols into esters and vice versa. There are a hundred or so esters in beer, and most of them tend to be volatile and highly aromatic, smelling of apples, bananas, pears, or just generally fruity. In large quantities, some of them (especially ethyl acetate) reek of nail polish remover. Ester formation is strain dependent; top-fermenting strains generate more esters, which is further aided by the generally higher temperatures of ale fermentation, so a brewer's first line

of control of ester flavors is choice of yeast and fermentation temperature (just 2 or 3 degrees difference may be noticeable). There are other factors as well, but it's very complicated. Higher pitching rate may raise or lower ester production, depending on the strain. Weizen yeast and some Belgian strains may be less estery if somewhat underpitched, but this effect seems to be small in most cases. Runaway ester production may happen if the yeast becomes stressed, as is common in high-alcohol beers, making them a special concern. Esters are not stable in beer and tend to fade away in aged beers.

FERMENTATION VARIABLES AND ESTER PRODUCTION

Temperature ↑   OG ↑   Pitching Rate ↑/↓   Wort O₂ ↓   Low Zn/Cu ↑

FUSELS

Fusels are longer-chain alcohols that are produced by yeast during fermentation. In small amounts they add complexity, but at high levels they can add rubbing-alcohol smells and harsh, hot tastes. They are especially a problem in stronger beers, and are exacerbated by higher fermentations. Good yeast health and proper pitching rates and wort oxygenation (specifically not overdoing either in this case) can prevent them from becoming a problem.

FERMENTATION VARIABLES AND FUSEL PRODUCTION

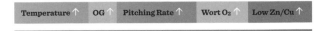

Temperature ↑   OG ↑   Pitching Rate ↑   Wort O₂ ↑   Low Zn/Cu ↑

GLYCEROL

This is a natural by-product of yeast fermentation, ending up in the finished beer at 500 to 1600 ppm, where it adds fullness and smooth character. It is sometimes added as a preservative in tropical countries.

Glycerol levels range from 50 to 1600 mg/L, and as a minor contributor to mouthfeel, its level is not commonly subject to manipulation by brewing or fermentation variables.

ORGANIC ACIDS

These are minor players in themselves, but they are precursors to ester formation and during normal fermentation drop the beer acidity by about 1.3 pH lower than wort.

Organic acids, such as pyruvic acid, citric acid, L-malic acid, acetic acid, and L-lactic acid vary widely from beer to beer, and while important for the final flavor of beer, are not commonly singled out for manipulation like esters and other chemicals.

PHENOL

This is a broad chemical family, whose flavors can range from a vague spiciness to the crisp peppery notes of saison yeast to the clove and allspice note of a classic hefeweizen, and even a certain earthy smokiness from some *Brettanomyces* yeasts. Less pleasant phenolic aromas may be medicinal, plastic, or even electrical fire in character. Except for wild yeast, which produces phenol in abundance, it is not a common off-flavor. In fact, the problem in styles like hefeweizen and saison is to get enough phenol into the beer. Phenol-producing strains have an active copy of a gene called the phenolic off-flavor (PAD1) gene. To produce phenolic aromas, yeast needs a precursor called ferulic acid. Special mashing techniques may be used to elevate the ferulic acid present in wort, but this is not a silver bullet. Phenol production is also sensitive to temperature, but this usually involves a complex balancing act, as the esters are also sensitive to temperature.

FERMENTATION VARIABLES AND PHENOL PRODUCTION

Temperature ↑/↓	OG NA	Pitching Rate ↓	Wort O₂ NA	Low Zn/Cu NA

SULFUR (SULFIDE AND SULFITE)

This is a pair of simple sulfur compounds that can be created by yeast from sulfur-containing amino acids or from inorganic water minerals like calcium sulfate. As with most sulfur chemicals, they are powerful odorants, hydrogen sulfide being the familiar rotten-egg aroma, and sulfite (sulfur dioxide) being a really pungent aroma of a match being struck. Both are highly volatile and are unlikely to remain in a beer beyond the first few sips. Excessive sulfur is rarely a problem with top-fermented beers. It is a special gift that lager fermentation brings, partially because lower-temperature fermentation less vigorously blows off volatiles. The silver lining is that sulfur compounds are good for beer stability, reducing some papery, oxidized flavors.

FERMENTATION VARIABLES AND SULFUR PRODUCTION

Temperature ↓	OG NA	Pitching Rate ↓	Wort O₂ NA	Low Zn/Cu ↑

VICINYL DIKETONES: DIACETYL AND 2,3-PENTANEDIONE

These are the buttery-smelling chemicals produced during fermentation. When yeast synthesizes a couple of amino acids, a precursor (acetolactate) leaks out of the cell and is converted into the potently aromatic VDKs. This is perfectly normal in all beer fermentations. During conditioning, VDKs are reabsorbed and converted to less noxious compounds. This requires active yeast and is more efficient at ale temperatures, so lagers (and some cool-fermented ales) are subjected to a "diacetyl rest" of two or three days at approximately 68°F/20°C toward the end of conditioning. While an identifiably buttery aroma is never a positive, diacetyl near threshold level may add a desirable richness to some English ales.

Diacetyl is also produced in great quantities by bacteria, especially *Lactobacillus* and *Pediococcus*. Buttery aromas are diagnostic of infections of that type, most often showing up in dirty draft beer systems.

FERMENTATION VARIABLES AND VICINYL DIKETONES/DIACETYL

Temperature ↑/↓	OG NA	Pitching Rate ↓	Wort O₂ NA	Low Zn/Cu NA

YEAST GROWTH *and* FERMENTATION

There are two distinct types of metabolic activity that the yeast can engage in: Harvesting energy or expending it. Catabolic activity involves assimilating energy, mostly from carbohydrate nutrients in the environment. Anabolic activity is the opposite; the cell is using energy, mainly for the creation of lipids and other biomass, essential for the creation of new yeast. These two types of cellular activity are employed in specific ways in two different sorts of yeast behavior: respiration and fermentation. In brewer's yeast, the presence of oxygen stimulates respiration, causing the yeast to switch over to fermentation, taking in sugars and breaking them down to create energy and, to our great benefit, releasing alcohol and CO_2, among other things, into the developing beer.

Before anything happens, yeast has to adapt itself to its new environment, which may differ from its previous one in sugar content, temperature, pH, and more. Oxygen begins to be absorbed to create fats such as sterols, which are necessary for the more active phase to come, as a crucial component of cell membranes. During this time, the yeast draws on its own glycogen reserves for nutrition. There is no increase in yeast numbers or drop in OG. This is called the lag phase, and it lasts just a few hours.

Once the yeast feels quite at home, it begins to absorb and metabolize sugars from the wort, making gravity drop. And it begins to make babies. Within six hours, about 90 percent of yeast cells will be budding, each bud becoming a new cell. By the time cell growth is over, the amount of yeast will have increased about fivefold. In all-malt worts, the amount of oxygen present at the beginning will be the limiting factor for how much yeast will be produced.

When the oxygen is depleted, new cell production stops and the yeast gets serious about gorging itself on sugar. Glucose is its preferred food, requiring the fewest metabolic steps and helper enzymes. In fact, glucose can actually be problematic, because if fed too much of it, yeast will not develop the permease enzymes needed to get maltose inside the cell, and will ferment maltose poorly, if at all. Fortunately, in all-malt worts, there is not a great deal of glucose, and much of it is used up in the growth phase. However, in beers with a lot of sugar (more than 15 percent), it may be a good idea to hold back some or all of the sugar until after the most vigorous phase of fermentation.

How rapidly fermentation proceeds is affected by a number of interdependent parameters: temperature, dissolved oxygen, pitching rate, wort gravity, and pressure (depth of tanks). It's complex, because oxygen solubility goes down at higher temperatures and higher wort gravities. This is another area where adopting good practices will keep you out of trouble. Plenty of good fresh yeast, pitched into well-oxygenated wort, and you'll have few problems, as long as everything is clean and sanitized.

More extreme beers will require some extra attention, as will lagers. But for most beers, pitching one package of yeast per manufacturer's direction will give you perfectly acceptable beers. However, most really great brewers feel they get noticeably better beer if a yeast starter is used, even for average-gravity beers. For strong beers and lagers, they're a necessity.

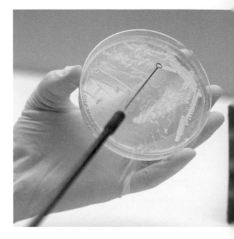

An advanced technique for most homebrewers, but plating yeast in a nutrient medium in a Petri dish is a necessary step in purifying yeast. Photo courtesy of White Labs.

Most yeast strains, even lagers, actually prefer temperatures around 90°F/32°C, but we normally ferment them cooler to reduce the amount of esters and higher alcohols to a more palatable level. Each yeast has a recommended temperature range that we are well advised to take seriously. Although it's not always simple or convenient, reasonably accurate temperature control is important if you want to be able to control the flavor and aroma of your beer. Lacking that, a good strategy is to find a yeast that will give good results at whatever ambient temperature you can manage, and just call that the house yeast. My homebrewing friends in Brazil should be making saisons, because that yeast actually prefers tropical heat. Lager, it should be noted, is impossible to make without good temperature control; it is necessary for maintaining a cool fermentation and cold conditioning, which creates the smooth clean flavors in that family of beers.

During fermentation, yeast activity is very vigorous; as sugars are metabolized, alcohol is excreted and CO_2 is expelled. The result is a thick, foamy head, and the beer can be seen churning as if boiling. It's pretty dramatic. This is also known as the primary fermentation. The conditions here will determine a good deal of the flavor and character of the beer, because once this activity subsides, the yeast personality of the beer has largely been determined, with only minor changes to come during conditioning.

These conditions will also determine how long the primary fermentation lasts. With plenty of yeast in an average-gravity wort, this can happen in a day or two. Three or four days is probably more typical, and a week or so for lager or high-gravity worts is the norm. At the end, fermentation slows down as the maltose is used up, and the yeast starts to work on the less readily fermentable maltotriose. Eventually, the foam will collapse and the surface will clear. When the yeast runs out of food, it will slowly fall to the bottom of the vessel and the beer will appear to darken as it becomes clearer.

The term for this slower phase used to be *secondary fermentation*, but that's not a reflection of what's really happening. The correct term is *conditioning* or *maturation*, indicating the fermentation is mostly done, but the beer is getting cleaned up, cleansed of "green" beer flavors like acetaldehyde and diacetyl.

The length of this stage varies by the same factors noted earlier, but is most dependent on wort gravity and temperature. An easy-drinking homebrew ale might need a couple of weeks or so before it's ready to bottle, while an average lager might need a month or six weeks. Bigger beers can take much longer. Anchor ages its Old Foghorn barley wine for six months or so before it leaves the brewery, and a similar timeframe is the historic lagering period for a doppelbock.

Standard practice for homebrewers used to be to transfer the beer to another vessel as soon as the primary fermentation was over. The idea was to get the beer off of the trub and dead yeast because it could impart a dirty, soapy flavor. This is a good instinct, and over time, those nasty flavors can develop. But for most beers that will be in the carboy for a month or less, transferring doesn't

Even an antique microscope, if it is in good condition, can be useful for examining yeast.

seem to make any difference, plus the additional handling is one more opportunity for exposure to oxidation and contaminants, not to mention another vessel to clean. For strong beers that require a long maturation, transferring is recommended; and moving from a large carboy to one the same size as the batch size minimizes the amount of beer exposed to the air.

YEAST TYPES

There are hundreds of different brewing strains in yeast banks around the world. The United States has two suppliers of pedigreed liquid yeast packaged for homebrewers, offering a few dozen strains that come from many of the world's most renowned and characteristic breweries. The choice of yeast can push a wort in a particular direction: fruity, spicy, woody, peppery, hoppy, or neutral. Most of Europe's beer traditions rely on specific yeast strains to add that final layer of unique personality to the beer. Without the appropriate yeast, there's not much to distinguish a Scotch ale from a Belgian dubbel from a German bock. Choosing the right yeast is as important a part of your recipe as working out a grist or a hop bill.

Dividing yeast strains by national origin is a good place to start, as they have been selected over the centuries to lend a particular character to the beer. This is an area where being a schooled beer connoisseur is really helpful because these complex yeast personalities can be difficult to explain in words. And while generalizations can be made about national beer traditions, within each one there is still a huge variation, so knowing your Fuller's from your Young's from your Whitbread's gives you an advantage when trying to choose from the many strains on the market.

With the choices available these days, one can brew almost any beer that can be imagined.

YEAST-STRAIN FLAVOR AND PERFORMANCE CHARACTERISTICS

ALCOHOL TOLERANCE

Most yeast can handle about 10 percent alcohol without any problem. High-alcohol beer types can go up to 12 percent or more as long as they're pitched in sufficiently large quantities into well-oxygenated wort. Normal wine yeasts can easily reach 15 percent or slightly more, while specialized yeasts for distillation, sake, or tokay wine, can tolerate 20 percent or more. Brewers making super-strong brews usually start with alcohol-tolerant ale strains in wort at around 1.100 (24°P), adding extra sugar and a specialized yeast when the normal yeast conks out. Rousing (stirring), along with extra oxygen, is sometimes necessary to ferment very high-alcohol beers.

AROMA

All the characteristics from esters to phenol and beyond. Lager yeasts have restrained aromas. Every ale strain has some amount of fruitiness, but only a few specialized ones produce noticeable phenol, giving spicy, sometimes peppery aromas. Each strain is different, so you'll just have to get familiar with them. It is also useful to know how each strain you work with responds to temperature, something that usually takes several batches (or split batches) to become familiar with. For more details see An Atlas of Beer Flavor and Character, page 40.

ATTENUATION

With yeast behavior, this is largely related to flocculence. A yeast that stays in suspension longer ferments more thoroughly. Beyond differences between strains, attenuation is greatly affected by pitching rate and wort aeration, as greater quantities of yeast are more effective at eating all the sugar in the wort. Alcohol tolerance of yeast obviously has an impact on attenuation of strong beers.

FLOCCULATION

This is the tendency for yeast cells to clump together and drop out of the beer, a process that involves the binding of special proteins and other chemicals on cells' surfaces. Some floccu-lence is useful, as it clears the beer, but with too much, the strain may be underattenuative, leaving the beer a bit sweet. So-called powdery or nonflocculent strains are highly attenuative, making a dry beer, but they may need to be fined with isinglass or gelatin in order to clear the beer.

TEMPERATURE RANGE/COLD TOLERANCE

Every yeast has a temperature range where it produces the most style-appropriate flavor. Below its working range, the yeast may go dormant; above it, estery and possibly phenolic flavors become too much. The high end is more a matter of personal preference and style norms, but the low end is a matter of yeast physiology, and the brewer has little choice over the matter.

Yeast produces a number of familiar flavors and aromas, including esters reminiscent of bananas, nail polish/solvent, pineapple, apples, and more; and phenolic flavors of pepper, clove, or other spices. The production of these flavors is governed by yeast strain and many different fermentation conditions.

Here's an overview of what to expect from the major categories of yeast.

BELGIAN YEAST

This is a large and especially varied category, with a lot of very distinctive yeasts. They can be divided into two types: estery and phenolic. The former is used in the majority of Belgian ales, from abbey to strong golden and dark ales. Many are very alcohol tolerant, a good thing for a tradition with so many strong beers. At the far end of the phenolic scale is saison yeast, especially the DuPont strain. It produces a dry, unsentimental beer with a sharp, peppery nose. It prefers high temperatures, and even at well over 90°F/32°C, it still doesn't make a lot of esters. It is believed to be related to red wine yeast, which has similar characteristics. Saison yeast likes a lot of oxygen and is famous for conking out halfway through the fermentation. Either give it a few more weeks, or finish the job with a neutral ale yeast. Either way, the flavor will be similar. In between are some yeasts that have a mix of estery and phenolic character.

TEMPERATURE RANGE: (estery type) Primary 65 to 72°F/ 18 to 22°C; (phenolic type) Primary 68 to 80°F/20 to 27°C
BEER STYLES: (estery type) The dazzling splendor and variety of Belgian ales—abbey, blonde, pale ale, strong golden, strong dark, and many eccentrics; (phenolic type) saison, witbier

ENGLISH YEAST

A wide range of yeasts from English, Scottish, and Irish brewery pedigrees is available. All have fruity ale characteristics, but there is a variety of different personalities as well as brewing characteristics like flocculence. In addition to specific flavors of their own, British yeasts are notable for changing the balance of the beer, enhancing certain characteristics such as maltiness or hop character. Some are now used for specific beers like stout; all probably originated as all-purpose ale yeasts. When choosing a yeast, it may be helpful to actually taste the beer that is brewed from it, if available, as written descriptions can give only limited information.

Flocculent strains aren't as attenuative, but they're better behaved and will settle out readily in the carboy as well as the finished package. Poorly flocculent yeast may need to be fined to get it to drop out and clear the beer. Cold tolerance varies; Scottish strains may be able to work a little cooler than English ones.

TEMPERATURE RANGE: Primary 65 to 70°F/18 to 21°C
BEER STYLES: All British styles; a wide range of American craft beer styles

EUROPEAN (RHINE VALLEY) YEAST

These are strains used to ferment Düsseldorfer altbier and Kölsch, and have a clean fruitiness. They also tolerate cold conditioning, so can be thought of as intermediate between ale and lager yeast in terms of performance and flavor charactistics, which is why such beers are often referred to as "hybrid" ales. There are a relatively limited number of strains available, with few differences between them.

TEMPERATURE RANGE: Primary 65 to 69°F/18 to 21°C; Secondary 44 to 48°F/7 to 9°C
BEER STYLES: Kölsch, Düsseldorfer Alt, cream ale, American wheat ale, sparkling ale

HEFEWEIZEN

This is the species *Torulaspora delbrueckii*, not regular brewer's yeast. Think of it as a housebroken wild yeast. It contains a working copy of the phenolic off-flavor (PAD1) gene, which allows it to produce some clove and allspice aromas along with plenty of banana and bubblegum. A large part of the art of using these yeasts is choosing and maintaining a temperature that gives you the exact aromatic mix you want for your beer. As little as a couple of degrees changes the balance of aromas.

TEMPERATURE RANGE: Primary 66 to 72°F/19 to 22°C
BEER STYLES: All Bavarian hefeweizens and weizenbocks; dampfbier, a sort of fake weissbier made from barley malt

LAGER

While there are several offered, the flavor is likely to be very similar. All lagers produce a relatively neutral-tasting beer, with few fruity or spicy flavors. In general, lagers are more apt to produce sulfury flavors, especially when underpitched or with yeast in the first generation. Water with a high sulfur/sulfate content can exacerbate this. Lagers really do need to be fermented cool and cold-conditioned for true lager character. They will produce acceptable beer at warmer temperatures, but it will have some fruitiness, so it won't taste like a lager.

Note that the drop from primary to lagering temperature should be gradual, to avoid shocking the yeast; 1 to 2°F/0.05 to 1°C per day is traditional.

TEMPERATURE RANGE: Primary 50 to 55°F/10 to 13°C; Secondary 40°F/4°C
BEER STYLES: Full range of lagers from Pilsner to doppelbock; steam beer

DRIED YEAST

Though it encompasses many strains, dried yeast deserves some discussion because there are a number of things that make it a bit different from liquid brewing cultures. From a brewer's standpoint, it is handy, inexpensive, transports easily, and is easier to use than liquid yeast. And it is capable of producing fine beer. However, most people in the hobby and the profession feel that all things being equal, a liquid strain properly handled will usually result in a better-tasting beer.

First, dried strains are chosen for their ability to withstand the dehydration process. Not every strain can handle this stress, so the link to a known brewery or specific beer type is broken. Brewers are seldom the most important market segment for dried yeast, so we often have to get in line behind bakers and distillers for resources. Because of the complexity of production, most dried yeast manufacturers offer just a few strains. British and American ale strains are available, and recently lager, weizen, and even Belgian strains have come on the market, so there is a lot more choice than there used to be.

Second, dried yeast may be a bit stressed. Because of this, it often has poor performance in areas like attenuation and overabundant esters or phenol. Dried yeast that has been used to ferment a batch and then saved and repitched into a new beer often performs better in this regard. Dried yeast also has a tendency to be a bit one-dimensional from a flavor standpoint. Some brewers have reported better results by using more than one dried strain, giving the beer a more complex aroma.

Dried yeast does require proper hydration to achieve best performance. Adding dried yeast directly into the beer will cause osmotic shock and very poor fermentation performance. To rehydrate, pour the dried yeast into a small amount (10 times yeast weight) of warm sterilized water at 86 to 95°F/30 to 35°C. Do *not* add sugar or malt extract; the yeast has enough food reserves to get going on its own. Bubbling or lack thereof is no indication of yeast viability. After 15 minutes, stir or swirl gently, allow to sit a few more minutes, then add to the wort.

Allowing dry yeast to rehydrate in clean warm water (not wort!) is essential for best performance.

WILD YEAST: ALIENS in YOUR BREWERY

If you want to explore the entire world of beer flavor possibilities, at some point you're going to have to get down and dirty with wild yeast and even certain bacteria. It is a complex subject beyond the scope of a general book like this, but there are some uses that don't require a biology PhD, so we'll cover the basics here.

Pure cultures of a number of exotic yeasts and bacteria are available, as are mixed cultures for specific beers such as lambics or Flemish sour brown ales. Many homebrewers get good results with a more casual approach—simply dumping in the dregs of commercial traditional lambics and waiting a few months. As long as your sanitization procedures are solid, brewing with exotic microorganisms can be as simple or complex as you like.

The following is a list of the more commonly used "wild" yeasts and other microbes used in brewing sour and exotic beers.

BRETTANOMYCES (OR *BRETT*)

This is the most common wild yeast used in brewing, and is useful in rustic Belgian ales where whiffs of barnyard or roasted pineapple are appropriate. Lambics, Flemish sour brown, and red ales also use *Brett*, but in combination with a number of other critters. *Brett* is a distant cousin of brewers' yeast and shares many of its characteristics, although there are some differences as well. *Brett* will ferment beer by itself, and some in the United States have experimented with 100 percent *Brett* beers. Normally it is added late in the fermentation process, or sometimes, as in the Trappist beer Orval, at bottling. *Brett* is a slow performer and likes to have a trickle of oxygen available—one reason it does well in oak barrels, which are largely transparent to oxygen. It is believed that the interior of oak trees is one of *Brett's* natural habitats. *Brett* works best when pitched in small quantities, so starters are not normally used.

Brett and other forms of wild yeast will form a whitish pellicle, or film, on top of the beer. It will easily ferment maltotriose, which ale yeast usually doesn't, along with the more complex sugar, maltotetraose. This can cause problems if not taken into account when bottling, as the beer can become overcarbonated. Maltotriose may be up to 10 percent or so of wort carbohydrate content, so for this reason it may be best to add the *Brett* to the fermenter and allow a few weeks to pass before bottling. Many wild yeasts can ferment dextrins, allowing the beer to become overcarbonated. Gushing, along with strong phenolic flavors, is indicative of a wild yeast infection.

Brett produces a bit more acidity than brewers' yeast, but it really doesn't make a beer sour. That takes bacteria like *Lactobacillus*, *Pediococcus*, and the vinegar-producing *Acetobacter*.

There are three types of *Brett* generally available, and although they are usually listed as separate species, this is not technically true. (However, I buy into the marketing fiction for the sake of simplicity.) Each has a specific range of flavors, although there seems to be a lot of variability from one supplier to another: *B. bruxellensis* is considered a medium-intensity strain, with some pleasant barnyard/horse-blanket character, and is the one used by Orval; *B. lambicus* is a higher-intensity subspecies of *B. bruxellensis*, with horse-blanket and fruity, cherry-pie aromas, occasionally showing some spicy/phenolic flavors; *B. anomalus* (*claussenii*) is the *Brett* species associated with wood-aged British old ales, and has a fruity aroma, sort of like roasted or overripe pineapple. There are many others, but they are not generally available except in truly wild cultures, in the laboratory, or perhaps living in your backyard.

TEMPERATURE RANGE: 60 to 70°F/16 to 21°C

BEER STYLES: Lambics and sour Flanders beers (mixed with other wild microbes); as exotic flavor accent in saisons or other eccentric or rustic Belgian specialties or Belgo-American ales; British old ales (*Brettanomyces claussenii*)

The dregs of homebrewed or commercial lambics can often be used to get a wild fermentation going.

LACTOBACILLUS

While a component of lambic fermentations, *Lactobacillus* is the star of the "wild bug show" in beers like Berliner weisse. It is notoriously difficult to culture in wort, as it prefers glucose, present in wort only at the beginning and in small quantities, and lactose, which is absent unless added in milk stouts. *Lactobacillus delbrueckii* is the species most often used in brewing; the cultures available to homebrewers are designed for direct pitching into beer, but may take several months to develop much acidity.

Most people who are really serious about *Lactobacillus* make a special starter medium that incorporates lactose and/or dextrose and some yeast nutrient like yeast hulls, sometimes with the addition of tomato juice, which creates the slightly acidic environment *Lactobacillus* prefers. For best results, it also needs to be incubated at about body temperature.

TEMPERATURE RANGE: 60 to 72°F/16 to 22°C

BEER STYLES: *Lactobacillus* is the defining characteristic for Berliner Weisse and some of the more obscure historical styles in Northern Germany, such as lichtenhainer, broyhan, and others. Probably also an important player in historic Belgian witbiers, described as having varying degrees of sourness, which is likely derived from *Lactobacillus*. Important in lambics, *Lactobacillus* comes as part of the commercially available mixed lambic cultures that provide good results with minimal fuss.

MIXED BELGIAN CULTURES

These are usually a blend of *Saccharomyces cerevisiae*, a few strains of *Brettanomyces*, and some *Pediococcus* and *Lactobacillus* bacteria that do the heavy lifting in acid production. Because those mixed cultures contain brewers' yeast, they can be used to do the total fermentation, but some brewers like to control the main fermentation with a particular yeast, then pitch the mixed culture later.

Be aware that *Lactobacillus* and *Pediococcus* are fairly sensitive to the antibacterial properties of hops, which are related to beta acids. A general rule of thumb is to keep the bitterness well below 10 BU, which is in line with style norms for lambics. More bitterness can be achieved, if desired, by using low-beta-acid hop varieties.

TEMPERATURE RANGE: 63 to 80°F/17 to 27°C

BEER STYLES: The yeast manufacturers usually recommend using the same cultures for either lambic-type beers or Flanders sour browns/reds, although Wyeast offers a "Roeselare" blend, which includes an oxidative sherry yeast, for this purpose.

Easy wild beer? Depends on what you mean by that! One can certainly add a packet of Brett to a beer at bottling. The key is knowing what characteristics of that beer will mesh well with the eventual Brett contributions. I think it's easier to grow Lactobacillus in a flask, by itself, rather than in the main wort. Blend it at bottling too, but generally to a highly attenuated beer, to minimize the risk of overcarbonation. Always use as attenuated a beer as possible with these critters. If you have access to a barrel, you can go all in.

JEFF SPARROW, author of *Brewing Wild Ales*

THE CARE *and* FEEDING *of* YEAST

Yeast is a hardy little beast, but like all of us, it has its preferences. For the most part, the conditions of normal brewing suit it just fine in terms of nutritive mix, temperature, pH, osmotic pressure, alcohol, and more. This makes it easy, because if we take care of just a few important things like pitching rate and proper wort aeration—and sanitization, of course—we don't have to worry too much about the health of our yeast.

There are a few possible problem areas though, that may require special action.

> *An ideal fermentation can make a poor recipe still taste good.*

CHRIS WHITE, founder and president, White Labs, co-author *Yeast: The Practical Guide to Beer Fermentation*

AVOIDING PROBLEMS WITH YEAST

PROBLEM: Low-gravity, high-adjunct beers may lack FAN (free amino nitrogen) and other nutrients.
SOLUTION: Add a yeast nutrient such as diammonium phosphate.

PROBLEM: Most worts are zinc deficient; some lack copper, too.
SOLUTION: Add zinc sulfate or a product like Servomyces to the boil. Copper wort chiller or brass valves provide sufficient copper; otherwise, a penny or two can be added to the boil kettle.

PROBLEM: High-gravity worts have high-osmotic pressure that is harmful to yeast.
SOLUTION: Add sugar or additional extract after fermentation has lowered wort-sugar content.

PROBLEM: High-alcohol concentrations are harmful to yeast.
SOLUTION: This is strain-dependent, so choose alcohol-tolerant yeast. Pitch larger quantities of yeast for high-alcohol beers. For superstrong beers, start with an alcohol-tolerant brewers' yeast, then to switch champagne or other wine yeast.

PROBLEM: High pressure is harmful to yeast.
SOLUTION: Carbonate beer only at the very end of fermentation. Large commercial brewery fermenters are much deeper than homebrew ones, so this is not often a problem for homebrewers.

PROBLEM: Lager yeast needs special handling, especially in stronger styles like the bocks.
SOLUTION: Always use higher pitching rates and good wort oxygenation.

PROBLEM: Rapid temperature drops cause yeast to go dormant.
SOLUTION: Make any temperature change gradual—no more than 5°F/3°C per day; with lagers, no more than 2°F/1°C per day.

Most homebrewers are quite happy to buy yeast and just follow the manufacturer's directions. And manufacturers wouldn't recommend this if it didn't get good results. But if you ask them, even they will say that, in general, the beer will probably be better if a starter is made and it is added rather than using packaged yeast. With strong beers (1.080[19°P]) and lagers, a properly sized starter should be standard operating procedure.

A starter is just a mini batch of beer designed to increase the volume and freshness of yeast used to ferment your main batch of beer. It's not too difficult to do. Most homebrewers make a starter of about a liter, and that's what the instructions here are for, but if you can get a larger flask, doubling this will give you even better results. Starters are unnecessary with dry yeast, and may even do damage. If you're concerned about having enough, just buy more—it's cheap enough.

How to Make a Yeast Starter

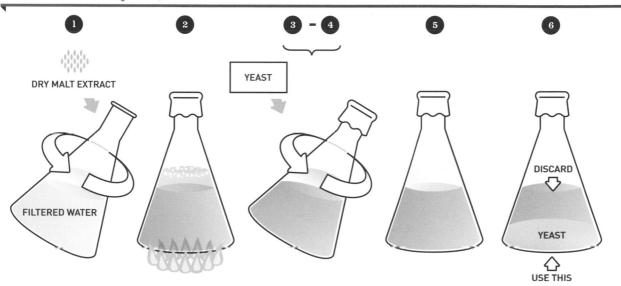

Most agree that beer is better when a starter is made and added, rather than using packaged yeast.

1

Fill a sanitized 2-L borosilicate laboratory flask (Pyrex or similar) half full of filtered tap water and add 3.2 oz/90 g of dry malt extract, swirling to dissolve. This will make a 1.034 (8.8°P) wort. Stronger is not better. Cover top of flask with aluminum foil.

2

Place on stove and heat to a boil, making sure extract is well dissolved. Maintain gentle boil for 10 minutes.

3

Remove from heat and allow starter to cool to ambient room temperature, somewhere close to 70°F/21°C.

4

Pour yeast into starter and replace foil. Shake for a couple of minutes to oxygenate the wort.

5

Maintain temperature. Give the starter a minute of shaking every couple of hours when it's convenient—you don't have to set the alarm for 3:00 aɴ. for this. An advanced method is to place the flask on a stir plate, with a stir bar in the wort. This agitation aerates and knocks the CO_2 out of the starter, both of which will speed and improve its performance.

6

Yeast activity should be visible in a couple of hours. Starter is best used at high kraeusen, most likely 18 to 24 hours after inoculation. When foam has subsided, starter will remain usable for a week or so. After the yeast starts to settle, the clear liquid above the yeast can be decanted if desired. After 18 to 24 hours, it should be fed with additional boiled wort.

PITCHING RATES

The pitching rate is an expression of the number of yeast cells added to the wort to start fermentation. Although in most circumstances, adding yeast according to manufacturer's recommendations provides a workable quantity of yeast cells, there are some circumstances where it is helpful to do a little calculating. High-gravity and lager beers benefit from an increased pitching rate, meaning more yeast for those situations. Larger batches, of course, require more yeast in proportion to their size.

A general rule of thumb for normal-strength worts is somewhere about 7 million cells per milliliter of wort for ales, and about 13 million cells per milliliter for lagers. With stronger beers, a more complex formula should be used: 0.75 million cells per milliliter per degree Plato for ale; double that for lagers.

YEAST PITCHING RATES FOR LAGERS AND ALES BY GRAVITY

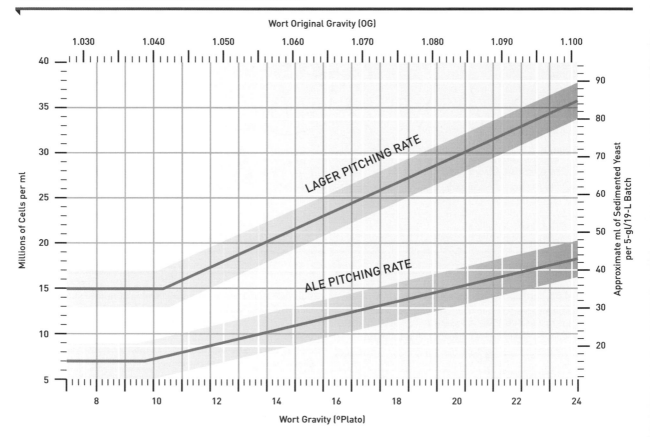

This graph shows pitching rates varying by wort gravity in both millions of cells per milliliter (left scale) and a very approximate amount of dense, sedimented slurry (right scale). Note that below about 1.040 OG (10°P), pitching rates remain the same as for stronger beers. Shaded zones around lines show acceptable range.

WORT AERATION

Closely related to pitching rate is wort oxygenation. Yeast needs oxygen to produce lipids that will be used to help build cell membranes, essential for good yeast health. Wort oxygen is in fact the growth limiter for yeast. As soon as it is used up, yeast turns its attention to fermenting the sugars in the wort. Just as with pitching rates, an adequate aeration rate will ensure a quick and vigorous fermentation, resulting in a clean and well-attenuated beer.

Standard practice for wort oxygen levels is 8 to 10 mg/L (ppm) for ales, and a little higher at 12 ppm for lagers. As with most industry norms, this is for normal gravity beers, under about 1.080 (19°P). As with pitching rates, bigger beers also demand more oxygen, compounded by the fact that O_2 is less soluble in sugar-rich worts. The minimum for a good fermentation in a normal beer is 5 ppm.

WORT AERATION LEVELS BY GRAVITY

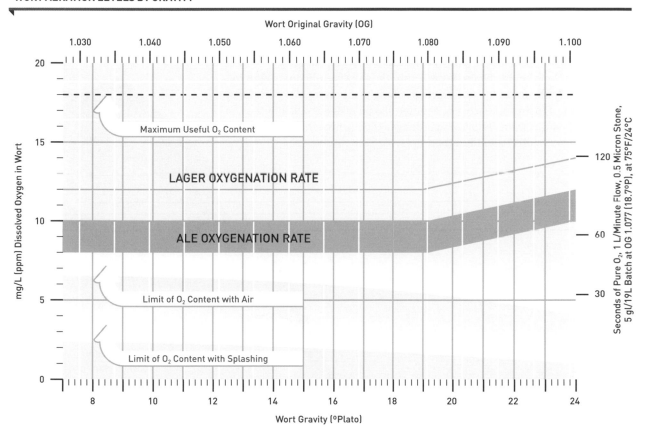

An adequate aeration rate will ensure a quick and vigorous fermentation, resulting in a clean and well-attenuated beer.

The ability to get good dissolved oxygen levels in your wort will be limited by your equipment. Entry-level brewers usually shake, splash, and stir their way to as much oxygenation as they can manage. Pro brewers use sintered aeration stones and pure O_2 and can dial in a precise amount of oxygen.

Shaking and other physical techniques normally reach about 3 ppm, far below what is ideal, but still far better than nothing. If your carboy can be capped and given a really vigorous shaking *safely* (plastic carboys only, please), then somewhat higher levels may be reached. I have seen figures for the venturi aerators going perhaps as high as about 5 ppm. Air is 21 percent oxygen; an aeration stone with an aquarium pump can hit about 8 ppm, a pretty comfortable level for most beers. It takes pure oxygen to reach higher levels than this. Pure oxygen is available to homebrewers, but this needs to be used carefully to avoid over-oxygenating.

With strong beers and some Belgian types such as saison, a second aeration might be helpful. There is a limit to how much O_2 can be taken up by the population of pitched yeast cells, so letting them go and bud off another generation of yeast creates new customers for another shot of oxygen. This is typically done around 12 or more hours after the initial pitching.

Wort aeration should always be done after the wort is chilled, so as not to cause oxidized flavor problems later; and solubility is better at low temperatures anyway. If using pure oxygen, aeration should take place before the yeast is pitched, as there is some small danger of poisoning the yeast with too much O_2. It's a small chance, but there's no reason to risk it.

Fitted with a sterile filter, an aquarium pump can be used to inject air into your wort for a faster, healthier fermentation.

YEAST UNLEASHED: PRACTICAL FERMENTING

By now your wort is in its fermenting vessel, hopefully residing somewhere close to the desired fermentation temperature. It's worth expending some effort to try to control the fermentation temperature because so many aspects of beer flavor are dependent on it. It isn't always easy. Five gallons/19 L of fermenting beer is a fairly large thing, and there's no easy, cheap, compact device to keep it at a constant temperature. In warmer areas, people use old refrigerators or retrofitted chest freezers. I use heated carboy carts in my Midwest U.S. basement. Another common method is to place your fermenter in a tub with 4 inches/10 cm of water in it, periodically swapping out frozen water bottles or blue ice to maintain a cool temperature. Insulation helps hold in the cool.

Use a yeast strain that works with your ambient temperature and do the best you can—you can always call it the *hausgeschmack*, or house flavor. If you can't manage active temperature control, try to minimize the temperature swings by putting it in a central part of the house or protect it with some kind of insulating cover.

Yeast will generate some heat, and in commercial breweries this can cause runaway temperatures if not actively cooled. In small vessels like ours, temperatures can rise between 2°F/1°C and 5°F/3°C depending on ambient temperature, strain, and other factors.

Once pitched, the beer will start to show some signs of activity in as little as 4 to 6 hours, but may take longer. Generally, you like to see some signs of activity by the next morning, but you have about 24 hours before you have to start panicking. Activity will typically show up as a cookie-like raft of foam in the middle of the vessel, then spread out and consume the entire surface, and rise up 2 inches/5 cm or so, although lagers show restraint here. At high kräusen, the maximum stage of activity, the top will be highly convoluted, and usually show patches of dark trub dotting the foam. The fermenting beer will look pale and very cloudy, and if you get close, you'll see a lot of activity swirling around in there.

This vigorous primary stage will usually last 2 to 4 days, sometimes more. It is dependent mainly on yeast strain, wort gravity, fermentation temperature, pitching rate, and wort oxygenation. Big beers take longer than small ones; cool fermentations take longer than warm ones.

The foam will diminish and eventually collapse and the surface of the wort will clear, although if this seems to be happening slowly, comparing the gravity from day to day can show when yeast activity slows to a crawl. At this point, most of the sugar has been used up and the conditioning phase begins. Some beer styles such as lagers and Rhine Valley ales require a gradual drop to a cooler temperature at this point, but most beers are conditioned at the same temperature as the primary.

Many traditional British fermenters incorporate special devices to force yeast up into a space from which it can be collected and re-pitched, assuring vigorous top-fermenting behavior. This setup was in a small brewery in Kent.

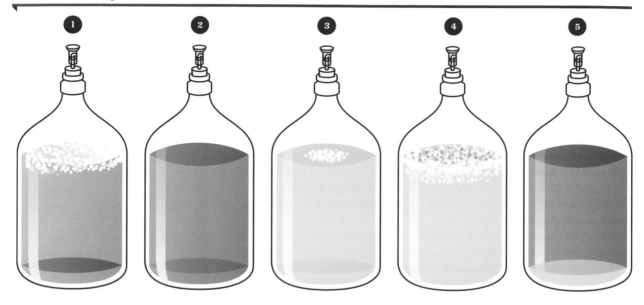

Fermentation begins with a carboy filled with chilled and slightly cloudy wort and yeast, and ends days or weeks later with a clear and dark looking brew.

1

Chilled wort and yeast in carboy with foam from aeration present. Wort will usually be slightly cloudy.

2

Foam subsides after 1 to 2 hours, and nothing appears to be happening. This is the lag phase, which may last 2 to 12 hours, sometimes longer.

3

Yeast activity begins as a circular raft on surface or sometimes several patches.

4

Full kräusen, with yeasty foam that can sometimes push all the way out of the carboy. Wort will appear quite milky at this point.

5

Yeast activity winding down and conditioning takes place. Wort will gradually clear over days or a few weeks, and beer will appear dark. When it gets to that point, it's ready to bottle.

Lager brewing requires precise temperature control. Most lager-brewing homebrewers use chest freezers fitted with accurate temperature controls for the extended cold-conditioning required.

CONDITIONING *and* MATURATION

Although at this point it looks as if it's going dormant, the yeast is still active, taking offensive aroma compounds like acetaldehyde and diacetyl back into its cell and changing them into less obnoxious compounds, greatly cleaning up the flavor and aroma of the beer.

Within a couple of weeks for most beers, the beer will start to drop bright, as brewers say, and take on a much darker appearance in the carboy as it clarifies. For most beers, this means it's time to keg or bottle. If you're using a non-flocculent strain, this may take an irritatingly long time. Finings such as gelatin may be helpful to speed this process up.

There are other methods that aid conditioning. Kräusening is a process in which a small amount of rapidly fermenting wort equal to about 10 percent of the batch size is added to beer during conditioning. The active yeast speeds up maturation and may increase attenuation. Normally used in lagers, it's not a complicated process, but since it needs freshly fermenting yeast, the donor and receiving batches must be well timed. For homebrewers it's a useful technique for making very strong beers, since the fresh and healthy yeast may be able to attenuate below what was possible with the original pitched yeast.

Beer requires from several days to several weeks for flavors to mature and clean up. During that time, the yeast drops out and beer appears to darken in the carboy. This one's ready to bottle.

FININGS

Finings are a method of clarifying beer that relies on chemical qualities to cause yeast, other solids, and haze particles to drop out of solution. There are two main categories: colloidal finings that use proteins such as collagen to bind and drag down particulates like yeast, and types that are designed to clear protein haze.

ENZYME FININGS (CLARITY FERM, BREWERS' CLAREX)

A new type of fining material that uses a protease enzyme to target the amino acid proline, which breaks up proteins and thus reduces haze. The side benefit is that gluten also contains proline and these finings reduce it to levels that can make the beer essentially gluten-free. Pectinase is sometimes used in winemaking and can be used in fruit beers to break down haze-forming carbohydrates that sometimes come along with the fruit. Enzyme finings are usually added at the beginning of fermentation.

GELATIN

This is simply household gelatin, which works in a similar manner to isinglass. It's not as effective, but it is much easier to deal with, cheaper, and has no shelf-life problem. Mix one packet of unflavored gelatin with a small amount of cold water and let stand until rehydrated; mix in some hot water, let stand for a few minutes, and then gently blend it with the beer. A day or two later, the beer should be bright.

ISINGLASS

This is a type of pure collagen, typically extracted from fish swim bladders or other body parts. It is the traditional fining used in English cask ales. It works by casting a wide protein net across the beer in the vessel, attracting and trapping yeast and other particles as it falls to the bottom, a process that usually takes a day or two. It's a perishable product that must be stored correctly and activated with an acid before use. Liquid preparations are traditional, but they store poorly. There are a number of forms available to homebrewers, so manufacturer's instructions should be followed for best results.

PVPP (POLYCLAR)

This works differently from isinglass or gelatin and is meant to remove not yeast and particulates but haze-forming proteins and polyphenols, most often in lagers, where chill haze can be problematic. Add it directly to beer toward the end of conditioning and it works best if the beer is cold. The recommended quantity is 5 to 10 grams per 5-gallon/19-L batch. Rehydrate it for an hour or so in sterilized water, then add it to the beer, mixing well. It usually takes a day or two to clarify. If you're also using gelatin, do that first, then chill and follow with Polyclar.

SILICA GEL

This is an inert quartz material that is used to remove chill haze in a similar manner to PVPP. Mix 6 to 10 grams per batch with some sterilized water, then mix into the beer and let stand 24 hours or a little more.

Chris Graham's Closed Wort-Transfer Method

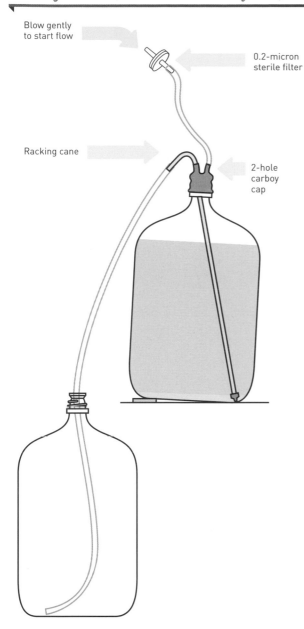

Blow gently
to start flow

0.2-micron
sterile filter

Racking cane

2-hole
carboy
cap

The sanitized destination carboy is flooded with CO_2 (if you have it available) to expel air, then fitted with a soft plastic carboy cap with two hose inlets. The transfer hose goes through one and all the way to the bottom, arranged so as to minimize splashing when the wort flows.

The carboy with the beer in it is fitted with the same type of cap, and the sanitized racking cane goes through one hole. Don't forget to attach the little plastic pickup doohickey to the bottom end of the cane.

Attach a 0.2-micron tubing filter to the other hole or stuff some cotton ball material into the tubing.

Place the source carboy so the highest possible liquid level is lower than the bottom of the source carboy. Tilt the source carboy on a small piece of wood (or this book!) so the cane tip ends up in the lowest part.

5

Blow gently into the filter. Pressure in the carboy should push beer into the hose and start the siphon. Once beer flows, stop blowing and let the carboy fill up. Remove the hose and fit with a fermentation lock.

To avoid possible contamination and oxidation issues, Chris Graham, at the brewing supply superstore MoreBeer, recommends a wort-transfer method that keeps exposure to air at a minimum.

CHANGES DURING FERMENTATION AND CONDITIONING

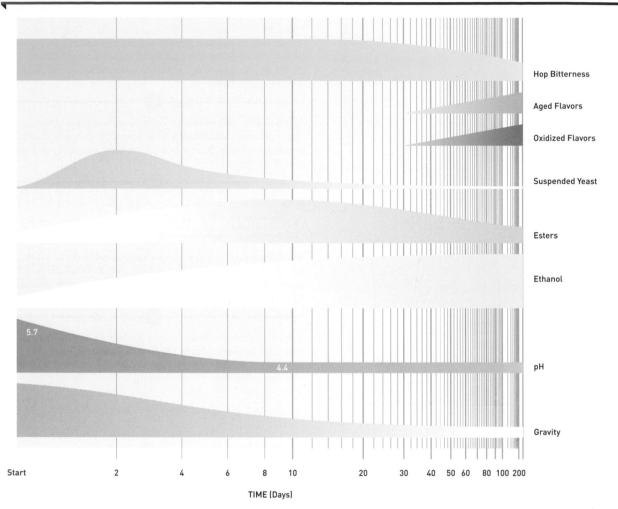

Hop Bitterness

Aged Flavors

Oxidized Flavors

Suspended Yeast

Esters

Ethanol

5.7

4.4

pH

Gravity

| Start | 2 | 4 | 6 | 8 | 10 | 20 | 30 | 40 | 50 | 60 | 80 | 100 | 200 |

TIME (Days)

This chart shows how flavors and other aspects of beer change over time. In the beginning, changes are day by day. Changes after packaging happen on a much longer time scale, over months and even years. This chart depicts a generalized beer and is intended to be instructive but not predictive.

Lagers, too, have longer conditioning times, although some modern lagers are produced in as little as ten days. Six weeks was the traditional lagering period for normal strength beers like Pilsners; doppelbocks could take six months. Be sure not to forget to do a diacetyl rest by raising the temperature to 65 to 68°F/18 to 20°C for a couple of days at the end of fermentation or the beginning of conditioning, when there is still some yeast in suspension.

There will be no outward sign to tell you when your lager is ready, so just take a guess, but don't be afraid to give it plenty of time. If you're lagering in bottles, be sure to leave the bottles at room temperature for a couple of weeks to allow the yeast to carbonate, which can also serve as a diacetyl rest. If you condition before bottling, the cold lagering temperatures will drop out the yeast, so you may need to add fresh yeast for bottle conditioning.

FILTRATION

Filtration is just a means of hastening what would happen anyway given sufficient time. Homebrewers aren't usually in a big hurry and there's no financial pressure to turn over the tanks and keep the beer moving out the door. So, filtration is something that's not often used by us nanoscale brewers. Good thing, too, because filters are expensive, troublesome, and a likely source for infections if not handled very carefully.

What's more, removing the yeast from beer actually strips away some protective effects. Yeast is an excellent oxygen scavenger, and helps beer from becoming oxidized. There's also something to be said for a product that's still a living thing. It will continue to age gracefully and evolve into different forms, much more elegant than a filtered product.

The other thing about filtration is that there are huge trade-offs, making it hard to come up with an ideal solution. A loose filtration may leave bacteria and some yeast in suspension, and can't do anything about chemical haze. Tight filtration can remove all the offending molecules, but it's going to take some color as well as body- and head-forming proteins with it.

For homebrewers who do wish to filter their beer, the type of plastic pad filters used by winemakers are perhaps the most common. Polypropylene cartridges that fit standard filter housings can also be used. The best choices for pore size are 1 micron and 0.5 micron. Both will remove yeast; the tighter filter will do a better job on haze, but may possibly strip a little protein and color out, although these effects are slight at this size. The size needed for sterile filtration is 0.2 micron, but this will remove a lot of body, head, and color.

For homebrewers wishing to speed up clarification of their beer, finings are easier to use and suit our needs better. See the Finings section on page 220 for details.

This Bass Pale Ale is more than 100 years old. Some strong beers can age gracefully for decades under good cellar conditions.

PACKAGING *and* SERVING YOUR BEER

Now we come to a fork in the road, as your batch needs to find a home either in a keg or a bottle. Most new brewers choose the bottle route, as the initial startup cost is much lower. Bottles have advantages, too. They're more portable and convenient, and it's great to have a stash with lots of different beers in bottles so you can enjoy them over time, especially with strong beers. Draft beer requires a more elaborate setup, including regulator, hoses, kegs, and more, and it is more cumbersome to haul around. The big advantage is ease of use. Just one big package and some hoses to clean, then transfer the beer, toss it in the fridge, hook it up to gas, and wait a week. It's much less tedious than the washing, sanitizing, rinsing, capping, and rinsing again for every one of the fifty-three bottles that constitutes a batch.

Of course, it's not an either/or situation. You can split a batch in all kinds of ways, and you can also fill bottles, growlers, or mini-kegs from the draft line to bring to parties, although these beers may be less stable than bottle-conditioned beer.

CAPPING IT OFF: BOTTLING

Bottled homebrew is normally bottle conditioned. A measured amount of corn sugar or dry malt extract is mixed with a small amount of water and boiled to form a thin syrup. This is added back to the finished beer as it is transferred to a bottling bucket, ideally with a spigot near the bottom, and gently stirred to make sure it is dissolved. After that, a bottling wand with a spring-loaded valve on the bottom is used to fill the bottles, and a capper applies some force to the crowns, crimping their edges around the lip on the bottle.

The amount of sugar needed depends on a number of things. First, how much carbonation is desired? Every style of beer has a certain amount of sparkle, from the *cremant* kiss of English cask ale to the blowzy fizz of hefeweizen and Belgian ales. Brewers talk about this dissolved gas in terms of volumes of CO_2, which literally means that a single volume of CO_2 gas would fill a particular volume (like a bottle) by itself, but in the case of carbonated liquids is actually dissolved in the liquid. Europeans measure grams of CO_2 per liter, a number about double the volume.

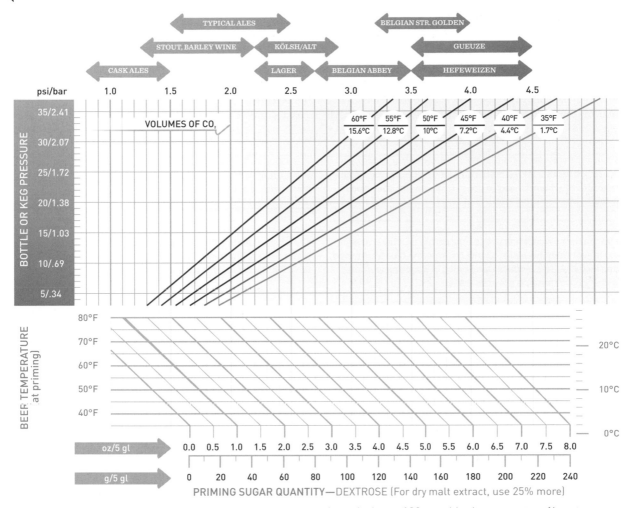

This chart shows the interplay of pressure, temperature, sugar quantity, and volume of CO_2, resulting in a vast range of beer types.

The top part of this chart shows carbonation ranges for a few major beer types. Below that is a pressure-times-volume chart. The intersection of a CO_2, volume and a diagonal temperature line can be read across to the left to give an approximate pressure. The bottom section is for finding the quantity of sugar needed to reach a given volume level. Read the vertical volume line down until it intersects with the beer temperature in the fermenter, then follow diagonally to get to the sugar content. Temperature is a factor here because more CO_2 from the original fermentation will be dissolved in colder wort, meaning less sugar will be needed to reach any given carbonation volume.

BOTTLING STEP-BY-STEP

This is the basic method used for homebrew bottle conditioning. Make sure the beer is finished with fermentation. The surface should be clear, and the beer should have a deep, transparent appearance, like black coffee, not café au lait. Check the final gravity with a hydrometer; it should be somewhere less than 25 to 30 percent of original gravity, depending on the beer. This is a disaster check to make sure the yeast didn't crap out with work still to do. Too much remaining sugar can mean exploding bottles once the revived yeast gets at it.

1

Prepare bottles by soaking them in a non-caustic alkaline cleaner, then sanitizing them. Chlorine needs to be rinsed; other types may not.

2

Set up the beer for racking, placing the carboy on a table or a stand higher than the vessel to which the beer will be transferred, tilting it slightly by placing a small block of wood or something under one edge to support it at an angle.

3

Sanitize the bottling bucket, hose, racking cane, and tip, as well as the bottling wand. Follow the closed-transfer method earlier on page 221 but place a few ounces (about 100 ml) into a clean saucepan; add the required quantity of sugar from the recipe or the preceding priming and carbonation chart, then bring to a boil, hold for 10 minutes, and add back to the beer to be bottled. If this is a strong beer or a well-lagered lager, it might be helpful to add fresh yeast. Dry yeast is okay, but rehydrate before adding it to the sugar mix. Half a packet should be plenty.

4

Move the rest of the beer to the bottling bucket. Check to make sure the valve on the bucket is closed before starting. When the sugar solution is cooled, it can be added and gently stirred into the beer. Try not to splash. Clean and put away the racking cane—you're done with it for now.

5

Move the carboy out of the way and put the full bottling bucket where the carboy was.

6

Sanitize the caps and drain, rinsing if necessary, and put them in a handy spot for bottling. Set up the capper slightly off to one side under the bottling bucket. It helps to have enough room on the table for at least half the bottles at one time.

7

Connect the sanitized hose and the bottling wand to the bottling bucket valve and start to fill the bottles. If you have someone to assist, you can set up an assembly line. Otherwise, fill a small batch, cap them, and then move them out of the way.

8

Rinse the bottles when capped, as a little beer always seems to spill. Write a code number and an abbreviation for the style on the cap.

9

Place the bottles in at least as warm a place as where you've been fermenting the beer—warmer, in the case of lagers. Carbonation should take a week, possibly two. (Put one beer into a plastic soda bottle so you can check pressure by squeezing; then drink that one first.) Enjoy!

Like it or not, science has shown that a great impression does make the beer taste better. This appetizing little setup was created and photographed by Mike Williams of Leeds, UK.

BOTTLE TYPES

Bottles should be crimp-on, not twist-offs as they don't seal as well. Heavy returnable bottles are great if you can find them. Sometimes it's nice to fill some champagne bottles for parties.

CAP CLOSURES
A twist-off bottle, left, and crimp-on, right. Try not to use the twist-off type, as they don't seal well.

CHAMPAGNE BOTTLES
Be sure to use American-style bottles that fit a standard 26-mm crown cap. European ones take a larger 29-mm cap that probably won't work with your capper unless you are Belgian or just a very geeky person. Some cappers have interchangeable crimping dies to handle different cap sizes.

CRIMP-ON BEER BOTTLES
Any of these are great. Small bottles, if you can find them, are great for strong beer.

SWING TOP
These make a nicer presentation, and seal well as long as the gaskets aren't worn out and compressed.

"CORK & CAGE" BOTTLES
Corks have the true old-school look, but require special equipment to compress the cork into the narrow neck to make a good seal. Plastic corks are available, but only fit some champagne-style bottles.

5-L MINI-KEG
These are meant for commercial beer but can work fine for homebrewing. They can be primed just like bottles or filled from a keg. CO_2 dispenser systems are available.

THE DELIGHTS *of* KEGGING

Many of us get impatient with the tedium of bottling after a year or two and start thinking about kegging our beers instead. It's a serious investment, but it delivers what it promises—great homebrew without the hassle of cleaning and filling bottles.

The standard for homebrewers is the 5-gallon/19-L stainless soda keg, but larger and smaller sizes exist. Two companies made these vessels: Champion and Cornelius; it's the latter that was adopted by homebrewers with the slang "Corny." You can buy new Cornys, but for now there are still used kegs available. All the parts are available from homebrew suppliers, so you can easily swap out or replace missing parts if you run across one at a flea market or yard sale. See the Keg and Draft Systems section on page 189 for more information.

Like any beer container, kegs and parts need to be well cleaned and sanitized before every use. Normal brewery cleaning materials are fine for this. Once clean and reassembled, hook up the gas line and fill the tank with CO_2. Then the beer can simply be racked into the tank and the hatch snapped shut. Always double-check that the quick-disconnect tank fittings are fully tightened. If not, you can force your whole batch out the loose fitting. It's another one of those ask-me-how-I-know moments.

Besides the Corny keg, you will need a source of CO_2 gas. The gas tanks actually hold CO_2 in liquid form, which means the tanks can hold quite a lot. There are several different sizes, from 2- to 50-pound/1- to 23-kg capacities. Either steel or aluminum is fine, but the aluminum ones are lighter and look spiffier. Both need to be hydro tested every five years and the date stamped into the metal on the shoulder. Larger tanks are more economical to fill and of course last longer, but smaller ones are easier to haul to parties. A 10-pound/4.5-kg tank is a good compromise. One thing about the valves—gas bottle valves are designed to seal both when opened and when closed (and not in between), so when you open it, twist the valve tightly all the way open.

I should mention again that a full gas tank has as much potential energy stored in it as a small bomb, so be careful when handling, and especially transporting. Tanks are designed to work in the upright position, so don't lay them down or you may get liquid CO_2 shooting through your system, and nobody's going to be happy about that. Pressure is typically several hundreds of psi/20 bar plus, and will remain the same until the liquid is gone, which means there is very little CO_2 left. Checking by weight is the best method to determine fill level; tanks are marked with a tare, or empty, weight. Just subtract this from the total weight and that's how much CO_2 is remaining.

"Siphon" jugs similar to this are still made, but you can't beat the charm of the classics.

The "Carbo-Cap" from Liquid Bread allows beer to be force-carbonated in common PET soda bottles for easy transport to parties and events when you don't want to haul a draft system.

CARBONATING IN THE KEG

The next thing is to carbonate the beer. Kegs can be primed and naturally carbonated, just like a big bottle, but this leaves a slug of yeast on the bottom. Those who do this usually cut 1 inch/2.5 cm or so off the liquid dip tube to avoid pulling up the yeast. Most of us skip the mess and just toss the keg in the fridge, hook it up to the gas, set the pressure to 12 psi/0.83 bar, and wait a week or so.

Does it matter whether you use natural or forced carbonation? No, not really. Gas solubility is a physical, not a chemical, process; gas is gas, no matter how it gets there. Beer connoisseurs prefer natural carbonation because it usually means freedom from two things that negatively impact beer flavor: filtration and pasteurization. Your beer, even if force-carbonated, probably is alive and unfiltered.

You can use the same CO_2 volume and pressure chart to figure out how much pressure to apply at what temperature. Gas is more soluble at lower temperatures, so in general, carbonation goes fastest at low temperatures. It is possible to speed things up instead of waiting a week by applying higher pressure and/or by shaking the vessel or using a carbonating stone, the same type that you may have used to aerate your wort.

If I'm in a hurry, I will set my regulator pressure to 50 or 60 psi/3.45 or 4.14 bar and come back in 24 hours, release the pressure, set the regulator back to its normal 12 psi/0.83 bar and check the beer. It usually needs more carbonation, so I repeat and check it again in 12 to 24 hours. Usually, by the second day, I'm set. When dealing with higher-than-normal pressures, make sure your hoses can handle it. It's also best to leave your liquid lines disconnected when force carbonating.

Another trick is shaking. Lay the keg on its side on the floor with the gas fitting at the bottom. Turn on the gas and lift the other end to get the liquid rocking back and forth. Every time you move the keg, you'll hear the gas hissing; that's the sound of CO_2 flowing in as it's dissolving in the beer. Do this for ten minutes, check the pressure, try again, until you get where you want. It's a pain, but you can get that keg to the party. Tonight.

A carbonating "stone" is how most breweries do it. We can use the small, finely sintered (0.5 micron) stainless stone that also serves as an oxygenator. The best way to use the stone is with a special Corny hatch that has a gas fitting on top and a line going to the bottom where the stone can be connected. If you're building one, be sure to use stiff tubing or weight it so the stone doesn't float to the top when charged with gas. You'll want to start the pressure low, maybe 1 or 2 psi/0.07 or 0.14 bar, and increase it slowly every couple of hours, bleeding off the pressure from the top every time you do. This should get your beer carbonated in a couple of days or slightly longer. When the carbonating is done, the special hatch can be swapped out for a standard one.

SERVING DRAFT BEER

Serving is just a matter of hooking up a hose and a tap. If you do it like most of us, without much thought, you will probably have your share of foamy beer. To serve draft beer in good condition, you have to get comfortable with system balancing. This is the foundation of good draft-system practice. What it means is that the pressure on the beer in the keg must match the resistance created by the tubing and valves of the dispense system. On the surface, liquid seems to run through hoses pretty freely, but actually there is a good bit of friction between the liquid and the tube wall; the smaller the tube, the greater the restriction.

Because we're pouring from a keg that's just in the fridge, homebrewers typically don't need very long lines. But a short line makes for too little restriction, which means we're standing there squirting glasses of foam. There are a couple of solutions: One is to use a longer piece of tubing and make it the smallest diameter draft line available—3/16 inch/5 mm. The following table gives an idea of the restrictive properties of hose and various fittings, so we can just add them up and come up with the tubing length. If in doubt, start with a longer length, and cut it down until you find the perfect balance. It should be obvious that every carbonation level requires rebalancing the system.

DRAFT-LINE TUBING AND ITS RESTRICTION PRESSURES

Type	Size		Restriction	
VINYL	3/16 inch/4.76 mm ID*	3 psi/ft		0.68 bar/M
VINYL	1/4 inch/6.35 mm ID	0.85 psi/ft		0.19 bar/M
VINYL	5/16 inch/7.93 mm ID	0.4 psi/ft		0.09 bar/M
STAINLESS	1/4 inch/6.35 mm OD**	1.2 psi/ft		0.27 bar/M

Note: These are generalized numbers; your supplier may have different values for the type of tubing they sell. Gravity adds 0.5 psi per foot/0.30 meter of vertical travel.

* Inside dimension
** Outside dimension

Some tap heads have an adjustment that helps vary flow, and this helps with fine-tuning. But there's no substitute for a well-balanced system. Another neat trick is to use one or two plastic epoxy mixer tubes, shoved in the liquid dip tube of the keg. These are basically dual spiral tracks that provide a lot of back pressure to give you a good amount of restriction in a compact form, perhaps 6 psi/0.41 bar per 6-inch/15-cm mixer. They are available cheap from industrial suppliers like McMaster-Carr (part number 74695A58).

The Brewers Association has a very detailed *Draught Beer Quality Manual* available as a free PDF on their website if you want more information.

Once you have the beer in a keg, you may want to put some of it into a bottle—some of us are never content! You can make this simple or complicated. If you just want to fill up a jug to take to a party, then you can do what they do in brewpubs. Just stick a piece of tubing on the end of the tap and shoot the beer into the container. I find it helpful to turn the regulator pressure down to about 2 psi/0.14 bar and bleed the keg, giving just enough pressure to push the beer out of the keg and into the jug. A 12-inch/30-cm piece of ⅜-inch-/ 10-mm-diameter stainless tube fits nicely into the opening on a plastic "cobra" tap. Cutting one end off at a 45-degree angle helps the beer flow easily into the container. Chances are you will get some foam, so you'll have to top up to get a full jug. How long will tap-filled jugs last? In the words of one Chicago pro brewer, "It's like milk, not like wine," meaning it will remain drinkable for a week or so, not much longer.

PET soda bottles (anything but root beer or grape!) work fine, and have the advantage that you don't have to haul them back home. A special cap called a Carbo-Cap is available with a Corny gas fitting that allows you to attach the gas line and re-pressurize. There are also plans online to make your own using a tire-filling Schrader valve. These setups are great for instantly carbonating beer. Just fill and cap, hook up the gas, invert the bottle, and shake the hell out of it. After some practice, you'll get a sense of how to gauge beer carbonation by the tautness of the bottle.

A piece of ⅜-inch-/10-mm-diameter stainless tube with the end trimmed at an angle can make filling growlers easier. It fits nicely inside of a standard "cobra" tap valve.

COUNTER-PRESSURE BOTTLING

A counter-pressure filler is designed to purge the bottle of air using CO_2, then fill under pressure to prevent foaming and preserve carbonation.

Counter-pressure filling is more complicated, but the beer will not have the yeast in the bottle that results from bottle conditioning. In addition to a liquid inlet, counter-pressure fillers use CO_2 to purge the bottle with gas before filling, reducing the oxygen in the package. Specifics vary from model to model, but the general scheme is to purge the bottle with CO_2 and then, under pressure, start the liquid flow. When pressure equalizes, the flow will stop. At this point a vent valve is opened (or the rubber stopper sealing the bottle is tilted or "burped"), bleeding off a little pressure and allowing more beer to flow. This is repeated until the bottle is full, then the filler is withdrawn and a cap applied, sometimes waiting until the foam rises to the top, expelling much of the remaining air.

CELLARING YOUR BEER

Most beer is meant to be consumed fresh. That's one of the benefits of brewing your own: you know exactly how old it is and how it has been handled, and that you're drinking it at its peak of perfection. For beers under about 6 percent alcohol, they're ready as soon as they clear out and you can get them bottled and carbonated, a process that will normally take four to six weeks, perhaps a bit longer at the stronger end. As the beer gets stronger, more time is required. Lagers, because they're fermented cool, take perhaps half again as long.

Really strong beers like barley wines can taste great when they're two or three months old, as long as you love a face full of resiny hops and sticky caramel malt—and many of you do, I know. But cellaring transforms an unruly young barley wine into an elegant and refined tipple. In barley wine's heyday, the beer then known as "October" beer was routinely aged for a year or two before being consumed. Stronger beers were aged for decades.

During an extended aging, several things happen. Hop bitterness decreases and the more green and edgy aspects of their aroma fades. Fruity, estery aromas fade as well. Protein complexes gradually settle out, making them less dense on the palate. The beer dries out and becomes more wine-like on the palate, but at the same time malt aroma becomes more intense, perhaps because other aromas are reduced. Some aged and oxidized flavors develop and, if the beer's a good one, these will be nutty and some leather-like rather than cardboardy. As Sierra Nevada's Ken Grossman said about aged Bigfoot, "It's a different beer, but it's still good." After a decade, old beers can develop some umami, even soy sauce flavors, as the yeast falls apart and releases amino acids into the beer. Beers on the yeast age much better than those without.

Suitable beer styles to age include barley wines, imperial stouts, and strong ales, and if dosed with *Brettanomyces claussenii* and given some oak to chew on, a proper old ale can be created. Other beers with *Brettanomyces* are often aged because that yeast is a slow-acting critter that may take many months to develop full flavor.

Appropriate cellar conditions are the same for any beverage: cool, constant temperatures 50 to 65°F/10 to 18°C, with moderate humidity. More important than a specific temperature is absence of frequent temperature swings, which can tire out a beer rapidly.

The chart on the facing page will give you some idea of what to expect. A 10 percent or stronger barley wine can easily last a decade or more. I have tasted beer from 1958 that I wouldn't have guessed was more than ten years old, and one from 1938 that was pretty much a ghost but still had some beer-like qualities.

San Diego homebrewer and wood-crafter Brian Mertz makes beautiful bottle-shaped tap handles.

WOOD- *and* BARREL-AGED BEERS

Now we are entering the category of extended techniques, which can be fun to play around with and can result in some stunning beers, though you do have to be careful. Aging in oak can add lush aromas of vanilla and toasted coconut or, in the worst circumstances, some harsh, woody, and astringent notes.

Barrels are cool, there's no denying that. But they're large and demand a lot of attention, so they're probably best as a club activity, or as someone's main brewing focus. The standard size for wine and bourbon is 50 gallons/190 L; if you want a smaller one, you'll have to buy it new, which means it will be pretty harsh and raw, better for taming a huge cabernet rather than a poor defenseless beer. Also, the surface-area-to-volume ratio is really good in the full-size barrel; smaller barrels mean too much wood contact.

Assuming you can deal with 50 gallons/190 L, there are two routes to go with barrels: bourbon or wine. Bourbon barrels have mature, vanilla aromas that are best with big beers like barley wines and imperial stouts. The resiny component of wood, called *lignin*, is transformed over time into vanillin, which flavors the bourbon, and now the beer. Barrels are fairly sterile as well, because of the high-proof alcohol they hold for three years or more.

The other use for barrels is wild-fermented beers. The wood is an ideal habitat for *Brettanomyces* and other wild yeast and bacteria, and wood's porosity to air means there's a trickle of oxygen coming in, which is also beneficial to the wild stuff.

BEER STORAGE TIME AND SHELF LIFE

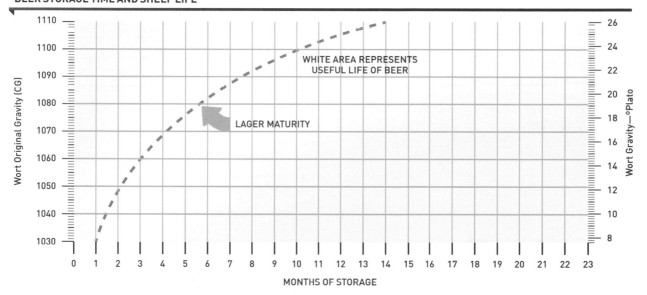

Many factors play into a beer's drinkability over time, as aging processes alter its taste and chemical makeup.

Either way, barrels need to be as fresh as possible, because when they dry out, they get leaky. A solution of potassium metabisulfite can be used to sweeten barrels. The common winemaking technique of a flaming sulfur wick should *never* be used in bourbon barrels, as the alcohol vapors inside can explode. I know one brewer who was on crutches for months from such an accident.

For bourbon-barrel beers, strong beer should be aged in the barrel for six months to a year, then kegged or bottled using fresh yeast. Sometimes brewers blend the aged beer with some fresh beer for a more subtle result. Another technique, borrowed from sherry wine, is called *solera*, in which only a portion is removed and replaced with fresh beer, so the batch grows more complex, year by year. Soleras may work out especially well for lambic and sour brown Belgian ales, as the complexity can grow as time passes.

If you want to make a bourbon-aged beer without the muss and fuss, you can start right now. Get some finger-size pieces of white oak, char them deeply with a torch, then drop them into a bottle of not-too-expensive bourbon. Allow these to age for a year, at which time you'll have some oak sticks you can add to a beer in the carboy during conditioning, along with some mighty fine bourbon to drink. I've currently got an experiment going with tequila and mesquite chunks; time will tell if that was a brilliant idea or a bust. In a pinch, there's nothing wrong with adding a shot or two of bourbon to your beer and skipping the more complicated technique. I promise not to tell anybody.

Oak cubes, spirals, and other forms are available, normally used for winemaking. These should all be used with a light touch, as even deeply toasted oak can have some pretty harsh flavors. From what I've tasted, it makes sense to add the wood chunks or cubes as early in the fermentation process as possible, as yeast activity seems to speed up the lignin-to-vanillin transformation and soften the harsh oaky flavors.

Facing page, row by row from top left: Homebrew labels by Fantastic Mykel, Dave Gallagher, Jim LaFleur, Łukasz Szynkiewicz, Szymon Tracz, Matteo Pellis/Alberto Bodritti, Mark McDermott, Kim Leshinski, Kim Leshinski, Matteo Pellis/Alberto Bodritti, Mark McDermott, and Jason McLaughlin.

KILL A MOCKINGBIRD

UNTING SAISON

ABV 5%
VOL 500 ml

BREWED BY RILEY'S
CRAFTED BY HAND

BEAR DOWN
BLACK IPA

HIGH WATER BREWERY

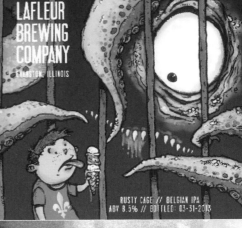

LAFLEUR BREWING COMPANY
EVANSTON, ILLINOIS

RUSTY CAGE // BELGIAN IPA
ABV 8.5% / BOTTLED: 03-31-2013

w stylu
and Pale Ale

a nr 25
a: 06.01.14
ane: 27.01.14

: 13.5 BLG
5.6% ABV
ca: 48 IBU

POCZWÓRNY NELSON

new zealand pale ale
single hop nelson sauvin

Skład:
Woda, słody: Pilzner
Monachijski II, Pa
Bursztynowy, Pszen
chmiel Nelson S
drożdże Safale U

ČESKA JEDENÁCTKA
-2014-

SIKORKA

BROWER

11,5 Blg
4,5% alk.

SHEE.P.A.

ENGLISH
INDIA
PALE ALE

33 cl e
alc. 6,3 % vol
OG 1063
BU 70

10-12

IME GROWN
ALE

RTHERN BREWER HOPS
FOR A TRUER TRIP.

HAIL TO THE ALE

BATCH No: 6
BOTTLED: 05-12
INGREDIENTS AND LIVE FROM CHICAGO, IL.
BREWED WITH ALL NATURAL, LOCALLY SOURCED
ABV: 8%

la Poire

A PEAR & FRENCH OAK SOAKED SUMMER SAISON

HAIL TO THE ALE

Not
Your Honey

PECORA NER

A
IM
S

33 cl
alc. 9
OG
BU

КРАПУТНИК
Советские Республика Толстопиве

Цховорядческий русский имперский
Толстовое пиво теперь Заварен к потреб-
ностям работнико.

DOUBLE CHOCOLATE
BROWNIE STOUT

CHAPTER

7

The Art and Science
OF THE
RECIPE

It is possible to make perfectly palatable beers by carefully following the directions of a kit.

We all start this way. Many delightfully memorable beers have been created by this method. But once you've got a few beers under your belt (or are a few belts into your beer), you may feel the urge to put a little more of yourself into your brews. If beer is art, how long can one be happy with paint-by-numbers?

Because of its technical nature, scratch brewing may be a little intimidating. That's why most people, even when making their own recipes, will look at some existing recipes to get a sense of proportion and to see how different beers are put together. Use a recipe as a framework that you can tear down to build something more personal in its place. This book is stuffed with recipes for just such purposes.

Building a recipe, like the rest of the brewing process, is a mix of fussy technical details and artistic vision; you really can't have great beer without both. Brewing is a very good way to give both hemispheres of your brain a real workout.

Beer is not just a faceless factory product anymore. Beer is art, a communication of the most intimate and profound sort. In my view, just a few short years ago this idea would have been laughable. At its best, it is a noble, delicious, and treasured beverage, the equal of any other form of liquid pleasure on Earth. Now it's your turn to conjure up something wonderful.

THINKING THROUGH YOUR GOALS

Before a recipe can be created, you need to ask a few questions. What's the purpose of it? Who will drink it? What is its relationship to the seasons? Is it a temporary passion or adding to your life's work? Does it answer some questions about ingredients, process, or history? Will it battle in the judging arena, or just rock the party? What sort of mood should it invoke? Is this beer about seduction, sedition, whimsy, or preordained destiny? Or none of the above?

And if your mind is a completely blank slate, then think back to some memorable beer experiences or flip through the recipes in this book or elsewhere to light the fuse.

Create a virtual beer in your head. We're overwhelmingly visual creatures, so picture it in living color, in a perfect glass, beads of condensation slowly trekking down the sides. Think about the aroma, perhaps some creamy caramel, maybe a whiff of toast, cut by a pine forest's worth of resiny hops and a dab of grapefruit. And the taste? Cool, then sweet and malty, then the clean bitterness of hops, building to a crescendo, tapering to a lingering, happy aftertaste. Yum. Now all you have to do is figure out how to make it happen.

This is where being a good taster really pays off. Having the chops to identify and give names to the dozens of flavors identifiable in beer creates a cabinet of virtual ingredients you can swap in and out with your nimble mind until a promising profile is conjured up. Then, it's just a matter of making it happen for real.

This visualization doesn't have to be purely mental. You can actually do some daydreaming in a glass by mixing different commercial beers together, and if the concept calls for it, spiking them with tinctures made of spices and other flavorings, until you arrive at a close approximation of the beer you'd like to brew. Think of it as rapid prototyping. It's helpful if you have some idea of how these blending beers are brewed, so dig up as much information as you can. Don't forget to take notes on the mixtures and quantities you use.

Dig out your tasting vocabulary, and maybe even some brewing ingredients, and start thinking about the major components of base malts and the specialty malts that will create the personality of the beer. Do remember that however developed our inner vocabulary is, it's usually not as nuanced and vivid as the real thing, so it's easy to get into a rut of thinking, for example, that all crystal malts or corianders taste more or less the same. Taste everything, all the time. This is a habit of successful brewers.

I usually start with the grain bill, but it's possible to start with the hops, the spice mixture, or any other defining characteristic. When thinking about the malt, try to define the signature malt character you would like to taste in your beer, and build the recipe around it. But whatever you do, don't add any ingredient out of habit. Make every decision a conscious choice.

You can aim for a symphony of malty flavors, balancing of rich warming maltiness with a whiff of sharp roastiness to create a balanced old ale or Scotch ale, for example. Or chunk up the austere purity of Pilsner malt with

A recipe always starts with a target concept: How do you want the beer to taste? Whether you take that target from a published style profile, from a desire to clone a commercial example, from a food pairing, or from a crazy idea that popped into your head, you still have to be able to envision and describe that final product. Then every choice you make in recipe formulation is based on getting to that point.

GORDON STRONG, Grand Master BJCP judge; three-time winner, AHA Ninkasi Award; and author of *Brewing Better Beer*

an overlay of Munich or Vienna. Maybe you want to do as one brewer did after hearing me rant on the subject, and put some of every kind of malt he could find into the beer and just be done with it. *That's* complex! The possibilities are endless, so it helps to have a plan. And it makes better beer.

INTEGRATING INGREDIENTS
and PROCESS

A beer's character is dependent not only on its ingredients. Brewing is all about process. Mash temperature and dilution have effects on attenuation. The mashing schedule also affects proteins in ways that have consequences for head retention and body. Various ingredients respond differently to the mashing process, so understanding each grain type will lead you to certain decisions depending on what's desired in the finished beer. That's why it's so important to match material and method.

For the most part, modern malt responds well to simple, single-step infusion mashes, so stick with this and you're safe. If you're digging up ancient recipes like decoctions from the catacombs, be aware that ingredients change and those old techniques won't give good results with most modern malts. A protein rest, for example, can change the perfect balance of proteins so carefully created by the maltster, resulting in a dearth of head- and body-forming mid-length proteins in the finished beer, so skip this step unless you're sure you need it.

The converse is also true. It's lovely to work with a traditional witbier grist with its unmalted wheat and oats, but it is highly dependent on a mashing procedure that brings the unmalted grain close to the boiling point. Even a step mash won't yield all that much in terms of extract and the creamy mouthfeel that is such an important part of the style. So look carefully at those old recipes and processes and make sure they are working together effectively.

Yeast and the way it's handled has an enormous impact on a beer's personality, so choose carefully and treat it well.

Will this beer or recipe piss off Garrett Oliver? Then I know I'm onto something.

NICK FLOYD, founder and chief dungeonmaster, Three Floyds Brewing, Munster, IN

Formulating a recipe is as much a thinking process as it is a feeling process. In my view, intuition is always at the start of a new recipe. Then you can put on your thinking cap and start doing the brew-technical math to nail down the brew's specifications and process parameters.

SABINE WEYERMANN, Weyermann Malting, Bamberg, Germany

RECORD KEEPING

All the details that will have a noticeable impact on the character of the finished beer may seem unforgettable in the moment; but I assure you that you will forget them by the time the beer is ready to drink. That's why it's a very good idea to write down as much detail as you can along the way. Brewing software will do it for you. The basic worksheet here can help structure the information and prompt you for the necessary information. A PDF version is available at www.chroniclebooks.com/masteringhomebrew.

Worksheet Instructions

TARGETS

Here is where you record target parameters, such as the OG (the density of the wort before fermentation begins), the alcohol content of the finished beer (in percent by volume), and the attenuation (the thoroughness of fermentation). Also record your target MCU (Malt Color Units, which use the °L of each grain multiplied by pounds, and a total added of all malt additions), and the SRM, meaning the color of the beer in the U. S. "Standard Reference Method." If you start with this number, go to the color chart on page 258 to find the corresponding MCU number and use that as a target for malt color in your recipe.

MASH TIME AND TEMPERATURE

Record time and temperature at intervals during the mash; connect the dots for a complete record. Decoctions are usually recorded with a dotted line. Record your start time at the bottom.

WATER

Record water quantity and treatment information here. If you removed any carbonate ions, mark in the "Boil & Decant" section. "Stand" is where you note the time water sat to allow free chlorine to evaporate. Use the "Filter" section to record whether the brewing water was filtered and if so, what type of filtration was performed. Next to "Other," record any other type of water treatment such as the addition of mineral salts.

MASH TYPE

Note specifics of strike water, temperature, and other mash and boil parameters here. Next to "Rest Temp," record your initial mash temperature. Next to "Diff," note the difference between your strike water temperature and the initial rest temperature of your mash. Use the "Decoc" sections to record quantities removed and boiled during decoctions. If you're measuring pH, record the mash resting pH in the "Mash pH" section, and record the wort pH (taken at the end of the boil) next to "Wort pH." Use the "Boil Start Time" to note the time it took for a full boil to develop. "Boil Length" is where you note the total boiling time. Next to "Irish Moss," note whether kettle finings such as Irish moss are used and if so, what quantity.

GRAINS AND ADJUNCTS

Use this section to include information about all grains and other fermentables. Below "%," list the percentage of each ingredient in the grain bill. Include all sugars and other fermentables as well. Below "Qty," list the quantity for each grain bill ingredient. For "Gravity," list the gravity contribution expected from each ingredient. Most homebrewers get between 70 and 85 percent of the potential extract and this efficiency must be taken into account when estimating gravity (see Gravity Calculations, page 255). Under "Malt/Grains/Adjunct @ %," list the corresponding ingredient. Under "Eff," make a note of the expected efficiency of the mash, used to help calculate the expected wort gravity. Under "G," "@CLR," and "CU":"G" is used to indicate grind; if your mill has a marked setting, write the setting used in this space. The "@CLR" space should be used to record the malt/grain color. "CU" is Color Units, the grain color is °L times pounds (or °EBC times kg if you're using the metric system). The two lines at the bottom of this section are used to calculate color. Add up the total malt color units (color in °L times pounds) for each grain, then add them up at the bottom of the column. Then, divide by the number of gallons to get a total MCU for the brew. Next, using the chart on page 258, find the SRM color that corresponds to your MCU, and make a note of it. You can work backward as well. Choose the color in SRM you would like to end up with, then use the same chart to find the MCU number corresponding to it, and make a note of it. Then, as you work out your grain bill, you will use your different malts to add color, typically using the darkest malt at the end of the calculation to make up for whatever color is still needed to achieve the MCU target.

HOPS

This section holds all information about hops and their usage. Use this to list any spices, herbs, or other flavorings as well. "@ ACID %" is alpha acid percentage and should be taken from the hops packages or, less accurately, from the numbers shows in the Hop Varieties in Detail section on page 86. "P/W" is where you indicate whether your hops are pellet or whole. BUs (Bitterness Units) are calculated from weight, alpha acid percentage, and utilization (see page 266). "Boil" is where you list the number of minutes of boiling for each hop addition. "Util Rate" is where you note the utilization rate expected for each hop addition. Add up the BUs from all the hop additions to get a total for the batch of beer and record next to "Total Estimated IBU."

FERMENT STAGE

This should be used to track the gravity of the beer before, during (if desired) and after fermentation. "Time" means time from start to fermentation. Original gravity chart on the left side can be used to translate gravity measurements and calculate alcohol. Don't forget to measure and record gravity when racking or bottling/kegging.

OTHER

Use this to make notes about the particulars of the yeast used and how it was handled. This section also can be used to keep track of priming and carbonation details. Next to "Yeast type/brand," note whether the yeast is dry or liquid; the manufacturer; and the brand or strain. Next to "Starter," indicate whether a yeast starter was used to grow up the yeast before pitching. In the "Priming" section, indicate the quantity and type of priming used to carbonate your beer when bottling. If you're kegging, this is a good place to make a note of CO_2 pressure, beer temperature, etc.

NAME

BEER STYLE

QTY

TARGETS			
OG	°P	Alcohol %/vol	Atten %
Color	Malt Color Units	SRM	
BU			

MASH TIME AND TEMPERATURE

TEMP °F

210							
200							
190							
180							
170							
160							
150							
140							
130							
120							
110							
100							
90							
80							
70							
60							
50							

TEMP °C

100 90 80 70 60 50 40 30 20 10

HOURS 0 1 2 3 4 5 6 7 8

START TIME

GRAINS AND ADJUNCTS

%	QTY	GRAVITY	MALT/GRAINS/ADJNCTS @ %	Eff.	G	@CLR	CU

MCU ◀ ÷ No. gals ◀

▲ ▲ ▲ TOTALS ↻ Corrected ➡ SRM

WATER

TREATMENT   Boil & Decant

Filter   Stand

Other

MASH TYPE

TOTAL lbs

STRIKE WATER QTY

qt/lb   @   °F/°C

– REST TEMP   – DIFF

DECOC 1

DECOC 2

MASH pH   WORT pH

BOIL START TIME

BOIL LENGTH

IRISH MOSS?

HOPS

QTY	oz/g	HOP VARIETY	@ ACID %	P/W	BOIL	UTIL RATE	BU

TOTAL ESTIMATED IBU

ORIGINAL GRAVITY

ALCOHOL POTENTIAL (%)

0	1000	0
1	1010	1, 2, 3
2	1020	4, 5
3	1030	6, 7
4		8
5	1040	9, 10
6	1050	11, 12
7		13
8	1060	14, 15
9	1070	16, 17
10	1080	18, 19
11		20
12	1090	21, 22
13	1100	23, 24
14		25
15	1110	26

GRAVITY (°PLATO)

FERMENT STAGE	DATE	ORIGINAL GRAVITY	°PLATO	% ALCOHOL POTENTIAL	TEMP.	TIME	VESSEL
PRIMARY							
RACKED							
RACKED							
BOTTLED							
KEGGED							

OTHER

YEAST TYPE/BRAND	
STARTER	
PRIMING	

TASTE NOTES

CAP

CODE

ART _and the_ BREWER

However technical we get—and for many of us this can be very technical indeed—it's important to keep in mind that beer is supposed to be about pleasure. So when facing those many decisions, even though you've got your technical hat on, it's crucial to consider the purely hedonistic aspects of the beer: What would be the most delicious thing to do here?

Pleasure lives in the deepest recesses of the ancient, emotional parts of our brain, shaped by long-forgotten experiences and manifested by uncontrollable flashbacks of pleasure, familiarity, and, occasionally, dread: pretty scary stuff for an engineer but pure mother's milk to an artist.

Science, useful as it is, cannot define what makes a great beer. The cheapest mass-market lager is equal in quality to Bigfoot Barley Wine from the point of view of science, maybe better. Is this a point of view you can trust completely? Science serves the art of brewing, and no more. Without the direction given by well-conceived artistry, science is of little use. Art must have the plan, the direction. Art must lead the way.

I tell my students at the Siebel Institute that the proper role of an artist is to mess with people's heads. It's a flip statement, but it helps people understand that beer, like any art, is a conversation, with meaning, language, a time dimension, and plenty of cultural and personal references.

If you are of a more technical bent, all this art talk might make you a bit queasy, but a considerable body of rational thought has accrued over the centuries concerning the creation of art. Far from being a jumbled morass, art has its own set of methods, techniques, and logic, a science of sorts. If you study any art form, from carved stone to jazz improvisation, you will find that the same kinds of aesthetic considerations are at work.

I have spent thirty-five years in art and design, and have been brewing since 1985. In that time, I have learned a few things about how to put things together in a pleasing way, and the tools it takes to do so.

Artists exist in a precarious psychological state. An ego is required to create art, but to honestly deal with criticism in order to grow requires losing your ego-driven pride. Discovering you are sometimes mistaken is painful, but this is the essence of learning and growing. It is a fine balancing act. Always leave yourself open to the notion that sometimes you are a complete idiot.

Take risks, and sometimes things will go wrong; learn from your mistakes and move on. What the hell, it's just a batch of beer!

Art is a conversation, which means the audience is just as important as the artist. It is important to deal with the way our beer is sensed and perceived. We have to be highly attuned to the human interface—the physiological and psychological factors that are our pathways into the mind of our audience.

> _They should express the feelings of their creator: happiness, sadness, tranquility, or excitment; and also the feelings of the people of the place where it was created and consumed. When Frédéric Chopin composed the_ Polonaises, _especially the no. 6, his family had just been arrested in Poland, and the song reflects his anger. When Picasso painted_ Guernica, _a German officer visiting his exhibition asked why he painted such an ugly painting. Picasso's answer was: "You did this to my painting." That's how I try to make my beers._

MARCO FACONE, owner and brewmaster, Falke Bier, Belo Horizonte, Brazil

What do we have to work with? Plenty. Molecules in the beer latch on to receptors in the nose and mouth, firing off impulses that travel up through multiple processing centers until they reach various parts of the brain. Aroma and taste are wired into the ancient instinctive and emotional parts of the brain first, and somewhat less directly into cognitive centers where we may ponder their significance or put a name on them.

Because they interface with such primitive levels of the brain, aromas have the ability to directly stimulate powerful psychological responses, memories, and emotions. This provides us with incredible leverage for art and probably accounts for much of beer's appeal, but at the cost of being quite unpredictable from person to person.

In addition to aroma and taste, other physical sensations play a role in the perception of beer, like the mouthfeel sensations of carbonation, body, fullness, and temperature. Certain chemicals have other effects: the astringency of polyphenols, the oiliness contributed by high levels of diacetyl, and the eye-watering effect of too much ethyl acetate (a common ester).

Our eyes play a larger role than we would like to admit. Certain taste expectations are created by a beer's appearance: the light maltiness of a pale beer, the roastiness of a stout. When wine judges are given red-tinted white wine, a bouquet of bramble, mulberries, and cherries is perceived rather than pear, passionfruit, and gooseberry. It's really important to get the color right because it sets such strong expectations. Or, as with the new crop of black IPAs and witbiers circulating these days, one can play with and confound those expectations.

There are many interactions between our senses, a phenomenon known as synesthesia. It is plenty obvious that aroma and taste often come together to form a sensation of "flavor," but the true picture is far more complex, often in some pretty weird ways. America's beer Yoda, Fred Eckhardt, tells us to "Listen to our beer." This isn't just Fred's way of telling us to look at things from every unexpected angle; it actually has some basis in scientific fact. Strange as it is, our senses of hearing and smell are connected. Workers probing the olfactory centers of rats noticed a spike on the recording equipment when a wrench was dropped; further study confirmed the link. Careful studies of wine by Qantas Airlines showed that the roar of jet engines seriously degrades our ability to enjoy wine, just more of the mysterious baggage of perception we all live with.

Houston's Foam Rangers put on one of the best homebrewing weekends anywhere, the Dixie Cup Competition. Bev Blackwood has been doing these hilarious conference logos featuring Fred Eckhardt for years. Don't miss the Saturday morning barley wine tasting—come in your bathrobe.

As a brewer, your role doesn't end with the beer itself; it includes every aspect, from whatever style you call it, to the beer's name and niceties such as labels. Studies by the food industry show that the aura surrounding products can actually make them taste better, and my experience in the design world bears this out and points to the importance of a good presentation: beautiful beer, served at the right temperature, in a nice glass, and with a killer story. All that says you care; it draws people in and makes them look for the positive qualities of the beer, seeking the best experience.

KNOW YOUR AUDIENCE (AND YOURSELF)

Art is interactive. Consider your audience right now and how they will react. Beer is not marble sculpture; it will not endure until future generations can evolve to appreciate your opus. It happens right now, and then is gone forever. Timid or avant-garde, hophead homebrewers or regular folks at a wedding, it is important to consider their limits.

TELL STORIES

A beer with a great story involves people more than one without. Plus, it helps them remember the experience and tell their friends about it. If your audience can help participate in the story-making process, so much the better.

PUSH YOUR AUDIENCE

It's your duty as an artist! You don't want to put them off, but you do want to challenge them a little. That's part of what people like about art. It brings them to new places, conceptually, and challenges their status quo. Making a change in people is the core of the gratification we feel as artists. Surprise them. Take an elegant, pale strong ale and throw some chanterelles into it. Take a huge, inky imperial stout and lighten it up with some maple syrup. Do something unexpected.

I studied music composition as a kid and during my attempt at college. That work frames my whole worldview now. I think of beer recipes in terms of range, dynamics, timbre, counterpoint, polyphony, consonance, and dissonance.

TONY MAGEE, founder and so much more, Lagunitas Brewing Company, Petaluma, CA

THE TOOLS *of the* ART

Painters, poets, musicians, and all other artists will recognize many of the following ideas about making art. Different disciplines may have different vocabularies but the underlying principles remain the same: rhythm, harmony, contrast, coherence, voice. These are the dynamic elements of any art that come together to create a unified whole, tell a story, and, we hope, move our audience.

I hope the following notions demystify the artistic process and make it more manageable. Some are deeply philosophical; others are just cheap tricks. All are useful but don't feel you have to do everything in every beer. Rules are meant to be broken.

THE BIG IDEA

Creative artists are always looking for the biggest idea that can tie everything together. The visualization process is helpful here because it forces you to think about what is important before getting bogged down in the minutiae. I often write a sentence or two, the sort of copy that might end up on a label. If it takes more than this, it may be too unfocused. At this point, you don't need the complete specs; that can come later. A big idea doesn't need any specifics beyond the sensory or emotional experience it can offer, like these, for example:

- An IPA that smells like the desert (or may be dessert!)
- A Belgian stout with the texture of cappuccino
- A red beer that reminds people of roasting marshmallows over the campfire
- A brown ale with some of the flavors of a fine cigar
- A summer dark beer that is crisp and refreshing (think of mowing the lawn in the dark)
- A pale lager with the punch and concentration of an IPA
- A fruit beer for grown-ups

DISCRETION/ECONOMY

Get rid of things that don't contribute. Not sure? Toss it out. Don't be afraid to understate; sometimes a work of art needs a little room to breathe. It's an old art school trick—finish your composition, and then take one thing away. We all like lots of flavor, but it's easy to overdo it and make a beer that is a tiresome novelty. Does your Big Idea hit them over the head with a sledgehammer made of hops? If so, how good does the third pint really taste?

CONTRAST/TENSION

Normally we think of beer as having "balance," but I find this term too static for what's really going on in the glass. The drinker's attention constantly changes from one aspect to another, and it is this variety of focal points that makes a beer interesting. It all has to form a coherent whole, but it is a dynamic system, and it helps to think in terms of contrast or tension between various elements.

The normal balancing act of beer plays the bitterness of hops against the sweetness of malt. But by now you should know that malt can have a wide variety of flavors and aromas, and not all of them come down on the sweet side of the equation. The darker the malt, the more its flavors—sharp, roasty, and bitter—come down on the same side of the equation as hops, with sweeter, malty flavors coming from the paler malts.

It's quite common for three elements to compete for a drinker's attention—hops vs. sweet malt vs. toasty malt, for example—which makes for a much more interesting beer. Aromatic elements have the potential to add dozens more points of interest, so some attention must be paid to how this complicated picture is all put together.

COMMON FLAVOR BLOCKS AND THEIR COMPONENTS

Malt Flavor Blocks

Possible Components for Recipe

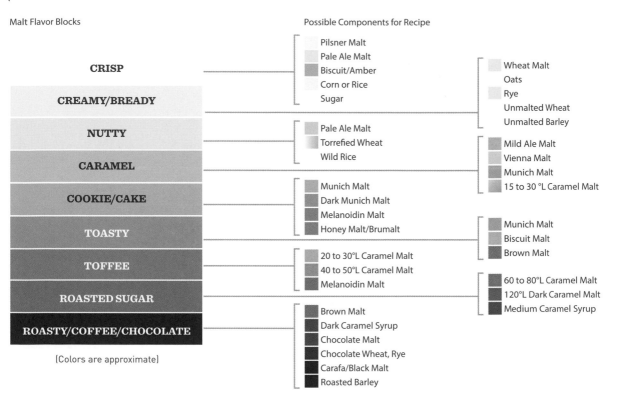

CRISP

CREAMY/BREADY

NUTTY

CARAMEL

COOKIE/CAKE

TOASTY

TOFFEE

ROASTED SUGAR

ROASTY/COFFEE/CHOCOLATE

(Colors are approximate)

Pilsner Malt
Pale Ale Malt
Biscuit/Amber
Corn or Rice
Sugar

Wheat Malt
Oats
Rye
Unmalted Wheat
Unmalted Barley

Pale Ale Malt
Torrefied Wheat
Wild Rice

Mild Ale Malt
Vienna Malt
Munich Malt
15 to 30 °L Caramel Malt

Munich Malt
Dark Munich Malt
Melanoidin Malt
Honey Malt/Brumalt

Munich Malt
Biscuit Malt
Brown Malt

20 to 30°L Caramel Malt
40 to 50°L Caramel Malt
Melanoidin Malt

60 to 80°L Caramel Malt
120°L Dark Caramel Malt
Medium Caramel Syrup

Brown Malt
Dark Caramel Syrup
Chocolate Malt
Chocolate Wheat, Rye
Carafa/Black Malt
Roasted Barley

Basic flavor categories combine to make up the complex taste of a beer. Note that some malt types can serve in more than one type of block. Additional blocks might be honey, raisin/dried fruit, cracker, and others, depending on the recipe needs.

MANAGING COMPLEXITY

It helps to break the grain bill into various components based on what they might contribute to a beer. The vocabulary of malt, as in the above chart, provides ideas we can use for these components.

A recipe may have a single malt flavor block or two, three, or possibly more, depending on the style. Each block can be made of a single malt type, or several. Piling on flavors within each block can be thought of as "layering," a term used in connection with cuisine, which is a strategy to create depth-of-flavor by using several similarly flavored elements rather than just one. An example might be a brown ale recipe employing a toasty component, a key aspect of such beers. It can be made purely from amber/biscuit malt, or that malt in combination with a smaller amount of a very dark caramel (Special B) malt, and/or a dab of brown malt. Or, as a caramelly block in a golden ale that can be made with purely Vienna malt, but for more complexity, a mix of Vienna and pale ale malt might be considered, possibly with other types such as Munich and pale caramel in small amounts for even more depth of flavor.

HIERARCHY

It's useful to consider the different flavor components as having some ranking of predominance. What is the primary flavor? What's the main counterpoint to that? The next layer? Deep subtleties? We are often more comfortable with this kind of structure than when everything is shouting at the same volume.

SCALE

When putting together complex recipes it is very important to keep the flavor intensities of the various ingredients in mind, as well as the context in which they are being used. Color is some indicator of this, but malts darker than chocolate actually become a little milder in flavor intensity, so be aware of that. Black malt can be used as a colorant in very pale beers, but in this case its use is well below 1 percent.

And don't forget to think about sub-threshold flavors. Just because someone can't pick out and name a flavor doesn't mean it's not there. Subtle flavors can add to or change the total flavor in subversive ways. This is especially true of spices; they often work best when most subtly used.

CRAFT

It should be obvious that the quality of execution can make or break a beer. Just as important as the recipe is a careful and fault-free execution of the concept. Odd aromas and harsh flavors can detract from even the best concept. Small errors in brewing can change the color, gravity, bitterness, and other attributes to something quite different from what was intended. Brewing is a game of details and the more you pay attention to them, the better your beer will be.

REFINE: LATHER, RINSE, REPEAT

There is no need to reinvent the wheel every time. The great jazz clarinetist Benny Goodman played his solos the same way every time, until he could find a way to improve them. Unless you happen to be a genuine genius like Louis Armstrong, it is usually better to improve on your successes.

I like to compare brewing a great beer to making a great sandwich—from the classic PB&J to a roast beef and cheddar to a double-decker club. Too much of any one thing throws the flavor off, and too much variety prevents you from tasting the signature flavor you were looking for in the first place. Simplicity, proportion, and restraint will help brewers brew great beer.

JOHN PALMER, aerospace metallurgist and author of *How to Brew*

Charlie Papazian is the visionary who founded the American Homebrewers Association, turning homebrewing from a secretive hobby to a well-organized global phenomenon. Photo by Edward Bronson.

IDEAS *and* INSPIRATIONS

Who knows where ideas come from? I've been an artist for more than three decades and I still don't know. Usually, they pop into your head, unannounced, mostly at the wrong time. They only rarely come when they are called.

One great tool for inventing beers it to put yourself into a particular time and place, whether real or imaginary. I find that this kind of role-playing allows the ideas to flow quite readily, often with surprising results. You can make up beers that might have been brewed at known times and places or you can take it a great deal further. This kind of fantasizing is not only a lot of fun, it is a good way to stretch your imagination and break yourself free of your usual patterns.

Just imagine . . .

- A monastery in southern Indiana where they brewed a dubbel called Two-X that was a strong version of the common beers once brewed in the Ohio Valley, but with a dab of molasses and sassafras added. A pawpaw tripel lightened with sorghum or maple syrup was a seasonal favorite.

- A mythic civilization that was a cross between the lands of *The Lord of the Rings* and a giant amusement park, kind of an "Elves Gone Wild" culture. Popular tipples might have included an ultra-pale springtime beer made from wheat with a sizeable addition of quince juice, dosed with ginger and woodruff; a wood-aged old ale with caramelized honey and aromatized with black truffles; and a velvety, ink-black barley wine seasoned with several types of flower blossoms, not all of which are legal at the present time.

- A secret community of brewers hidden in the caliphate of fourteenth-century Baghdad. One beer was laced with thyme honey; seasoned with exotic spices such as saffron, jasmine, myrrh; and colored a burgundy red with Syrian rue (Google that one). A stupefying and very sweet barley wine was made with a number of additions of date or sometimes grape syrup, seasoned with cardamom. It was served with a small disk of gold leaf floating on top of the foam.

- A secret order of brewing knights in France, who made off with brewing secrets from the ancient Middle East. Brewing in a regular seasonal progression for secret ceremonies and private meetings, these descendants of crusaders kept alive a tradition of the legendary beers of the ancient world in secret until the present day. Egyptian Red Beer of Sekhmet, Babylonian Strong Emmer and Date Beer, Sumerian Black-ened Raisin Ale, and Yellow Soma Ale were among the most memorable.

- What the Vikings and the Native Americans in Martha's Vineyard might have brewed together?

- The first beer brewed on Mars?

- What Elvis would have brewed if he were an ardent homebrewer?

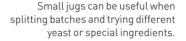

Small jugs can be useful when splitting batches and trying different yeast or special ingredients.

STRUCTURING *a* BEER

Let's look at the list of malts and adjuncts known as the grain bill first, and deconstruct a few beers to see how they might be put together. It's useful to think about them in terms of their broad characteristics before getting to the nerdy details of particular styles. The following graphics should help you visualize the different ways that each type of beer can be put together.

RECIPE STRATEGIES FOR LIGHT-COLORED BEERS

While the base malt must be a very pale type such as Pilsner malt, even the lightest beers can benefit from the added complexity of additional malts or adjuncts. The trick is to do it without adding too much color. Sugar and adjuncts like corn or rice thin out the body and make a beer lighter on the palate, a strategy painfully obvious in mass-market lagers, but quite useful in Belgian strong golden ales and tripels. Adjuncts like wheat and oats that improve head retention and add creaminess don't threaten the hue. With darker malts, it's simply a matter of watching the quantities. Vienna is probably the best choice and can be used up to 20 percent and still be in the gold range. Munich and caramel malts up to about 30°L are about as dark as you can go without shifting the color into the amber range, and those should be used sparingly, say less than 5 percent.

PALE AND GOLDEN BEERS

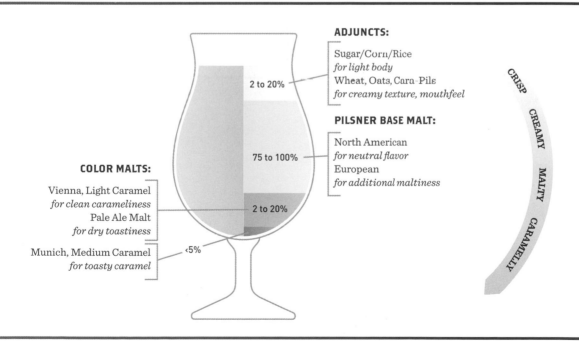

ADJUNCTS:
Sugar/Corn/Rice
for light body
Wheat, Oats, Cara-Pils
for creamy texture, mouthfeel

2 to 20%

PILSNER BASE MALT:
North American
for neutral flavor
European
for additional maltiness

75 to 100%

COLOR MALTS:
Vienna, Light Caramel
for clean carameliness
Pale Ale Malt
for dry toastiness

2 to 20%

Munich, Medium Caramel
for toasty caramel

<5%

CRISP
CREAMY
MALTY
CARAMELLY

RECIPE STRATEGIES FOR AMBER BEERS

Mid-colored beers offer the greatest number of possibilities. As with pale beers, raw grain and sugar adjuncts have a number of uses and don't affect the color in most cases. The first decision is base malt. Some amber beers such as Märzen derive all or most of their color from a colored base malt such as Munich or Vienna. In general, this produces beers with deep malty-caramelly flavors, possibly with hints of toastiness, especially if Munich malt is involved.

At the other end of the strategy range is to use a Pilsner malt base, color it with a roasted malt, which will produce a very crisp-tasting beer that sits lightly on the palate. This is a traditional strategy for some producers of Düsseldorf-style altbier.

In the middle are the rich possibilities of mid-colored malts such as Munich, melanoidin, and amber/biscuit, which offer a range of flavors from toasted caramel to fresh-baked cookies to sharp toastiness.

AMBER BEERS

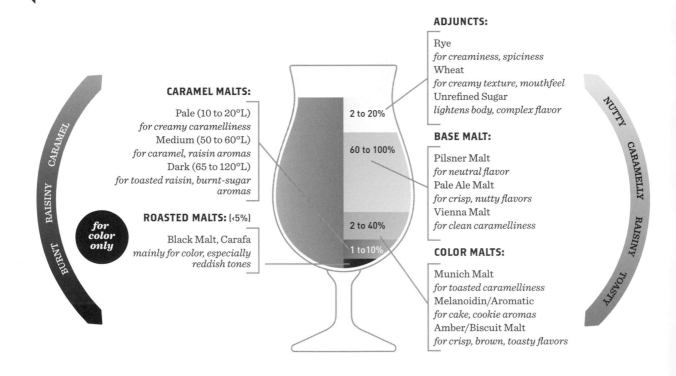

ADJUNCTS:
Rye
for creaminess, spiciness
Wheat
for creamy texture, mouthfeel
Unrefined Sugar
lightens body, complex flavor

CARAMEL MALTS:
Pale (10 to 20°L)
for creamy caramelliness
Medium (50 to 60°L)
for caramel, raisin aromas
Dark (65 to 120°L)
for toasted raisin, burnt-sugar aromas

2 to 20%

60 to 100%

BASE MALT:
Pilsner Malt
for neutral flavor
Pale Ale Malt
for crisp, nutty flavors
Vienna Malt
for clean caramelliness

ROASTED MALTS: (<5%)
Black Malt, Carafa
mainly for color, especially reddish tones

for color only

2 to 40%

1 to 10%

COLOR MALTS:
Munich Malt
for toasted caramelliness
Melanoidin/Aromatic
for cake, cookie aromas
Amber/Biscuit Malt
for crisp, brown, toasty flavors

BURNT RAISINY CARAMEL

NUTTY CARAMELLY RAISINY TOASTY

RECIPE STRATEGIES FOR RED AND BROWN BEERS

Caramel malt has its own universe of flavor personalities, running through a spectrum starting at caramel, moving to raisiny, dried fruit flavors, and then, as it gets darker, into the kind of burnt-sugar flavors that remind us of toasted marshmallows. The actual picture is far more complex than this, as every maltster will produce caramel malt in a different way, resulting in a huge range of flavor possibilities out there. So, if caramel malt is to form an important part of the flavor profile of a beer, taste what's available and find the one that best suits your vision.

Red beers are pretty distinctive, and normally feature the burnt-sugar flavors of medium- to dark-caramel malts, often with additional color from some sort of black malt. Both of these malts have more reddish tones than other malt types.

Black malts can be used in this color range simply to add a little more color, darkening a beer without adding a lot of flavor.

RED AND BROWN BEERS

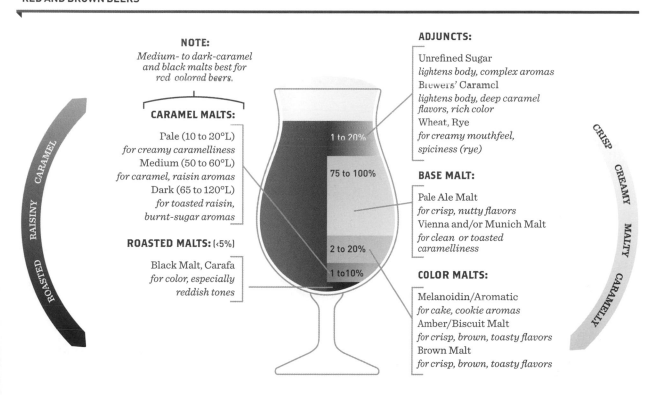

NOTE:
Medium- to dark-caramel and black malts best for red colored beers.

CARAMEL MALTS:
Pale (10 to 20°L)
for creamy caramelliness
Medium (50 to 60°L)
for caramel, raisin aromas
Dark (65 to 120°L)
for toasted raisin, burnt-sugar aromas

ROASTED MALTS: (<5%)
Black Malt, Carafa
for color, especially reddish tones

ADJUNCTS:
Unrefined Sugar
lightens body, complex aromas
Brewers' Caramel
lightens body, deep caramel flavors, rich color
Wheat, Rye
for creamy mouthfeel, spiciness (rye)

1 to 20%
75 to 100%
2 to 20%
1 to 10%

BASE MALT:
Pale Ale Malt
for crisp, nutty flavors
Vienna and/or Munich Malt
for clean or toasted caramelliness

COLOR MALTS:
Melanoidin/Aromatic
for cake, cookie aromas
Amber/Biscuit Malt
for crisp, brown, toasty flavors
Brown Malt
for crisp, brown, toasty flavors

ROASTED · RAISINY · CARAMEL

CRISP · CREAMY · MALTY · CARAMELLY

RECIPE STRATEGIES FOR BLACK BEERS

Sure, you can make a porter or stout by mixing 10 percent black malt with 90 percent pale, but how interesting will it be? For me, what makes a stout interesting is what's in the middle, colorwise. There are lots of malt and adjunct types that can be used here to give a black beer a seriously interesting personality.

Adjuncts like oatmeal, rye, and unmalted grain can add smooth, creamy textures that counter the sharpness of roasted grains, and this is an old traditional strategy. Guinness still uses 30 percent flaked barley for this reason (as well as cost). As in other styles, choosing a darker base malt can give the beer some caramelly underpinnings. Mild ale malt is perfect for the task, and very traditional in English stouts and porters, as well as mild ale.

Roasted malts vary considerably. Chocolate malt is misnamed. It is actually quite tangy and coffee-like, so I recommend caution. Black (patent) malts are often very chocolatey; roasted unmalted barley has a penetrating espresso flavor; no wonder it's often paired with the creaminess of flaked barley. The

BLACK BEERS

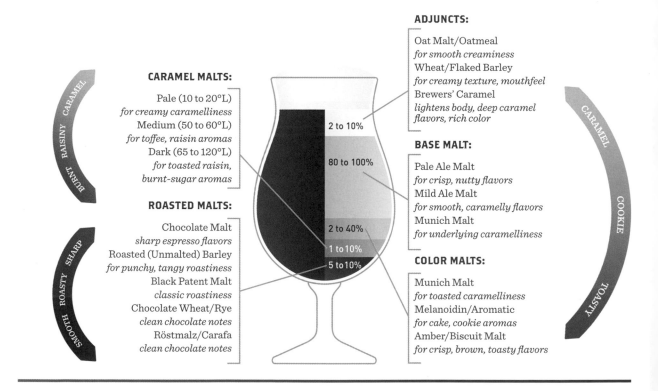

CARAMEL MALTS:
Pale (10 to 20°L)
for creamy caramelliness
Medium (50 to 60°L)
for toffee, raisin aromas
Dark (65 to 120°L)
for toasted raisin, burnt-sugar aromas

ROASTED MALTS:
Chocolate Malt
sharp espresso flavors
Roasted (Unmalted) Barley
for punchy, tangy roastiness
Black Patent Malt
classic roastiness
Chocolate Wheat/Rye
clean chocolate notes
Röstmalz/Carafa
clean chocolate notes

ADJUNCTS:
Oat Malt/Oatmeal
for smooth creaminess
Wheat/Flaked Barley
for creamy texture, mouthfeel
Brewers' Caramel
lightens body, deep caramel flavors, rich color

BASE MALT:
Pale Ale Malt
for crisp, nutty flavors
Mild Ale Malt
for smooth, caramelly flavors
Munich Malt
for underlying caramelliness

COLOR MALTS:
Munich Malt
for toasted caramelliness
Melanoidin/Aromatic
for cake, cookie aromas
Amber/Biscuit Malt
for crisp, brown, toasty flavors

2 to 10%
80 to 100%
2 to 40%
1 to 10%
5 to 10%

BURNT · RAISINY · CARAMEL

SMOOTH · ROASTY · SHARP

CARAMEL · COOKIE · TOASTY

Germans make a softer version of roasted malt so as not to interfere with the smooth malty character of their lager styles; Carafa is the Weyermann trade name. They come in a range of colors, and are offered in dehusked versions, which are extremely smooth and mellow.

Mid-colored malts counteract the bitterness of roasted malt, and can beef up the weight and sweetness of these very dark beers, like putting sugar and cream in your coffee. This is where it's helpful to visualize what the character of the finished beer will be, and choose malts that best suit that vision. Are you looking for roasted fruit flavors like plum pudding? Something soft and cappuccino-like or brisk and espresso-ish? Pure dark liquid chocolate? Then, find those same flavors and textures in ingredients and build your recipe.

THE NUMBERS GAME

A friend I taught to brew wanted, as a matter of principle, to control the beer simply by feel, and not measuring. If he wanted it stronger, he filled the mash tun a little higher. If he wanted it darker or hoppier, he added colored malts or more hops than normal. With some practice he was able to make what he wanted. None of these calculations are absolutely necessary for good beer.

All forms of predictive beer calculation are fraught with problems, from pretty reliable gravity numbers to very approximate color estimates. As you've probably figured out by now, brewing is pretty complex. Hop utilization varies by boil vigor and temperature, wort pH, hop form, time, wort gravity, and more. Hops themselves may vary from their stated alpha acid analysis and degrade over time at different rates depending on variety and storage conditions.

The more you look at the science, the more you conclude it's hopeless. There are a couple of reasons it is not. First, for any brewhouse, conditions are likely to be similar from brew to brew. So with some experience, formulas can be adjusted to more closely match reality. Second, we are limited in our ability to discern small differences in hop rates, perhaps between 5 and 10 BUs in gently hopped beers, possibly more in a very bitter beer. This all means you can trust hop calculations to get you close to the ballpark, especially if you've brewed with the calculations a few times, and you adjust the numbers to reflect the results you're getting in practice. The same is true for malt and gravity calculations.

You may decide to skip some of this in some or all of your brewing, but if you are trying for a very particular beer, calculating the basic parameters is quite useful, despite the lack of precision. The more ingredients in your beer, the more this is true. For competition brewing, where stylistic accuracy is of paramount concern, it is essential.

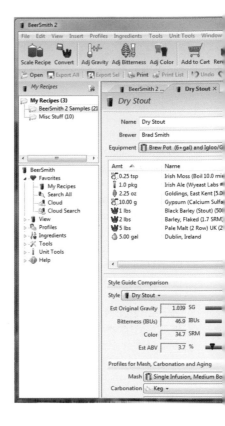

Most common brewing calculations can be easily handled by brewing software such as the popular BeerSmith. Image courtesy of Brad Smith/BeerSmith.

Now it's time to build a recipe. Start with the basic parameters:

- Original gravity and/or alcoholic content
- Color
- Bitterness

It's also good to have some thoughts on:

- Attenuation level (sweet, medium, dry)
- Hop aroma intensity

Sorry, art guys, we're in the world of math here, but if I can do it, so can you. It's just a bit of quick work with some charts and a pocket calculator, but it is increasingly common to use brewing software to make the calculations. These computer programs can figure and track all the important brewing variables and make it easy to try various choices until your recipe is the way you want it. Although there are a number of different packages, ProMash is the standard for the PC world. There have been many different ones for Macs, but BeerSmith has become the de-facto standard for all computer users.

There are two main areas of calculations to be done: the grain bill and hop usage. Both involve breaking the recipe into its component parts, calculating the contribution of each, and adding them all up. Each source of extract and hop has one or more numbers that represent its potential to add something to the beer. For malt, it is typically color and available extract. For hops, it's the alpha acid content. These are multiplied by weight, factored into the volume of the recipe, assigned efficiencies that are based on the performance of your system, and *voilà!* a recipe.

Calculating alcohol level is a bit more complex, as it depends both on the original gravity of the recipe, but also on the degree of fermentability, which depends on how the beer was brewed—specifically the fermentability of the wort, and also the performance of the yeast.

CALCULATING *the* GRAIN BILL

This is a fundamental calculation for pretty obvious reasons. To make a beer of a particular strength and color requires a carefully orchestrated selection of malts in very specific quantities that will all add up to the desired result. You will also be making choices about flavor, so there are a lot of different goals that have to be reconciled. It's not as complicated as it sounds; a logical approach helps make short work of it.

GRAVITY CALCULATIONS

Calculating gravity is pretty straightforward. Every malt type has a specification that shows how much of its weight, at maximum, will end up as gravity in the beer. In the malt listings in chapter 3, I've converted this to the gravity points added by 1 pound in the standard 5-gallon batch, or ½ kg in 20 L. This is for laboratory mashes that represent the best-case scenario, which home-brewing is not. Most of us feel lucky when we reach 85 percent or so; some processes like "no-sparge" mashing are much lower. The typical homebrewer ranges between 70 and 80 percent for normal, all-malt batches. All-grain recipes in this book are calculated at 75 percent efficiency. Your results may vary, and if they do, raise or lower the quantities to get the right end result.

It will be helpful to know the efficiency of your mashing system. If you've brewed a batch already, then just go back and recalculate, then compare your results against the laboratory analysis numbers. Divide the actual gravity by the lab figures, and you'll get a number below 1, that will be your percentage. If you have brewed several batches, it might be worth recalculating several of your most different recipes to see how your process varies from batch to batch. Settle on an average efficiency number you can use for calculations.

The two charts on pages 256 and 257 can be used to quickly find the amount of grain or other fermentable ingredient required to hit a certain gravity target. Start on the first chart. Find the grain, extract, or sugar you're planning on using—they are arranged by how much extract they can contribute. For extract or sugar, the yield will always be 100 percent, but each type of malt will give up extract at different rates depending on how efficient your system is. Follow the line where your grain of choice is, and read across to the column that represents your system's efficiency. If you haven't calculated it, here are some hints:

- Most beginner all-grain homebrew systems are around 70 percent efficient, so start there.
- No-sparge systems are a little less efficient; try 60 percent.
- Mini-mash yields are typically about 50 percent.

What do I think about when formulating a recipe? What's the simplest way to make it happen? A recipe is as much about process as ingredients. How well do I know the yeast? What's the lowest gravity I can start at and get the flavors I want?

STAN HIERONYMOUS, author of *Brew Like a Monk* and *Brewing with Wheat*

This analog calculator is wortproof and handy in the brewhouse. A similar version exists for hops.

TYPICAL GRAVITY CONTRIBUTIONS FOR VARIOUS INGREDIENTS IN 5-GAL/19-L BATCH

	ACTUAL GRAVITY CONTRIBUTION PER 1 POUND/454 G PER 5 GL/19 L										
% SYSTEM EFFICIENCY	**100**	**95**	**90**	**85**	**80**	**75**	**70**	**65**	**60**	**55**	**50**
Sugar (zero moisture—see listings for specifics)	1.0094				Normally utilized at 100%						
Dry Malt Extract	1.0091				Normally utilized at 100%						
Malted wheat, unmalted corn, rice, wheat, barley, rye	1.0078	1.0074	1.0070	1.0066	1.0062	1.0059	1.0055	1.0051	1.0047	1.0043	1.0039
Two-Row Pils Malt, Lager Malt, Pale Ale Malt	1.0073	1.0069	1.0066	1.0062	1.0058	1.0055	1.0051	1.0047	1.0044	1.0040	1.0037
Vienna Malt	1.0071	1.0067	1.0064	1.0060	1.0057	1.0053	1.0050	1.0046	1.0043	1.0039	1.0036
Mild Ale Malt, Munich Malt, Melanoidin Malt; Dark Munich, Aromatic, Melano, Honey Malt, Brumalt/Brew Malt	1.0070	1.0067	1.0063	1.0060	1.0057	1.0053	1.0049	1.0046	1.0042	1.0039	1.0035
Liquid Malt Extract	1.0070				Normally utilized at 100%						
Cara-Pils, Carafoam (ultra-pale caramel malt)	1.0067	1.0064	1.0060	1.0057	1.0054	1.0050	1.0047	1.0044	1.0040	1.0037	1.0034
Amber Malt; Biscuit, Victory (Briess) Brown Malt, Pale Caramel/Crystal, 10 to 30°L Caramel/Crystal, Medium Caramel/Crystal, 40 to 80°L Caramel/Crystal, Caramunich	1.0066	1.0063	1.0059	1.0056	1.0053	1.0050	1.0046	1.0043	1.0040	1.0036	1.0033
Chocolate Malt, Pale Chocolate, Coffee Malt, Röstmalz; Carafa (Weyermann), Black Malt; Black Patent Malt	1.0061	1.0058	1.0055	1.0052	1.0049	1.0046	1.0043	1.0040	1.0037	1.0034	1.0032
Extra Dark Caramel/Crystal, 100 to 140°L	1.0057	1.0054	1.0051	1.0048	1.0046	1.0043	1.0040	1.0037	1.0034	1.0031	1.0029
Oat Malt	1.0050	1.0048	1.0045	1.0043	1.0040	1.0038	1.0035	1.0033	1.0030	1.0028	1.0025

(Left margin label: FERMENTABLE)

When you're in the right efficiency column, make a note of the number. This is the actual gravity contribution of a grain or a fermentable ingredient found by first determining the percent system efficiency that 1 pound/454 g of your chosen grain will add to 5 gallons/19 L of beer. Locate this extract number on the diagonal lines on the graph on the facing page. Start at a quantity and read across to the diagonal, then follow the vertical line down to read an estimated gravity; or start with a gravity target, then read upward to the diagonal, then left across to find a grain quantity. Note that this chart also includes metric grain quantities; just read to the right rather than the left. Degrees Plato are along the top if you prefer.

Every grain needs to be calculated separately, as each has a different amount of gravity it can contribute. The estimated grain contribution number can then help determine either the original gravity or the fermentable grain amount. When we've added it all up, we can estimate the alcohol content by using the combination chart on the lower left corner of the recipe worksheet.

WORT GRAVITY ESTIMATOR

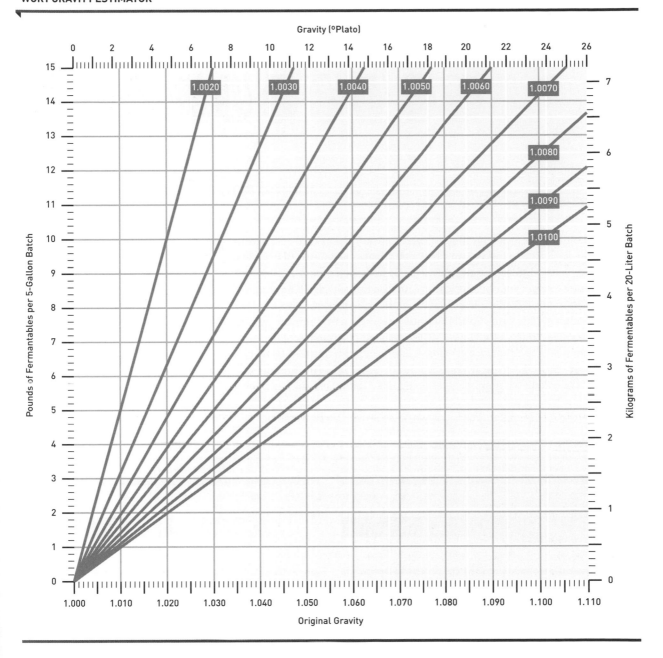

CALCULATING COLORS

BEER BY THE NUMBERS

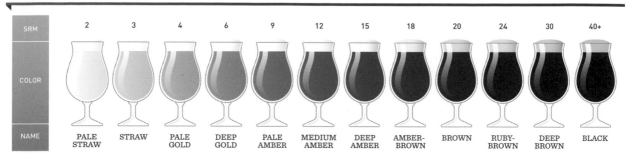

SRM	2	3	4	6	9	12	15	18	20	24	30	40+
NAME	PALE STRAW	STRAW	PALE GOLD	DEEP GOLD	PALE AMBER	MEDIUM AMBER	DEEP AMBER	AMBER-BROWN	BROWN	RUBY-BROWN	DEEP BROWN	BLACK

This chart is a rough guide to beer color as expressed by the numbers. As with the malt chart, the numbers have been simplified, and these styles exist as a range. Note that no universally agreed-on verbal terms exist.

The final color of a beer can be affected by a large number of hard-to-quantify factors, like variation in ingredients, boil vigor, heat source, wort pH, hot and cold breaks, yeast, differences in analytical methods, and others. It's not real science, but it can get your beers close to a chosen target range. The essence of beer color recipe calculation is to multiply the color times the weight, then divide by gallons. This sums up all the malts' colors for a preliminary number sometimes called Malt Color Units (MCU). Because of a number of factors, this number needs to be corrected before it can correlate to finished beer color. At the palest end of the scale, it's reasonably accurate, but as the numbers get higher, the calculated number gets much higher than the actual beer color, so by the time the calculated number reaches 300, it's three times as high as the real predicted beer color. The following chart provides a conversion.

MALT COLOR UNITS TO SRM CONVERSION

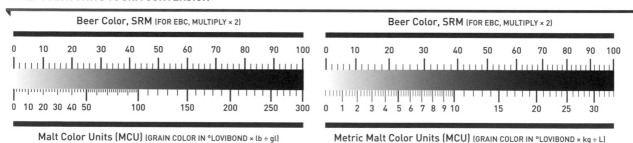

The U.S. Standard Reference Method (SRM) is a numerical index for labeling beer colors.

So add up the malt colors and divide by the number of gallons to get the MCU. Locate that number on the chart and read across the scale to a corrected estimated SRM color (and double those numbers if you're working in the EBC). I use this conversion for the color in the whole recipe, so if you're shooting for an SRM target, then use the chart to find your corresponding MCU target.

When working out a grain bill, especially when calculating color, I find it best to start with the middle-colored grains, those between 5 and 80°L. Choose an amount based on the flavor you'd like to add, and see where the color comes out, and also what their contribution to gravity will be. Subtract their gravity contribution from your intended total to see how much gravity you still need to get from your other malts or adjuncts. Based on that number, find the amount of those grains needed to reach the target gravity, calculate the amount, and see how much color those pale grains will contribute. Subtract the pale grain color and the middle grain color from your total color target to find out how much color you still need. Either use a very dark malt to adjust, which normally will not contribute enough gravity to require recalculation of your pale malts, or add more of your middle malt(s) and then recalculate your pale malt to get a correct total. The calculated color should end up getting you pretty close. Here's an example.

GRIST FORMULATION FOR RED ALE

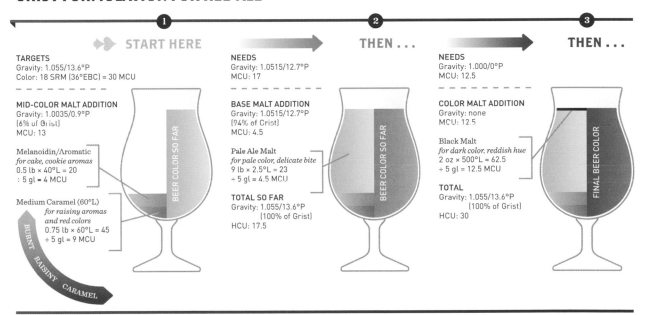

1 START HERE

TARGETS
Gravity: 1.055/13.6°P
Color: 18 SRM (36°EBC) = 30 MCU

MID-COLOR MALT ADDITION
Gravity: 1.0035/0.9°P
(6% of Grist)
MCU: 13

Melanoidin/Aromatic
for cake, cookie aromas
0.5 lb × 40°L = 20
: 5 gl = 4 MCU

Medium Caramel (60°L)
*for raisiny aromas
and red colors*
0.75 lb × 60°L = 45
÷ 5 gl = 9 MCU

BURNT RAISINY CARAMEL

BEER COLOR SO FAR

2 THEN . . .

NEEDS
Gravity: 1.0515/12.7°P
MCU: 17

BASE MALT ADDITION
Gravity: 1.0515/12.7°P
(94% of Grist)
MCU: 4.5

Pale Ale Malt
for pale color, delicate bite
9 lb × 2.5°L = 23
÷ 5 gl = 4.5 MCU

TOTAL SO FAR
Gravity: 1.055/13.6°P
(100% of Grist)
HCU: 17.5

BEER COLOR SO FAR

3 THEN . . .

NEEDS
Gravity: 1.000/0°P
MCU: 12.5

COLOR MALT ADDITION
Gravity: none
MCU: 12.5

Black Malt
for dark color, reddish hue
2 oz × 500°L = 62.5
÷ 5 gl = 12.5 MCU

TOTAL
Gravity: 1.055/13.6°P
(100% of Grist)
HCU: 30

FINAL BEER COLOR

You'll notice that the mid-colored malt is actually a block of two different malts, Caramel 60 and melanoidin. The melanoidin is there to reduce the sometimes over-the-top burnt-raisin character of caramel malt and to provide some complementary flavors, for greater depth.

HOPS *in the* RECIPE

Hops provide a counterpoint to the sweet, malty flavors of malt. Without them, beer would be pretty hard to drink. Hops can capture our imagination, make a beer more refreshing, sharpen the appetite, bring even the sweetest beer into balance, or take a starring role of their own. We love them because they make beer come alive.

The first step in your calculation is to consider what role the hops will play in your beer. Are they there just for balance, in the background? Are they an active element sharing the stage with the malts as one of several focal points vying for people's attention? Or are they front and center, with the rest of the beer backing them up?

You'll need to zero in on a desired bitterness level, expressed in Bitterness Units (BU). Few of us have the capability to actually measure this, but as the international standard, it's the common language we work with. Be aware that what is overpowering in a lighter beer may be quite subtle in a much stronger one. It's useful to consider the ratio of BU to gravity: As the original gravity of a beer goes up, so should the bitterness level.

Pick an IBU target based on the BU:GU ratio and what's appropriate for the style and your own personal vision. You will also need a vision for how prominent the aroma must be. There is no standard numerical measure of hop aroma, so this has to be qualitative: barely there, supporting, evenly balanced, hops on top, and totally freaking hopcentric.

Finally, you need to think about the aromatic character, which means choosing varieties and growing locations. For some classic styles, this is nearly automatic: Saaz for Czech Pilsners, Hallertau for German ones. For more freewheeling beers, there are a lot more choices. While national origin and genetic relationships can be helpful, this is an area where personal choice and experience really come into play. Sometimes you just gotta go with what you like. But it's also important to keep trying new things, especially these days with new hops showing up in every crop.

You can also use nontraditional hops to add complexity or twist the personality of the more traditional ones. Saaz, for example, can be mixed with some Citra, resulting in a brighter aroma that still works in a Pilsner. Hallertau can be mixed with Northern Brewer to make the flavor a bit more dry and neutral, or with Celeia or Pacific Jade to shift the tone away from the herbaceous character of the Hallertau.

Today's recipes demand a wide choice of hops for different aromas in creative or traditional beers. A well-stocked shop should carry at least a couple dozen varieties.

HOP BITTERNESS VERSUS WORT GRAVITY (BU:GU RATIO)

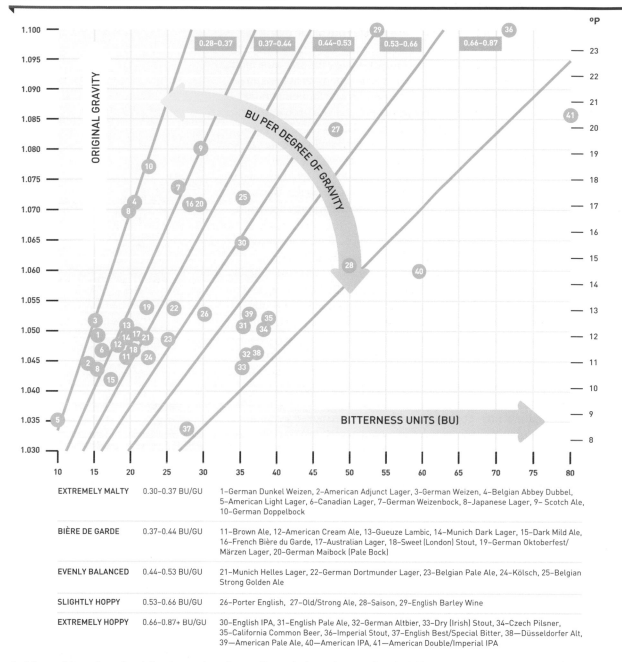

EXTREMELY MALTY	0.30–0.37 BU/GU	1–German Dunkel Weizen, 2–American Adjunct Lager, 3–German Weizen, 4–Belgian Abbey Dubbel, 5–American Light Lager, 6–Canadian Lager, 7–German Weizenbock, 8–Japanese Lager, 9– Scotch Ale, 10–German Doppelbock
BIÈRE DE GARDE	0.37–0.44 BU/GU	11–Brown Ale, 12–American Cream Ale, 13–Gueuze Lambic, 14–Munich Dark Lager, 15–Dark Mild Ale, 16–French Bière du Garde, 17–Australian Lager, 18–Sweet (London) Stout, 19–German Oktoberfest/Märzen Lager, 20–German Maibock (Pale Bock)
EVENLY BALANCED	0.44–0.53 BU/GU	21–Munich Helles Lager, 22–German Dortmunder Lager, 23–Belgian Pale Ale, 24–Kölsch, 25–Belgian Strong Golden Ale
SLIGHTLY HOPPY	0.53–0.66 BU/GU	26–Porter English, 27–Old/Strong Ale, 28–Saison, 29–English Barley Wine
EXTREMELY HOPPY	0.66–0.87+ BU/GU	30–English IPA, 31–English Pale Ale, 32–German Altbier, 33–Dry (Irish) Stout, 34–Czech Pilsner, 35–California Common Beer, 36–Imperial Stout, 37–English Best/Special Bitter, 38—Düsseldorfer Alt, 39—American Pale Ale, 40—American IPA, 41—American Double/Imperial IPA

In this graphic, various classic brews are plotted according to their gravity as well as their bitterness. The ratio of the two gives some idea of the balance of the beer, as more malt in a beer demands more hops to back it up.

Sometimes the goal is just to support and even stay out of the way of the malt flavors, so in those cases, we're using hops mostly for bitterness and will choose neutral hops that may have some complementary flavors to the malts.

Personally, I am inclined to use good-quality aroma hops, or at least dual-use hops all the way through, and this strategy works well for homebrews that are not massively hopped, but in hoppy beers it can be a problem due to the sheer mass of hop vegetation in the boil, particularly with whole hops. For us homebrewers, wasting a little money is not a big deal, but commercially, this is just foolish.

Even with high alpha bittering hops, it is a good idea to match the character of the hops to the rest of the hop bill. Magnum works well in German or Czech beers, and there are other European types of high alpha hops that work great for English or Belgian beers.

Most of us buy hops in those little 1-ounce packages, and we get into the habit of using one, two, three of them for bittering, and another one, two, three for aroma. Nothing wrong with beer made this way, but I find it much more useful to think about the total BUs desired, then divide them up and allocate the proper percentages of total BUs for each hop addition. Doing so allows you to vary the aromatic impact from the hops you use. If you get most or all of your BUs from the 60-minute addition, you get very little aroma. Getting more of your bittering from later additions ensures that you get more aroma in the final beer.

A beer like Düsseldorfer alt will use hops only for the full boil, because little or no hop aroma is desired in this style. Pilsners and pale ales will hop all the way through for a mix of bitterness and aroma. Hops boiled for 5 minutes have only a 5 percent utilization, which means you have to use five times as much as those boiled for 1 hour. In this scenario, you get a lot more aroma and the overall impact of the hops will be bigger and more complex.

With the popularity of hop flavor and aroma in modern beers, both commercial brewers and homebrewers are pushing this to extremes, often relying on late addition or even whirlpool hops for all of the bittering. This technique is sometimes known as "hop bursting." While a commercial brewery may get between 10 and 20 percent utilization for hops added after the boil has ceased, homebrew levels are likely to be somewhere below 5 percent. Calculating is the same as any recipe, but the far lower utilization rate allows very large hop quantities for a boatload of aroma.

So, decide how many hop additions you want, and what BU or percentage of the total you want from each different boil time. Normally you'll make one hop addition at the beginning of the boil for bitterness, and a second one at or near the end for aroma, which may also contribute a little bitterness. Two additions should be enough (unless you want a super-hoppy beer) and will make your hop calculations a little simpler. Brewers often add a third, at somewhere around 20 to 30 minutes, and of course, hops can be added continuously if desired, although it's not clear what this accomplishes beyond just a great story.

Hops were traditionally dried in unique cylindrical kilns called oast houses. Note the steerable chimneys at the top of these in Kent, England.

STRATEGIES FOR BITTERING VERSUS AROMA

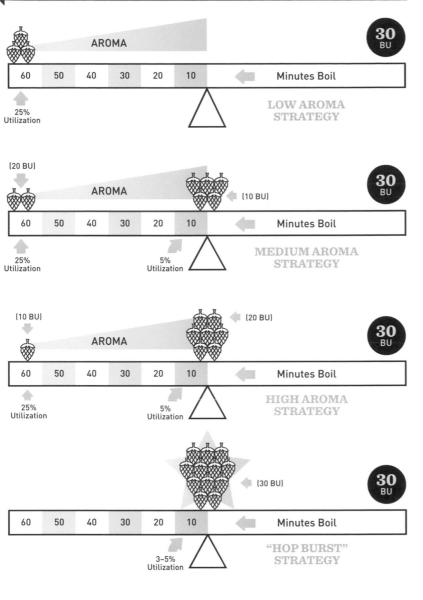

LOW AROMA STRATEGY

AROMA

60 50 40 30 20 10 — Minutes Boil

25% Utilization

30 BU

MEDIUM AROMA STRATEGY

(20 BU)

AROMA (10 BU)

60 50 40 30 20 10 — Minutes Boil

25% Utilization — 5% Utilization

30 BU

HIGH AROMA STRATEGY

(10 BU)

AROMA (20 BU)

60 50 40 30 20 10 — Minutes Boil

25% Utilization — 5% Utilization

30 BU

"HOP BURST" STRATEGY

(30 BU)

60 50 40 30 20 10 — Minutes Boil

3–5% Utilization

30 BU

These graphics show some different approaches to achieving bitterness and the effect they may have on aroma. All four produce the same bitterness, but when all the hops are added for the whole boil, there is much less aroma to start with because of the smaller quantity needed, and what *is* there tends to evaporate during the lengthy boil. The high-aroma approach can reduce the need for more complex techniques like dry-hopping. Note: Mid-boil hop additions have been eliminated for the sake of clarity here, but most beer recipes can be formulated using only full-boil and late-addition hops.

CALCULATING HOP ADDITIONS

Once you have a vision for your hops, you need to create a hop bill that will satisfy your objectives. First, think about your bitterness target. The IBU level depends on these things:

- Hop quantity and form (pellet or whole)
- Hop bitterness (alpha acid percentage)
- Boil time
- Wort gravity
- Many other factors that can't be calculated

The first four will be used to predict the bitterness from different hop additions. Quantity is obvious: Use more, get more. Pellet hops yield about 25 percent more bitterness than whole. The stated alpha acid will decrease over time, so for year-old hops, knock off 25 percent or so. Boil time and wort gravity are the two main predictors of something called *utilization*, a measure, expressed as a percentage, of how much of the hop's available alpha acid actually ends up in the beer. Other factors include wort pH, boil vigor, yeast performance, and others, but fortunately these are often similar from batch to batch, so you can ignore them. If you consistently get less hop bitterness than expected, you can lower the utilization rate, or vice versa. See the hop utilization charts, opposite and on pages 266 and 267 for more information.

As with malt, if you're using brewing software, these calculations are all taken care of for you. As for quantities, I prefer to work in grams, as they are smaller. Fractions of an ounce are pretty clumsy.

For any one addition, here are the steps:

1 Break down the recipe into different additions: 60, 30, 5 minutes, etc.
2 Assign a BU number to each, making sure they add up to the desired total.
3 For any one addition (I like to start with the aroma hops), choose your hop and note its alpha content.
4 Find the utilization rate on the following chart.
5 Plug in the utilization and the alpha acid percentage to the nomogram and find the quantity of hops needed to hit the BU you want for each addition.
6 Mark the quantity and time for each hop addition on your recipe worksheet.

You will need to do this for each hop addition. The estimator chart is a quick way to figure out how much hops to use as long as you're using pellet hops in a normal gravity wort.

HOP UTILIZATION BY BOIL TIME

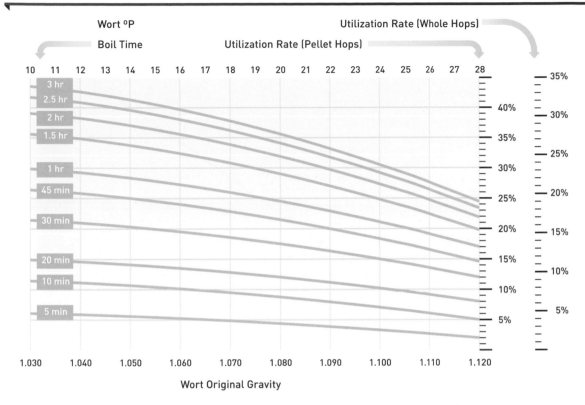

This chart shows approximate hop-utilization rates for whole hops incorporated into worts of varying gravities. The longest-boiling hops have the highest rate of utilization; the shortest ones, the lowest. Find where the wort gravity intersects with the curves representing boil times, and read across to the scale for pellet or whole hops.

HOP-BITTERNESS ESTIMATOR NOMOGRAM

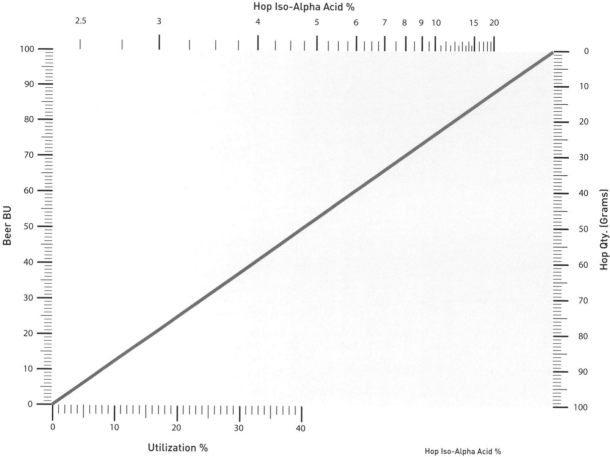

To calculate bitterness, first draw a line (———) from your chosen hop alpha acid % to the Utilization % you expect to get from this addition. Then, using the point where the first line crosses the gray diagonal as a pivot point, start from either the desired Beer BU and draw a second line (———) through the pivot over to the Hop Quantity scale, or start with a hop quantity and draw the line through the pivot in the other direction to find the required quantity to achieve that bitterness level.

Note: This chart is based on a standard 5-gallon/19-L batch. If you are brewing larger or smaller volumes, adjust the quantity based on that size (10 gl = 2x, 3 gl = 0.67x, etc.).

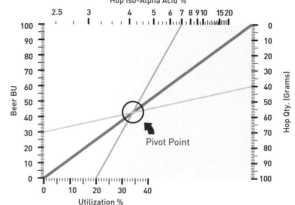

Pivot Point

QUICK-AND-DIRTY HOP-QUANTITY ESTIMATOR

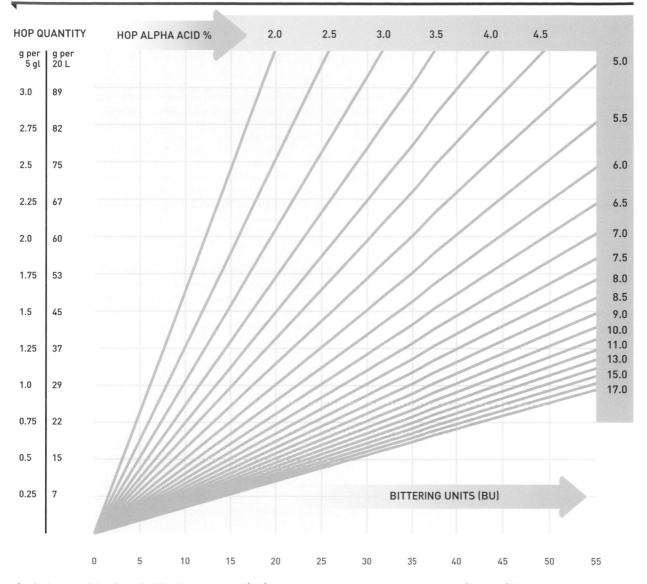

On the bottom of the chart, find the bitterness level (BU) you want to reach. Trace that figure upward on the chart until it intersects with the diagonal line representing the alpha acid content of the hops you wish to use. At the point where they intersect, trace left until you reach the vertical scale along the left side.

Hop quantity can be read on g/5 gl or g/20 L. This chart assumes a 23% utilization rate, equal to a 1-hour boil in 1.050/12.4°P or lower-gravity wort.

Refer to the utilization chart on page 265 for an idea of how boil time and wort gravity affect utilization. When mixing hop types, decide how many BUs you want from each hop variety, and figure separately. Figure only hops boiled 30 minutes or more.

THINKING THROUGH A RECIPE

There are many ways of working through a beer recipe. The following passages from some outstanding brewers should be helpful in seeing how different brewers think through a recipe—and how many similarities there are.

" I was inspired (as always!) by a recent bottle of Orval to make a well-attenuated, perceptively bitter beer. I had some yeast/*Brett* blend. I didn't have the same hops, so instead of the Goldings, I used some lovely Mt. Hood, and my beer would be like a forest, not a flowerbed. This was also the first time I used the bulk of kettle hops at 40 minutes remaining, as at Orval. And I kept it a bit paler, for no good reason. So there you have my pale, bitter forest, inspired by Orval, with *Brett* character yet to develop, though it doesn't taste or smell like Orval! "

JEFF SPARROW, author of *Brewing Wild Ales*

" I was thinking about how smoke character and phenols from fermentation often clash horribly, so I wanted to come up with a Belgian-inspired beer that was a good example of marrying smoke and phenols.

I began to visualize a beer with a base malty character, dark but not roasty, of moderate alcohol character, but enough to be warming. The smoke would need to blend in with the yeast quality, so I would try using fruitier strains, ones with lighter levels of spicy phenols. When I do these sorts of mental exercises, I also try to imagine the flavors and aromas of the beer when it is done. I think that relying on this type of sense memory can give you a fairly realistic idea of how the concept may turn out.

So that led me to a Belgian dark recipe of moderate strength, with the appropriate amount of smoked malt. I spent a lot more time thinking about what yeast to use, what sort of alcohol volume (ABV) I would want, and how to ferment the beer properly for the desired effect. In the end I tried several different yeasts and used taste testing to guide me further in yeast selection and refinements to the amount of smoked malt.

When doing a flavor description of a future beer, break it down: visual, aroma, taste, mouthfeel, and body. Then use what you already know—what do you know about your brew? Well, you brewed it, right? Break that down into its raw materials and define the flavors that come from them. Here are your buckets: grain bill, hop bill, spices and/or fruits, brewing yeast, and special processes. "

JAMIL JAINASHEFF, award-draped homebrewer and co-author of *Yeast: The Practical Guide to Beer Fermentation*

Every recipe should start in your head by visualizing the mix of flavors, textures, and aromas desired.

" I have a Dubbel with a malt bill of:

- Munich malt—for body, aroma, and malt sweetness, plus an orange-amber color.
- Special B—the darkest of the Belgian crystal malts. It has a big, roasted, sweet-caramel and nutty flavor. In large amounts it will actually give a plum- or raisin-like flavor!
- Biscuit malt—with a toasted aroma of Saltine crackers or warm biscuits and a garnet-brown color.
- Chocolate malt—for a dark color and rich, dark chocolate flavor.

And a hop bill of:

- Goldings—mild and delicate, it lends an earthy/herbal/light note; classic English type.
- Saaz—classic noble hop from the Czech Republic, provides lots of clean, earthy, spicy, and peppery notes.

Then I added:

- Dark candi sugar—It doesn't change the beer flavor but increases the alcohol and adds to the crispness.
- Grains of paradise—a vibrant blend of ginger, cardamom, and white pepper.
- Trappist yeast strain (fermentation and bottle conditioning).

Now comes the thoroughly kick-ass flavor description of the brew:

My Belgian Dubbel with its warm hickory hue and soft haze bursts out of the gates with aromas of dried plums and raisins, caramelized bananas, Bazooka bubblegum, cocoa nibs, and gentle hints of earthy spice from the noble hop addition. On first taste you notice the sweet deep chocolate malts. As the beer evolves, prickly pepper and spicy phenols along with the higher ABV warm the palate all the way to your tummy. Even a beer as high alcohol as this still has the full body and creamy texture that you'd expect from a traditional Dubbel. All it takes is a few sips from this beer and a delicious wedge of Trappist cheese and you'll fall back in time to those great brewing abbeys of Belgium.

If this is the type of description you give the next time someone asks, "What's your beer like?" who in their right mind wouldn't leap at the chance to try your homebrew?! **"**

LAUREN SALAZAR, beer blending and sensory specialist, New Belgium Brewing Company, Fort Collins, CO

". American Brown Ale, with hints of roast, coffee, caramel, toffee, and a subtle bitterness. Now overlay the herby flavors of sage, thyme, bay, and a touch of cumin with dried mushrooms like chanterelle or porcini to play off the roast and umami created in this style profile.

- Lemongrass, ginger, Thai palm sugar, and chiles infused into a Belgian Strong Golden style. The ester flavors dance with the heat of the ginger and chiles while the lemongrass and palm sugar keep the brew from being too spicy or like a ginger ale.
- Roasted Chinese five-spice seasoning added to the boil, whirl-pooled and "dry spiced" into an Imperial Stout or Coffee Stout. Add some converted sweet rice to the mash and some figs and persimmons to the secondary. The extra depth of flavor that these spices and additives could create across the palate and at the bar/restaurant is exciting.
- Start with a Kölsch style and overlay the flavors of the Caribbean. Think sugarcane and cooked yams added to the mash; then pineapple, tamarind, and a touch of allspice added to the end of the boil. **"**

SEAN PAXTON, The Homebrew Chef

Clockwise from top: Thai palm sugar, lemongrass, star anise, and fresh ginger.

OTHER FLAVORINGS

I am thrilled by the willingness of modern homebrewers to use any and all available herbs, spices, fruits, vegetables, and more in search of new and unique flavors for their beers. Dropping in a little orange peel and coriander to a witbier can be pretty simple, but without the right approach and a lot of attention to detail, eccentric ingredients can cause a lot of problems as well.

Each specialty ingredient comes with its own tradition, chemistry, flavor, methodology, and personality. Understanding the flavors and intensities, along with the best way to extract them and integrate them into a recipe, takes some experience.

SPICES *and* SEASONINGS *in the* RECIPE

Hops are not the only seasoning used in beer. The modern brewer has a large spice cabinet and should get to know the dozen or so spices and herbs most commonly used in beer. Coriander, orange peel, black pepper, and grains of paradise are among the most common. Pumpkin and Christmas beers often use culinary mixes, including cinnamon, ginger, nutmeg, and allspice. Check a cookbook for ratios common in baking, as those are likely to work well in beer.

There are many different approaches to incorporating spices into your recipe, ranging from sledgehammer to sublime. The Belgian approach is one of subtlety. Success comes when you taste the beer and think, "I can taste a spice, but which one?" Often the purpose of the spice is to add a little nuance to the malt and hop flavors, enhance crispness and drinkability, or augment or twist the flavors the yeast is contributing. The last thing you want is somebody saying, "It sure tastes like nutmeg, all right."

If done with a light hand, adding seasonings is a good way to give a beer a local or national character. By incorporating some flavorings associated with an ecosystem or a cuisine, you can create a beer with real connections to a place. Such beers are often stunningly good with the local food.

Many spices like vanilla and black pepper have the ability to enhance, mask, or modify other flavors. What's more, spices and other aromatic ingredients can have a sensory and even emotional effect at far below their threshold value, the level needed to actually pick out an individual flavor. It takes plenty of time and effort to become deeply familiar with the wide world of spices and how their flavors work in different beers.

As always, construct the rest of the recipe to receive the special ingredients gracefully. If you're making a gingerbread beer, make sure the beer has the taste and texture of cake before you add the ginger and other spices. If you're making a beer that's reminiscent of a margarita, make sure the body, malt character, and acidity of the beer are where they should be before you drop in the lime peel and agave, or you'll have a real mess on your hands.

The same preparation is called for when using coffee and chocolate. Their roasty characters can be enhanced and supported with malts that have

Our worst recipe disaster was a spiced hefeweizen we did back in '96. Black pepper amplified by the hefeweizen yeast, with lavender buds, too. It was like tongue-kissing Laura Ashley.

SAM CALAGIONE, founder, Dogfish Head Craft Brewery, Rehoboth Beach, DE

An assortment of Amazonian barks at a market in Belém, Brazil, near the mouth of the Amazon.

undergone much the same kilning process. These are expensive ingredients with delicate aromas, so you'll want the brew to taste as much like the special ingredient as possible before dropping in the nibs, beans, or extracts. At the same time, you want to stay away from malt or hop choices that will trample the delicate nuances of those pricey specialty ingredients.

RECIPE CONSIDERATIONS *for* FRUIT BEERS

Unlike spices, fruit in beer is not about subtlety. You want to have your fruit jump out of the glass and announce itself in a clean, clear voice. It's not always easy. Using sufficient quantities of fruit is expensive and can be messy in the brewery. In addition, certain fruits such as peaches and strawberries may not ferment gracefully and can fade quickly, making it hard to get true character even with great fruit. As with spices, each fruit has a whole set of characteristics that a brewer must learn about to deal with successfully. The information here is just the briefest introduction to the topic.

Although getting enough fruit in the beer is a common concern, the beer itself needs some serious thought *before* you put the fruit in. It's a fine balancing act. The beer should shine through but at the same time support and showcase the fruit. There are many ways beer can work with fruit. Will the beer be biscuity like pie dough or Danish pastry crust, or perhaps caramelly like a sauce? Will it be roasty and chocolatey as in a Black Forest cake or just provide some structure or sweetness along the lines of a fine wine? Some malts, like the mid-colored caramels, have raisin or prune aromas that can tie to and enhance the fruit flavor that's already there. Hops may have citrus, apricot, passionfruit, or even wine and melon aromas, so choose wisely. And don't forget that yeast itself has a lot of fruity flavors. Trying to make a banana bread ale? You'd be a fool not to use hefeweizen yeast.

Some acidity to balance and brighten the fruit is crucial. Some fruit supplies its own acidity, but sometimes the brewer needs to find a way to add it.

The other really important thing that affects fruit flavor is acidity. It is well known in the wine world that the right acid level is critical to a bright, snappy fruit character and, in fact, acid levels are one thing that determines when to harvest. The term *flabby* describes a dull and lifeless-tasting wine without enough acidity to support the fruit. The same thing can happen to fruit beer. Many fruits have sufficient acidity for good flavor, while others do not. Some acid malt, up to 5 percent, can be added to the recipe, and acid such as lactic, phosphoric, or even lemon juice can be used in the fermenter. Final adjustments can be made at kegging or bottling; but when you are tasting uncarbonated beer, remember that CO_2 dissolved in beer is fairly acidic, so you'll probably need to add less acid than you think.

Acidic beers such as lambics and Flanders sour ales make great bases for fruit ales. The old-school way is to use a lambic-style mixed culture that

Fruit beers are among the most beautiful of all brews and are best served in a tall, fancy glass.

includes some *Lactobacillus* and *Brettanomyces*. Both will contribute some acidity, but the bulk of it comes from the *Lactobacillus*. Be aware that these are slow-acting creatures that require months to achieve a strong sour or wild character.

And finally, be aware that we all drink with our eyes. A fruit beer with little or no color will definitely be perceived as more insipid than it really is. Some deep-colored fruits like elderberries or herbs like hibiscus flowers may be added just for their color. They often add herbal, floral, or wine-like character as well.

YEAST *and* FERMENTATION CHOICES

Just as with fruit and spices, yeast brings a particular range of flavors and aromas to a beer. To a certain point, yeast selection is guided by tradition— a weizen yeast to make a hefeweizen, for example. But even in beers tied to tradition, the brewer needs to carefully consider the choices, imagining the contributions the yeast will make, and make sure they are harmonious. Yeast is a living dynamic system containing a world of possibilities. Even small changes to temperature can make big changes to the flavor of the finished beer. Talk to anyone who brews great hefeweizen, and they will tell you that at least one of their secrets is choosing and maintaining a particular temperature that gives them just the right balance of the many flavors that yeast is capable of churning out.

Be aware of how attenuative the strain is, as this affects the balance of the beer. Highly flocculent strains are usually the most attenuative. With strong beers, be sure that the selected yeast will tolerate the levels of alcohol expected, and observe all the normal special procedures such as pitching rate and wort oxygen levels that are important in high-alcohol beers.

Style appropriateness and national character is only the first step, but it is a good place to start. Highly flocculent strains are the least attenuative. With a little detective work, most strains can be traced to their commercial brewery origins, which offers further clues to their character. Each different strain will produce a range of flavors and aromas of its own, and this will vary by temperature. Yeast suppliers usually offer detailed information on the character of their yeast, so read and abide by their guidelines unless you have a good reason for pushing the envelope.

In addition to contributing its own flavors, yeast affects the character of everything else in the recipe, from hops to malt. This is an area that takes a long time to get familiar with. Take heart, because as long as you make sure your yeast is well taken care of and working in a clean environment, the beer will be good at the very least. But if you get it right, optimizing the relationship between yeast and recipe can turn a good beer into a dazzling one.

Facing page, row by row from top left: Homebrew labels by Jim LaFleur, Fantastic Mykel, Matteo Pellis and Alberto Bodritti, Max Cassini, Łukasz Szynkiewicz, Kim Theesen, Dave Gallagher, Fantastic Mykel, Eric Monson, Kamil Raczynski, Szymon Tracz (fox), Kevin Bastian, Jim Behmyer, Craig Stacey and Ashley Brandt.

LAFLEURILLUSTRATION.COM
773-218-9680

...AMN CUP OF...

LAFLEUR BREWING COMPANY
EVANSTON, ILLINOIS

...OFFEE

...PER // OATMEAL STOUT WITH BOW...

JUNGLE CAT BLACK STOUT

Beeeer BREWERY

...ata fermentazione non...
...ata rifermentata in bottiglia...

FAKE SHEEP

FRUIT AL...
CON UVA
ARNEIS

33 cl e
alc. 6.5 % vol
OG 1062
BU 20
8-10

imbottigliata i 02...

Ingredienti acqua, malto d'orzo, u...
Arneis del Roero 20 %, luppolo, li...

Conservare in verticale a riluogo fresc...

...rma deposito naturale sul fon...

Birrificio
EL GRANO

A.P.A.
...AIN AMERICA

Bikini

12.5° blg   5.2 % alk.

ye olde red eye
Irish Nut Red Ale
K.R.Theesen
home-brewer
Beer Quest
22 Feb

...SYCHIC MEDIUM
...IBBEL   DUBBEL

TRANSCENDENTAL BELGIAN ALE ...% VOL

...WED BY ...EY'S
...REWING CONCERN LTD
...ASTICITYLABEL.COM

CRAFTED BY HAND
TORONTO ONTARIO CANADA

Captain Traceplant
IPA 2.0
"the Porch Strikes Back"

Pale   Ale

HIGH WATER BREWERY

WET BEAR

WITBIER

PIWKO WYPRODUKOWANE
W DOMKU PRZEZ RACZKI

SKŁAD:

słody: Heidelberg, pszeniczny
pszenica, płatki owsiane
curacao, kolendra
skórka słodkiej pomarań...
chmiele: Lubelski, Halle...
drożdże Fermentis S-3...

ZABUTELKOWAN...
19.03.2014

12° BLG
Ok. 4.5 alk.

NZ RED LAGER · 2014

μbrowar Sieniczno

Lis

6% alk.
14° Blg

Good Day Sunshine
Double IPA with Citra Hops for Days

EST. 2013 | Lisle, Illinois | 12 fl oz | ...% abv | Bottled on

BLACKBIRD BREWIN...

Turkish delight

Admiral Sasquatch

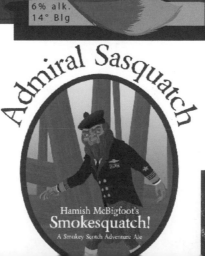

Hamish McBigfoot's
Smokesquatch!
A Smokey Scotch Adventure Ale

F.T. BROWNBRANDT'S
RAS KÖL...

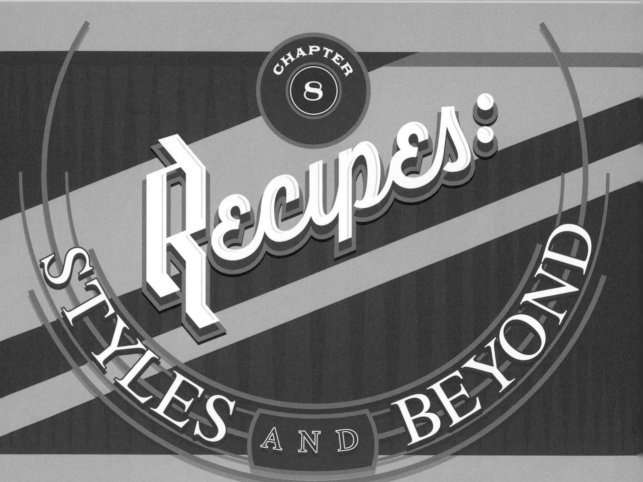

CHAPTER

8

Recipes:
STYLES AND BEYOND

❧ This chapter goes behind the theory and practice of brewing to the highly personal world of recipes.

I've tried to cover as wide a range as possible, from orthodox versions of classics like English bitter and Belgian dubbel to modern craft brews to ingredient-driven beers from around the world and my own take on a full year's worth of seasonal beers. That's a lot of territory, so there are many beers that don't get a full recipe workup. There should, however, be enough detail and historical background to make a pretty good attempt. Remember, my goal is to teach you how to make your own creatively delicious recipes, not keep you chained to mine.

The recipes in this chapter are all designed to make great-tasting beer. They are put together as simply as possible, but not dumbed down in any way. For the classic styles, I have tried to stick to traditional ingredients and recipe approaches as an educational tool. There certainly are many different ways to brew even the most hidebound styles, as present brewing practice around the world will attest. In a general book like this, it is impossible to present the fine details of something so complex as the culture of brewing. This book is just the beginning. There is a lot of great information out there.

CALCULATIONS *and* ASSUMPTIONS

All of the recipes here share the same assumptions about utilization, bitterness, and other parameters. All of the values used for malt, hops, and other ingredients are the ones found in the tables in chapter 3. You should be aware that there will be some variation in practice, and you may eventually feel the need to try to make adjustments to compensate for the many variables of ingredients and process. These break down into two areas: brewery-to-brewery variation, and changes in raw ingredients due to agricultural and production factors or limitations on what is actually available on the market, which may differ from what I've specified. Fortunately, it is possible to compensate for both issues.

For ingredients, check to see that what you're using is a reasonably close match to what's in the recipes. If a malt is darker or lighter than what is specified in the recipe, that may have visible effects. In that case, use a little more or less of the darkest malt in the recipe to compensate. Fortunately, the extract yield from one batch of malt to another varies only slightly, so generally, that's not a big concern. Hops may vary by 50 percent from year to year, and lose about one-third of their bittering power after a year of storage. And, of course, if you can't get a certain hop you'll have to substitute, and the most similar hops in terms of character won't necessarily match in terms of bittering power. If a hop is twice as bitter, use half as much in the recipe.

Everybody's brewing system is different. The utilization rates for malts are a guess based on the kind of efficiencies typical for homebrewers, but yours may well be different. This is one of the reasons it is so important to keep good records. Even after a single brew, you can go back and check your results against the recipe's expectations. If your beers are higher or lower in gravity, you can use less or more grain the next time. Malt extract should be pretty consistent, so efficiency is always 100 percent. Hop bitterness can't easily be measured, so a trained palate is helpful. If you feel your beers are more or less bitter than expected, adjust the hop quantities in future batches until you feel you're meeting expectations.

Grain yield efficiencies are as follows in the recipes:

- All-grain recipes are calculated at 75 percent of laboratory extract.
- Grains in mini-mash recipes are calculated at 60 percent of laboratory extract.
- Grains in steeped grain recipes are calculated at 50 percent of laboratory extract.

Percentages of grain bills are as a percentage of extract rather than a percentage of total weight. You can expect small rounding errors that may add up to a little over or under 100 percent. This is especially true when there are multiple choices on color and flavor malts. Some metric quantities have been rounded up or down slightly for sanity's sake and may not precisely equal the pound amounts.

Writer Michael Jackson was the first author in modern times to take beer really seriously. In addition to being a catalyst for the whole craft-beer movement, his work helped crystalize our modern notion of beer styles. Photo by Edward Bronson.

Alcohol content in the beer is dependent on a particular gravity target, but there's more to it than that. Not all worts are equally fermentable. In all-grain brewing, mashing temperature is the main method used to control this. Malt extracts vary in their fermentability, so they may produce different results than you're looking for. Further, yeast performance affects attenuation, and this varies by strain, fermentation temperature, and other factors.

All of the recipes in this book are for 5-gallon/19-L batches; so if you're brewing 20-L batches, all ingredient quantities should be multiplied by 1.05 if you want the exact same results. Obviously, larger batches should be scaled up appropriately.

All hop quantities are in grams, which are easier to use than fractions of ounces.

BREWING METHODS *in the* RECIPES

Full-mash recipes are given first, and in nearly every case, a steeped-grain extract or a mini-mash recipe is given as well. There are just a few beers that don't produce great results with simplified procedures, so that's perhaps some added incentive to step up to all-grain brewing. Here is an overview of the procedures used in the recipes you'll find in this book.

EXTRACT PLUS STEEPED-GRAIN (page 119)

This is mostly extract and uses a grain bag filled with malts like caramel that yield useful extract with a simple steeping as the rest of the (extract-based) wort is brought to a boil. Anything in the recipe called "extract" should be added to the kettle with the hot water, while the rest of the grains should be crushed and put into grain bags and added to the wort as it is heating, and then removed before the wort boils.

MINI MASH (page 127)

This conducts an actual mash at a small scale, using the important flavor malts for the recipe and sometimes some enzyme-rich Pils malt to speed things along. After an hour at about 150°F/66°C, the wort is drained to the rest of the extract-based wort

coming to a boil in the kettle. As with the steeped-grain method, all the extracts should go into the brew kettle; all the other grains should be crushed and made into the mini mash. Give the mini mash a head start, and only start heating the wort after about 45 minutes of mashing.

ALL-GRAIN INFUSION MASH (page 130)

Most of the all-grain procedures are simple infusion mashes. The temperature of the main rest for saccharification changes from recipe to recipe, which affects how sweet or dry the beer will be. Don't forget to pay attention to this detail. More complicated procedures are recommended in those few cases where a simpler mash won't give good results—witbier, for example. These will be referenced in the recipes.

You will not insult me by changing the recipes to suit your own experience or whim. It is my hope that you will learn enough to far surpass my efforts here. I look forward to tasting the results.

ABOUT STYLES

Ah, styles! There, I've already said something controversial. By the time I'm done with the next few paragraphs, I am hoping I will have annoyed everybody.

There are probably more disagreements over styles than anything else in brewing. In one camp, you have purists who view the current style guidelines as manifestations of inexorable progress toward perfection, the beers themselves as somehow fixed and immutable as the heavens. Some view the regions outside the style boundaries as barren, barbarian country, and in places there are even laws preventing entry into this forbidden zone. To live in a world without styles would be to descend into the madness of beer anarchy. Without common language, we live in a meaningless Babel.

In the other camp are those who see styles as arbitrary and unnecessary, a crutch for unimaginative minds and a barrier to the spirit of the true artist. Staying within established guidelines cuts one off from the incredible richness of possibility, and why would you want to do that? IPAs and Pilsners have been done to death. It's time for something new in the twenty-first century. Move forward or die.

Scholars of beer history would say that styles are simply a snapshot in time, and the more you try to pin them down, the less defined they are. Any reference to style must include a date stamp as well, because they change, often very rapidly, in response to many societal, political, technological, and agricultural factors.

Everybody's wrong, of course, and everybody's right. A true point of view requires you to make peace with contrary facts and suspend rigid thinking. After all, beer styles are the products of human imagination, so you can't expect them to be perfectly rational.

Styles do have their uses. They function as a shared language, a kind of shorthand that allows for easy communication, so important when we, as brewers, are trying to manage the expectations of people who drink our beers. Just say "pale ale," and a whole host of characteristics pops into mind. It's the way language works. One term speaks for a host of others. It's the nature of our brains to do this.

The historians point out that people often have incorrect notions of styles. There are lots of reasons for this. Part of it is the blind men and the elephant problem; we each have a point of view. If your only experience of Scottish ales is reading about them in books and tasting them in the United States, you will get a shockingly different view when you actually go to Scotland. Our view of Scottish ales as dark, malty, and a little sweet is a bit warped, and if you think Scottish beer has peated malt, then you're way off the mark. If you really care about a particular brewing tradition, go see what it's like in its home. You'll be amazed how wrong you can be.

The other problem is that our literature is filled with lovely folktales that masquerade as history, and even a writer as gifted and influential as Michael Jackson was wont to pass them along uncritically. Trying to correct these myths is like trying to replace the foundation of a large building brick-by-brick—a slow, perilous, and thankless task. I know I've made my share of mistakes in this area. For a lot of reasons, it's very hard not to. The incorrectness of the current state of many described styles detracts from their authority and even their usefulness. Otherwise they really are arbitrary and pointless for anything other than slicing up competition categories.

Styles are more a matter of tradition now rather than necessity. In the past, a beer existed because it was what you could brew from local ingredients, with whatever technology you had available, to suit the needs of your constituency. With few limitations beyond the demands of the marketplace, it's easy to make almost any kind of beer at every brewery. If you are trying to master a style, it's helpful to look at the limitations that led to its creation. Study agriculture and climate, look at tax systems, energy sources, transportation methods, packaging, and marketing; styles are shaped by all these factors and many others. It's quite a nice way to learn history.

Tradition is a loaded word, for sure. On the one hand, it creates a sense of continuity, a connection with the ancestors and a celebration of one's heritage, which can be very comforting. But tradition can be like lederhosen—cool flash from the past, but as trousers, they're kind of stiff and itchy. And so, a conflict. Tradition is inherently anti-change; that is just about its only feature. Art, not so much. I love tradition and all the richness it can provide, but at the same time, it needs to be allowed to live and breathe, and this means change; it's a very delicate balancing act. Reinvention is the path I prefer.

Like 'em or not, it is indisputable that learning to work within the limitations of styles will make you a better brewer, sharpening technical skills needed to really control the brew, as well as developing an aesthetic vision. Make a great Pils and you'll know you can make a clean beer and learn a few things about the importance of base malt. Brew a great bitter and you'll develop some tricks for coaxing subtlety and depth from meager ingredients. We have a lot to learn from the classics, for sure. For most brewers, it's worth the effort. And if you want to win awards, that's pretty much what the game is.

Whatever your point of view, styles exist, so, you'll have to come to terms with them in one way or another, or forever remain a rebel. You have to decide.

A TIMELINE of BEER HISTORY and TECHNOLOGY

A vast range of beer styles and technologies have evolved throughout the long and exciting history of beer brewing.

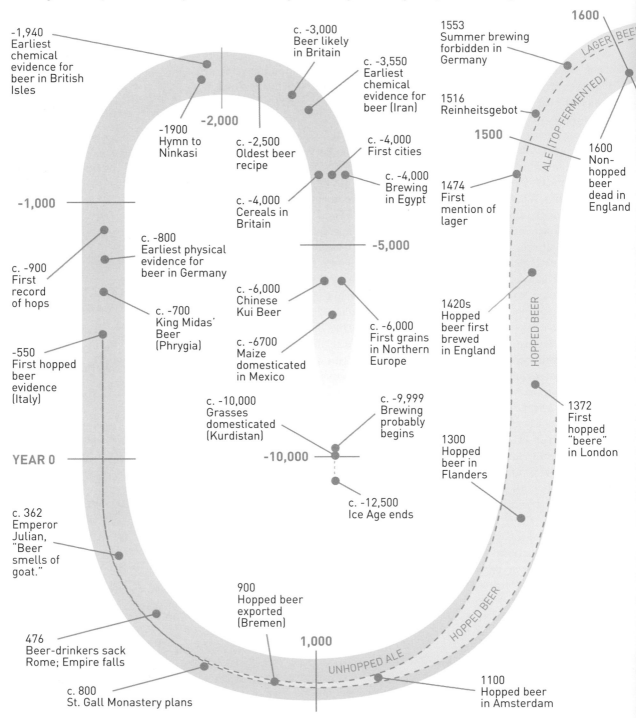

-1,940
Earliest chemical evidence for beer in British Isles

c. -3,000
Beer likely in Britain

c. -3,550
Earliest chemical evidence for beer (Iran)

1553
Summer brewing forbidden in Germany

1600

LAGER BEER

ALE (TOP FERMENTED)

-2,000

-1900
Hymn to Ninkasi

c. -2,500
Oldest beer recipe

c. -4,000
First cities

1516
Reinheitsgebot

1500

1600
Non-hopped beer dead in England

c. -4,000
Brewing in Egypt

1474
First mention of lager

-1,000

c. -4,000
Cereals in Britain

c. -800
Earliest physical evidence for beer in Germany

-5,000

c. -900
First record of hops

c. -6,000
Chinese Kui Beer

1420s
Hopped beer first brewed in England

c. -700
King Midas' Beer (Phrygia)

c. -6,000
First grains in Northern Europe

HOPPED BEER

-550
First hopped beer evidence (Italy)

c. -6700
Maize domesticated in Mexico

c. -10,000
Grasses domesticated (Kurdistan)

c. -9,999
Brewing probably begins

1372
First hopped "beere" in London

YEAR 0

-10,000

1300
Hopped beer in Flanders

c. 362
Emperor Julian, "Beer smells of goat."

c. -12,500
Ice Age ends

900
Hopped beer exported (Bremen)

476
Beer-drinkers sack Rome; Empire falls

1,000

HOPPED BEER

c. 800
St. Gall Monastery plans

UNHOPPED ALE

1100
Hopped beer in Amsterdam

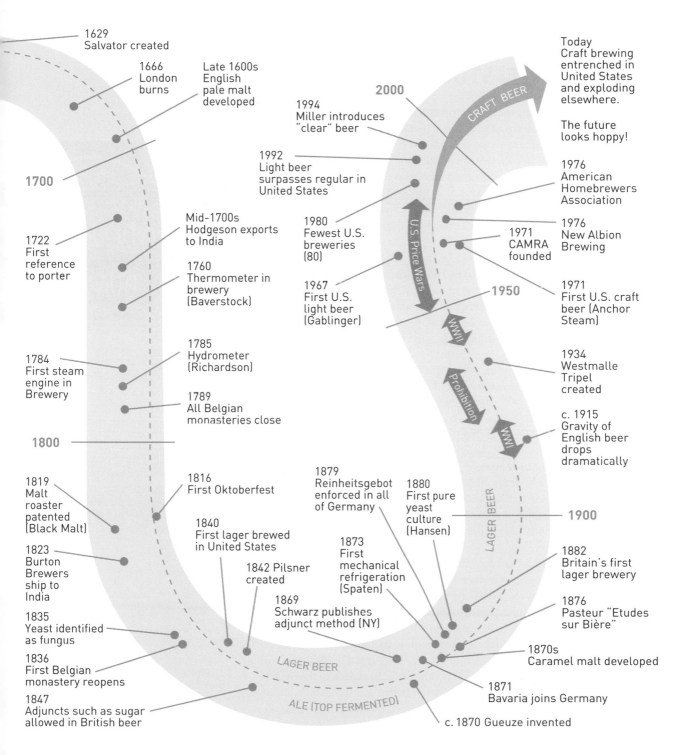

1629
Salvator created

1666
London burns

Late 1600s
English pale malt developed

1994
Miller introduces "clear" beer

2000

Today
Craft brewing entrenched in United States and exploding elsewhere.

The future looks hoppy!

1992
Light beer surpasses regular in United States

CRAFT BEER

1976
American Homebrewers Association

1700

1722
First reference to porter

Mid-1700s
Hodgeson exports to India

1760
Thermometer in brewery (Baverstock)

1980
Fewest U.S. breweries (80)

1967
First U.S. light beer (Gablinger)

U.S. Price Wars

1950

1976
New Albion Brewing

1971
CAMRA founded

1971
First U.S. craft beer (Anchor Steam)

1784
First steam engine in Brewery

1785
Hydrometer (Richardson)

1789
All Belgian monasteries close

WWII

Prohibition

WWI

1934
Westmalle Tripel created

c. 1915
Gravity of English beer drops dramatically

1800

1819
Malt roaster patented (Black Malt)

1816
First Oktoberfest

1879
Reinheitsgebot enforced in all of Germany

1880
First pure yeast culture (Hansen)

LAGER BEER

1900

1823
Burton Brewers ship to India

1840
First lager brewed in United States

1842 Pilsner created

1873
First mechanical refrigeration (Spaten)

1882
Britain's first lager brewery

1835
Yeast identified as fungus

1869
Schwarz publishes adjunct method (NY)

1876
Pasteur "Etudes sur Bière"

1836
First Belgian monastery reopens

LAGER BEER

1870s
Caramel malt developed

1847
Adjuncts such as sugar allowed in British beer

ALE (TOP FERMENTED)

1871
Bavaria joins Germany

c. 1870 Gueuze invented

A BREWER'S OVERVIEW *of* BEER STYLES

Caveats and cautionary notes aside, here's how you might think about beer styles and a sampling of recipes for making them.

ENGLISH ALE, STOUT, *and* PORTER

Brewing has been going on in the British Isles since 3000 B.C.E. or possibly earlier; this is a nation with beer deep in its bones. Modern British ales surely bear little resemblance to those ancient brews, although our picture of the early beers is pretty murky. Britain was the last place in Europe to cling to unhopped ales, eventually switching to hopped beer introduced by Flemish immigrants beginning about 1400 or so. By 1600, the unhopped beers were gone, although lightly hopped "amber" beers persisted for another century or more. The beers we enjoy today developed in fits and starts over the past few hundred years.

The story of modern British beer begins out in the countryside; those strong, amber-colored, highly hopped beers inspired considerable devotion. These were October and March beers, named for the month of their brewing, the former from freshly harvested malt and hops. These beers, especially the ones brewed on private estates, had the reputation as the best beers in England. By the early nineteenth century, they would move into the cities and morph into pale ale and IPA.

Britain's first big revolution was porter. This dark beer, which burst on the scene around 1720, was brewed from briskly kilned brown malt from Hertfordshire, north of London. It was brown, hoppy, pretty cheap, and available in several strengths. It found instant success especially among working classes like the specialized manual laborers, the porters, for whom it is named. Porter rode the tide of industrialization, and by 1750 the need for extended beer aging in mass quantities brought in moneyed players who obliged the public with huge amounts of porter. The beer itself changed dramatically in response to technological advancements, economics, and public taste, but would remain popular for another century. One variant, stout, is still with us today, and porter, extinct for a generation, has made a comeback as a specialty beer.

The history of British beers is convoluted and hard to follow, aggravated by the constantly changing nomenclature. The word *mild*, for example, once simply referred to any beer that had not undergone extended aging; by the twentieth century it applied only to light and dark versions of very low-gravity, lightly hopped beers. Today, the pale version is pretty much gone, leaving only the dark, which is again being brewed at higher strengths as well as low. Pale ale and bitter started out as different things, but today, if there is a difference, it's impossible to define and is contradicted by what's in the marketplace. The same goes for the subcategories of ordinary, special, ESB, and others,

Country-based homebrewed ales once had the reputation as being the best in England.

with no precise definitions outside the rarefied realm of beer competition guidelines. To further complicate things, a whole series of more lightly hopped K beers paralleled pale ales and bitters before being subsumed by them.

Such fluidity of language has always been a feature of English. If you like to be super-precise about the meaning of words, this will make you crazy. Best to just sit back and enjoy the inconsistencies over a well-pulled pint.

The beers change as well as the names. Porter was a different thing in every generation for most of its history, changing in recipe, seasoning, hopping, color, and terminology due to market and technological changes. And of course there were several different subtypes of porter being brewed at any one time. Like elsewhere, economic forces, prohibitionist sentiments, and historic events like poor harvests and wars shaped the beers in dramatic ways, often quite rapidly. WWI was a nexus of many of these factors; British beers were dramatically weaker after the war, and have never returned to anything close to their nineteenth-century strengths.

It is helpful to think about British beers in three big categories: pale, brown, and black. Within each, there are subdivisions of varying strengths, colors, and hop rates, but in terms of their formulation, beers in any one group share a lot. Once you grasp the basic idea of the broader style groups, it becomes pretty easy to adjust gravity, hop rates, and grist to move among the substyles as well as your own interpretation of how the beers should taste.

Many of us have a sort of dreamy-eyed view of English ales—rich, all-malt, antique beers that against all odds have stood the test of time. But the reality is that the same market and political forces that drove American mass-market beers to the edge of wateriness have also been at work in the United Kingdom for the past century or more. The truth is, that while there are some all-malt examples, the vast majority are quite light-bodied, the result of corn, sugar, and other adjuncts. Economics aside, it makes sense when you think about how a beer like bitter is actually consumed: in imperial pints, three or four at a go. A beer needs to be pretty light on its feet to keep its fans standing after such a session. The magic of this style at its best is that despite the delicateness, the best examples also find a way to be profound and enjoyable, pint after pint.

While the British style guidelines drop everything into neat little categories, commercial designations are a good deal more capricious.

THE PALE ALE FAMILY

Let's start with the base, pale ale malt. In the old days, beers were brewed from this malt alone, and it is possible to brew quite a delicious beer purely from pale malt. As always, you want the absolute best quality you can find for this. Pale malt is kilned to a color of 2.5 to 3.5°L, and by itself it will produce a deep gold beer. Flavor should lean just slightly toward a crisp toastiness, with additional nutty flavors tossed in. Most English brewer's malt is made from modern barley cultivars, but some heirloom varieties exist. Maris Otter is an older strain that makes complex and delicious beers; Golden Promise is a strain most often used in Scotch whisky, but also makes fine beer.

You may want some adjuncts to lighten the body as well as to add a touch of creaminess and improve the head. Corn sugar is the cleanest body-thinner, but unrefined sugar like Muscovado can also add an extra layer of flavor, and is quite traditional in English beers beginning around 1850. Liquid sugars like Lyle's Golden Syrup or light molasses (small quantities!) can also be used. Any of those can be added directly to the boil. Malted or torrefied wheat or flaked barley can add a creamy texture and improve the head. On the nontraditional side, wild rice makes a great addition, bringing a bit of nuttiness to the beer. It must be cooked as for eating before adding to the mash. The range for all of these is 5 to 20 percent of the extract.

Then we need to think about how we want to push the malt character. Here's a list of useful flavor malts for English bitters and pale ales.

AMBER/BISCUIT

Adds a crisp toastiness and a little color; 2 to 15 percent.

CARAMEL MALT

Lighter shades up to 40°L or so are best here, as darker versions lean toward burnt sugar that seems pretty out of place in a bitter or pale ale. Be aware that different maltsters' versions often taste dramatically different, so try to taste what's available to you and make your decisions based on that; 2 to 10 percent, but use restraint, as they can be heavy.

HONEY MALT

Less aggressive flavor than caramel, but definitely light caramel notes; 2 to 10 percent.

MELANOIDIN

Adds deep, cookie-like flavors and some color; up to 8 percent.

PILS

Cuts the slight toastiness of pale ale malt, lightens the color. May be used up to 100 percent in the case of golden/summer bitter.

VIENNA, MUNICH

Not traditional, but adds a rich caramelliness, with a slight toasted-cookie edge in Munich; 10 to 30 percent.

ORIGINAL GRAVITY AND COLOR OF PALE ALE FAMILY

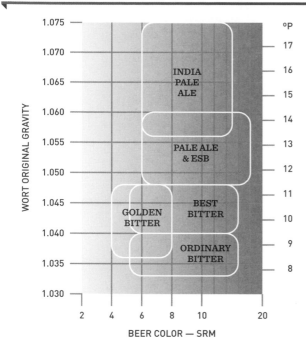

This graph is based on Beer Judge Certifcation Program (BJCP) guidelines, created for the purposes of competitions. Real-life categories are not nearly so clean cut, but this helps lay out the beers as they relate to one another as well as gravity and color parameters.

There is a broad range of bitterness in these beers, but hopping in this category should be noticeable at the very least, and can be quite aggressive. Southern England has long been home to some very fine and distinctive hops, and all English-style pale ales should reflect that national character. English hops such as Kent Goldings are often characterized by bright, green, grassy aromas with some spiciness. Fuggles have an earthier flavor, which is why they were more often used in dark beers in the past. Don't overlook newer hops like First Gold and Challenger, among others. When hopping, be aware of the ratio of bitterness to gravity, as it takes a lot less bitterness to balance a 1.035 ordinary bitter than a 1.060 pale ale.

Beer Name and Type		Original Gravity/°P	Estimated Alcohol by Vol.	Approx. BU	Color	Weeks to Drink
Multiple Personality Bitter or Else a Pale Ale or Else an ESB		1.044/10.9°P	4.8%	37/moderate	Gold to amber/ 6–12 SRM	3–5

Qty	Ingredient	OG/°P	%	**All-Grain Mashed Version**
8 lb/3.7 kg	Maris Otter pale ale malt	1.0440/11	100	Infusion mash (page 130) 60 min @ 154°F/68°C, then mash out
or				
6.7 lb/3 kg	Pale ale malt	1.0378/9.5	86	
6.5 oz/184 g	Amber malt	1.0009/0.2	2	
3 oz/86 g	40°L caramel malt	1.0009/0.2	2	
3 oz/86 g	Torrefied wheat	1.0044/1.1	10	
or				
5.2 lb/2.4 kg	Pale ale malt	1.0308/7.7	70	
2 lb/909 g	Pils malt	1.0104/2.7	24	
7 oz/199 g	Wheat malt	1.0026/0.07	6	

Qty	Ingredient	OG/°P	%	**Alternate Extract + Steeped-Grain Version**
2.5 lb/1.1 kg	Dry pale malt extract	1.0370/9.3	84	Standard E + SG Procedure (page 119)
13.5 oz/386 g	Dry wheat extract	1.0044/1.1	10	
9.5 oz/270 g	20°L caramel malt	1.0018/0.5	4	
3.5 oz/99 g	40°L caramel malt	1.0009/0.2	2	
or				
2.5 lb/1.1 kg	Dry pale malt extract	1.0365/9.1	83	
13.5 oz/386 g	Dry wheat extract	1.0053/1.4	12	
9.5 oz/270 g	Honey malt	1.0022/0.6	5	
or				
4.5 lb/2 kg	Dry pale malt extract	1.0413/10.3	94	
11.2 oz/318 g	Cara-Pils malt	1.0027/0.7	6	

Hops

Qty	Name	Alpha	IBU	Minutes	
					Yeast: Your choice of British ale yeast
24 g	East Kent Golding	5.5	20	60	**Fermentation Temperature:** 62 to 68°F/17 to 20°C
19 g	East Kent Golding	5.5	12	30	**Carbonation:** Medium low/2 volumes/
28 g	East Kent Golding	5.5	5	5	2.5 oz (71 g) priming sugar
or					
18 g	Palisade	8.0	22	60	
12 g	Challenger	7.5	10	30	
25 g	Challenger	7.5	5	5	

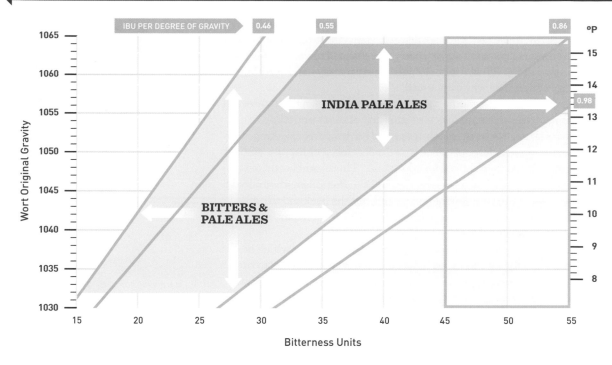

The gravity and bitterness range for these classic styles have a fair amount of desirable bitterness. As the gravities go up, more hops are needed to achieve the same perceived malt–hop balance. Diagonal lines are BU:GU ratios.

Yeast is another key component. There is a wide range of strains available, most traced to a particular brewery. Their impact on beer flavor and aroma is quite dramatic. Aside from its own fruity and occasionally spicy aromas, yeast can enhance a beer's malt or hops, or even bring out woody, nutty characteristics.

Bitters and pale ales are deceptively simple. Just a few ingredients, pretty light gravities—there's really nothing dramatic about them, and I guess that's the point. And as easy as it is to toss a serviceable one together, it is just as hard to create something that is not only complex and captivating, but also delicate and easy to drink—a true test of the brewer's art.

STRONG ALES, OLD ALES, AND BARLEY WINES

This category is so loose as to be little more than the description the title above offers. Sadly, these beers are not much in vogue these days, but a couple of hundred years ago much soppy poetry was devoted to them. They were considered some of the finest fruits of English gastronomy—and certainly can be worthy of that title when done well.

Color may range from pale amber to nut brown. Hopping in the eighteenth century was massive, and waned by the beginning of the twentieth.

In commercial use, the term is loosely applied but properly speaking, an old ale is one that has undergone an extended oak aging, picking up a vinous, mature flavor referred to in the old texts as "stale." This was not sourness; the old books are filled with bizarre remedies for that. *Brettanomyces* undoubtedly played a role in the transformation, drying out the beer and adding complex fruity and earthy aromas. The *B. claussenii* strain in particular is associated with English old ales.

Most English barley wines are basically ramped-up pale ales, which is fitting, because the style we know as India pale ale that was shipped to the English colonies was originally the pale, strong, hoppy brew called October beer, which matches a modern description of a barley wine pretty closely.

BRITISH BROWN AND MILD ALES

Although there are plenty of paeans to nut-brown ales in the literature of British drink, you really have to go back to pre-industrial days to find a widely popular beer there properly called brown ale. Brown ale seems to have been reinvented around 1900 after a long absence, but remained a specialty item in most places, although it did enjoy some popularity in England's north. A form of brown called mild ale achieved greater celebrity and was actually the most popular beer in England from WWI until the 1960s. Weak, cheap, and chestnut-colored, by the 1990s, mild had lapsed into an old man's beer. Today, authentic examples remain elusive. Although they are delicate beers, they have their charms and deserve a wider audience. Fortunately, both mild and brown ale have been reinterpreted by modern craft brewers in England as well as in the United States.

Although they look different, dark mild and brown ale have some similarities. Both may be brewed at a number of different strengths, although twentieth-century mild was exceedingly weak and watery. Both use a minimum of hops, barely enough for balance, with little or no aromatic character. Like bitters, they are intended for quaffing, not sipping. Mild is the darker of the two, with a beautiful ruby-brown appearance. Brown ale is often barely brown at all, overlapping with some of the darker pale ales. There is some geographic trending as well, with brown ales being more associated with the north of England and mild with London and the south. Despite their color and roasty/toasty flavors, both should be relatively light on the palate, without a lot of sweetness or heavy texture: think thirst-quenching dark beer.

English gentlemen drank their strong October beers from small glasses like this, toasting their health, the Queen, and lord knows what else.

Beer Name and Type		Original Gravity/°P	Estimated Alcohol by Vol.	Approx. BU	Color	Weeks to Drink
Faded Glory Mild Ale		1.037/9.3°P	4 %	20/moderate	Ruby-brown/ 24 SRM	3–5

Qty	Ingredient	OG/°P	%	**All-Grain Mashed Version**
5.5 lb/2.5 kg	Mild ale malt	1.0300/7.6	81	Infusion mash (page 130)
13 oz/370 g	Flaked barley	1.0037/1.0	10	60 min @ 154°F/68°C, then mash out
6.5 oz/185 g	80°L caramel malt	1.0185/4.7	5	
2.5 oz/71 g	Brown malt	1.0007/0.2	2	
2.5 oz/71 g	Röstmalz	1.0007/0.2	2	

Qty	Ingredient	OG/°P	%	**Alternate Extract + Steeped-Grain Version**
2.5 lb/1.1 kg	Dry pale malt extract	1.0259/6.5	70	Standard E + SG Procedure (page 119)
13.5 oz/386 g	Dry wheat extract	1.0074/1.9	20	
9.5 oz/270 g	Honey malt	1.0019/0.5	5	
3.5 oz/99 g	120°L caramel malt	1.0007/0.2	2	
5.5 oz/156 g	Röstmalz	1.0011/0.3	2	

Hops

Qty	Name	Alpha	IBU	Minutes	
					Yeast: London ESB Ale (WLP002 or Wyeast 1968)
12 g	Northern Brewer	8.5	16	60	**Fermentation Temperature:** 62 to 68°F/17 to 20°C
15 g	U.S. Hallertau	4.5	4	10	**Carbonation:** Medium low/2 volumes/2.5 oz (71 g) priming sugar

For base malts, the beers diverge. Brown ale needs some real toastiness, best accomplished with amber/biscuit malt, which can form up to half the recipe, in combination with pale ale malt. Smaller amounts of brown, melanoidin, or dark caramel malts can be used to add complexity. Mild seems truest to style when brewed with mild ale malt, a more highly kilned malt than pale, and this lends a profoundly rich and caramelly aroma. For color, usually some black malt is used, perhaps with small amounts of dark caramel, brown, chocolate, and even biscuit or melanoidin malt for complexity. A dehusked/debittered black malt, typically used in German beer, can give a smoother roasted component than typical black malt. The use of adjuncts, either as body thinners or head improvers, is much the same as for the pale ales.

Fuggles are the traditional hops for dark beers, but Northern Brewer and Northdown also work nicely. Typically, hops get a single addition for the full boil, with no late hopping.

As with the pale ales, yeast is important here. In general, I find that a malt-accentuating strain like the so-called London ESB (Fuller's) yeast really brings these beers to life, although you may have your own ideas about what you are trying to achieve.

Through much of the twentieth century, the dimpled pint mug was iconic for dark mild ale, the working man's choice.

STOUTS AND PORTERS

This is another big happy family. Porter was the craze of eighteenth-century London and was always brewed in a number of strengths and hop levels, one of which was called "stout"—not the strongest one, by the way. Over a couple of hundred years of history, the basic idea of a super-dark beer gets morphed and twisted, split and rejoined, in response to public needs and whims, as well as economics and politics. This makes trouble for us today when we want to absolutely, positively know what a stout is, and when it's not a porter. Having spent a lot of time hitting the books on this, I can tell you that there are no absolutes, only snapshots, slices of time that reveal a certain temporary order eventually carried away by the tide. In a way, this is liberating because it means a stout can be any beer that's really dark, and porter is always just a bit lighter than that.

Because the dark color and roasty tastes define these styles, it's easy to think that's all there is to them. The specific character of the roasty component is certainly important, but what differentiates a great stout from an ordinary one is everything but the roasted malts. Without something going on underneath all that inky darkness, these beers can get boring real fast. Guinness knows this. The pungency of roasted unmalted barley is countered by a big dose (30 percent!) of raw unmalted barley, which smooths out the sharp roastiness. Then they add a few percent of an oak-aged beer for some aromatic complexity and a bit of acidic tang. For a beer of 3.8 percent alcohol, it's profound.

As far as grists, we have the same component blocks to work with as with other beers:

1 base
2 color
3 middle malts for complexity
4 adjuncts as needed for texture, body, and head-retention

The trick to brewing good stouts and porters is to make sure there's plenty of depth to keep them from being a one-note drink. Texture, especially creaminess, is also important, as it helps to balance the sometimes-acrid nature of roasted malts. No wonder oatmeal stout is a popular substyle.

The base is often pale ale malt, but historically the somewhat darker mild ale malt was more often used. It offers a deep caramelly underpinning to build your beer on. Vienna malt is similar and can be substituted if mild ale malt is not available. Although not traditional, Munich malt can be used for all or part of the base with similar effects.

Top to bottom: Brown, pale chocolate, chocolate rye, Carafa/röstmalz, black patent, and roasted unmalted barley show the many choices for adding color and roast character to stouts, porters, and other dark beers.

As for the roast component, there are a number of choices that can be used singly or blended together to balance each other's character and/or achieve greater depth:

BLACK PATENT MALT

The standard for most stouts. Deep espresso flavors.

ROASTED UNMALTED BARLEY

Traditional in Irish dry stout, this has a very sharp, bright character.

DEBITTERED/DEHUSKED ROASTED MALT

Usually from German sources (röstmalz/Carafa), these offer a smoother bittersweet chocolate character and are typically available in up to three different colors.

CHOCOLATE, PALE CHOCOLATE

The palest of the roasted malts, chocolate actually has a very sharp and biting flavor, so take care to avoid harshness in the finished beer.

CHOCOLATE WHEAT OR RYE

Despite the name, these are truly black malts, and may offer some alternative roast character.

BROWN MALT

Not roasted but kilned, this was the original malt used to make porter. It has a rich, round, deeply toasted flavor, sort of a mocha type of character. Use it, and people know that you brewed a porter, not a stout.

With the exception of brown malt, these roasted malts are normally used in quantities of 10 percent or somewhat less in stout recipes, and probably in the 5 to 7 percent range for porters. Brown can be used up to 20 percent or even higher.

Then there's what's in the middle. A mess of biscuit for toastiness, melanoidin for cookie-like flavors, and caramel malts for a variety of flavors from, well, caramel in the lighter-colored ones to raisins and prunes in the 40 to 60°L range, then toasted marshmallows and burnt sugar in the 80°L and up versions.

Don't forget about adjuncts. With the exception of Irish stout, stouts can be pretty full-bodied, so they don't often need body-thinners like sugar, although that can be a nice addition to high-gravity versions, as a way of improving drinkability. I do like wheat in a stout or porter, which can be used in high percentages—up to half the grist—but this is not anything supported by history, just in case you're worried about that kind of thing. Oatmeal is a classic, and even has a style dedicated to it. Toast the oats first and you'll get a lovely aroma as well as a creamy texture. Sweet, or "milk," stouts often have lactose (milk sugar) added to them, which leaves some residual sweetness in the finished beer.

Other types of beer appear hideous in these Irish cobalt glass goblets, c. 1830, but stouts and porters contrast gloriously.

Porter began as a really hoppy beer, perhaps in the 50 to 80 BU range for some of the bigger ones; but in a couple of centuries it's become a very malty drink. Over the decades, this has happened to some of the stout styles as well, although Irish stout has a good deal of bitterness, especially in its relatively low-gravity draft forms. Except in American versions, it's rare to have much hop aroma in a modern stout or porter, so hop choice is not a big deal. You could just set the dial to "Fuggle" and you'd be all right, but you would also do well with Northdown, Northern Brewer, or even the clean bitterness of Magnum or Hallertau.

PORTER AND STOUT SUBSTYLES

MILD/BROWN AND ROBUST PORTER

Charlie Papazian (author of *The Complete Joy of Homebrewing*) admits to pulling these two porter categories out of thin air for homebrew judging categories back in the early 1980s, but there wasn't much to go on then. Porter was dead in its homeland and pretty much everywhere else except the Baltic region. So, modern porter is a reinvention, not a continuation. The two porter substyles don't really correspond to any historical realities, but the idea is that the mild porter is softer, lighter on the palate, sort of a souped-up brown ale, and the robust is a kind of junior stout, with some brisk roastiness, just a bit less of it than a true stout. Generally, you want to brew them just like a stout, but cut the black malts in half or so. Porter should be dark chestnut brown, but not black.

BALTIC PORTER

While technically a lager, its formulation falls into this category. It's pretty big, a bit sweet, and super smooth due to the use of debittered roasted malt. Hopping is low to medium at 20 to 40 BU and focuses on continental hops rather than English ones.

IRISH DRAUGHT STOUT

This is a light-bodied, low-alcohol stout made with a good dose of unmalted flaked barley and roasted unmalted barley as the roast component. The flaked barley is a bit tough to handle in large amounts without special adjunct procedures, so perhaps malted wheat and/or a dash of rye might supply the needed creaminess. Shoot for a light body. A percent or so of acid malt can approximate the soured beer that Guinness uses. Hopping is high for the gravity, maybe 30 or 40 BU.

IRISH EXPORT AND FOREIGN EXPORT STOUT

These are the same beer formula brewed at slightly different strengths. Roasted unmalted barley should be used here as well. Hopping can be vigorous, from 40 to as high as 60 BU in the stronger versions.

OATMEAL STOUT

This is a normal-strength beer with some flaked or malted oats added. Hopping is normally low-ish, at 28 to 30 BU. Black malt is the normal roast component, but debittered malt can make it even smoother, if that's what you're after.

IMPERIAL STOUT

Think big. Really big. Monstrously, ridiculously big—at least 1.090 (21.5°P). Load up on the hops, too. That's the way the Russian imperial court liked it and people still do.

Beer Name and Type	Original Gravity/°P	Estimated Alcohol by Vol.	Approx. BU	Color	Weeks to Drink
Leprechaun's Ladder Irish Stout	1.060/14.7°P	6.3 to 6.5 %	50/high	Blackish-brown/ 40 SRM	5–7

This is a pretty classic recipe, presented as an export-strength version. For the lighter draught version, simply multiply all quantities by 0.75, which will give you a 1.045 (11.2°P) wort. To make the stronger foreign extra version, multiply all quantities by 1.25, which gets you 1.075 (18.2°P), or by a larger multiplier for an even stronger beer. The acid malt simulates the tang of the wood-aged beer that is blended into Guinness.

Qty	Ingredient	OG/°P	%	**All-Grain Mashed Version**
8.2 lb/3.7 kg	Pale ale malt	1.0462/11.5	77	Infusion mash (page 130)
1.2 lb/544 g	Flaked barley	1.0072/1.8	12	Infusion, 60 min @ 150°F/66°C, then mash out
6 oz/168 g	Acid malt	1.0018/0.5	3	
1.1 lb/499 g	Roasted unmalted barley	1.0048/1.3	8	

Qty	Ingredient	OG/°P	%	**Alternate Extract + Steeped-Grain Version**
4 lb/1.8 kg	Dry pale malt extract	1.0360/9.0	60	Standard E + SG Procedure (page 119)
2 lb/907 g	Dry wheat extract	1.0185/4.7	31	
1 lb/454 g	Acid malt	1.0024/0.6	4	
9.5 oz/270 g	Roasted unmalted barley	1.0030/0.7	5	

Hops

Qty	Name	Alpha	IBU	Minutes	
					Yeast: Irish Stout (WLP004 or Wyeast 1084)
					Fermentation Temperature: 62 to 68°F/17 to 20°C
21 g	Nugget (or Galena)	13	35	60	**Carbonation:** Medium/2.5 volumes/4 oz (113 g)
21 g	Nugget (or Galena)	13	15	10	priming sugar

SCOTLAND AND ITS BEER TRADITIONS

While we think of them as dark and malty, most Scottish ales actually resemble English ales more than they conform to our imagined picture. Even Scotch ale, the strong, sweet, and lightly hopped brew that defines the Scottish approach, was a creature of the twentieth century, modeled on Burton ale and exported around the world in vast quantities.

Sometime during the nineteenth century, the Scots created a unique nomenclature system based on barrel prices in shillings. So you'll see references to 60 and 80 shilling ales, written "60/–" and "80/–," and each grade has a name such as "light" or "export" as well. The shilling designations are rarely seen there now and mostly live on in American beer judging style descriptions.

This doesn't mean there are no uniquely Scottish styles, though. The strong Scotch ales known as "wee heavy" and a scaled-back version of the same idea called an "export" can be found. Both put the emphasis on malt and have a very neutral fermentation character due to uniquely Scottish yeast strains working in the cool northerly climes.

BRITISH ALE STYLES BY THE NUMBERS

BEER STYLE	OG	°Plato	Alcohol % Vol.	Attenuation %	Color SRM	BU
ORDINARY BITTER	1.033–1.038	8–9	2.4–3	Dry to medium	8–14	25–55
BEST/SPECIAL BITTER	1.038–1.046	9.5–11.4	3.3–3.8	Dry to medium	8–14	25–55
ESB	1.046–1.060	11.4–14.7	4.8–5.8	Dry to medium	8–14	25–55
PALE ALE	1.044–1.056	11–14	3.8–6.2	Crisp, dry	5–14	20–50
IPA	1.050–1.070	12–17	4.5–7.5	Crisp, dry	6–14	40–60
GOLDEN/SUMMER BITTER	1.036–1.048	9–12	3.6–5	Crisp, dry	4–8	20–28
SCOTTISH LIGHT 60/–	1.030–1.035	8–9	2.5–3.2	Light, dry	10–25	25–35
SCOTTISH HEAVY 70/–	1.035–1.040	9–10	2.8–3.2	Moderate	9–19	12–20
SCOTTISH EXPORT 80/–	1.040–1.057	1–14	3.4–4.8	Moderate	10–19	5–30
SCOTCH ALE/WEE HEAVY/120/–	1.072–1.085	17–20	6.2–8	Full, sweet	10–25	25–35
NORTHERN BROWN ALE	1.040–1.052	10–13	4.2–5.2	Dryish	12–22	20–25
MILD ALE	1.040–1.052	10–13	4.2–5.2	Dry	12–22	20–25
ENGLISH STRONG/OLD ALE	1.061–1.092	15–22	5–9.5	Medium to full	12–30	30–65
BARLEY WINE	1.083–1.125	20–29	6.8–10	Medium to full	10–22	40–60
PORTER	1.040–1.065	10–16	4–6.5	Medium	20–50	20–40
IRISH DRY STOUT	1.038–1.048	9.5–12	3.8–5	Dry	40+	30–40
IRISH FOREIGN EXTRA STOUT	1.056–1.075	14–18	5.5–8	Medium to full	30+	30–65
LONDON/SWEET STOUT	1.045–1.056	11–14	3–6	Sweet to full	40+	15–25
OATMEAL STOUT	1.038–1.056	9.5–14	3.8–6	Creamy	25–40	20–40
IMPERIAL STOUT	1.079–1.124+	19–29	7–12	Medium to full	45+	50–80

English pubs are among the most glorious in the world.

GERMAN ALES, HYBRID ALES, and WEISSBIER

The fact that ales are often referred to as *alt*, or "old," beer gives some indication that top fermented beers were the original brews, with lagers coming a couple of thousand years later, at least. The Bavarian lager juggernaut rolled over the rest of Germany in the nineteenth century as it did in the rest of the beer world, but it couldn't snuff out all of the ale styles brewed in the north. In places like the Rhineland and in the vicinity of Berlin, these ales still survive. Even in lager-soaked Bavaria, one ale—hefeweizen—has coexisted alongside lager for many centuries.

However, lager has had its influence on these survivors. Except for wheat beer, German top-fermenting yeast is extremely neutral in character and, in the case of Düsseldorfer alt and Kölsch, even submits to a bit of cold conditioning. For this reason, Rhine beers are sometimes referred to as top-fermenting lagers. Wheat beer, with its distinctive fermentation character, has remained proudly untouched by lager tradition.

GERMAN ALES: ALT AND KÖLSCH

Although different in the glass, alt and Kölsch have a lot in common. They are both middling-strength table beers, usually with simple recipes, fermented at coolish temperatures with a softly fruity ale yeast, and lagered to further smooth out the flavors. Kölsch is a blonde beer, an ale counterpart to a lager like helles, but with a distinctive fruitiness and a subtle hop bouquet. It is normally made mostly from Pilsner malt, sometimes with small amounts of wheat to improve head and texture, and possibly small amounts of lightly colored malts like Vienna for a little complexity.

Düsseldorfer alt is its shadowy twin—deeply amber and briskly bitter, a crisp and refreshing dark beer. There are two very different ways to put together an altbier grist: one with Pils malt and a bit of debittered roast malt for color and a crisp roasty flavor; the second approach is to use a Munich malt base for a richer, toasted caramel flavor with a fatter texture, and if needed, a pinch of black malt to deepen the color. These two approaches can be combined, so anywhere in between can make a good altbier.

Altbier is a bitter beer, between 25 and 48 BU, but hop aroma is not desirable. Noble hops, especially Spalt, are most appropriate for both styles. Kölsch is less bitter at 18 to 25 BU, but some hop aroma character makes for a nice beer. World versions of noble hops can work if they're not overly aggressive.

Brewing Rhine Valley ales is pretty straightforward: a single infusion mash with low mash temperatures in the 144 to 148°F/62 to 64°C range makes a well-attenuated beer with a light body and good drinkability. Fermentation takes place at 60 to 69°F/18 to 21°C, with a cold conditioning at about 45°F/7°C.

Kölsch is served in a small, delicate glass called a "stange." Düsseldorfer alt comes in a shorter version along similar lines.

NORTH AMERICAN HYBRID ALES

There are two older North American ale styles generally referred to as "hybrid" ales because they combine characteristics of ales and lagers. Cream ale originated in the East and moved as far west as Ohio, where it still can be found as a slim shadow of its former self. Originally, cream ale may have been a blend of lager with a strong, hoppy "stock" ale that was a common product of most lager breweries before Prohibition. Blending allowed breweries to offer more products than they actually brewed, and cream ale would have been a refreshing, yet substantial and flavorful product. Cream ales came back after Prohibition, but because stock ales mostly did not, the trend was to use the company's lager at a slightly higher strength, sometimes with a dash more hops and occasionally sweetened before being pasteurized—a sad end for what must have been a pleasantly drinkable beer. Homebrewers and some small breweries are making revival versions using mostly malt

Beer Name and Type	Original Gravity/°P	Estimated Alcohol by Vol.	Approx. BU	Color	Weeks to Drink
Not Your Uncle Fritz's Steam Beer Steam Beer/California Common	1.052/12.9°P	5.6%	37/med. to high	Amber/8 SRM	5–7

Anchor's 1971 reformulation of its famous Steam beer was not based on traditional Steam beers, but was cooked up homebrew style from the ingredients available at that time. This leaves us with a problem: a style definition based on a single (and very modern) beer. This is a somewhat more backward-looking pre-Prohibition version. A more interesting sugar such as Demerara or piloncillo may be substituted (use 10 percent less) for the flaked rice or corn. Black malt was a common colorant in nineteenth-century American beers.

Qty	Ingredient	OG/°P	%	All-Grain Mashed Version
6.5 lb/2.9 kg	Pils malt	1.0338/8.5	65	Infusion mash (page 130)
2 lb/907 g	Vienna malt	1.0104/2.7	20	60 min @ 150°F/66°C, then mash out
14 oz/393 g	Flaked corn or rice	1.0052/1.5	10	
8 oz/227 g	Honey malt	1.0024/0.6	5	
1 oz/28 g	Debittered black malt	—	—	

Qty	Ingredient	OG/°P	%	Alternate Extract + Steeped-Grain Version
5.3 lb/2.4 kg	Dry pale malt extract	1.0444/10.9	85	Standard E + SG Procedure (page 119)
11 oz/312 g	Rice syrup	1.0052/1.3	10	
10 oz/284 g	Honey malt	1.0024/0.6	5	
1 oz/28 g	Debittered black malt	—	—	

Hops

Qty	Name	Alpha	IBU	Minutes	
					Yeast: San Francisco Lager (WLP810 or Wyeast 2112) or other strain
19 g	Cluster	7.0	20	60	**Fermentation Temperature:** 58 to 65°F/14 to 18°C
18 g	U.S. Hallertau	4.5	9	30	**Carbonation:** Medium /2.5 volumes/3.5 oz (99 g)
33 g	U.S. Tettnang	4.5	4	5	priming sugar
33 g	U.S. Hallertau	4.5	4	5	

with a little corn, moderately hopped with a nice noble hop aroma, perhaps tinged with some North American varieties. Fermentation with lager yeast at ale temperatures, like the Steam beer to follow, would be appropriate.

Steam beer is the other hybrid style, a result of brewers in the Mountain and Pacific regions of the western United States brewing beers with lager yeast but without ice for cooling, resulting in some ale characteristics. Once refrigeration arrived, around 1880, lagers could be properly fermented, so Steam beer began a long slow decline. By the 1960s, there was only one: Anchor. It was a mess of a beer by then, with lots of sugar as adjunct and very irregular quality. Fritz Maytag and his crew at Anchor Brewing Company reformulated it from the ground up in 1971, resulting in the first genuine craft beer in the United States, but one bearing little, if any resemblance to historical Steam beers. The mix of Northern Brewer hops on top of a caramel malt character is a modern classic, and the basis of all "California Common"–style descriptions.

THE KING OF WHEAT BEERS: GERMAN HEFEWEIZEN

The wheat beer called hefeweizen is widespread in Germany, but is still most popular in its home, Bavaria. A second wheat style from northern Germany (Prussia, actually) is Berliner weisse. The terminology is confusing so let's sort it out. *Weizen* means "wheat," but is applied only to the Bavarian style. *Weisse* means "white," and is more loosely applied to all wheat beers because of their cloudy appearance. *Hefe* means "yeast," so *hefeweizen* means the unfiltered form with yeast in the bottle or keg. *Kristal* indicates a filtered Bavarian style. Sometimes you see *hefe-weisse*, meaning the same thing as hefeweizen. *Dunkel* means "dark" and, of course, *bock* means the same thing it does in German lager brewing: a stronger beer.

All of these styles are brewed with malted, rather than raw, wheat. Bavarian hefeweizen will usually be at least 50 percent, and as much as 70 percent, malted wheat; Berliner weisse is somewhat less at 33 to 50 percent malted wheat.

Wheat beers often benefit from a protein rest, a step of 20 to 30 minutes at 122°F/50°C, and even more from a decoction. Production of the clovey phenolic compound 4-vinyl guiacol depends on a chemical called ferulic acid that is produced in the mash. While there is usually enough ferulic acid in a normal mash, some brewers employ a special mash step of 10 minutes at 113°F/45°C, which encourages formation of ferulic acid. Depending on the circumstances, it may be beneficial to you or not.

Bavarian weizen employs a unique species of yeast, *Torulaspora delbrueckii*. In the wine industry this yeast is used to add complexity; in beer it imparts highly distinctive aromas of clove, banana, and bubblegum. This yeast is highly sensitive to fermentation temperature, so good temperature control is key to creating a particular aromatic profile. Let the temperature wander, and you are at the mercy of its whims.

Hefeweizen is best served in a tall, curvy, half-liter glass.

Berliner Weisse is the traditional sour wheat beer of Berlin, often called the Champagne of the North. It is a part of the great family of white ales that follows the northern coast of Europe. Brewed from 50 percent or so of malted wheat, it is fermented with a conventional ale yeast as well as lactic acid bacteria that create a sharp sourness and a yogurty aromatic twang. In earlier days, Berliner weisse was brewed without boiling the wort at all, which ensured that some *Lactobacillus* survived to do the souring. By the late nineteenth century, the practice was to boil half the wort with the hops, and to ferment the unboiled fraction with *Lactobacillus* separately, combining them before packaging. *Brettanomyces* was also present in historical weisse, but this would have manifested itself only after an extended time in the bottle.

GERMAN WHEAT-BEER STYLES: GRAVITY BY COLOR

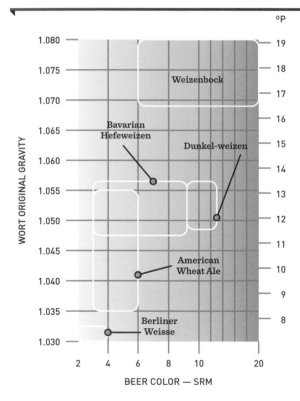

Here, classic German wheat beer styles are clearly organized by color and gravity ratios. American wheat ale added for comparison.

Supposedly based on a Flemish noble, Gambrinus, shown on a nineteenth-century chromolith poster for Pilsner Urquell, is a German invention who serves as the champion of all things lagery.

Beer Name and Type	Original Gravity/°P	Estimated Alcohol by Vol.	Approx. BU	Color	Weeks to Drink
Land of the Giant Gnomes Pale and Dunkel Weizen	1.052/12.8°P	6.3 to 6.5 %	50/high	Hazy straw/ 2.5 SRM	5–7

With only the pale wheat/extract, this is the pale version, but if all the ingredients including the darker malts are used, this will be a stronger dunkel-weizenbock. Many intermediate variations are possible, as are stronger and darker versions. Pay particular attention to the fermentation temperature; this is key to controlling the profile of fruity and spicy aromas. Every 2 degrees or so makes a noticeable difference.

New Glarus founder and brewmaster Dan Carey has a neat trick. A few percent of smoked malt added to the recipe enhances the phenolic character of the yeast without making the beer taste smoky. If you like your hefeweizens on the spicy side, try 1 or 2 percent of smoked malt swapped out for some of the Pils.

Dunkelweizenbock Version	1.076/18.4°P	6.3 to 6.5 %	15/low	Amber/ 10 to 12 SRM	5–7

Qty	Ingredient	OG/°P	%	All-Grain Mashed Version
6 lb/2.7 kg	Malted wheat	1.0354/8.8	68 (47)	Wheat Beer decoction mash (page 134),
3.2 lb/1.5 kg	Pils malt	1.0166/4.2	32 (22)	60 min @ 150°F/66°C, then mash out
1 lb/500 g	Rice hulls	—	—	
For Dunkelweizenbock, also add				
4.3 lb/2 kg	Dark malted wheat	1.022/5.6	28	
8 oz/227 g	45°L caramel wheat malt	1.0023/0.5	3	
1 oz/28 g	Chocolate wheat malt	—	—	

Qty	Ingredient	OG/°P	%	Alternate Extract + Steeped-Grain Version
4 lb/1.8 kg	Dry wheat extract	1.0416/10.4	80 (64)	Standard E + SG Procedure (page 119)
2 lb/907 g	Dry pale malt extract	1.0104/2.7	20 (16)	
For Dunkelweizenbock, also add				
1 lb/454 g	45°L caramel wheat malt	1.0040/1.0	6	
1 lb/454 g	Dry pale malt extract	1.0093/2.4	14	
1 oz/28 g	Chocolate wheat malt	—	—	

Hops

Qty	Name	Alpha	IBU	Minutes	
21 g	Tettnang	4.5	10	60	**Yeast:** Bavarian Hefeweizen (WLP351 or Wyeast 3638 or others)
21 g	Tettnang	4.5	5	10	**Fermentation Temperature:** 66 to 70°F/ 19 to 21°C
					Carbonation: High /3.5 volumes/6.5 oz (184 g) priming sugar

Dampfbier is a rustic specialty popular in parts of Bavaria and in the Black Forest region. Essentially, it is ersatz weissbier. Wheat was forbidden for commoners to use in brewing, but those with a taste for wheat ales would brew them anyway, using 100 percent malt. Supposedly backyard hops were also used for an additional rustic touch, and that's part of the fun of them, I think. Hop rates can be a little higher than in a hefeweizen. If you want to get all non-Reinheitsgebot about it, a few percent of oats can add some creaminess.

HYBRID ALE AND WHEAT BEER STYLES BY THE NUMBERS

BEER STYLE	OG	°Plato	Alcohol % Vol.	Attenuation %	Color SRM	BU
KÖLSCH	1.042–1.048	10.5–12	4.8–5.3	Low to med.	4–5	18–25
DÜSSELDORFER ALTBIER	1.044–1.048	11–12	4.3–5	Crisp, dry	11–19	25–48
AMERICAN CREAM ALE	1.044–1.052	11–13	4.2–5.6	Med. to dry	2–4	10–22
STEAM BEER/CALIFORNIA COMMON	1.048–1.056	12–14	4.3–5.5	Crisp, dry	10–14	30–45
GERMAN DAMPBIER (STEAM BEER)	1.047–1.056	11.8–14	4.9–5.5	Med. to dry	3–9	15–25
BAVARIAN HEFEWEIZEN	1.047–1.056	11.8–14	4.9–5.5	Creamy, dry	3–9	10–15
DUNKELWEIZEN	1.048–1.056	11.8–14	4.8–5.4	Creamy, dry	9–13	10–15
WEIZENBOCK	1.066–1.080	16–19.5	6.9–9.3	Medium	15–20	18–29
BERLINER WEISSE	1.028–1.032	7–8	2.5–3.5	Dry, tart	2–4	3–6

LAGER

It is a sad fact that the true history of lager beer has never been written, so we are left to conjecture and fantasy. The common tale about monks fermenting in alpine caves doesn't make sense for a lot of reasons. It's hard to haul grain up the mountains, and equally difficult to get the beer down to where there are people to drink it. They're cool, but caves are far above the temperatures needed for lagering unless a lot of ice is added. Lager's development was probably spurred by bans on summer brewing, leaving the beer to ferment in poorly heated breweries in cold weather. This probably happened before 1500, but we know very little more than that.

The concept of a special beer brewed in the winter and stored for use in the summer is widespread in Europe, and likely of great antiquity. Summer has long been a season for brewing only small, quick beers used for hydration and refreshment. The winter beers, being stronger, have always been special.

It has long been known that lager yeast is a hybrid between ale yeast and another, closely related species, which was unknown. Recently that partner was located, living in sugar-filled galls on birch trees in Patagonia. This poses a problem for historians, as Magellan didn't make a note of that place until 1520, almost fifty years after our first solid documentation of bottom-fermenting beer. I am guessing that *Saccharomyces eubayanus*, the cold-tolerant yeast that hybridized to form lager yeast, will be found in a more convenient location. Or else our history in this case is wrong—which wouldn't be the first time.

It is also not well known what the early lager beers were like, but there is a good likelihood that they were reddish-colored beers, early versions of the dunkels that would make Munich famous in the beer world. Stronger versions called bocks probably have been brewed for many centuries. The first doppel-bock, Salvator, is said to have originated at the Paulaner monastic brewery in 1629. Most other lager styles were created in the nineteenth century, and by 1900, the familiar mix of European lagers we see today was in place.

The nineteenth century witnessed massive technological changes as well as social ones. German porters and schwarzbiers developed, at least partially in response to the success of English porter. The amber Vienna style was popularized by Anton Dreher in that city around the middle of the century. The first Oktoberfest happened in 1810, and while it was a helluva party, the amber beer that today bears its name wasn't brewed in Munich until Spaten cooked up a batch in 1872. The Bohemian city of Plzen set the brewing world on fire with the world's first pale lager in 1842. Toward the end of the century, Pilsner and its imitators had spread everywhere, first to northern Germany and then to the rest of northern Europe, including England, and beyond. By 1900, even the hidebound Bavarians had managed to coax a mellow pale lager—helles—out of the chalky Munich water. There has been limited stylistic development in lager since then, except in the United States, with light beer and its derivatives.

As far as recipes, lagers tend to be quite simple. Many lager grists contain one ingredient only, a holdover from the days that every town or region had its own style of malt and that's what the beer was made from. With great malt, you really don't need anything else, so resist the urge to pile stuff on to the grain bill. Caramel malts, if used at all, need to be handled with a deft touch, as they can take over quickly and obscure more delicate malt characteristics, making the beer kind of ponderous. Plus, they have nothing to do with traditional lager styles.

Historically, lagers were brewed with decoction mashes, which involve removing and boiling a portion of the mash, then returning it to the mash to effect a temperature rise. There are lots of good reasons the old timers did it this way, but most of those are not the case anymore. Most modern malt is designed to work best with single infusions, so decoctions can actually do more harm than good, stripping away valuable body- and head-forming proteins. If you want the six hours of fun a genuine *dreimaischverfahren* triple decoction can provide, you'll have to seek out some undermodified malt to do it with.

The other thing that makes lager brewing more challenging is fermentation. Temperatures need to be controlled fairly precisely, because without cool fermentations and cold conditioning, it's just ale, no matter what the ingredients. Lager yeast also needs to be pitched at greater quantities than ale, just as with brewing a strong beer. Also, it's important to raise the temperature for a couple of days toward the end of cold conditioning to allow buttery compounds to be reabsorbed by the yeast, a step known as a diacetyl rest.

The pilsner glass's ancient form still serves up a cool golden pilsner admirably.

The following list covers the classic lager styles in their idealized form. Be aware that there may be some regional variation, and also that styles—even classic ones—are still changing in response to consumer demand and technological factors. Of course, it is possible to make beers that do not fall exactly into these narrow categories, as commercial breweries sometimes do, and so can you.

BOHEMIAN PILSNER

This is the original Pilsner, and some examples are still brewed with a triple-decoction mash, which adds a rich, caramelly character that is an important part of the style. Up to 20 percent Vienna malt or around 5 percent light-caramel malt can add some of this caramelliness. Bitter it with a clean, neutral hop like magnum, and toss in a load of Saaz hops for aroma. Dry-hopping is not traditional, but adds even more hop character. While the normal style guidelines emphasize the somewhat stronger export versions at 1.044 (12°P), the Czechs are more likely to be found drinking a lighter version at 1.041 or 1.048 (10 or 11°P), the weaker of the two being by far the most popular. More luxurious pale lagers at 1.053 to 1.057 (13 to 15°P) also exist and can be a special treat.

GERMAN PILSNER

Drier and paler than Bohemian Pilsner, this is always brewed purely from Pils malt and hopped with noble hops—Hallertau character preferred. Most are brewed precisely at 1.048 (11.9°P), the way they teach it at the Weihenstephan brewing school.

MUNICH HELLES

Munich brewers in the late nineteenth century had a difficult time re-creating a proper Pilsner, a raging phenomenon at the time. This is what they came up with, a similar malt bill but with much lighter hopping, a combination that worked with Munich's chalky water. Hop aroma is present, but much less pronounced than either Pilsner style.

DORTMUNDER EXPORT

Dortmund was a brewing city famous for a beefy lager that has now become a rare breed, more common in the United States than in its home these days. It is intermediate in character between a helles and a German Pilsner, so, a pretty evenly balanced beer, but brewed at a stronger gravity, about 1 percent higher in alcohol. "Export" beer as a somewhat stronger pale lager still exists in Germany, although its connection to Dortmund is long lost. This style, in fact, is gaining ground as the new pale Oktoberfest brew.

AMERICAN PRE-PROHIBITION LAGER

American mainstream beer in the nineteenth century wasn't necessarily always of super-high quality, but it had more color and definitely more hops in addition to the corn or rice used to lighten its body. These have attracted a small cult of homebrewers and are even brewed by some craft brewers looking for fun and quaffable beers. Authentic brewing would include six-row Pils malt plus an adjunct mash with corn or rice grits, although up to 10 percent of flaked corn can be added in a normal infusion mash. For extract versions, rice syrup or corn sugar can be used, but they lack the flavor added by corn. Cluster hops for bittering would have been universal in the old days, with European aromatic hops used for aroma in more luxurious examples. American-grown European varieties like Saaz, Hallertau, and Tettnang should work nicely.

AMERICAN ADJUNCT LAGER

These are extremely delicate beers, and as such are very difficult to brew. Even premium versions today use 25 percent adjunct, and cheapo versions up to 50 percent. These quantities require an adjunct mash, which makes them a test of skill and an appealing challenge worth tackling.

AMERICAN LIGHT LAGER

In commercial production, amylolytic enzymes derived from *Aspergillus* fungus are used to convert all available starch to fermentable sugar. This makes the beers as light in calories as possible for any given alcohol content. As these enzymes may not be available in small quantities, homebrewers have reported success using the dietary supplement Beano. This supplement has similar characteristics and can break starches into sugars. Hopping is minimal. Dry beer is exactly the same process, but at a higher alcohol level; ice beer is even stronger.

AMERICAN MALT LIQUOR

I'm not sure why I'm even talking about this style, as it is usually a very cheap product intended for intoxication and little else. However, some homebrewers find it amusing to brew them and honestly, if some care and good ingredients are used, the results can be enjoyable. Commercial examples typically use the legal maximum of 50 percent adjuncts—usually corn or invert sugar. Hop aroma is not true to style, but makes the style a lot more enjoyable, so suit yourself.

MÄRZEN/VIENNA/OKTOBERFEST/SPEZIAL

This is a group of closely related amber lagers with slightly different characteristics. All originated in the mid-nineteenth century with connections to Vienna, its original home, and Munich. Vienna is a normal-gravity beer, while the others are about 1 percent stronger in alcohol. Märzen and Oktoberfest used to be synonymous, but in the last decade or so they have been diverging. To accommodate public taste, brewers are making Oktoberfests paler every year, so some versions are as pale as a beer called *spezial*, which is a helles brewed 1 percent higher in alcohol. Some brewers now make Oktoberfests and Märzens. Confused? Yeah, comes with the territory.

As far as brewing, Vienna should be based on Vienna malt, up to 100 percent of the grist, or possibly lightened with some Pils malt. The darker Märzen can use a mix of Vienna and Munich malts, possibly with some Pils as well if a paler version is desired.

MUNICH DUNKEL

This is the original red beer of Munich, although changes to malting technology in the mid-nineteenth century led to the creation of modern Munich malt, which would have changed the flavor profile of the beer. Although it can still be found in Bavaria these days, it has largely been displaced in favor of the paler beers modern palates seem to prefer. Munich malt is by far the preferred base, although some röstmalz is often used to deepen the color. Decoction mashes were the norm historically, but modern brewers find them too costly in time and energy.

CZECH DARK LAGER

Although famous for Pilsners, Czech brewers often make amber and dark lagers (and ales, too) ranging from amber to near black, and ranging in strength from 1.040 to 1.066 (10 to 16°P). As elsewhere, the paler beers tend to be the hoppier. Saaz hops rule for aroma, even in these dark beers.

SCHWARZBIER

These black lagers are associated with places in and around Bavaria, especially Köstritz, Kulmbach, and Augsburg. They are porter-like in character, and may even have some connection to that English style. Ladislaus von Wagner, in his 1877 brewing textbook, refers to "Englischer Köstritzer." Munich is a good base, and color should come from the smooth, clean tasting röstmalz. Hopping is moderate, adequate for balance and neutral in character. Hop aroma is not a part of the historic style, but may be pleasant nonetheless.

BALTIC PORTER

No mistaking this for a present-day stout; these are definitely brown, not black. Thick, chewy, smooth, and sweet, Baltic porter is both a stronger schwarzbier and a darker bock. Their smooth malty lager character lacks the fruit and spice of an ale. At 5.5 to 8.5 percent or more alcohol, you can feel the effects pretty quickly, putting them into the class of beers known as "velvet hammers."

Beer Name and Type	Original Gravity/°P	Estimated Alcohol by Vol.	Approx. BU	Color	Weeks to Drink
Motek Welwetu* Baltic Porter * Polish for "velvet hammer"	1.075/18.2°P	6.8 %	40/med. to high	Dark brown/ 35 SRM	8–12

As with many styles, Baltic porter offers opportunities for enlightened deviance. Swap out half the barley malt for malted wheat, and the milkshake texture is epic. Licorice abounded in the old English porter recipes and fits well here. Additions of black pepper, ancho chile, star anise, or toasted oatmeal would all create enjoyably twisted versions.

Qty	Ingredient	OG/°P	%	All-Grain Mashed Version
13 lb/5.9 kg	Munich malt	1.0660/16.1	88	Infusion mash (page 130)
2 lb/907 g	Amber/biscuit malt	1.0074/1.9	10	Infusion, 45 min @ 155°F/69°C, then mash out
8 oz/227 g	Debittered black malt	1.0020/0.5	2	

Qty	Ingredient	OG/°P	%	Alternate Extract + Mini-Mash Version
6.8 lb/3.1 kg	Pale dry malt extract	1.062/15.5	83	Standard E + MM Procedure (page 127)
1 lb/455 g	Pils malt	1.0043/1.1	6	
1.5 lb/680 g	Melanoidin malt	1.0055/1.4	7	
8 oz/227 g	40°L caramel malt	1.0019/0.5	2	
8 oz/227 g	Debittered black malt	1.0018/0.5	2	

Hops

Qty	Name	Alpha	IBU	Minutes	
					Yeast: Your choice of lager strain
					Fermentation Temperature: 55 to 60°F/13 to 16°C, then cold-condition for a month at around 40°F/4°C
21 g	Magnum	14.0	33	60	**Carbonation:** Medium/2.5 volumes/3.5 oz (99 g) priming sugar
75 g	Lublin (Saaz OK)	4.0	7	5	

MAIBOCK/HELLER BOCK

By law, bock beers are always at least 1.066 (16°P) in Germany. This is a gold to amber strong lager, associated with the month of May, and it indeed makes a fine late-spring tonic. Look at a blend of Pils and Vienna malts, possibly with a bit of Munich if a slight cookie-like edge is desired. Hopping can be moderate; aroma character is desirable, but it should definitely be noble in character.

DARK (DUNKEL) BOCK

This is a bit of a ghost of a style, and is extremely rare in Germany, but enjoyed by homebrewers and beer enthusiasts in the United States and elsewhere. Evidence from old paintings would suggest that bock was more commonly an amber beer than a brown one for at least a couple of hundred years, but that's just one more unknown tidbit from brewing history. Recipes should be just a beefed-up Munich dunkel, simple as that.

DOPPELBOCK

Brewed to a minimum of 1.074 (18°P) by law in Germany, this springtime brew is super big, rich, and malty. Munich malt is a good base, and it really is just an even stronger version of the Munich/bock family, with brewing pretty much the same, although higher gravity means normal procedures for strong beer fermentation should be followed.

LAGER STYLES: ORIGINAL GRAVITY BY COLOR

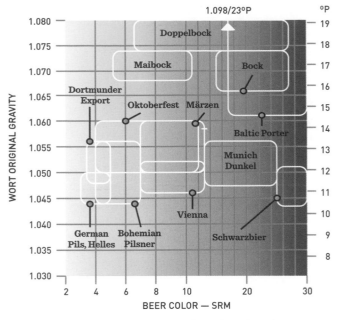

Here, lager styles are clearly organized by color and gravity ratios.

LAGER BEER STYLES BY THE NUMBERS

BEER STYLE	OG	°Plato	Alcohol % Vol.	Attenuation %	Color SRM	BU
BOHEMIAN PILSNER	1.044–1.056	11–14	4–5	Medium	3–7	30–45
GERMAN PILS	1.044–1.051	11–12.5	4–5	Crisp, dry	3–4	30–40
MUNICH HELLES	1.044–1.053	11–13	4.5–5	Crisp, dry	3–4	18–25
DORTMUNDER EXPORT	1.048–1.056	12–14	5–6	Medium	3–5	23–29
AMERICAN PRE-PROHIBITION LAGER	1.045–1.052	11.3–12.9	4.0–4.9	Medium	3–5	25–40
AMERICAN ADJUNCT LAGER	1.040–1.046	10–11.5	3.8–5	Crisp, dry	2–4	5–14
AMERICAN LIGHT LAGER	1.024–1.040	6–10	3.5–4.4	Super dry	1.5–4	5–10
AMERICAN MALT LIQUOR	1.050–1.060	11–15	5–6	Super dry	2–5	12–23
MÄRZEN	1.050–1.060	12.5–15	5.3–5.9	Medium	7–15	18–25
VIENNA	1.042–1.052	11.4–12.8	4.5–4.8	Medium	7–15	18–25
OKTOBERFEST	1.050–1.060	12.5–15	5.3–5.9	Medium	4–12	18–25
MUNICH DUNKEL	1.044–1.052	11–13	3–3.9	Medium	15–25	16–30
SCHWARZBIER	1.044–1.052	11–13	3–3.9	Medium	25–30	22–30
BALTIC PORTER	1.061–1.098	15–19	5.5–9.5	Medium	17–30	20–40
MAIBOCK/HELLER BOCK	1.066–1.074	16–18	6.5–8	Full	5–11	15–30
DARK (DUNKEL) BOCK	1.066–1.074	16–18	6.5–8	Full	15–30	12–25
DOPPELBOCK	1.074–1.081	18–19.5	6.5–8	Very full	12–30	12–30

BELGIUM

Let me start by saying that much of what you know about Belgium is probably wrong. Like the rest of beer history, we have some lovely old stories that have little to do with the truth. It might be best to run through a backward history of Belgian brewing to get a more accurate picture.

If you read this timeline carefully, you can see some of our notions about Belgian beer are wrong. With the exception of witbier, lambic, and the sour Flemish dark ales, most of what we see as typically Belgian was more influenced by beers from outside its borders: pale and Scotch ales, and lagers like Märzens, bocks, and even Pilsners. These beers served as the templates for abbey and Trappist beers and many other Belgian beers created between the World Wars. Strong beers like tripel are really mid-twentieth-century inventions. Having a true picture of the origins of Belgian beer gives us a better picture of how to brew it.

Belgian beer can appear pretty intimidating. If we had to perform turbid mashes and ferment spontaneously for all of them, there would be very few Belgian-style homebrews. Luckily, you don't need to be an Iron Brewer to cook up most Belgian beer types. Extracts or simple infusion mashes work quite nicely for everything but lambics and witbiers, which traditionally use large percentages of unmalted wheat, requiring intensive mashing with a brief boiling. However, there are workarounds for those.

So much of the Belgian-ness of these beers is due to the unique personalities of Belgian yeast strains. It almost doesn't matter what you brew; if you ferment it with a Belgian yeast, you get a Belgian-tasting beer. Half of all Belgian artisan beers aren't in any particular "style" anyway, so it really is hard to go too wrong. You do want to choose your yeast carefully. There's quite a range available in terms of ester and phenol profiles, fermentation characteristics, and alcohol tolerance. Some styles like saison are highly dependent on a very specific fermentation character; use the wrong yeast, or the right one at the wrong temperature, and you miss the mark entirely.

As a general rule, Belgian beers are more about malt than hops. The paler beers generally use a high-quality European Pils malt as a base. Darker beers may use Munich or Vienna malt as a base, colored and flavored with the cookie-like goodness of mclanoidin/aromatic. Some employ caramel malt for dried fruit flavors, like raisins and prunes. It is rare to have too much sharp toastiness. Generally, Belgians like their beer smooth.

The Brewers' Guild Hall, the only guild hall on Brussels' Grand Place serving its original purpose, also houses a museum of beer and brewing.

A BACKWARD HISTORY OF BELGIAN BREWING

TODAY
Seventy percent of all Belgian beer is exported; only 15 percent is artisan or classically Belgian in style, and the rest is industrial Pilsner.

1978
Belukus imports Duvel to United States. The next year, Merchant Du Vin imports Lindemans.

1974
First specialty beer bars open in Belgium.

1965
Lambic and gueuze appellations created.

1965
Pierre Celis opens De Kluis, starts brewing Hoegaarden witbier.

1958
Last witbier brewery in Hoegaarden, Tomsin, closes.

1950
Exports are 0.05 percent of Belgian beer production.

1934
The first pale tripel, Westmalle, is created.

1932
Westmalle registers Trappistenbier appellation.

1926
Orval opens for the first time since the seventeenth century. Brewery opens 1931.

1920
Chimay starts selling beer to public.

1919
Belgian government forbids on-premise sale of spirits like jenever.

1917–1919
WWI. Horrific devastation. Roasted beet seeds used to color beer.

1908
Half of all beer in Wallonia is under 1.020 OG (5.1°P).

1907
3,387 breweries in Belgium!

1902–1903
Henri Van Laer stages Contest for the Improvement of Belgian Beer. Big success the next year when secret recipes are allowed.

1890–1900
Belgian brewers unable to compete with larger importing breweries.

c. 1887
The first Belgian brewing school, École Brasserie Supérieure de Brasserie, founded at the Catholic University of Louvain.

1886
Belgium's first lagers, a pale bock and a dunkel, are brewed by Great Koekelberg brewery.

1885
Dutch mash tun tax system finally repealed.

c. 1870
Gueuze lambic invented, packaged in machine-made champagne bottles.

1851
Belgium's great nineteenth-century brewer G. Lacambre says, "Belgium is a wheat beer–brewing country."

1839
Belgian independence! Mash tun tax remains.

c. 1836
G. Lacambre reinvents witbier with modern adjunct-mash process.

1836
First Belgian monastery brewery, Westmalle, opens after French revolution.

1822
Dutch take over, institute weird tax on mash tun volume.

1789
French Revolution. All monasteries close.

c. 1400
First hopped beer in Belgium.

c. 1300
Bruges brewers' guild formed.

c. 700 B.C.E.
Celtic tribes brewing beer in Belgium.

Lightness on the palate is another important consideration. Nearly all of the stronger beers employ sugar of some kind, in quantities up to 20 percent of the recipe in the strongest ones. For pale beers, it's often just pure corn or invert sugar, which adds no flavor of its own. Paler unrefined sugars like Demerara or the pale Thai palm sugar work, too, and add a layer of rich flavor even as they thin the body. Darker beers are often colored and flavored with either brewer's caramel syrup or a special brown sugar made especially for that purpose. Even though much of Belgium's sugar comes from beets, there's no magic in that. Before it's refined, beet sugar has a flavor that one old British brewing book described as "nauseous." Beautiful as they are, there's nothing at all special about the giant crystals of sugar. They're cheap in Belgium, but not here. Don't waste your money.

Some of the paler Belgian styles have a bit of hop bitterness and aroma, but the Belgian-American hybrid IPAs can ramp up to 60 or 70 BU. Generally, a European hop character is desirable, although Lacambre does mention a recipe using large amounts of "pungent American hops," so there's some very old precedence for that. In pale beers, the mix of Saaz and Styrian Goldings is classic, so anything along these lines is fine, including the modern "super Styrian" types. Darker beers can do well with a neutral hop like Northern Brewer, while earthier English types like Fuggle and clean high-alpha hops like Magnum can work as well. It's very rare to have any hop aroma showing in a dark Belgian ale. Belgium's history with Germany has been problematic, so there's not much use of German hops.

Many Belgian beers use spices to create interesting aromatic profiles and to augment and change the yeast character. Notice I didn't say " . . . to make the beers taste like spices." Although stating a hard and fast rule for Belgian beer is tricky, spices should be so subtle that it is difficult to name them individually. Spices are most characteristic in witbier, where a subtle blend of coriander, bitter orange (think marmalade), and perhaps other seasonings gives the beer a complex perfume. Wit is probably the only style in which spices are mandatory, but they are frequent in saison, where peppery notes are augmented with things like grains of paradise and, well, pepper, and strong dark ales where things like star anise, licorice, and even cumin can find a happy home.

Spicing is difficult to get right. Different varieties and origins of the spices make a big difference, as does freshness and, of course, all of that needs to be matched to the beer, so getting the quantity right can be a challenge. I recommend vodka-based tinctures added at bottling or kegging in a very controlled manner. For more details see the Herbs and Spices section of chapter 3.

BELGIAN PALE ALE

This is essentially the same as English pale ale, but with reduced hopping and fermented with Belgian yeast. Perhaps a little less pale malt and a little more Vienna for less toast and more caramel. Can be all-malt or up to 10 percent adjuncts. Spicing is not all that traditional, but can be tasty if it's really subtle. There are Belgian pale ale yeasts available; look for those with Antwerp origins. Fermentation temperatures may be a little lower for a less estery aroma profile.

BELGIAN BLONDE AND STRONG GOLDEN ALES

These are pretty similar styles, differing mainly in alcoholic strength. Pils malt is the usual base; blondes may be all-malt, but the strong golden always uses a neutral-tasting adjunct like corn sugar to lighten the body. Saaz and Styrian Goldings are common choices for hops, but other noble and super-clean hops are appropriate here.

ABBEY AND TRAPPIST BEERS

It's important to know that *Trappiste* is an appellation—a term of origin rather than an actual style. Trappist ales tend to reflect the character of the regions they come from, so it's difficult to draw generalizations about that wild bunch. Abbey beers do conform to a general pattern with a dark dubbel and a pale tripel. Both employ sugar to lighten the body, as drinkability is always important. Tripels are mostly Pils malt, although some Vienna can be used to add a bit of color and caramelly aroma. Hopping can be similar to the category above. Dubbels tend to be all about the mid-colored malt. Recipe philosophies go from the cookie-like aromas of melanoidin to the raisiny flavors of mid-colored caramel malt to the soft chocolatey character added by brewer's caramel rather than dark malt. Hops are there just for balance. Stick to neutral types. Because of the high alcohol content, make sure you have an alcohol-tolerant yeast and observe the usual procedures for fermenting strong beers.

BELGIAN STRONG DARK ALE

This category really is as vague as it sounds, and that's the beauty of Belgian beer. As long as it's strong and dark, it qualifies. In terms of recipe, think of them as Dubbels ramped up to Tripel strength and beyond, although it's a little more common to see spicing in this style, and thick, chewy all-malt versions are not unheard of.

SAISON

This is a middling-strength blonde brew with a kiss of hops and a strongly peppery/spicy yeast character. Its history is pretty garbled. The only "saison" mentioned by name in the nineteenth century books is from Liège, a city near Belgium's eastern border, famous for waffles. Liège saison was very low in gravity and poorly attenuated, brewed from malted spelt with oats and sometimes buckwheat or broad beans added. Fontaine and Perrier-Robert in their 1996 book on Belgium's brewing history describe it as a 1.040 gravity (10°P) "blend of an old acid beer (formerly fermented in wooden casks) and top-fermented beer brewed between April and May." It is currently categorized as a "farmhouse" beer, although there is not much evidence this was the case, as most small breweries in Belgium appear to have been village-based commercial enterprises rather than by-products of agriculture.

Whatever the case, brew them from very pale Pils malt, with up to 20 percent wheat if you like, and possibly very small amounts of Vienna for some richness. Saison should always be very dry on the palate, so use sugar for stronger versions. Hop bitterness and aroma are part of the character—it is Belgium's hoppiest style. Above all, a proper saison yeast should be used, at fairly high temperatures; the Dupont brewery ferments around 95°F/35°C. It's a tough fermentation, prone to slowing down before full attenuation. Either give it a few more weeks or add some ordinary ale yeast to finish the job. Saison yeast likes to be well aerated, too.

Beer Name and Type	Original Gravity/°P	Estimated Alcohol by Vol.	Approx. BU	Color	Weeks to Drink
Dubbel Vision Belgian Abbey Dubbel	1.072/17.3°P	8.2 %	25/med. to low	Black/16 SRM	6–8

This is a variable recipe that offers the possibility of three different mid-colored malts, each with a different flavor. The melanoidin gives a dry, cookie-like aroma; the caramel contributes dried fruit flavors; and the caramel syrup offers molasses and chocolatey notes. Use one of them, or mix 'n' match as you like for greater complexity, but try to stay at about 1 pound/454 g total or slightly more for a somewhat darker beer. Multiply everything in this recipe by 1.25 and you get to 1.090 (22°P), which puts you into strong dark territory.

Qty	Ingredient	OG/°P	%	**All-Grain Mashed Version**
6.5 lb/2.9 kg	Pale ale malt	1.0369/9.2	51	Infusion mash (page 130)
4.3 lb/2 kg	Munich Malt	1.0216/5.5	30	60 min @ 150°F/66°C, then mash out
1.3 lb/590 g	Sugar (your choice)	1.0010/0.3	15	
2.4 oz/68 g	Röstmalz (Carafa II)	—	—	
Plus				
10 oz/184 g	40°L caramel malt	1.0029/0.7	5	
Or				
1 lb/454 g	Melanoidin malt	1.0047/1.2	5	
Or				
8 oz/227 g	Belgian dark I candi syrup	1.0024/0.6	5	

Qty	Ingredient	OG/°P	%	**Alternate Extract + Steeped-Grain Version**
6.2 lb/2.8 kg	Pale dry malt extract	1.0576/14.2	80	Standard E + SG Procedure (page 119)
1.2 lb/544 g	Sugar (your choice)	1.0110/0.3	15	
2.4 oz/68 g	Röstmalz (Carafa II)	—	—	
Plus				
1 lb/454 g	40°L caramel malt	1.00471.2	5 (approximately)	
Or				
1 lb/454 g	Melanoidin malt	1.0047/1.2	5 (approximately)	
Or				
8 oz/227 g	Belgian dark candi syrup	1.0024/0.6	3 (approximately)	

Hops

Qty	Name	Alpha	IBU	Minutes	
					Yeast: Your choice of Belgian Abbey or Trappist
					Fermentation Temperature: 68 to 74°F/20 to 23°C
13 g	Northern Brewer	8.0	15	60	**Carbonation:** High/3.5 volumes/6.5 oz (184 g)
53 g	Saphir	3.5	10	5	priming sugar

BELGIAN BEER STYLES BY THE NUMBERS

BEER STYLE	OG	°Plato	Alcohol % Vol.	Attenuation %	Color SRM	BU
BELGIAN PALE ALE	1.040–1.055	10–13.6	3.9–5.6	Medium	4–14	20–30
BELGIAN STRONG GOLDEN ALE	1.065–1.080	16–19.2	7–9	Super dry	3.5–5.5	25–45
BELGIAN STRONG DARK ALE	1.064–1.096	16–23	7–11	Med. to full	7–20	20–50
BELGIAN ABBEY DUBBEL	1.062–1.080	15–19.2	6–7.8	Low to med.	10–20	15–25
BELGIAN ABBEY TRIPEL	1.075–1.090	18–22	7.5–9.5	Med. dry	3.5–6	25–38
SAISON	1.055–1.080	13.5–19	4.5–8.1	Dry	6–12	20–45
BELGIAN WITBIER	1.042–1.055	10.2–13.6	4.2–5.5	Creamy, dry	2–4	15–20
GUEUZE LAMBIC	1.044–1.056	11–14	5–6	Ultra dry	6–13	11–23
SOUR BROWN/SOUR RED/OUD BRUIN	1.044–1.057	11–14	4.8–5.2	Sweet/sour	12–18	15–25
BIÈRE DE GARDE	1.060–1.080	15–19	6–8	Med. to full	6–12	25–30

WITBIER

This is a personal favorite. When done right, it's a mesmerizing combination of pale hazy color, rocky foam, creamy texture, spicy fragrance, tangy zip, and extreme complexity, somewhat magical for its quite ordinary gravity. It is part of a large family of white beers that once were popular all along Europe's northern coast. Similar beers were once widespread in Belgium, and made places like Leuven and Hoegaarden famous as brewing towns.

The classic witbier recipe is 50 percent "wind-" or air-dried six-row malt, 45 percent unmalted winter wheat, and 5 percent oats. Because of the large proportion of unmalted grain, this recipe requires an adjunct mash (see Adjunct Mashing, page 137) to get good extraction and flavor; step infusions don't cut it. The solution is to use a larger percentage of malted wheat—between 60 and 70 percent—along with the 5 percent oats and the rest six-row Pils malt. If you use a step mash with a protein rest, you'll get a pretty acceptable facsimile. Don't forget the rice hulls, as this can be a rather gloopy mash.

Much of the coriander on the market has a distinct vegetable aroma, and can give your beer a tang of old hot-dog water. Be choosy; Indian varieties are always nice, and there are others that can be pleasant in different ways. The same applies to orange peel. Sour oranges are hard to find in their raw state, so chipped, dried peel can be used. I have found that some of the big chunks of orange peel sold for brewing add a pithy bitterness that is pretty harsh. Marmalade and triple-sec are both decent sources of bitter orange aroma. There is often a "mystery spice" added to witbier. Try chamomile, cardamom, elder flowers, grains of paradise, and black pepper and see what you like.

BIÈRE DE GARDE

Not strictly Belgian, but from the corner of France with a similar brewing tradition, and similar beers continue to be brewed in Belgium as well. These slightly strong, top-fermented ales came into their own, spurred by the success of Belgian specialty beers in the decades after WWII. There are amber and blonde versions, the latter being increasingly dominant. Both are malty and lightly hopped, with little aromatic character. Yeast character is somewhat subdued compared to Belgian ales, so perhaps a bit lower fermentation temperature is appropriate, 62 to 68°F/17 to 20°C.

Beer Name and Type	Original Gravity/°P	Estimated Alcohol by Vol.	Approx. BU	Color	Weeks to Drink
Wit de Nit Belgian Witbier Made Easy	1048/11.9°P	4.8%	20/low	Hazy straw/ 2–3 SRM	3–4

This is a simplified recipe designed to get the maximum witbier character, especially the creamy/wheaty aspect, with as simple a brewing process as possible. The raw wheat used in traditional recipes requires an adjunct mash (page 137) but larger quantities of malted wheat can help compensate for it. The flour tossed in the kettle can add some of the starchy haze traditional turbid mashes also provide. For a super-easy extract version, use 25 percent more wheat extract and skip the mini mash—this provides a pretty enjoyable witbier if you do everything else right.

Qty	Ingredient	OG/°P	%	**All-Grain Mashed Version**
5 lb/2.3 kg	Malted wheat	1.0288/7.3	60	Infusion mash (page 130)
3.1 lb/1.4 kg	6-Row Pils malt	1.0144/3.7	30	60 min @ 150°F/66°C, then mash out
1 lb/454 g	Instant or puffed oats	1.0050/1.3	10	
1 lb/454 g	Rice hulls	—	—	
2 oz/59 g	All-purpose flour*	—	—	

*Make into slurry with cold water, and then add to kettle during boil.

Qty	Ingredient	OG/°P	%	**Extract + Mini-Mash Version**
2.9 lb/1.3 kg	Dry wheat malt extract	1.0359/9.0	75	Standard E + MM Procedure (page 127)
14 oz/408 g	6-Row Pils malt	1.0041/1.0	9	
8 oz/227 g	Instant or puffed oats	1.0040/1.0	8	
8 oz/227 g	Cara-Pils malt	1.0040	8	
2 oz/59 g	All-purpose flour*	—	—	

* Make into slurry with cold water, and then add to kettle during boil.

Hops and other seasonings:

Qty	Name	Alpha	IBU	Minutes	
20 g	Northern Brewer	7	20	60	**Yeast:** Belgian wheat strain such as Wyeast 3942 or White Labs WL400, or your favorite Belgian yeast
14 g	Freshly ground coriander*	—	5	—	**Fermentation Temperature:** 68 to 72°F/20 to 22°C
8 g	Bitter orange peel**	—	—	5	**Carbonation:** Medium high/3.0 volumes/5.2 oz (147 g) priming sugar
6 g	Chamomile	—	—	5	

* Source your coriander carefully. Much of it has a sharp, cilantro-like vegetal aroma. Indian and Chinese varieties usually brew well.

** Make sure your orange peel doesn't have much white pith attached. Marmalade is actually great to use in this situation—perhaps 15 g per batch.

NEW AMERICAN CLASSICS

By the 1970s, the term *American beer* was synonymous with something bland and monotonous, an unholy trinity with white bread and processed cheese. For many Americans, travels in Europe pounded that point home in a very painful way.

Combine that somewhat embarrassing gastronomic history with the sort of cultural inferiority only a former colony can have and you get a mix of strange emotions that clouds our thinking about aesthetic matters. Europe still has authority and plenty of prestige, and marketers work hard to make sure we feel that way. In the general market, there's still something special about those green-bottle Pilsners from across the sea, even if they are stale and skunky.

Brewers outside Europe look to Britain and Germany for a sense of order and righteousness, and to the Czechs for elegance born of simplicity and great ingredients. Belgium provides inspiration and permission to be an individual. Great places to start, but to me, brewing strictly traditional beers is like playing in a cover band. The sounds might be groovy enough, but are you saying anything? Fortunately these days, we are starting to realize that not being European can be a great asset, because we can respect and draw inspiration from tradition, but not be ruled by it. We can invent a new kind of beer.

AMERICAN CRAFT BEER STYLES

Ales were the flavorful antidote to the sea of mass-market lager that had swept everything else away in America. These are beers inspired by Europe, but brewed from memory of brief encounters while on summer vacations without any real interest in brewing classic styles authentically. The goal was something bold, brisk, lively, and packed with flavor. Since all the commercial versions began as homebrews, you'll find that ubiquitous homebrew ingredient, caramel malt, in most examples. Their thirst for hops unsatisfied by industrial lagers, brewers piled on the bitterness, with a special relish for the tangy, grapefruity new high-alpha hop varieties emerging in the 1970s and 1980s. These are unapologetically brash, fun, and in-your-face beers, a true reflection of the people who made them their life's work.

Love it or hate it (I'm in the latter camp), the shaker pint—originally designed as half a cocktail shaker—has become synonymous with craft beer.

AMERICAN AMBER, PALE ALE, AND IPA

This is a family of related styles that differ in strength and hop character, but have a lot in common. Inspired very broadly by English ales, most recipes are based on pale ale malt, getting additional color and some chewy caramel and raisin flavors from medium-caramel malts. Adjuncts are rare. In amber, hops are there mainly for balance, but depending on the brewery can have a fair amount of bitterness.

AMERICAN AMBER, PALE ALE, IPA, AND RED ALES, PLUS THEIR IMPERIAL FORMS: ORIGINAL GRAVITY BY COLOR

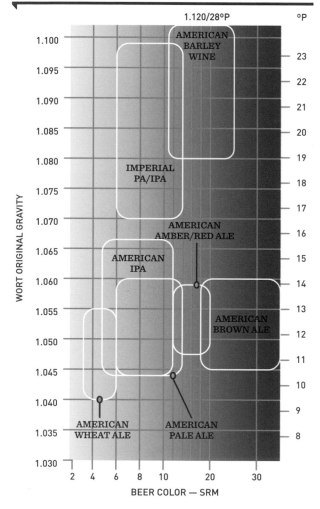

Here, amber ales, pale ales, IPAs, and red ales are clearly organized by their color and gravity ratios.

This family of beers is essentially scaled-up homebrew, as the ubiquitous caramel malt attests. So, they respond well to simple infusion mashes and extract-plus-steeped-grain approaches.

The workhorse yeast in this brew is often referred to as "Chico" because of its association with Sierra Nevada, but it actually comes from the old Ballantine's brewery in New Jersey, one of the few old-school American breweries to feature ales rather than lagers. They closed in 1972, but the yeast lives on. It is hardy, easy to use, and somewhat alcohol tolerant, and makes great beer, but it is sensitive to cool temperatures. English ale yeast strains can work nicely, but Chico is the classic.

RED ALES

Here's another example of a rapidly changing beer style. Back in the mid-1990s, there was a minor fad for them, and big breweries even jumped on the red-ale bandwagon with beers like A-B's Red Wolf Lager. At that time, they were light in body, reddish amber as one would expect, and very lightly hopped. Over the years red ale has become increasingly hoppy; today's reds are about as hoppy as pale ales or IPAs, and tend to be richly malty, with an intense burnt-sugar character coming from the dark-caramel malt that also gives them their reddish tint. Today's reds are also a bit stronger than earlier examples, and, of course, imperialized versions abound.

From a brewing and hopping standpoint, they're the same as the American pale ales, the difference being a good amount—up to 10 percent—of 60 to 80°L caramel malt, often with a small amount of roasted malt added to deepen and enhance the red color. A subset of these beers with 5 to 20 percent rye in the grist is becoming popular, and may eventually define the style. Yeast and fermentation is the same as with the pale ales and related styles.

AMERICAN BROWN ALES

While the competition guidelines tend to define these more narrowly, in reality this is a giant brown blob of beers where almost anything goes as long as it's got a brown color. Some are barely browner than amber ale, with soft toastiness and a hint of hops. Others are chestnut in color and fairly strong, pushing the fuzzy boundary with porter, reminding us that in its day, porter was itself a brown ale. Hops are all over the map, with a particular American brown ale claimed as their own by Texas (make that Houston) homebrewers.

Even though there's a lot of variety, the malts tend to be less about caramel and more of the toasty types, especially amber/biscuit. Super-dark 120°L caramel malts may also be used, along with small amounts of brown or chocolate malts. Brewing and fermentation run pretty much the same as the pale ale group.

Beer Name and Type	Original Gravity/°P	Estimated Alcohol by Vol.	Approx. BU	Color	Weeks to Drink
Sweet Georgia Brown Ale, American Style	1.0525/13°P	5.3 %	38/med.	Brown/ 19 SRM	3–5

This recipe actually straddles the fence between English and American brown styles. Cut the brown malt back to 8 oz/227 g, drop the bittering hops to half, and eliminate the aroma hops and you've got a classic English brown. Many American browns are bigger and more aggressive than this, so feel free to pile on the malt and hops—just stay away from too much caramel malt unless you want to turn it into a red ale. This beer can be a great base for fine Southern ingredients like sorghum, toasted pecans, and sweet potatoes, or Northern ones like wild rice.

Qty	Ingredient	OG/°P	%	**All-Grain Mashed Version**
3 lb/1.4 kg	Pale ale malt	1.0165/4.2	31	Infusion mash (page 130)
4.6 lb/2.1 kg	Mild ale malt	1.0235/6.0	45	60 min @ 150°F/66°C, then mash out
2 lb/907 g	Amber/biscuit malt	1.0093/2.4	18	
3.2 oz/91 g	Brown malt	1.0009/0.2	2	
6.4 oz/181 g	Torrefied wheat	1.0021/0.5	4	

Qty	Ingredient	OG/°P	%	**Alternate Extract + Mini-Mash Version**
3.1 lb/1.4 kg	Pale dry malt extract	1.0284/7.2	54	Standard E + MM Procedure (page 127)
1 lb/454 g	Wheat malt extract	1.0090/2.3	17	
1 lb/454 kg	Pale Ale malt	1.0043/1.1	8	
2 lb/907 g	Amber/biscuit malt	1.0077/2.0	15	
8 oz/227 g	Honey malt	1.0019/0.5	4	
5 oz/142 g	Brown malt	1.0012/0.3	2	

Hops

Qty	Name	Alpha	IBU	Minutes	
					Yeast: Your choice of English or American ale yeast
					Fermentation Temperature: 62 to 68°F/17 to 20°C
44 g	U.S. Fuggle	4.5	30	60	**Carbonation:** Medium /2.5 volumes/3.5 oz
50 g	Glacier (Styrian OK)	5.8	8	5	(99 g) priming sugar
28 g	Cascade	5.0	—	—	

Beer Name and Type	Original Gravity/°P	Estimated Alcohol by Vol.	Approx. BU	Color	Weeks to Drink
Squidward's Inky Ale Oatmeal Stout	1.052/12.8°P	5.2 %	40/med. to high	Black/38 SRM	4–6

This is a super-luscious and creamy oatmeal stout, with many layers of maltiness. The mild ale malt lays own a rich caramelly base, and the toasted oats provide a cookie-like aroma while the wheat piles on the creaminess and adds an amazing head. Hops are fairly neutral here. You could easily change it up with some West Coast hops or even some citrusy New Zealand varieties.

Qty	Ingredient	OG/°P	%	**All-Grain Mashed Version**
7 lb/3.2 kg	Mild ale malt	1.0369/9.2	71	Infusion mash (page 130)
2 lb/907 g	Malted wheat	1.0078/2.0	15	60 min @ 150°F/66°C, then mash out
2 lb/907 g	Oatmeal	1.0026/0.7	5	
2 lb/907 g	Oatmeal, toasted golden	1.0026/0.7	5	
8 oz/227 g	Chocolate rye	1.0021/0.5	4	

Qty	Ingredient	OG/°P	%	**Alternate Extract + Mini-Mash Version**
6.2 lb/2.8 kg	Pale dry malt extract	1.0372/9.3	72	Standard E + MM Procedure (page 127)
1 lb/454 g	Pils malt	1.0056/1.4	11	
1.5 lb/680 g	Melanoidin malt	1.0055/1.4	11	
8 oz/227 g	40°L caramel malt	1.0019/0.5	3	
8 oz/227 g	Debittered black malt	1.0018/0.5	3	

Hops

Qty	Name	Alpha	IBU	Minutes	
					Yeast: Your choice of English or American ale yeast
					Fermentation Temperature: 62 to 68°F/17 to 20°C
18 g	Magnum	14.0	33	60	**Carbonation**: Medium /2.5 volumes/3.5 oz (99 g)
65 g	Lublin (Saaz OK)	4.0	7	5	priming sugar

AMERICAN PORTER AND STOUT

Like the brown ales, this group is so variable that one hardly knows what to say about it. In general, they're not much different from English versions except for the hopping, which in most cases tends to be more aggressive. Both the BJCP and World Beer Cup/GABF guidelines somewhat arbitrarily divide porter into "mild" or "brown" and "robust" subcategories, and some breweries do in fact brew to those guidelines, but there are plenty that do not. I guess part of it depends on how badly you want a medal.

You should pay attention to the hop varieties to make sure what you use works with the dark malt flavors and aromas. The citrusy, grapefruity varieties generally don't work as well as more herbal types such as Northdown, Willamette, Northern Brewer, and even U.S. Hallertau. For yeast and fermentation, again, same as for the pale ale group.

IMPERIALIZATION

In keeping with the over-the-top nature of American cultural endeavors, high-strength "double" or "imperial" beers of every type, from Pilsner to stout, have gushed forth from our brew kettles for the last decade or so. The term is not new. Originating as a factual designation on big stouts or porters brewed for the Imperial Court of Russia, by 1900, the term was used in Britain and the United States for any extra-high-grade beer, although not always indicative of high strength. Modern-day American brewers rediscovered the term, and it has stuck.

Any imperial beer tends to be just an amped-up version of the original style, so there's not a lot to be said in terms of recipe except for: use more of everything. One thing to consider, though, is body. As the malt level increases, so does a beer's heaviness. At the very least, mashing a little lower and longer will aid fermentability and make a drier beer, as will using some sort of brewer's sugar.

AMERICAN-STYLE ALES BY THE NUMBERS

BEER STYLE	OG	°Plato	Alcohol % Vol.	Attenuation %	Color SRM	BU
AMERICAN PALE ALE	1.044–1.060	11–14.7	4.5–6.2	Medium	6–14	28–40
AMERICAN IPA	1.044–1.067	11–16.3	5.5–6.5	Dry	5–12	35–70
DOUBLE/IMPERIAL IPA	1.070–1.099	17–23.5	6.9–10.5	Crisp, dry	6–14	65–100
AMBER/RED	1.048–1.059	12–14.5	4.5–6	Medium	11–18	30–40
AMERICAN BARLEY WINE	1.080–1.120	19.3–28	7–12	Med. full	11–18	50–100
AMERICAN BROWN ALE	1.045–1.060	12–14.5	4–6	Medium	18–35	20–45
AMERICAN WHEAT ALES	1.040–1.055	10–13.5	3.0–5.5	Light to med.	3–6	15–35

AMERICAN WHEAT ALE

These delicate and genial beers taught a lot of people how to enjoy craft beer back in the 1990s and they remain popular with beginners today. They differ from German weissbiers mainly because a conventional ale yeast is used, so they lack the banana and bubblegum aromas of the German types. They usually use 30 to 40 percent wheat, as opposed to the 50 to 70 percent found in the Bavarian recipes. Although not a hoppy style, American wheats do have higher rates than the Germans, with whiffs of American hop aroma pleasantly acceptable.

The grist is a mix of U.S. Pils malt and malted wheat, with small amounts of Vienna and/or pale caramel malt to add depth without too much color, as these are blonde beers, not amber. Mashing is usually a single infusion, although they may benefit from a protein rest to break up the proteins from the wheat and improve the head. Hopping should be delicate and reasonably refined; personally, I like Tettnangs for wheat beers. The clean fruitiness of Glacier also works nicely. That said, a new bolder,

hoppier style is becoming much more popular. This features bitterness in the 30–40 BU range, and a ton of late-addition or dry hops of decidedly American character from grapefruit to lemon or passionfruit to floral.

Any conventional ale yeast will do. In my opinion, fermentation with an estery Belgian yeast improves the complexity of this style considerably, but then that puts it outside the guidelines, doesn't it?

A subset of this style incorporates a little honey (5 to 10 percent) into the recipe to lighten the body a bit and add some flowery aromatics. Choose your honey carefully; coarse phenolics are not welcome here. It is best to add the honey after the most vigorous phase of fermentation, so as not to blow off too much delicate aroma. Honey wheats may be pale, but as often as not they have a little caramel malt added for some color and weight, although this must be done with a deft touch.

Beer Name and Type	Original Gravity/°P	Estimated Alcohol by Vol.	Approx. BU	Color	Weeks to Drink
Danky Panky XXX Pale Ale	1.074/18°P	7.3 %	120/stupid-high	Pale amber/9 SRM	6–8

Dank is a word used to describe high-grade marijuana, all hairy and gooey with resin. The term has recently been applied to the hyper-hoppy West Coast IPAs, so I'll do my best to cook up a really sick 'n' sticky version for all you young bong-boys out there. For additional dankiness, add 50 to 80 metric grams of hops to the mash.

Qty	Ingredient	OG/°P	%	**All-Grain Mashed Version**
10 lb/4.5 kg	Pale ale malt	1.0547/13.5	74	Infusion mash (page 130)
8 oz/227 g	Honey malt	1.0024/0.6	3	60 min @ 147°F/64°C, then mash out
8 oz/227 g	40°L caramel malt	1.0024/0.6	3	
1 lb/454 g	Flaked rye	1.0060/1.5	8	
1 lb/454 g	Thai palm sugar	1.0090/2.3	12	

Qty	Ingredient	OG/°P	%	**Alternate Extract + Steeped-Grain Version**
5.5 lb/2.5 kg	Pale dry malt extract	1.0416/10.4	56	Standard E + SG Procedure (page 119)
2 lb/907 g	Dry wheat malt extract	1.0185/4.7	25	
1 lb/454 g	Honey malt	1.0033/0.9	4	
8 oz/227 g	40°L caramel malt	1.0016/0.4	2	
1 lb/454 g	Thai palm sugar	1.0090/2.3	12	

Hops

Qty	Name	Alpha	IBU	Minutes	
					Yeast: California Ale Yeast
					Fermentation Temperature: 62 to 68°F/17 to 20°C
25 g	Chinook	12.5	37	First wort*	**Carbonation:** Medium/2.5 volumes/3.5 oz
25 g	Columbus	15.0	50	60	(99 g) priming sugar
38 g	Palisade	7.5	30	30	
61 g	Mt Hood	4.5	15	10	
113 g	Simcoe	13.0	—	—	
28 g	Mt. Hood	4.5	—	Dry hop	
28 g	Simcoe	13.0	—	Dry hop	

* Hops added to kettle as it begins to fill with wort (page 128)

FREAKIN' THE EURO LAGERS

Perhaps you have noticed that the discussion so far about American variants of Euro-beers has all been about ales. For some mystifying reason, few American brewers are willing to challenge the imposing rigidity of classic lagers. Perhaps the Reinheitsgebot has some mysterious supernatural power to hold brewers in its thrall. Whatever the mechanism, this ancient goatskin has intimidated us all into keeping to the straight and narrow—even though it technically doesn't even apply to Germans themselves anymore. Or, maybe it's because German and Czech beers are perfection personified, the pinnacle of the ten-thousand-year march to beer destiny? Nah.

Anyway, as fabulous as a classic lager can be at times, they are by no means sacrosanct. So let's put our warped points of view to work and see what we can come up with. Here are some of mine.

FLAKY LITTLE GRANOLA LAGER

This takes a perfectly respectable Dortmunder export lager and bumps up the crunchy-creamy factor by using 4 percent each of flaked oats, flaked rye, and flaked barley. A similar percentage of honey malt adds that toasted sugary flavor, and 1 percent light molasses adds a nutty layer. Original gravity should be about 1.055 (13.6°P). Mashing would benefit from a protein rest and some rice hulls to speed filtration. Hop as you would a classic lager, although the apricot fruitiness of Simcoe would be a nice touch. Shoot for 30 to 35 BU, but suit yourself—the beer police aren't watching. Honey, toasted hazelnuts, and coconut are optional.

NAMIBIAN PALE LAGER

The Germans never had the vast colonial empire the other major European states had, but did hold some African territories late in the nineteenth century. It's interesting to think what they might have done to a Pilsner-style beer to make it hold up to the rigors of a sea voyage. To a base of 100 percent Pils malt brewed to a gravity of 1.068 (16.6°P), I'd add a boatload of fine Spalt or Hallertau hops. Let's say 60 IBU, which comes out to 3 ounces/90 g an hour for a 5-gallon/19-L batch, plus another 3 to 4 ounces/90 to 120 g right at the end of the boil. Feel free to dry-hop this batch as it lagers. You could give the same beer the Czech treatment by using Saaz hops instead of the German varieties.

NOVEMBERFEST

Picture a rich, creamy Oktoberfest dialed up a notch for the chillier winds of November. We're shooting for 1.063 (15.5°P). Start with Munich (and a little Pils if you like), but add about 10 percent dark Munich or melanoidin, and about 2 ounces/60 g of Carafa for a little extra color. Eight ounces/225 g of molasses will add a layer of complex flavor and lighten the body just a little. I'd keep the hopping relatively light on this one.

TRIPEL MAIBOCK

I love the malty aroma and hop-tinged taste of maibock, but I am often underwhelmed by this style. What if we take a page from Belgian brewing and add some sugar for a crisper palate and double up on the hops? I would add 10 percent high-quality pale ethnic sugar, perhaps Thai palm, a.k.a. coconut sugar. Gravity should be in the Tripel range at 1.080 (19.3°P). Hop with Perle for bittering (1 ounce/30 g will get you 30 IBU), and finish with massive amounts of Saaz or the American Ultra. I'd definitely recommend dry-hopping with more Saaz or something more frisky.

Beer Name and Type	Original Gravity/°P	Estimated Alcohol by Vol.	Approx. BU	Color	Weeks to Drink
Angry European Red Lager	1070/17°P	5.5–6.5 %	65 IBU	Red amber/ 18 SRM	10–12

In the 1990s, red ales were iconic for the industrial breweries' ham-handed attempts to grab a piece of craft-beer glory. Consciously or not, craft brewers have since taken red ale to a place they know the big brewers won't follow: into the land of juiced-up, over-hopped ales of no small gravity. Here's a recipe one of my Chicago cohorts and I recently brewed together on American Homebrewers Association Big Brew day.

Qty	Ingredient	OG/°P	%	**All-Grain Mashed Version**
6.3 lb/2.9 kg	Vienna malt	1.0324/7.3	46	Infusion mash (page 130)
4 lb/1.8 kg	Munich malt	1.0200/5.1	29	60 min @ 147°F/64°C, then mash out
2 lb/907 g	Melanoidin malt	1.0096/2.5	14	
8 oz/227 g	120°L dark caramel malt	1.0022/0.6	3	An extract + mini mash can be made by substi-
1 lb/454 g	Wheat malt	1.0058/1.5	8	tuting 5.7 lb/2.6 kg amber dry malt extract for the Vienna and Munich malts.

Hops:

Qty	Name	Alpha	IBU	Minutes	
5 lb/28 g	Perle	8 % AA	33	60	You could lager this, or if you can't manage tem-
2 oz/57 g	Hallertau	3.5 % AA	22	30	peratures well enough for a true lager, use one of the European ale yeasts and do a conditioning
2 oz/57 g	Saaz	2.5 % AA	20	10	as cool as you can manage. The beer will mature in roughly half the time this way.

Katarzyna Haptaś brews with Marcin Kamiński and creates these thrilling labels for their Cztery Bapy (Four Paws) home-brewery in Warsaw, Poland.

PLANET HOMEBREW

Over the last few decades, homebrewing has undergone an amazing transformation from a disjointed and rather primitive hobby to the sophisticated and well-connected community we have today. We're proud of what we've built in North America, and are excited to see that crazy passion affecting brewers elsewhere. Legions of hobbyists, connoisseurs, and entrepreneurs are rising up everywhere, no longer willing to put up with the lack of variety and vapidity of industrial beer and, as a result, good beer is exploding all over the world. Homebrewing is now a global movement.

It's just one more sign that we're all becoming a lot more like each other. We get the same Internet, watch a lot of the same TV shows, listen to the same music, and even share each other's food. As the middle class rises, people jump at the chance to travel abroad, and that further breaks down barriers. Today's global homebrewers are inspired by the great classic brewing traditions of Europe, but also by the feast of variety and excitement going on in the United States. And more often than not, they are adopting the U.S. model as the one to build on.

Wherever you find it, homebrewing attracts the same kind of curious, open-minded, passionate, and creative enthusiasts. It's fundamental to our pursuit, a bond that we all share. It is the hobby's most valuable asset. We are passionately stricken by the beer bug, and will employ all our resources to make that happen. That's a constant.

There are some differences as well. Although homebrew shops are popping up, they are still rather rare, so access to supplies can be somewhat limited. Hops have always been an international product and as such can be mail-ordered. Quality malt producers like Weyermann have a footprint in most regions, and South America now has its own micro maltster making a full range of products. Yeast is the biggest problem. Liquid types don't travel well, and live cultures always draw a lot of scrutiny at customs. As a result, most brewers, even many commercial ones, use dried yeast. This is not a bad thing in itself, but these strains have a tendency to emphasize a single characteristic, like ester or phenol, and tropical fermentation temperatures make it worse. Equipment is another big problem, as many developing countries impose gruesome import duties, so gear is not only hard to get, it's crazy expensive as well.

In most places outside the United States, there is simply less critical mass swirling around good beer. This means fewer commercial craft beers, less experience with judging and competitions, fewer homebrewing clubs, and not as many places to drink good beer. These are all problems homebrewers faced in the United States, and eventually grew out of, so we can expect great things in the near future from brewers around the world.

The future of Beer? Heretics, weirdos, creativity. The world is more borderless and intertwining, united in our diversity.

SAM CALAGIONE, founder, Dogfish Head Craft Brewery, Rehoboth Beach, DE

As Rio de Janeiro beer-shop owner Leo Oliviera shows, devotion to great beer is spreading to all parts of the world.

The homebrewing scene is most lively and creative where local beer tradition is the least interesting, which was certainly the story in the United States a few decades back. There is still a lot of interest in the European classics, and folks are brewing them for pleasure as well as the challenge of achieving a certain set of characteristics, and why not? Those beers are classic for good reasons. But now they also have the example of U.S.-style brews, from hop monsters to fruit beers, barrel-aging, and beyond. All of this serves as inspiration, but not idolatry. Brewers everywhere are working to find their unique voices, changing things up to take advantage of local flavors and ingredients, working to seduce local palates and fit into the local culture and cuisine. It's getting to be a very tasty world.

ITALY

This ancient land is home to some great wine and one of the best food cultures on Earth. However, since the days of the Roman Empire, Italians have never considered beer as anything particularly artsy. Things have changed. In Italy's north, a vibrant and creative craft-brewing scene has been established. Here, the craft brewers are out ahead of the homebrewers, leading with innovation, but homebrewers and beer enthusiasts are organizing rapidly, trying to build a community and empower themselves to make great beer.

To some degree, inspiration comes from Italy's incredibly diverse and creative wine culture. In addition, the creative Belgian approach resonates with many Italian brewers. Spices and non-traditional ingredients are common, although there are plenty of straight-up classic styles as well. Homebrewers are still something of a rare breed. The lack of a large pool of expertise has had an effect on both beer quality and the ability to develop a sizable following of rabid fans. A beer enthusiast group called MOBI (Movimento Birrario Italiano) spreads information and enthusiasm.

A recent excavation discovered the earliest known evidence for hopped beer, found in a sixth century B.C.E. context in Liguria, a region in which wild hops can still be found. It turns out that beer may be more Italian than everybody thought.

The penetrating aroma of this ancient grape variety makes it perfect for flavoring beer.

Italy has a very exciting and artistic good beer scene.

Beer Name and Type	Original Gravity/°P	Estimated Alcohol by Vol.	Approx. BU	Color	Weeks to Drink
Lampo Bianco (White Lightning) Witbier with Muscat Grape Juice	1.045/11.2°P	5.8%	19/moderate	Gold/5.6 SRM	6–8

This recipe was inspired by a Duchessa—an Italian saison brewed by a craft brewery called Del Borgo in Borgorose, a bit north of Rome. The Del Borgo recipe uses 50 percent juice from Sangiovese grapes, the variety used in Chianti. It features a beautiful white wine nose and a soft, beery texture on the palate. I decided to change this up and make it a witbier and use a highly aromatic grape variety, muscat, used in Italy to make low-alcohol sparklers as well as dessert wines. I collaborated with San Diego master homebrewer Harold Gulbransen on this recipe, which I am unable to improve on, so here you are.

Qty	Ingredient	OG/°P	%	**All-Grain Mashed Version**
3.5 lb/1.6 kg	U.S. two-row Pils malt	1.019/4.8	42	Infusion mash (page 130)
4.1 lb/1.9 kg	Malted wheat	1.024/6.1	51	60 min @ 154°F/68°C, then mash out
8 oz/227 g	Flaked oats	1.0033/0.9	7	

Qty	Ingredient	OG/°P	%	**Alternate Extract + Steeped-Grain Version**
2.1 lb/950 g	Dry pale malt extract	1.020/5.1	45	Standard E + SG Procedure (page 119)
2.6 lb/1.2 kg	Dry wheat extract	1.024/6.1	51	
8 oz/227 g	Cara-Pils	1.0024/0.6	5	

Hops and Seasonings

Qty	Name	Alpha	IBU	Minutes	
8 g	Chinook	11.1	12.7	60	**Additional Ingredients:** One 46-oz/1.4-L can of muscat grape juice concentrate, added to fermenter at the end of the primary
10 g	Simcoe	11.9	6.2	10	
14 g	Columbus	12.0	0.0	0	**Yeast:** Belgian Wit Ale (WLP550 or Wyeast 3944 or 3942)
12 g	Indian Coriander	–	–	2	
2 g	Cardamom (Whole Pod)	–	–	2	**Fermentation Temperature:** 75 to 78°F/24 to 26°C
3 g	Dried Ginger	–	–	2	**Carbonation:** Medium high/3.0 volumes/5.5 oz (156 g) priming sugar
2 g	Lemon Zest	–	–	2	

I found a lot of small commercial brewers making chestnut beer in Italy, but nobody there seemed all that excited about the notion. This is explained by the fact that the Italian government subsidizes chestnut beers as a rural development program, going so far as to pay for an entire brewery to focus on them. Indeed, I found them to be lackluster for the most part, with little chestnut flavor other than a coarse astringency.

Still, I wondered if it was possible to make a delicious-tasting chestnut beer. With the help of another San Diego homebrewer, Guy Shobe, I found out that it is. Roasting the chestnuts first is the key. Use dried chestnuts (I found them at an Asian market) and roast them in the oven at 350°F/177°C until they develop a pinkish, pale tan color and a deep nutty aroma. Break them up with a hammer and crush them as finely as you can. I used an old coffee grinder for this. To add another layer of flavor, try chestnut honey. It's a dark and intense honey, so it's best used in moderation.

Beer Name and Type	Original Gravity/°P	Estimated Alcohol by Vol.	Approx. BU	Color	Weeks to Drink
Dado Duro (Hard Nut) Brown Ale with Chestnuts and Honey	1.055/13.6°P	5.7%	16/low	Brown/ 17 SRM	4–6

Qty	Ingredient	OG/°P	%	All-Grain Mashed Version
3.6 lb/1.6 kg	Pale ale malt	1.022/5.8	40	Infusion mash (page 130)
3.4 lb/1.5 kg	Malted wheat	1.019/4.8	35	60 min @ 154°F/68°C, then mash out
8 oz/227 g	Melanoidin malt	1.0033/0.9	6	
8 oz/227 g	40°L caramel malt	1.0033/0.9	6	
8 oz/227 g	Black malt	1.0033/0.9	6	
1 lb/454 g	Roasted chestnuts (see text)	1.0033/0.9	6	

Qty	Ingredient	OG/°P	%	Alternate Extract + Steeped-Grain Version:
2.6 lb/1.2 kg	Dry pale malt extract	1.024/6.1	44	Standard E + SG Procedure (page 119)
3 lb/1.4 kg	Dry wheat extract	1.0275/6.9	50	
8 oz/227 g	Super pale caramel (Cara-Pils)	1.0033/0.9	6	

Hops

Qty	Name	Alpha	IBU	Minutes
9 g	Northern Brewer	8.0	11	60
112 g	Northern Brewer	8.0	5	10

Additional Ingredients: 1 lb/454 g chestnut honey, added to fermenter after primary fermentation
Yeast: London ESB (Fuller's strain) (WLP002 or Wyeast 1968)
Fermentation Temperature: 64 to 68°F/18 to 20°C
Carbonation: Medium/2.2 volumes/3 oz (85 g) priming sugar

Chestnuts are widely used in Italian brewing, partly due to government agricultural subsidies. Chopped, roasted dried chestnuts (above) are ready for the mash.

SCANDINAVIA

This region is a fascinating mix of the modern and the very ancient. It's the home of IKEA and many other icons of modernity. In design this isn't so bad, but what *modern* means in beers is the same sad sea of bland international Pilsners as everywhere else on the globe. In fact, the yeast strains now used to make nearly all the beer on the planet were first isolated and purified—a very modern idea—in Denmark at the Carlsberg and Tuborg facilities.

But miraculously, the ancient brewing traditions linger on. In Finland, a rye beer called sahti is still brewed by farmers using hollowed-out logs and juniper branches as mash tuns, and this is even produced commercially on a small scale. On the Swedish island of Gotland, a smoky beer called Gotlandsdricka is still brewed, and rustic brewing traditions are still very much alive in rural Norway.

Fulfilling my lifelong dream of harvesting bog myrtle in a Danish bog.

Beer Name and Type	Original Gravity/°P	Estimated Alcohol by Vol.	Approx. BU	Color	Weeks to Drink
Valkyrie Tears Scandinavian IPA with Bog Myrtle	1.072/17°P	6.8%	77/high	Deep gold/ 6 SRM	8–12

Beer enthusiasts in far Northern Europe love a good IPA. I find the aroma of bog myrtle (Myrica gale, or porse, in Danish) particularly enchanting, and a really good partner with hops. It's a bit hard to find, but there are mail-order sources and it is fairly common in damp places in Alaska and elsewhere in the far north. Leaves are commonly sold, but they have some astringency. The tiny conelike flowers have a much more refined and intense aroma, and they are the parts used in Denmark to flavor porse schnapps. Add 10 to 20 grams (depending on freshness/intensity) of leaf with the finishing hops.

Qty	Ingredient	OG/°P	%	**All-Grain Mashed Version**
6 lb/2.7 kg	Pale ale malt	1.036/9.0	50	Infusion mash (page 130)
7 lb/3.2 kg	Vienna malt	1.036/9.0	50	Infusion, 60 min @ 154°F/68°C, then mash out

Qty	Ingredient	OG/°P	%	**Alternate Extract + Steeped-Grain Version**
7.3 lb/3.3 kg	Dry pale malt extract	1.0673/16.4	93	Standard E + SG Procedure (page 119)
1 lb/454 g	Honey malt	1.0047/1.2	7	

Hops and Seasonings

Qty	Name	Alpha	IBU	Minutes	
25 g	Cascade	5	14	First Wort	**Yeast:** California Ale (WLP 001/Wyeast 1056) **Fermentation Temperature:** 62 to 66°F/17 to 19°C **Carbonation:** Medium/2.2 volumes/3 oz (85 g) priming sugar
17 g	Columbus	15	35	60	
15 g	Cascade	5	8	30	
4 g	Columbus	15	7	30	
70 g	Riwaka or U.S. Saaz	5.5	10	5	
10 g	Bog myrtle/sweet gale	—	—	5	

Beer Name and Type	Original Gravity/°P	Estimated Alcohol by Vol.	Approx. BU	Color	Weeks to Drink
Smøkesbørd Swedish Smoked Ale with Juniper	1.052/12.6°P	5%	25/low	Brown/ 16 SRM	4–6

This beer is inspired by the fresh, smoky real ale of Nårke Kulturbryggeri, in Örebro, Sweden. It's a hybrid of an English brown ale and something more primal, with the flavors of smoke up front and juniper lurking in the background. Here, the recipe calls for the cherry-smoked malt from Briess, but feel free to smoke your own—birch would be most Swedish. For another Nordic touch, a large handful of juniper branches with berries can be boiled in the mash water.

Qty	Ingredient	OG/°P	%	All-Grain Mashed Version
3.1 lb/1.4 kg	Briess cherrywood-smoked malt	1.0156/4.0	30	Infusion mash (page 130)
3.1 lb/1.4 kg	Pale ale malt	1.0156/4.0	30	60 min @ 154°F/68°C, then mash out
3.4 lb/1.5 kg	Amber/biscuit malt	1.0156/4.0	30	
1 lb/454 g	Melanoidin malt	1.0047/1.2	10	

Qty	Ingredient	OG/°P	%	Alternate Mini-Mash Version
3.7 lb/1.7 kg	Dry pale malt extract	1.0345/8.7	66	Standard MM Procedure (page 127)
2 lb/907 g	Smoked malt	1.0098/2.5	19	
1 lb/454 g	Honey malt	1.0047/1.2	9	
11 oz/318 g	120 to 150°L caramel malt	1.0030/0.8	6	

Hops

Qty	Name	Alpha	IBU	Minutes	
					Yeast: English or Scottish Ale (your choice)
					Fermentation Temperature: 62 to 66°F/17 to 19°C
8.5 g	Northdown	8.5	11	60	**Carbonation:** Low to medium/1.8 volumes/2 oz (57 g)
23 g	Fuggles	4.5	6	10	priming sugar

Scandinavian beer is utterly dominated by the large breweries, which have a large chunk of the craft segment as well. A few huge retailers own the marketplace, and taxes are ruinously high. Norway has the embarrassing distinction of having the highest beer taxes in the world, something like U.S.$1.50 per 12-ounce/355-ml bottle. In Sweden, only the state liquor stores sell beer over 3.5 percent alcohol by volume—even weaker than the 3.2 percent (by weight that's 4 percent by volume) beer in many U.S. states. Scandinavians have lots of good reasons to homebrew.

The Scandinavian good-beer scene looks a lot like the U.S. one—creative brewers trying to make something interesting, loving the wild and bracing flavors of North American hops, but at the same time embracing the ancient flavors of smoke, juniper, and bog myrtle, and respecting the centuries of porter-brewing before beer became utterly Bavarianized there.

We are very interested in traditional home-brewed Gotlandsdricka from Sweden and sahti from Finland. A unique Scandinavian beer has to stay small scale or it will very soon lack the character it started with.

H. G. WIKTORSSON AND BERITH KARLSSON, husband and wife owners of Nårke Kulturbryggeri, Örebro, Sweden

BRAZIL

The beer market in this exotic, vivid, wild, diverse country is dominated by AB InBev, which, in stark contrast to its vibrant culture, cuisine, and people, is every bit as uninteresting as industrial beer everywhere.

Craft brewing started in the 1990s, but was not accompanied by a home-brewing scene until more recently. Many of the early craft breweries were pretty Germanic, brewing timid all-malt beers with just the barest whisper of hops. But that's old news. Brazil's beer scene is expanding rapidly in size and concept. There's a palpable sense of excitement and a desire to make bold, delicious beers that reflect the liveliness of the country as a whole. At this point, inspiration comes as much from U.S. craft beers as it does from European classics.

The country is a treasure trove of fascinating natural products that can be absolutely delicious in beer and new Brazilian brewers are experimenting with them, searching for combinations that are fun and interesting, but at the same time profoundly delicious and not just tiresome novelties.

Brazil is a paradox, a country where relatively expensive craft beer faces the cheapest most profitable beer on Earth. Our mission is to prove every day that "money has no ideas." Here, as in many parts of the world, we used to have a big beer diversity. We want our beer forest back. We want our beer scene to reflect the luscious forests that surround us.

MARCELO CARNEIRA DA ROCHA,
founder and owner, Cervejaria
Colorado, Riberão Preto, Brazil

The produce market in Belém, Brazil, offers a bewildering array of exotic, wild-harvested products.

Some ingredients of interest that may be available in the United States:

CUMARU (*Dipteryx odorata*)

More widely known by its seed, the tonka bean, this spice contains coumarin, an aromatic substance with some toxicity, however it is legal in France for culinary uses like chocolate. One-half to one bean (5 to 10 g) per 5-gallon/19-L batch is a perfectly safe amount, as long as you're not drinking more than a couple of beers a day. (Here's the math on this. Science: there may be problems above 6.1 mg per day for a 135-pound/143-kg person. The Federal Institute for Risk Assessment published an alternative limit of 0.1 mg coumarin per 2 pounds/1 kg of body mass per day, which is considered harmless as average intake. According to this scale, a person of 110 pounds/50 kg could afford to eat 5 mg of coumarin per day. Tonka beans have 10 percent coumarin. Beans weigh about a gram each. If all the coumarin from the bean goes into the beer, that means 100 mg per 5-gallon/19-L batch, or not quite 2 mg per 12-ounce/355-mL beer.)

Cumaru is pretty potent in terms of aroma; I would consider one bean per 5-gallon/19-L batch as the upper limit for aroma. It has a deep aromatic quality, a bit vanilla-like, but heavier with something of the character of cherry pits (kirsch) as well. Should do best in a dark beer.

HONEY

Brazil has 300 species of bees, many of them stingless. Exotic honeys include jatai from stingless bees, honeydew, acacia, pepper tree (*Schinus molle*), as well as wildflower honeys with many different characters. None of these is easy to find, but should be well worth experimenting with.

RAPADURA SUGAR

This is simply sugarcane juice, boiled down to a thick syrup and poured into molds. It is similar to the Colombian piloncillo found in Latin markets in the United States, but has a brighter, more grassy flavor. Uses include body thinning on stronger beers and IPAs, especially doubles.

TROPICAL FRUIT

Many of these, like papaya, mango, and passionfruit, are familiar fruits cultivated throughout Latin America. Cashew juice, made from the fruit attached to the nut, is a popular breakfast beverage and has a complex, delicious flavor somewhat similar to mango. More exotic Amazonian fruits such as açaí, bacurí, or taperabá are worth seeking out.

TROPICAL HARDWOOD

As would be expected from a country that harbors one of the largest forests on Earth, there is a lot of exotic wood in Brazil. A huge range, including Brazil-nut (castanha de Parà), imburana, jequitibá, ipê, grápia, bálsamo, amendoim, jatobá, guanandi, pau-Brasil, cabreúva, tibiriçá, garapeira, and cerejeira, are used to make vats in which the local sugarcane rum, cachaça, is aged. Tanks often are built from staves of many different woods. Ipê and jatobá (and some others) are internationally available for use as flooring and rot-resistant decking. They have pleasant aromas, suitable to use in chunks added to a fermenter for some exotic wood character.

Left to right: Brazilian cumaru, rapadura sugar, and cashew fruit.

Beer Name and Type	Original Gravity/°P	Estimated Alcohol by Vol.	Approx. BU	Color	Weeks to Drink
Monkey Toes Brazil Nut Dark Ale with Rapadura Sugar, Conditioned on Ipê Wood	1.066/16.1°P	6.3 %	32/medium	Dark brown/ 20 SRM	6–8

This recipe was inspired by a really fantastic beer by homebrewer Ricardo Rosa that was later brewed in a small batch at Cervejaria Colorado—"We had a thousand dollars worth of nuts in there!" The original version was aged in a barrel made of Brazil nut wood, which in Brazil is called castanha de Para, or "chestnut of Para," after its native state in Brazil's north. In the United States, ipê wood is widely available for use in decking and outdoor furniture. Just a handful of scrap wood cut down to fit into a carboy should be sufficient to add a delicate perfumy wood character.

Qty	Ingredient	OG/°P	%	All-Grain Mashed Version
5.7 lb/2.6 kg	Pale ale malt	1.0320/8.0	48	Infusion mash (page 130)
6 lb/2.7 kg	Munich malt	1.0300/7.6	45	60 min @ 154°F/68°C, then mash out
12 oz/340 g	Honey malt	1.0033/0.9	5	
4.8 oz/136 g	Chocolate rye	1.0041/0.3	2	

Qty	Ingredient	OG/°P	%	Alternate Extract + Steeped-Grain Version
6.5 lb/2.9 kg	Dry pale malt extract	1.0594/14.6	90	Standard E + SG Procedure (page 119)
1 lb/454 g	Honey malt	1.0044/1.1	7	
8 oz/227 g	60°L caramel wheat malt	1.0022/0.6	3	
4.8 oz/136 g	Chocolate rye	—	—	

Hops

Qty	Name	Alpha	IBU	Minutes	
15 g	Magnum	14	28	60	
15 g	Cascade	5	8	30	
5 g	Columbus	15	7	30	

Additional Ingredients: 8 oz/227 g of lightly toasted Brazil nuts, crushed in food processor, added to mash, or added to steeping malts. Approximately 4 oz/113 g of ipê wood, cut into pieces small enough to fit into a carboy, boiled to sanitize and added to fermenter.
Yeast: Scottish Ale (WLP 028/Wyeast 1728) or other ale of your choice
Fermentation Temperature: 62 to 66°F/17 to 19°C
Carbonation: Medium/2.0 volumes/2.5 oz (71 g) priming sugar

These Imburana wood tanks are used to age the Brazilian sugar-cane liquor, cachaça, in Riberão Preto, São Paulo State.

ARGENTINA

It is not a coincidence that the tango, with all its brooding passion, is central to the artistic life of Argentina. It is a place that cultivates a serious, even dark, side to the national character and where people take perverse pride in the fact that Buenos Aires has more psychologists per capita than any other place on Earth. They think of Buenos Aires as the most European city in the Western Hemisphere and the city is chock-full of Beaux-Arts buildings designed by Parisian architects in the late nineteenth century—one tasty wedding cake after another, as far as the eye can see.

And man, they love their sweet stuff! The streets are just about paved with *dulce de leche* (milk caramel), practically oozing from every pastry shop window.

Quilmes, an AB InBev brand, utterly dominates the commercial beer marketplace. Craft beer is still just getting rolling, and is still far less than 1 percent of the market. There is a lot of enthusiasm for homebrewing, thanks in part to a pretty gloomy economy. The level of skill and community organization is growing rapidly. Somos Cerveceros is a large, well-organized homebrewing club based in Buenos Aires.

My trip there was commemorated by a special pale ale brewed with yerba maté, the ubiquitous herb tea consumed incessantly in Argentina. It has a pleasant herbal quality that blends nicely with beer. It needs no special recipe; just replace some of your aroma hops, gram-for-gram, with the maté.

A beer called Dorada Pampeana, or "Pampas Gold," survives from the very beginnings of Argentine homebrewing, decades ago. In those days, anyone who wanted to brew had to beg a brewery to sell a bag of lager malt and some local Argentine hops, grown way down south in Patagonia. These hops are a little rough around the edges. Liquid yeast was—and still is—difficult to obtain there, and so a dry yeast called Nottingham was most often used. Dorada Pampeana is considered a test of skill among homebrewers. Making a tasty beer from these three ingredients is challenging, but that's the point. Life is difficult, but if you have enough passion, you can turn it into something delicious.

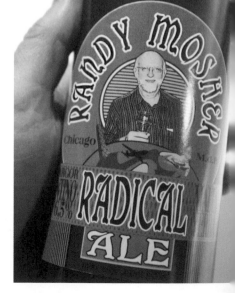

Nothing more weirdly flattering than having your face on a beer label. Brewed using yerba maté by my friends in Argentina.

Beer Name and Type	Original Gravity/°P	Estimated Alcohol by Vol.	Approx. BU	Color	Weeks to Drink
Vida Dulce (Sweet Life) Porter	1.056/13.8°P	6%	22/medium	Dark brown/ 20 SRM	6–8

I was invited to a beer festival in the Argentinean beach-resort city of Mar Del Plata, and informed that there would be some homebrewers waiting for me. I was led to the middle of the room where two 10-gallon/38-L systems were going full tilt, one with a porter and the other a brown ale. The brewers anxiously asked, "Mister Randy, Mister Randy, what should we add?" It was Sunday afternoon, and of course we had to think of something that we knew we could get, so we settled on black pepper and a pinch of nutmeg for the brown ale, and—drum roll, please—2.2 pounds/1 kg of dulce de leche for the porter.

Qty	Ingredient	OG/°P	%	**All-Grain Mashed Version**
7.5 lb/3.4 kg	Mild ale malt	1.0398/10	71	Infusion mash (page 130)
2 lb/907 g	Amber/biscuit malt	1.0093/2.4	17	60 min @ 154°F/68°C, then mash out
1 lb/454 g	Brown malt	1.0047/1.2	8	
8 oz/227 g	Chocolate malt	1.0022/0.6	4	

Qty	Ingredient	OG/°P	%	**Alternate Extract + Mini-Mash Version**
5.2 lb/2.4 kg	Dry pale malt extract	1.0493/12.2	88	Standard E + MM Procedure (page 127)
1 lb/454 g	Honey malt	1.0047/1.2	8	
8 oz/227 g	60°L caramel wheat malt	1.0022/0.6	4	
4.8 oz/136 g	Chocolate malt	—	—	

Hops

Qty	Name	Alpha	IBU	Minutes	
25 g	Argentine Cascade	5	16	60	**Additional Ingredients:** 1.1 lb/500 g dulce de leche, purchased readymade or made by heating unopened cans of sweetened condensed milk in a pan of simmering water for 2.5 hours. **Yeast:** London ESB (Fuller's strain) **Fermentation Temperature:** 62 to 66°F/17 to 19°C **Carbonation:** Medium/2.5 volumes/3.5 oz (100 g) priming sugar
15 g	Argentine Cascade	5	6	30	

Dulce de leche is a sweet milk caramel confection ubiquitous in Argentina. By the way, it's delicious in beer.

NUEVO LATINO CERVEZA *en* CHICAGO

Current beers in Latin America are simply international lagers that have little or nothing to do with the culture and cuisine there. In Chicago, my partners and I at 5 Rabbit Cerveceria are reimagining Latin-American beer. It's an interesting challenge because you have to go a very long way back to find any indigenous traditions; but a flexible point of view helps, using past and present inspirations to create twenty-first-century beers that are fun and tasty. Offerings include a passionfruit witbier with fresh lime peel, a Oaxacan dark ale with piloncillo sugar and a dab of ancho chile, and a bent Oktoberfest beer with dulce de leche and some very subtle spices including Mexican cinnamon.

In trying to conceptualize some dark beers, the notion of a Mexican black witbier popped up, flavored with mesquite and aromatized by white sage, the perfumy herb sacred to native people all over the region. Done right, the beer would smell like a desert campfire. San Diego homebrewer Harold Gulbransen came to my aid with a delicious version, even going to the trouble of smoking the malt in his barbecue smoker.

> *Beer made with hibiscus, spearmint, piloncillo, tamarind—these are classic ingredients in my culture that I want to include. Also I'd like to use tequila barrels to age beer, or do something with mezcal even with pulque.*

RODOLFO ANDREU, Cerveceria Primus, Mexico City, Mexico

With an actual brew, it can be several weeks or longer before you find out how the flavors are working. While there's no substitute for actually brewing, you can learn a lot by spiking a base beer with teas, vodka tinctures, extracts, fruit purées, acids, and other components that may be employed in the final recipe.

Beer Name and Type	Original Gravity/°P	Estimated Alcohol by Vol.	Approx. BU	Color	Weeks to Drink
Smoke Signals Sonoran Black Ale with Mesquite-Smoked Malt and White Sage	1.064/15.7°P	6.3 %	20/low	Dark brown/ 16 SRM	6–8

Qty	Ingredient	OG/°P	%	**All-Grain Mashed Version**
7 lb/3.2 kg	Smoked malt	1.0368/9.2	57	Infusion mash (page 130)
4 lb/1.8 kg	wheat malt	1.0175/4.5	27	
1 lb/454 g	Carastan malt*	1.0047/1.2	7	60 minutes @ 153°F/67°C, followed by mash out. If
8 oz/227 g	Caramunich malt	1.0023/0.6	4	you're so inclined, a 15-minute protein rest before
8 oz/227 g	Flaked oats	1.0022/0.6	3	saccharification at 122°F/50°C might yield a little
4.8 oz/136 g	Debittered black malt	1.0005/0.2	1	more creaminess from the wheat and oats.

* A unique, toffee-flavored 30 to 37°L caramel malt made by Bairds Malt.

Qty	Ingredient	OG/°P	%	**Extract + Mini-Mash Version**
2.3 lb/1 kg	Dry pale malt extract	1.0220/5.6	34	Standard E + MM Procedure (page 127)
3.2 lb/1.5 kg	Dry wheat malt extract	1.0300/7.5	46	
2 lb/907 g	Smoked pale malt*	1.0075/1.9	12	
1 lb/454 g	Carastan malt (see above)	1.0030/0.8	5	
8 oz/227 g	Caramunich malt	1.0014/0.2	2	
4.8 oz/136 g	Debittered black malt	1.0004/1.0	1	

* This will add minimal smoke. For more, consider re-smoking on home smoker (see page 71).

Hops and Seasonings

Qty	Name	Alpha	IBU	Minutes	
15 g	Chinook	11	18	60	**Yeast:** Belgian Lachouffe strain Wyeast 3522, WLP550
15 g	Hallertau	3	2	10	**Fermentation Temperature:** 68 to 72°F/20 to 22°C
14 g	Indian coriander seeds, cracked	—	—	2	**Carbonation:** Medium/2.5 volumes/3.5 oz (100 g) priming sugar
12 g	White sage leaves	—	—	2	

White sage, a desert plant sacred to Native Americans, has an exotic, slightly perfumy aroma. Photo by Harold Gulbransen.

While many different woods can be used to smoke malts, mesquite offers the dry, pungent aroma of the Southwest.

AUSTRALIA *and* NEW ZEALAND

The scene Down Under, which is still picking up steam, is the closest thing to American-style homebrewing I have seen. The clubs are well organized, there is a lot of interest in BJCP judging, and brewers are making a wide variety of styles based both on European classics and American craft beers, with uniquely Australian styles such as sparkling ale in the mix.

Craft brewing has been under way since about the early '90s. The pattern there has been to sell out to larger business interests as soon as some degree of success is attained; consequently, there is a layer of corporate craft brewing that is a little different than in the United States, where craft breweries tend to be more independent. As the twenty-first century progresses, a new crop of more free-spirited entrepreneurs has popped up, and the beers are becoming bolder and more flavorful.

Because the Australian landmass separated from the rest of the world 96 million years ago, it developed a unique community of plants and animals unlike anywhere else on Earth. For brewers and cooks alike, this means a treasure chest of spices, herbs, honey, and exotic woods to choose from. Some experimentation has been done, but much work remains to make sense of this incredible variety of flavors and to find ways to make compelling and uniquely Australian beers from them.

Native herbs and spices include Tasmanian pepperberry, which is a wild roller-coaster ride of flavor ranging from fruity to juniper to a stinging prickly heat to a weird, lingering sweetness. I can say with certainty that it's the strangest thing I've ever tasted. I'm thinking it might be great in some kind of Southern Hemisphere saison.

And there are others, like lemon myrtle (*Backhousia citriodora*), which has a super-clean, bright, lemony aroma that would be the perfect seasoning to blend with some citrusy hops for a really bright, happy summer ale, perhaps based on a classic sparkling ale. Aniseed myrtle (*Backhousia anisata*) has a pleasant anise aroma as its name would imply. One of the more complex and interesting native herbs is strawberry gum, which has a bright, fruity, berry-like aroma with a little sharp, fresh-cut oak character as well.

Roasted wattleseed (*Acacia victoriae*) has an aroma described as similar to both vanilla and coffee, but I find it also has a nice dark-roasted peanut butter scent as well. In cooking, it is typically used in desserts. It's comfortably at home in brown ales and porters, an example of which is included here.

> *With the development of newer hop varieties in Australia and New Zealand, such as Galaxy (AU) and Nelson Sauvin (NZ), there is a greater chance of a regional style developing with brewers showcasing the wonderful flavors and aromas of these new varietals and realizing the best way to do this is with simple malt bills for pale ales and Pilsners.*

PHIL YEUNG, Australian homebrewer and club organizer

In case you were wondering, homebrewing is just as nuts Down Under.

Beer Name and Type		Original Gravity/°P	Estimated Alcohol by Vol.	Approx. BU	Color	Weeks to Drink
Wattle Itbee? Roasted Wattleseed Brown Ale		1.050/12.4°P	6%	16/medium	Dark brown/ 20 SRM	6–8

Wattleseed comes from various species of the acacia tree. When roasted, it develops an intense, nutty aroma a little like dark-roasted peanut butter. The base beer is a creamy brown ale that shows off the wattleseed nicely and enhances its nutty character. For a variation, add 1 pound/454 g of macadamia honey to the fermenter once the primary is winding down.

Qty	Ingredient	OG/°P	%	All-Grain Mashed Version
8.5 lb/3.9 kg	Vienna malt	1.0445/11.1	89	Infusion mash (page 130)
12 oz/340 g	Amber/biscuit malt	1.0035/8.8	7	60 min @ 154°F/68°C, then mash out
1 lb/454 g	80°L caramel malt	1.0015/1	3	
4.8 oz/136 g	Black malt	1.0005/0.1	1	

Qty	Ingredient	OG/°P	%	Alternate Extract + Mini-Mash Version
4.8 lb/2.2 kg	Dry pale malt extract	1.0440/11	88	Standard E + MM Procedure (page 127)
1 lb/454 g	20°L caramel malt	1.0044/11	9	
8 oz/227 g	80°L caramel malt	1.0022/0.4	2	
4.8 oz/136 g	Black malt	1.0005/0.1	1	

Hops and Seasonings

Qty	Name	Alpha	IBU	Minutes	
5 g	Galaxy	14	9	60	**Yeast:** Most any British yeast will do. I like the Fuller's strain (London ESB) for its malt-accentuating character.
55 g	Galaxy	14	7	30	**Fermentation Temperature:** 64 to 68°F/18 to 20°C
14 g	Roasted wattleseed	—	—	2	**Carbonation:** Medium/2.5 volumes/3.5 oz (100 g) priming sugar

Several of these indigenous ingredients can be sourced from sellers on eBay or Amazon, but www.outbackchef.com.au is a handy single source for many native ingredients.

In addition to herbs and spices, Australia and New Zealand are home to some really fabulous honeys. Leatherwood honey is the most popular variety, exotic and complex, with some savory, herbal, and floral qualities. Macadamia honey is pale and super-rich, with a heavy flavor that comes across as caramelly. Yellow box (a type of eucalyptus) has an elegant floral perfume; another eucalyptus, iron bark, makes a honey with caramelly, nutty overtones. Way out in the outback, the native stingless bee produces the very rare sugarbag honey, which has a really complex wine-like aromatic profile. New Zealand has an altogether different set, including tawari, manuka (tea tree), honeydew, and rata, to name-drop a few.

And I'll just leave you drooling with this list of native fruits, all of them virtually unobtainable outside of their homeland: black apple, burdekin plum, Cedar Bay cherry, Davidson's plum, desert lime, finger lime, midyim, native raspberries, quandong, and riberry. Plenty of great things to look forward to, don't you think?

Various species of acacia yield tiny seeds that, when roasted, offer deliciously nutty flavors.

INGREDIENT-DRIVEN BEERS

Beyond the excitement of exploring new flavors, there is a lot of interest in making beers that reflect their location and celebrate the produce and culture of a particular place. From Rio to Tokyo to Bologna to Springfield, brewers want their beers to resonate with local flavors and sensibilities, and they're using everything they can get their hands on to make this happen.

From the very beginning we liked our beer with a lot of flavor. The people of the ancient Middle East had a big spice cupboard and it's likely they put it to good use. Spices like coriander, cinnamon, and cumin—all still used in brewing—are well documented. Many of them surely found their way into ancient beer.

Modern analytical techniques like chromatography have revealed details of the chemistry of ancient food and drink, including beer. Researcher Patrick McGovern was responsible for the work behind the Dogfish Head historical beers, Midas Touch and Chateau Jiahu. His book on ancient beverages, *Uncorking the Past: The Quest for Wine, Beer, and Other Alcoholic Beverages*, is fascinating reading.

HERB *and* SPICE BEERS

Residues from vessels have demonstrated that the ancient tribes of northern Europe used herbs such as sweet gale (*Myrica gale*), juniper, and meadow-sweet (*Filipendula ulmaria*) in their beers and meads, and these are still used today in farmhouse brews such as Finnish sahti. In Scotland, the Picts were famous for the use of heather blossoms as a beer seasoning.

Before circa 900 C.E., hops were largely unknown in beer, so other substances lent their bitterness and flavor. A seasoning mix called *gruit* was the monopoly of the local bigwig; its high price and mandatory use constituted an early beer tax. A trio of wild herbs including sweet gale is usually cited as the backbone of gruit, along with more common culinary spices like nutmeg, juniper, and others. Gale has a pleasant resiny taste, and finds use in Scandinavian and Scottish historical beers, and actually makes a nice addition to a beer like saison. The other two herbs, yarrow and *Ledum palustre*, are unpleasant tasting and mildly toxic, so there is clearly a lot about gruit beer we don't understand. The switch to hopped beer in Europe began about the year 1000 and was complete by 1500, although the use of sweet gale continued in the backwoods until modern times.

The easiest way to incorporate spices and herbs into a beer is to add them to the end of the boil with the finishing hops. Be cautious about quantities; you can't remove them once they're in the beer. If you undershoot, you can place some spices in a fine-mesh bag and steep in the conditioning beer for a few days or weeks. This method takes advantage of the fact that alcohol is an excellent solvent, and pulls out some of the aromatic compounds water alone might have a hard time extracting.

Beer Name and Type	Original Gravity/°P	Estimated Alcohol by Vol.	Approx. BU	Color	Weeks to Drink
Mackenzie's Windsor Ale c. 1820 English Spiced Ale	1.091/21.8 °P	8.0–8.4 %	63/high	Deep gold/ 6 SRM	8–10

This is one of those rustic English country ales that has a lot in common with what we think of as Belgian brewing. It was taken from Mackenzie's *5000 Receipts* (Philadelphia, 1851), but the recipe resembles an earlier one in Morrice's *Practical Treatise on Brewing the Various Sorts of Malt Liquors* (London, 1819). It's a mouthful.

Qty	Ingredient	OG/°P	%	**All-Grain Mashed Version**
15.5 lb/7 kg	Maris Otter pale ale malt	1.091/21.8	100	Infusion mash (page 130)
2 oz/57 g	Honey, end of the boil	—	—	60 min. @ 153°F/64°C, then mash out

Qty	Ingredient	OG/°P	%	**Alternate Extract + Steeped-Grain Version:**
9 lb/4.1 kg	Dry pale malt extract	1.082/19.7	90	Standard E + SG Procedure (page 119)
8 oz/227 g	Honey malt	1.0044/1.1	5	
8 oz/227 g	25°L caramel malt	1.0044/1.1	5	
2 oz/57 g	Honey, end of the boil	—	—	

Hops and Seasonings

Qty	Name	Alpha	IBU	Minutes	
60 g	E. Kent Golding	5.5	45	90	**Yeast:** Your favorite London ale yeast
20 g	E. Kent Golding	5.5	11	30	**Notes:** Ferment at normal cellar temperatures (60 to 68°F/16 to 20°C). This would be a good
80 g	E. Kent Golding	5.5	7	5	candidate for some extended wood aging, if desired. Serve at low carbonation levels, ideally
4 g	Indian coriander	—	—	5	as real ale in cask or bottle.
2 g	Grains of paradise	—	—	5	
10 g	Ground licorice root	—	—	5	
4 g	Bitter orange zest	—	—	5	

At racking, add 1.5 g each of ground ginger and ground caraway.

Another useful method for adjusting herb and spice flavor is to make a tincture. Add ground spices to about double the volume of cheap vodka, allow them to soak for a week or two, then strain through a coffee filter and judiciously add to the beer at kegging or bottling. The advantage of a tincture is that the mix can be tested in advance and adjusted in the right quantity. To do so, use a pipette or syringe calibrated in $1/10$-ml increments and a shot glass or similar small measure. Try adding different amounts to the same or a similar beer, and then do the simple math required to scale up to the full batch. Liqueurs such as triple sec can be used in place of the vodka, but in that case you need to measure and account for the sugar present.

SPICED BEERS IN JOLLY OLD ENGLAND

Spiced beers were widespread in pre-industrial England, but by the early eighteenth century, a law was enacted that specified only malt and hops be used, and a tax was paid on these ingredients. Wealthy landowners, who maintained breweries on their property to lubricate staff and family, were not subject to these limitations. Consequently, the recipes of these house breweries abounded with alternate seasonings, including coriander, ginger, grains of paradise, orange peel, licorice, and other spices. Rare old books like the *London and Country Brewer* are full of fascinating recipes and are available for free on the Internet.

Licorice was especially popular in darker beers such as porter, and one early-nineteenth-century brewing writer noted that if it didn't have licorice in it, then it wasn't really porter. Both powdered root and a solid extract called *Spanish juice* (identical to modern brewer's licorice) were used to give the beer an unctuous quality and sweetish finish. Capsicum (chile pepper) is also common in the old eighteenth-century porter recipes.

THE BELGIAN APPROACH

We tend to think of the traffic between England and Flanders as unidirectional—after all, it was the Flemish who first brought hops to England when they began moving into Kent around 1400. But in the nineteenth century, boatloads of English and Scottish beer was shipped into Flanders and local brewers would have taken notice. In his monumental tome *Traité Complet de la Fabrication des Bières* (Brussels, 1851), G. Lacambre mentions coriander, grains of paradise, orange peel, and a number of others and says, "of course we all understand these are English spices." So the history we think we know is not as solid as we would like to believe.

The Belgians developed a taste for these "English" brewing spices, and they are still found in many Belgian beers, including saison, strong dark ales, and the many eccentric beers unrelated to any style. The Belgian touch with spices is a light one. Spices are used to augment the flavors of the ingredients or yeast, and give the beer a unique twist. If you can pick out an individual spice, the brewer is doing something wrong.

Witbier is always spiced to some degree, with orange peel and coriander as the base. Pierre Celis once confided to me that his "secret" ingredient was chamomile. You never know whether such a nugget from a crafty old brewer like Pierre is a gift or a trick to throw you off track, but he wasn't kidding. I've brewed witbier with and without, and can confirm that chamomile adds a soft Juicy Fruit gum aroma characteristic of Celis's witbiers.

Using coriander seed can be tricky. Much of the coriander for sale through culinary sources has a strong vegetal quality—think: stale hot-dog water (coriander is the primary seasoning in hot dogs). This can wreck the mood of your delicate witbier, so choose your coriander carefully. I have found six or

The sour orange (left) has a much more intense aroma than the typical sweet type (right). It is also known as bitter Seville or, when harvested green and unripe, Curaçao orange.

Beer Name and Type	Original Gravity/°P	Estimated Alcohol by Vol.	Approx. BU	Color	Weeks to Drink
New Claude of Zeply Belgian Grand Cru (whatever that means)	1066/16.1°P	6.0 to 6.5 %	28 IBU	Deep amber/ 14 SRM	6–8

This is a strongish Belgian-inspired spiced amber wheat ale brewed by me and my original brewing partner, Ray Spangler. It was served as the AHA conference beer way back in 1990 and always was a tremendous crowd-pleaser.

Qty	Ingredient	OG/°P	%	All-Grain Mashed Version
2 lb/907 g	Pale ale malt	1.0110/2.8	16.5	Infusion mash (page 130)
4 lb/1.8 kg	Munich malt	1.0200/5.1	30.0	Mash 1 hour @ 152°F/67°C.
1.5 lb/680 g	Melanoidin malt	1.0072/1.6	11.0	
4 lb/1.8 kg	Wheat malt	1.0230/5.8	34.5	**Note:** Mini-mash recipe can be made by substitut-
1 lb/454 g	Oatmeal, toasted*	1.0043/1.0	6.5	ing 3.5 lb/1.6 kg of amber dry extract for the pale
4 oz/113 g	120°L caramel malt	1.0011/0.2	1.5	and Munich, and mashing the rest of the ingredients

for an hour at 150°F/66°C and adding the drained,
sparged wort to the extract.

* Until it smells like cookies

Hops

Qty	Name	Alpha	IBU	Minutes
16 g	Northern Brewer	8	20	60
10 g	Northern Brewer	8	8	30
13 g	Coriander (Chinese or Indian)	–	–	
67 g	Tangerine zest	–	–	

Spice Potion Mix

Qty	Name
67 g	Indian coriander
28 g	Tangerine zest
2 g	Long pepper, cracked (substitute black pepper if unavailable)
2 g	Star anise, whole
4 g	Cassia buds, whole or crushed
28 g	Crushed cocoa nibs (optional)

Yeast: Belgian wheat or Abbey strain

Notes: Mix this all with enough cheap vodka to generously cover, and allow to stand for about a week. Drain through a coffee filter and add to beer at bottling or kegging. If you're spice-shy, do a test with 1 ounce/30 ml of beer and a pipette or syringe, Trying varying amounts of the potion until you determine the desired level of dosing, then scale up and add the appropriate amount.

more different types, each with its own, distinct aroma. For brewing I prefer the pale, oblong Indian variety (mild, fruity, a little citrusy) or the small Chinese types (pungent, piney, almost menthol). Coriander is cheap and easy to find at all kinds of ethnic markets, so go out there and get a snootful.

Orange peel is most often from the Seville orange, known as Curaçao, in its green, unripe form. It is sold to brewers as chunks of whole peel, that have the potential to impart a "pithy" bitterness to the beer. Culinary spice suppliers like the Spice House offer a coarsely ground dried zest which is quite nice. If you live near a Caribbean neighborhood, you may be able to find fresh sour oranges. The peel of two oranges, shaved off with a potato peeler, will season a barrel of beer. A workable substitute can be made from two parts sweet orange to one part grapefruit peel.

Darker beers may use licorice, star anise, or cumin to add a little mystery. Spices like grains of paradise, black pepper, long pepper (*Piper longum*, a close relative of black pepper), or even mustard seeds can add aromatic top-notes that complement the phenolic dryness of many stronger pale Belgians. Saison de Pipaix even uses a "medicinal lichen" (my guess is *Pulmonaria lobelia*) as a seasoning, so it can get pretty wacky out there.

In his beer-making treatise, Lacambre also mentions elderflower (*Sambucus nigra*), another herb with a strong English connection. It has sweetish floral and grassy aromas, especially appropriate for lighter and more delicately flavored beers. It is very popular in Scandinavia for liquors and soft drinks, especially when mixed with apple flavors. Makrut (a.k.a. kaffir) lime leaves can be used, *sparingly*, to impart a pungent citrusy note, also best in pale beers.

AMERICAN HERB AND SPICE BEERS

Early Americans were much more likely to be sipping rum, cider, or whiskey than beer. The lack of quality brewing ingredients meant that beer was often brewed "of pumpkins and parsnips and walnut-tree chips," as the old ditty goes. The use of a mildly toxic plant called wood sage (*Teucrium canadense*) as a bittering agent was common before the Germans brought their "modern" lager to these shores. The *Wahl-Henius Handy Book* (1906) mentions a brown ale called Pennsylvania Swankey that was seasoned with aniseed. In Alaska, Sitka spruce tips are so rich in vitamins and sugar that native people used them as a spring tonic and early settlers often added them to whatever homebrew they made. Alaskan Brewery founder Geoff Larson became fascinated by the idea, and uses spruce tips to season Alaskan Winter Ale. It is sweetish and deeply fruity, not the piney mouthful that one might expect.

The Reinheitsgebot-toting Germans threw all that out when they started brewing here, and their "pure" style of beer still dominates the market nearly 170 years later.

It wasn't until the resurgence of homebrewing in the late 1970s that beers with alternate seasonings were regularly brewed in the United States. And with many homebrewers turning pro, those notions came right along with them into their commercial breweries. Like Dogfish Head's Sam Calagione, many were brewing with tiny systems, which meant they had to brew a batch nearly every day to keep the taps flowing. Calagione says, "I got bored with the same old beers. I would wander into the kitchen and ask, 'Whaddya got?' and then throw that in the brew pot."

Holiday brews were the first to emerge. Inspired by English traditions of "wassailing," these dark, warming brews are cornucopias of spice: cinnamon, nutmeg, ginger, allspice, and more. Anchor's Our Special Ale was one of the earlier ones. The Anchor staff is sworn to secrecy on this, but it's clear that the beer changes year by year. The mystery is part of the pleasure. Be cautious: Heavily spiced holiday brews can be overbearing, so use restraint. Making a tincture of herbs in cheap vodka is a good way to draw out the flavors of spices; and test dosing the mix in 1 ounce/30 ml of beer makes it easy to get the right quantity into the beer. After straining through a coffee filter, the tincture can be added at bottling or kegging.

The shockingly high prices of hops have led brewers to look for bitter substitutes. In various times and places, gentian, wormwood, quassia, blessed thistle, and many other plants have been used. In the last couple of years, New Belgium has produced seasonal beers bittered with wormwood and dandelion. Many of these hop substitutes can be searingly bitter and can contribute a bitterness that's much harsher and less pleasant than hops, so test batches are definitely in order here, too.

Small-scale brewing is part of a global trend in food, and reflects a fusion of the local and the exotic, formed by our diverse experiences and expressive of the curiosity and passion of the people behind the products. This attitude makes for some very personal expressions, sometimes a risky approach, but with the potential for high art.

Craftsman Brewing's Mark Jilg has been making a Triple White Sage for several years, using the outdoorsy-scented herb gathered from the San Gabriel Mountains above Pasadena. The resulting beer tastes of the place in a way few beers can. A bit south in Orange County, Patrick Rue's The Bruery uses spices to good effect in several Belgian-inflected beers. Their Tradewinds Tripel is seasoned with Thai basil; Orchard White contains lavender in addition to the more orthodox coriander and orange peel. At Elysian in Seattle, Dick Cantwell cooked up an exotic IPA called "Avatar," scented with whole jasmine flowers. During his time at Archipelago Brewery in Singapore, brewer Fal Allen used local ingredients like calamansi and pandan fruit for beers that resonate with the local culture and cuisine. Once you start looking, there are unlimited possibilities: ginger, lemongrass, woodruff, ginseng, sweet flag, vanilla, and many, many more.

CREATIVE FRUIT BEERS

There are two main approaches to making fruit beer. One is the brewpub style: light, breezy, fruit-tinged ales, most often in the wheat ale style. The second approach is to pile on the fruit and try to create something more profound, with the intensity and nuances of a fine wine.

The light and summery fruit beers are quite easy to make—just dump in ½ pound per 1 gallon/59 g per 1 L of your favorite fruit to an American wheat ale, hit it with some acidity if needed, pop open the beach umbrella, and enjoy. Raspberries, cherries, blueberries, peaches, and apricots are the most popular, but this approach works with more exotic fruit. Witbier provides a somewhat more complex base. There's nothing wrong with these easy fruit ales—no sin in keeping it simple. Here are a few ideas to get the juices flowing.

MANGO AMERICAN WHEAT

Mango has such a luscious flavor, it's surprising that beers using this tropical fruit are not more common. Frozen purée is available in Latin markets. One package (usually 14 oz/400 g) is a good place to start. Add this to a 1.045 (11.2°P) wheat beer made with 40 to 50 percent wheat, with the remainder Pils malt. Simcoe has a nice tropical fruit aroma, but some New Zealand hops would lend a Southern Hemisphere zing: Motueka, Rakau, or Riwaka.

LYCHEE WITBIER

This Asian fruit has a sublimely perfumy, rose-like aroma that demands a very delicate beer, so the witbier on page 312 should be perfect, although you may want to reduce the spices a bit, or maybe substitute ginger for the orange peel. The flavor is available as a concentrated syrup used to make cocktails and bubble tea. About a liter for a batch should be good. Try the New Zealand hop Nelson Sauvin or the Japanese Sorachi Ace. This will be super-pale. If some pink color is desired, add a handful of hibiscus petals to the boil.

APPLE PIE AMBER ALE

Start with a beer that tastes like crust—pale malt, plus a bit of both 20 and 40°L caramel malt, plus a little amber/biscuit for a slight toastiness. One pound/454 g of acid malt will brighten things up. To this, add a couple of cans of thawed frozen apple juice concentrate after the primary. The rich and creamy flavor of macadamia honey (1 to 2 pounds/454 to 907 g) tops the whole thing off. Look for a hop with some spiciness, maybe Styrian Golding or Glacier. A gram or two of Ceylon cinnamon can add the requisite spicy touch.

BLACKCURRANT MILD ALE

Blackcurrant is hugely popular in Europe, and deserves to be much more popular elsewhere. Mild ale, though dark, is actually a delicately flavored beer that suits our purposes here and, laced with blackcurrant, should pour an impressive purplish ruby color. Start with the mild recipe on page 289. Flavor is available as Ribena fruit drink concentrate, maybe two or three 600-ml bottles per batch, depending on how much blackcurrant flavor you want. Tasmanian pepperberries are optional, but would add a nice, complex fruity/peppery zip. Use just a gram or two crushed and added at the end of the boil, as they're pretty potent.

Yellow Manila mangos, smaller that the more common variety, offer an intense and elegant mango flavor in beer.

The other option is to make a fruit beer as complex and enchanting an experience as any wine; a beer *por meditazione*, as they say about certain wines in Italy. For these, there is no way around it: You will need to use a lot of fruit, and structure the beer and fermentation to bring it out in the best possible way. Some more ideas:

CHERRY-POPPIN' DOPPELBOCK

Adding fruit to a Bavarian lager is so not Reinheitsgebot, and actually makes me feel a little bit naughty and in need of the kind of spanking a beer like this can mete out. Start with a great big pile of Munich malt, shooting for 1.075 (18.5°P) with maybe ¼ pound/ 113 g of röstmalz to deepen the color. Hops should be light and neutral. To this, add at least 2 pounds/907 g of cherries per 1 gallon/ 3.8 L. Here in the Midwest, we like the Montmorency sour cherries that taste like pie. If you have access to sour dark cherries, those can be great, too. If you can't manage an actual lager, this will work just fine with an altbier or Kölsch yeast—we're adding fruity aromas anyway. Either way, cold conditioning will smooth out the flavors.

BLACK RASPBERRY SAISON

This may be something you have to brew in the summer when fresh farmers' market berries are available, as purées and frozen black raspberries are not readily available on the consumer market. The earthy, peppery saison yeast character should be the perfect foil for the deep and fruity perfume of blackberries. Freeze, then thaw the berries, and then add after the primary and allow the beer to sit on the fruit for a week or two. Use no less than 1 pound per 1 gallon/454 g per 3.8 L, and double that or more if you're feeling frisky. Some red raspberries can be added for complexity and a touch of tartness. Pacific Jade would be an interesting choice for hop aroma, but go easy. No matter what, this beer will be a stunner— luminously purple, with a shocking violet head.

PASSIONFRUIT DOUBLE IPA

One of the reasons passionfruit works so well in beer is that some of its aromas are quite similar to those found in modern high-alpha hops. It seems right at home. Start with a mix of Pils and pale ale malt, use a little 20°L caramel malt and some honey malt. Look at hops with tropical aromas: Simcoe, Riwaka, Nelson Sauvin, Motueka, Pacifica, and others. Pile them on, maybe 70+ BU, and plenty of aroma. I would use no less than two 14-ounce/397-g packages of thawed frozen passionfuit puree; up to four might be possible.

VEGETABLE-FLAVORED BEERS

A wide variety of vegetable produce can be used in beer without ever resorting to broccoli. Many of the flavorings in this category can actually be thought of as spices. Whatever they are, just ignore the labels and enjoy the delicious range of possibilities when incorporated into suitable beers.

PUMPKIN

Here's a secret: pumpkin beer is really about getting the spices right. At least in the United States, our main experience with pumpkin is pie, and that always includes a classic mix of spices. Here's a good place to start: 8 grams cinnamon, 2 grams cloves, 2 grams nutmeg, 4 grams ginger, 2 grams allspice. You can cut this in half for a more subtle and drinkable beer, or step off in a different direction with spices like star anise, Chinese flower pepper, pink peppercorns, grains of paradise, coriander, cassia buds, sassafras, cardamom, black pepper, long pepper, and mace.

Here are a few vegetable beer concepts to consider.

SMOKIN' HATCH IPA

Take your favorite big IPA recipe, about 1065 (15.9°P) or so, but use 2 pounds/907 g of smoked malt in place of the pale. Then, add two to four freshly roasted New Mexico Hatch green chiles (poblano works, too) at the end of the boil. Hop using something green-tasting like Columbus or Amarillo, maybe finish with Kent Goldings or First Gold. If you like, add half a dozen sage leaves or a few needles of rosemary for an outdoorsy aroma.

PUMPKIN BELGIAN AMBER

Some Belgian ales are so perfectly spicy, they're just ready to have pumpkin dropped into them. Start with an even mix of Pils and Munich malts and add just 1/4 lb/113 g of 40°L caramel malt for a little fruity/raisiny character. Hopping should be light at about 20 BU, and Styrian or something related. Spices can be added with the finishing hops, a mix something like this: 10 grams crushed coriander; 5 grams Ceylon cinnamon; 2 grams grains of paradise; 2 grams cassia buds; 1 gram star anise and 10 grams powdered or sliced licorice root (or 5 grams brewers licorice stick). Two pounds/907 g of roasted pumpkin can be added to the boil (see roasting directions on page 113).

SWEE'PO RED ALE

Take Angry European Red Lager recipe from page 320, cut the hop quantities in half and add 1 to 2 pounds/454 to 907 grams of candied sweet potatoes to the boil, and one-quarter of a vanilla bean (or 1/2 tsp/2.5 ml vanilla extract) at the end of the boil along with the finishing. Combined with the dark caramel malt that provides a burnt-sugar flavor, the vanilla completes the illusion of the toasted marshmallows crowning Aunt Ida's famous yam dish. Ferment with your favorite ale yeast.

Beer Name and Type	Original Gravity/°P	Estimated Alcohol by Vol.	Approx. BU	Color	Weeks to Drink
Abbey Toadex Chocolate Quad	1.0910/21.7°P	10 %	30/medium	Chestnut brown/ 32 SRM	8–10

This is inspired by the great dark beers of Rochefort. They're already very chocolatey because of the dark candi syrup added; the actual chocolate added should be exactly like icing on the cake. A dab of bourbon adds a woody/vanilla touch.

Qty	Ingredient	OG/°P	%	**All-Grain Mashed Version**
16 lb/7.3 kg	Munich malt	1.0820/19.8	90	Infusion mash (page 130)
1.5 lb/680 g	Belgian dark II candi syrup	1.0093/2.4	10	60 min @ 150°F/66°C, then mash out

Qty	Ingredient	OG/°P	%	**Alternate Extract + Steeped-Grain Version**
6.5 lb/2.9 kg	Dry Pale malt extract	1.0773	85	Standard E + SG Procedure (page 119)
1 lb/454 g	Honey malt	1.0044	5	
1.5 lb/680 g	Belgian dark II candi syrup	1.0093	10	

Hops

Qty	Name	Alpha	IBU	Minutes	
25 g	Northern Brewer	8	24	60	
32 g	Pacific Jade	13	6	5	

Additional Ingredients: 8 oz/227 g of roasted cocoa nibs, added to the secondary and allowed to sit at least a week. Also, 1 tablespoon of bourbon added at packaging.
Yeast: Alcohol-tolerant (WLP 540/Wyeast 1762) or other Abbey/Trappist ale of your choice
Fermentation Temperature: 66 to 70°F/19 to 21°C
Carbonation: Medium/2.5 volumes/4 oz (113 g) priming sugar

SCREW STYLES

I have no problem holding a two-sided view of beer styles. The classic styles are fascinating, important, delicious, and absolutely the foundation for everything we do in the Western tradition of beer. Understanding how they work and where they come from informs a brewer's ability to go forward with new things that work from a sensory perspective, as well as broaden and enrich the tradition as a whole. That's a really worthy goal. But I certainly don't mind ignoring, twisting, or stomping all over their petty little rules when it suits me.

Once you leave the comfort and safety of existing styles, you are working without a net to some degree. With a style, countless brewers and their customers have worked out all the fine points, so the limitations that define a style are to some degree a set of rules for how to make it balanced, beautiful, delicious. When you're freestylin', you need a strong internal compass to guide you through all the qualities possessed by a great beer and to figure out ways to achieve that with every recipe.

So where does inspiration come from for a style-free beer? Peter Bouckaert of New Belgium came up with a beer inspired by the architecture of a museum, so there is pretty much no limit to where these ideas can come from. Here's a list of mine.

- Variations on some existing style
- Fascination with a particular ingredient
- Historical tidbit that suggests a lot of possibilities
- Turning up or down the volume on certain recipe parameters
- Agricultural inspirations
- A specific cultural context
- Seasonality or some other type of usage occasion
- Custom brewing for a specific audience
- Cuisines
- The desire to create a specific emotional response
- The sounds, sights, and other sensations of a different art form

BREWING *with the* SEASONS

A lively parade of seasonal beers is a delicious way to be a little more in touch with the rhythm of the land, the weather, and the mood. Some styles are associated with specific seasons; others simply taste just right at a particular point in the year.

> *I like to roam outside of my own industry and find where there are potential creative overlaps: food, music, art, wine, travel. I also like collaboration with companies I believe in, so we can learn from them, what their creative process is. That widens the possibilities for us.*

SAM CALAGIONE, founder, Dogfish Head Craft Brewery, Rehoboth Beach, DE

This season has most commonly been associated with bock beer; but from Belgium to Finland to Russia there is a tradition of spring, or more specifically Easter, beers. You can't call this a style. These *Paasbiers* range from the archaic Scandinavian dark wheat or "white" beers called *hvidtøl* to Belgian confections nearing 10 percent alcohol. Flavors range from the spicy blonde of Belgium's De Dolle Bos Keun (Easter Bunny) to the chocolate-tinged Synebrykoff Easter beer from Finland—a colorful range of goodies for your Easter basket, to be sure. Here are a few springtime beer possibilities:

DOBBELT-ØL

While the traditional Paasbiers might have bumped up the 1.8 to 2.8 percent alcohol levels of regular Hvidtøl just a tad, evidence exists for stronger types. We're talking about a sweet, porterish brew that's very rich and nourishing. Start with a base of Pilsner malt and aim for a gravity of 1.055 (13.6°P). Subtract the contributions of the other ingredients to figure out how much Pilsner malt (or pale extract) you need to make up the difference. Historically, these beers contained a certain amount of caramel syrup, so add about 1 pound/454 g of dark Belgian brewers' caramel right into the kettle. One pound/454 g of dark crystal malt like Special B adds an inner richness; 4 ounces/113 g of German röstmalz will add a ruddy depth.

Hopping should be modest at about 25 BU. I like a neutral-tasting hop such as Northern Brewer for chocolatey beers. Speaking of chocolate, we're within striking range, so if you want to turn this into the ultimate liquid chocolate bunny, add about 1 pound/454 g of cocoa nibs to the secondary and some toasted coconut to complete the Easter-egg illusion. Alternately, a few grams of caraway takes a cue from aquavit and can add a characteristically Scandinavian touch.

INDIA WHEAT ALE

Think of this as a transitional beer, bridging the gap between the blustery days of March and true weissbier season, which starts mid-May. Nothing too complicated about the recipe: 50 percent good-quality pale malt, 40 percent wheat malt, and the rest can be your choice of Munich or a slightly darker malt such as melanoidin/aromatic. Gravity can span the range from 1.055 (13.6°P) to a double version at 1.070 (17°P).

Hopping needs to be aggressive, but not too wild in character. Go with one of the newer, mellow, low-cohumulone varieties such as Glacier or Simcoe. I always enjoy the taste of Tettnangs in wheat beer or you can mix 'n' match. Bitterness should be at least 50 BU, with a big load of aroma, either using late kettle additions or dry-hopping. As an alternative, you might substitute 2 to 4 pounds/907 g to 1.8 kg of the pale malt with German rauchmalz or home-smoked malt. Although this might seem like an odd choice, it actually bumps up against a once-popular Prussian/Polish style called a grätzer that was pale, smoky, and bitter.

SAISON DU PRINTEMPS

Tweaking this farmhouse ale in the direction of a maibock—deep gold with caramelly touches—gets us in the 1.065 to 1.070 (16 to 17°P) range. Equal parts Pilsner and Vienna malts (or ⅔ Pils + ⅓ Munich) make the bulk of the grain bill. We can thumb our nose at the Reinheitsgebot by adding 1 to 2 pounds/454 to 907 g Thai palm sugar to thin out the body as it adds a layer of aroma.

Hopping should be modest, from 30 to 40 IBU. Saaz and Styrians can't fail, but other high-class hops will work as well. Avoid anything too extreme. A little herb or spice is welcome, as long as it doesn't dominate. Grains of paradise offer a mystical peppery bite. To borrow from another beverage—May wine—a few grams of woodruff adds a sweet herby note. Chamomile, orange peel, sweet gale, or ginger could take the beer in several different directions.

Although any Belgian yeast will bump up the character, it is saison yeast that separates this style from all other Belgian blonde ales. It's a cranky, uncooperative yeast, so be prepared to deal with it on its own terms. First, it likes it hot—around 80°F/27°C. I use a heated pad with a thermostat under my carboys and keep a close eye on the temperature. Second, this yeast needs a lot of oxygen. Commercial breweries often aerate the second day, although I've had good results without taking this step. Third, it's s-l-o-w. Most commercial breweries add their regular ale yeast after two or three weeks and get it over with. If you're willing to wait a couple of months it will eventually do its business and drop out.

It's hot and you need something refreshing and thirst-quenching, not huge and alcoholic. Think: picnics, fishing, barbecue, lawn bowling, quick rolls in the hay. The beer has to work for every occasion. Making light yet flavorful beers can be done, but you have to pay attention to the details. Let's see how many ways you can make a lawnmower beer.

AL'S PALS PRE-PRO CREAM ALE

This style was originally made by mixing a strong, oak-aged stock ale and an adjunct lager. Of course, you can do this exact technique, but obviously you have to plan way in advance. To re-create the blended beer, try a recipe that's 35 percent Pils malt, 45 percent pale ale malt, 10 percent wheat malt, 8 percent 40°L caramel malt, and a couple of percent of sour malt for a little tang. I recommend about 35 BU with a clean bittering and a U.S. noble hop like Crystal or Ultra in fairly large quantity as a finishing hop. A small amount of toasted oak (2- to 3-inches/5- to 7.5-cm square of surface area) added to the primary can give a nice oak character or you can just cheat and add about 1 ounce/30 ml of bourbon or rye whiskey to simulate the barrel aging.

RHINEBOTTOM BLACK KÖLSCH

I know there is a dark Rhine ale right down the river in Düsseldorf, but can you imagine the feud if the Köllners ever decided to break with tradition and get into the dark-beer business? Yowie. Köln's version would still be soft and fruity, with just the barest hint of roasty goodness. Recipe should be 80 percent Pils malt, 15 percent Vienna, 5 percent wheat, and just a dab (0.2 ounces/6 g) of Sinamar, that liquid malt-based coloring goo from Weyermann.

BILLY'S BONG-SMOKED WIT

White beers once came in a dazzling variety of forms, including smoked ones like the grätzer from West Prussia that was brewed from 100 percent wheat malt and Lichtenhainer, the sour smoked weisse from Thuringia. They're not all white, either; some are ruddy brown. Start with 60 percent wheat malt and add 2 to 5 percent sour malt depending on how much tartness you want, about 2 pounds/907 g dark Munich or melanoidin for color, and the remaining percentage should be smoked malt. Hopping should be light and noble, although the grätzers were around 40 BU. And if you've got some hemp seeds lying around, toast them, crush them, and add them to the mash.

DUMPSTER-DIVER OATEN HONEY GOLDEN ALE

Most of the honey beers out there are quite useless, designed to promise but not deliver on great honey flavor. We'll use caramelized honey for coloring and to layer the honey flavor. Using 1 pound/ 454 g of honey, follow the directions on page 76 for making caramel, but skip the inverting step (honey is already invert sugar). Cook the honey until it turns the color of molasses and add to the kettle. Use 5 percent oats, toasted golden, plus pale ale malt to make up a gravity of 1.052 (12.8°P). For that hippie touch, you can add a box of cereal to the mash, too. Hop to about 20 BU with Glacier or some other Styrian type, although there's no harm in a higher rate. Ferment with the Ardennes strain, WLP550 or Wyeast 3522, or other Belgian strain. When fermentation slows down, add 2 pounds/907 g of good, aromatic honey. If you have the patience, this is a good candidate for a secondary fermentation with *Brettanomyces*.

Autumn gets one thinking about the harvest and bigger, darker beers. Amber and brown beers always seem classic at this time of year, but there are lots of other options.

DÜSSELKÖLSCHFEST MASHUP

Start with a base of half Vienna, half Munich malt, and shoot for about 1.065 (13.6°P), just a bit higher than normal for a Märzen. Keep it simple. Use Spalt or Tettnang hops, about 40 BU, with 1 ounce/28 g at the end for aroma. Ferment using a Kölsch strain at coolish temperatures, 55 to 60°F/13 to 16°C, with as cool and long a conditioning as you can manage. One pound/454 g of torrefied wheat or flaked rye can add a little extra creaminess. If you're so inclined, this beer can handle a higher hop load.

BELGIAN AMBRÉE

Take a standard witbier or saison recipe, bump up the gravity, if needed, to about 1060 (14.7°P), and replace some of the Pils malt with 1 pound/454 g of melanoidin malt or half that amount of 40°L caramel malt. Spices can be a little richer and rounder: small amounts of star anise, ginger, Ceylon cinnamon, Chinese flower pepper (prickly ash), and black pepper can all work, alone or in a blend. Use a yeast appropriate for the original style.

❄ WINTER

This is a time for rich, warming beers. While barley wines and spiced holiday beers are the ones that jump to mind, there are many other possibilities.

MONSTER MASH BROWN ALE

Take the Sweet Georgia recipe on page 315 and multiply all the grains by 1.5, which will get you to 1.070. Add 1 pound/454 g of Indonesian gula jawa dark palm sugar, which will bump up the gravity to 1.079. If you feel the need for spices, consider licorice, Szechuan flower pepper, star anise, black pepper, and allspice. You can make a tincture and try it out before committing. Belgian yeast even makes it more of a confection.

RED VELVET ALE

This recipe aims to re-create the luridly colored chocolate cake of the same name. Aiming for a gravity of 1.067 (16.3°P), start with a base of Vienna malt, and layer on 8 ounces/227 g each of honey malt and 60°L caramel malt, plus 10 ounces/284 g Belgian brewer's caramel (Dark II = 160°L). One pound/454 g of flaked rye adds a creamy touch. Hopping should be neutral and light at 20 to 30 BU. For a really red color, 2 ounces/55 g of hibiscus flowers can be added at the end of the boil. Yeast is up to you. Add 8 ounces/227 g of cocoa nibs after the primary and allow them to sit for one to two weeks as the beer settles clear. Better than the cake!

Left to right: Homebrew labels by Randy LaCoille, Dave Gallagher, Łukasz Szynkiewicz, Dave Gallagher, and Charles Wiseman (2).

Beer Name and Type	Original Gravity/°P	Estimated Alcohol by Vol.	Approx. BU	Color	Weeks to Drink
Blanche de Noire Dark Witbier	1067/16.3°P	6.4%	20/low	Chestnut brown/ 30 SRM	4–5

What's black and white and beer all over? It could only be a dark witbier. It's a lip-smacking sundae of a drink: soft and creamy, overlain by a gentle cocoa roastiness, topped off with the fruity complexity of a Belgian yeast strain. It is profound and fascinating, but at around 6.5 percent alcohol, it won't knock you over, important if you're interested in a second one. If you're not yet familiar with this style, you're missing out.

Qty	Ingredient	OG/°P	%	**All-Grain Mashed Version**
4.7 lb/2.1 kg	Vienna malt	1.0241/6.1	36	Infusion mash (page 130)
5 lb/2.3 kg	Malted wheat	1.0293/7.4	44	60 min @ 152°F/67°C, then mash out
1.5 lb/680 g	Melanoidin malt	1.0070/1.8	10	
1 lb/454 g	Instant oats	1.0047/1.2	7	
8 oz/227 g	Carafa II	1.0022/0.6	3	
1 lb/454 g	Rice hulls	—	—	

Qty	Ingredient	OG/°P	%	**Extract + Mini-Mash Version**
2.6 lb/1.2 kg	Pale dry malt extract	1.0235/6.0	35	Standard E + MM Procedure (page 127)
2.9 lb/1.3 kg	Dry wheat malt extract	1.0268/6.8	40	
1 lb/454 g	Pilsner malt	1.0041/1.1	6	
2 lb/907 g	Melanoidin malt	1.0070/1.8	10	
8 oz/227 g	Instant oats	1.0040/1.4	6	
9 oz/256 g	Carafa II black malt	1.0022/0.6	3	

Hops and Seasonings

Qty	Name	Alpha	IBU	Minutes	
17 g	Northern Brewer	8	20	60	**Yeast:** Belgian wheat strain such as Wyeast 3942 or White Labs WL400, or your favorite Belgian yeast
14 g	Freshly ground coriander*	—	—	5	**Fermentation Temperature:** 68 to 72°F/20 to 22°C
14 g	Powdered licorice root	—	—	5	**Carbonation:** Medium high/3.0 volumes/5.2 oz
3 g	Star anise	—	—	5	(147 g) priming sugar

* Source your coriander carefully. Much of it has a sharp, cilantro-like vegetal aroma. Indian and Chinese varieties usually brew well.

Beer Name and Type		Original Gravity/°P	Estimated Alcohol by Vol.	Approx. BU	Color	Weeks to Drink
Shiverey Winter Saison		1066/16.1°P	7.5 %	21/low	Amber/12 SRM	6–10

Qty	Ingredient	OG/°P	%	All-Grain Mashed Version
3 lb/1.4 kg	Pils malt	1.0165/4.2	25	Infusion mash (page 130)
5 lb/2.3 kg	Munich malt	1.0250/6.3	38	60 min @ 148°F/64°C for an hour; mash out.
1 lb/454 g	Melanoidin malt	1.0046/1.2	7	
8 oz/227 g	Flaked oats, toasted*	1.0025/0.6	4	
8 oz/227 g	Buckwheat, toasted*	1.0025/0.6	4	
4 oz/113 g	Brown malt	1.0013/0.3	2	
1.5 lb/680 g	Panela/piloncillo (partially refined cane sugar), added to kettle	1.0135/0.3	20	

* Toast for approximately 20 min @ 300°F/150°C, or until a nice cookie aroma starts coming from your oven.

Qty	Ingredient	OG/°P	%	Extract + Steeped-Grain Version:
4.5 lb/2 kg	Pale dry malt extract	1.0438/10.9	66	Standard E + SG Procedure (page 119)
1.5 lb/680 g	Panela/piloncillo	1.0135/3.4	20	
1 lb/454 g	Honey malt	1.0033/0.9	5	
8 oz/227 g	Flaked oats, toasted*	1.0020/0.5	3	
8 oz/227 g	Buckwheat, toasted*	1.0020/0.5	3	
8 oz/227 g	Brown malt	1.0014/0.4	2	

* Toast for approximately 20 min @ 300°F/150°C, or until a nice cookie aroma starts coming from your oven.

Hops and Other Seasonings:

Qty	Name	Alpha	IBU	Minutes	
12 g	Northern Brewer	8	14	00	**Yeast:** Saison Wyeast 3724 or White Labs WLP 565
24 g	Northern Brewer	8	5	5	**Fermentation Temperature:** 70 to 80°F/21 to 27°C (Note: Use these high temperatures only with the
15 g	Saaz	5	2	5	saison strains. With other Belgian yeasts, ferment
9 g	Orange Peel	—	—	5	10 to 15°F lower.)
9 g	Indian Coriander	—	—	5	**Carbonation:** Medium high/3.0 volumes/5.5 oz
1 g	Whole star anise	—	—	5	(156 g) priming sugar

BREWING *the* PERFECT PARTY BEER

As homebrewers, we are often called upon to brew something special to celebrate a milestone: a wedding, a graduation, or just surviving another year in the cubicle. When the audience is made of beer maniacs, it's easy—anything goes. The real test of a brewer is to please those habituated to beer that is cold, golden, and canned, while at the same time upholding your homebrew oath to always brew something interesting. As a brewer, it's a great trick to make a lighter beer that is satisfying, quaff after quaff.

It's obvious why you don't want to brew a double imperial pale ale or bourbon doppelbock for the uninitiated. The intensity of these beers is like an electric shock to people unfamiliar with their charms, and that won't win you any converts. The trick is to hook people ever so gently and then, with a tug, set the hook. Who says you can't change people? I've seen it happen over and over. And so the movement grows.

Everybody loves great malt. Pils, Vienna, and Munich all have their charms, as does pale ale malt. Avoid a lot of caramel, which can sit heavily on the palate, and the sharper, roasty-toasty malts like amber, brown, and chocolate. Honey malt and its cousin melanoidin offer some nice color and flavor, without too much heaviness.

We also want a clean and pleasant hop presence; use super-clean bittering varieties like Magnum and high-quality, low-alpha varieties to maximize aroma.

These accommodations still leave us a nice window in which to operate: pale-to-amber color, medium-to-dry palate, low-to-medium bitterness, and a nice, fresh dose of hop aroma.

Beer styles such as Dortmunder, Vienna, bitter, and witbier are easy to enjoy as they are. You may also forge into the land between the styles and create something all your own. When I was first starting out, I brewed a beer called Wifey's Tender Ale, a delicate amber ale with a kiss of hops; it always disappeared quickly in the presence of friends trying to come to terms with my strange, new hobby. Think about your audience, then select the malts, hop profile, and yeast character to make this the perfect beer designed to tickle the taste buds of your partygoers. Don't give up and make a beer you think only other people would want to drink. Satisfy yourself, and the beer will be better. You *can* do both.

So let's put together our perfect autumn party beer. As an easy-drinking session beer, we'll be shooting for a target of about 1.046/11.4°P. This should ferment out to give us an alcohol content of around 4 percent by volume.

The choice of hops will help determine the national character of your beer. English hops such as East Kent Goldings will, of course, create an English bitter or pale ale character; continental hops will tilt the beer toward the Germanic. Belgians are caught in the middle and, of course, with all the idiosyncratic hop varieties from New Zealand and elsewhere, all bets are off. Let's follow the middle path and go with a mix of Saaz and East Kent Goldings.

Top to bottom: Wedding homebrew labels by Tom Fitzpatrick, Courtney Hoem/Arlyn Hoem/Luann Fitzpatrick, Luann Fitzpatrick, and Kim Leshinski.

Beer Name and Type		Original Gravity/°P	Estimated Alcohol by Vol.		Approx. BU	Color	Weeks to Drink
Anyfest'lldo Ale Party Beer		1.046/11.4°P	4.4%		22/low	Pale amber/ 10 SRM	3–4

Qty	Ingredient	OG/°P	%	All-Grain Mashed Version
3 lb/1.4 kg	Pilsner malt	1.0155/4.0	34	Infusion mash (page 130)
2 lb/907 g	Pale ale malt	1.0111/2.8	24	60 min @ 150°F/66°C; mash out.
2 lb/907 g	Malted wheat	1.0120/3.1	26	
1.5 lb/680 g	Melanoidin malt	1.0070/1.8	16	

Qty	Ingredient	OG/°P	%	Extract + Steeped-Grain Recipe
2.9 lb/1.3 kg	Pale dry malt extract	1.0271/6.8	59	Standard E + SG Grain Version (page 119)
1.5 lb/680 g	Wheat malt extract	1.0140/3.6	30	
1.5 lb/680 g	Honey malt	1.0049/1.3	11	

Hops

Qty	Name	Alpha	IBU	Minutes	
					Yeast: Really, do I have to tell you everything? **Fermentation Temperature:** Follow manufacturer's recommendations
14 g	Glacier	5.8	12	60	
16 g	Saaz	3.5	6	30	**Carbonation:** Medium/2.5 volumes/3.8 oz
43 g	Saaz	3.5	4	5	(108 g) priming sugar

Searching for a complex, but restrained malt profile, let's go with a mix of Pils malt and a slightly darker base malt such as pale ale or Vienna. A portion of wheat will add a little creaminess and great head retention, which can sometimes be lacking in lighter beers. On top of that, we'll drop a dollop of honey malt, giving a shimmery amber color and an inviting depth.

Yeast is the other major factor that influences what character the beer will have. By this point in the book, I don't need to elaborate. Choose whimsically and/or wisely.

Put it all together with your best technique and roll out the barrel for your family and friends. If you do it right, all you'll have to haul home are the empties.

Troubleshooting

This chapter is designed as a guide to identifying problems and pinpointing their cause.

Unfortunately, most brewing problems are difficult to fix. Most of the time, you have to wait until the next batch to get it right. But if there is a fix, you'll find it in this chapter.

Instruments for measuring can be a great benefit, but they can cause a lot of mischief when they are not accurate. Cheap homebrew thermometers are notoriously inaccurate. Make sure you have one you have full confidence in.

It is also helpful to understand that one needs to be careful about all kinds of measurements and timings. A little slop here and there, and it's easy to be off by 10 percent, which can add up to a tastable difference in the finished beer.

You should also be aware that all brewery predictions are dependent on plenty of variables over which you may have little control; there's a high likelihood that your results will differ somewhat from the predictive formulas in this book—or anywhere else for that matter. Over time, you'll need to calibrate your system and make adjustments to your recipes, especially in terms of mashing efficiency and hop bitterness, so the final beer matches your expectations. Give your system another check whenever you make major changes in equipment or process.

INGREDIENTS, RECIPES, *and* BREWING

Any time you are dealing with agricultural ingredients, there is going to be some variability. While these inconsistencies are slight, sometimes they can cause problems especially in the unlikely event they are mislabeled by manufacturers or sellers. More important, every type of ingredient has a certain behavior and needs to be treated in particular ways for best results.

YIELD

Lower than expected
- Check grain grind (see Grain Crushing, page 120).
- Too much wort collected, or too much wort left behind in the mash tun? Use only as much brewing liquor as you need to end up with the amount needed for your batch, accounting for the expected loss from evaporation and other effects (see page 132).
- Check recipe and math.
- Check thermometer accuracy.
- Runoff too fast (less than 30 minutes)?

Higher than expected
- Check recipe and math.

SPARGING

Too fast
- Grain grind too coarse?
- Mash bed channeling?

Too slow
- Grain grind too fine, especially husks?
- Bed compacted from initial fast runoff.
- Make sure mash at sparge is at least 145°F/63°C.
- Huskless adjuncts? Use rice hulls.
- Sticky adjuncts may benefit from glucan rest.
- See Lautering and Sparging, page 140, for discussion of slow/stuck sparge.

BOILING

Boilovers
- Kettle too small? Needs minimum 30% of final volume; 50% or more is better.
- Let boil 10 minutes before adding hops, then add just a portion, let stabilize, and then add the rest of the first charge.
- Have a spray bottle full of water nearby and hit the foam whenever it threatens.

Weak boil
- Stove not strong enough. Split batch into two pots.
- Some cowl or shield around burner if outdoors to keep flame from getting windblown.

YEAST *and* FERMENTATION BEHAVIOR

Getting a good fermentation depends on careful handling of yeast, some control over temperature, appropriate selection of strain, and scrupulous attention to cleaning and sanitization. Good basic procedures as outlined in chapter 6 will assure that your yeast troubles are few and far between.

FERMENTATION

Smack packs not proofing?
- Check package expiration date.
- Make sure temperature is within recomended range.
- Any sudden temperature drops?

No start in 24 hours?
- Beer too cold? Warm it up.
- Any sudden temperature drops? Repitch.
- Dry yeast properly rehydrated? See Dried Yeast, page 209.
- Rehydration temperature too high for dry yeast? See Dried Yeast, page 209.
- Check yeast package expiration date.
- Check with hydrometer; sometimes stealthy fermentation occuring without obvious signs.
- Pitch new yeast if needed.

Sluggish fermentation
- Make sure proper quantity of fresh yeast was pitched.
- Check that temperature is correct for yeast strain. Either too high or too low can cause problems.
- High adjunct (corn, rice, sugar, honey)? May need nitrogen (FAN) yeast nutrient.
- Saison? See Belgian Yeast, page 208.
- *Brettanomyces*? See *Brettanomyces*, page 210.
- Low zinc or copper?
- Dry yeast properly rehydrated? See Dried Yeast, page 209.
- Fix for most problems: Be patient or pitch new yeast. There is no simple way to decide what to do, but if there is visible activity, you can just wait it out. In most cases, though, there is no harm in adding new yeast.

Underattenuation
- Check if temperature is correct for yeast strain. Too high or too low can both cause problems.
- Any sudden temperature drops? Don't do that!
- Double-check mash temperature and procedure.
- More than 10% caramel/crystal malt? Usually too much.
- Saison? Probably just slow (see Belgian Yeast, page 208.) Pitch different yeast to finish the job if you can.
- Flocculent strain? Rousing may help.
- Alcohol above 10%? May need alcohol-tolerant yeast added to restart.
- Check extract brand. Some have lots of unfermentables.

Overattenuation
- Double-check mash temperature and procedure.
- Saison or *Brett*? High attenuation is normal.
- Accompanied by phenolic, electrical-fire aroma? Could be wild yeast. Toss the batch.
- High percentage of sugar in recipe.

Film (pellicle) on surface
- If *Brettanomyces*, then it's normal; otherwise, wild yeast (infection).
- Mold fairly common with fruit beer. Keep flushed with CO_2 (mold needs air). Don't allow the beer to sit too long on the fruit.

SENSORY PROBLEMS

This category covers a wide range of possible problems. With aroma, more often than not there is a yeast issue; check the information in chapter 6 on yeast aromas and their origins. If you are getting weird aromas frequently, it's time to have a serious look at your methods and materials for cleaning and sanitization, and also your yeast-handling habits.

AROMA

Creamed corn/DMS
- Slow boil, or boiled with lid on? Don't do that!
- Long time to chill? Don't do that, either.
- Feeble boil? Ditto above.
- If intense, can be symptomatic of infection. Toss.

Cheesy, stinky feet
- Hops old or stored warm?

Lack of hop aroma
- Sufficient quantity of aroma hops?
- Hops reasonably fresh?
- Add dry-hop to secondary and/or keg.

Buttery/diacetyl
- Conditioned long enough?
- Sudden temperature drop?
- Remember diacetyl rest in lager (see page 203).
- In large amounts, symptomatic of infection.
- Dirty tap line?

Acetaldehyde (grassy/appley)
- Long enough conditioning?
- Sudden temperature drop?

Sulfur/rotten egg/burnt match
- A certain amount is normal in lager fermentation, so ignore it as it dissipates quickly after pouring. It can be bothersome in large quantities.
- Healthy yeast?
- Sufficient yeast quantity?
- Check sulfur/sulfate levels in well water. Copper in contact with wort during brewing may reduce sulfur.
- Can be caused by zinc deficiency.

Estery/fruity (lagers)
- Watch that temperature—not too high (see page 202).
- Check thermometer, temperature control.

Estery/solvent
- Fermentation temperature too high for strain?
- Strong beer? See page 202 for high-alcohol procedure.
- Stressed or damaged yeast?

Fusel/rubbing alcohol
- Fermentation temperature too high for strain?
- Strong beer? See Fusels, page 202 and pages 214 to 215 for proper pitching and wort aeration rates for high-alcohol beers.
- Stressed or damaged yeast?

Animal, goaty
- Usually symptomatic of infection.
- Dirty draft lines?

Skunky
- Fermenter exposed to daylight or fluorescent light?
- Don't use clear or green bottles for packaging or, if you do, protect them from light.

Soapy/yeast-bitten
- Common result of yeast autolysis (disintegration). Transfer from primary and off the dead yeast (lees) after 4 weeks.
- Can come from lipids in cold break material (rare); a complex issue to fix.
- Can be related to lack of yeast vigor/health.
- Observe good practice on pitch rate, aeration, etc. Moderated at higher fermentation temperatures.

Ballpoint-pen aroma
- A certain tangy aroma from stale malt extracts. If you can't be sure of liquid extract freshness, use dry extract.

Cidery
- Stale extract?
- High percentage of sugar?

Barnyard/horse blanket
- *Brettanomyces* added intentionally? Normal and desirable.
- No *Brett* pitched? Then it's an uninvited guest. If you like the flavor, drink it. If not, dump it.

Sourish, vinegary
- Acetobacter infection. This bacteria needs oxygen to function.
- Most plastic is O_2 permeable, as is wood. Use only glass or O_2-barrier plastic for extended storage.

APPEARANCE

Phenolic/plastic/ Bakelite
- Some saison strains show a bit of this, in a pleasant way. In large amounts, or if unpleasant in character, symptomatic of wild yeast infection or possibly damaged yeast. Toss it, as it will only worsen.

Chlorophenolic/ Band-Aid
- From free chlorine in unfiltered tap water.
- Lack of complete rinsing of chlorine sanitizer.

Ashtray, campfire, burnt
- Scorching in mash or boil. Black marks in flame pattern on pot bottom are a giveaway. Use heat diffuser on thin stainless pots, or use stainless pot with heat-spreading bottom.
- Home-toasted malts must mellow for 2 weeks before using.
- Be cautious with chocolate malt; it can be harsh.

Moldy
- Damp storage conditions for malt or hops?
- Mold aromas go right through plastic.
- Plastic fermenters on wet or earth floor?

Papery/cardboard/ oxidation
- Symptomatic of oxidation.
- Watch hot-side aeration (splashing, etc.) in brewhouse.
- Avoid scorching or kettle caramelization.
- Beware splashing when transferring beer.
- May be a problem in counter-pressure bottling.
- Keep storage temperatures low: < 70°F/21°C.

Sherry
- Oxidation, common in aged beers.
- Keep storage temperatures low: < 70°F/21°C.

Soy sauce
- Common in very old beers.
- Keep storage temperatures low: < 70°F/21°C.

Color too light
- Check recipe and calculations.
- Mislabeled grain?
- Too-coarse crush?
- Too-short steep? Try longer soak before
- removing grain bag.
- Add a small amount of black malt tea or Sinamar malt color concentrate.

Color too dark
- Check recipe and calculations.
- Mislabeled grain?
- Liquid extract can't make a super-pale beer.
- Too much kettle caramelization? Shorten boil time; use heat diffuser with stainless pots.

Beer is cloudy
- Adequate time for clarification?
- Powdery yeasts may require fining (see Finings, page 220).
- Presence of starch from incomplete mash. Check thermometer to make sure mash temperatures are correct.

Cloudy-beer style is clear
- Next time, add flour to boil kettle (see page 312).
- Flocculent yeast strain? Next time, change to less flocculent strain.

Chill haze
- Common in all-malt beers served cold.
- Requires filtration or PVPP fining to eliminate.
- Ignore—not harmful. Will settle out in time.

Poor head
- Don't use protein rest with most malts.
- Do use protein rest for wheat beers.
- Oils from nuts and other specialty ingredients can be a problem.
- Be sure glassware is clean and well rinsed of detergents.

Ropy, like glue
- Rare infection. Toss it.

TASTE

Too bitter/ not bitter enough
- Check recipe, math, quantities, boil times.
- Inaccurate alpha percentage on package.
- Water chemistry can affect taste—check it.
- Old hops = less bitterness (see Hops' Form and Function, page 79).
- System variables—adjust up or down for next time.
- Make sure boil is vigorous for best utilization.

Harsh hop bitterness
- Check water chemistry, especially with pale, hoppy beers (see page 97).
- Some hop varieties cleaner than others.

Metallic
- Avoid iron equipment; iron/blood taste can occur.
- Check for iron in well water.
- Rare but possible with copper and brass.
- Can come from lipid oxidation. Make sure malts are stored dry.

Salty/mineral
- Rare, but check water and mineral additions.
- Never use softened water for brewing—too much sodium.
- Adding $MgSO_4$ to match historical Burton water can cause this. It's not needed.

MOUTHFEEL, TEXTURE, AND ASTRINGENCY

Husky/grainy
- May be oversparged (see Lautering and Sparging, page 140). Pay attention to proper water quantities for the batch size.

Husky/phenolic/ astringent
- Canadian or tropical 6-row malts? Common in these types.
- More than 60% 6-row? Too much.

Hot alcohol
- Fermentation temperature too high for strain?
- Strong beer? See pages 214 to 215 for proper pitching and wort aeration rates for high-alcohol beers.
- Stressed or damaged yeast?

Lacking body
- Don't do a protein rest unless you're sure you need one.
- Check mash thermometer.
- Wheat, oats, rye can add some creaminess next time.
- Some malt extracts have this problem.

Lacking creaminess (wheat ale)
- Use more wheat malt. Up to 100% if you want.
- Protein rest would probably be worthwhile.
- Unmalted wheat requires special mashing (see Adjunct Mashing, page 137).

Too sweet or dry
- Check thermometer to make sure mash temperature is correct.
- Watch amount of caramel/crystal malt. 10% max for most beers.

PACKAGING *and* SERVING PROBLEMS

Most of these issues have to do with too much or too little carbonation. With bottle-conditioned beers, make sure priming sugar quantities are accurate, and that there is some healthy yeast present, not always the case for strong or long-conditioned beers.

With draft systems, you are reliant on regulators and especially gauges that may be damaged or inaccurate, so they can be a common culprit in incorrectly carbonated beers. Perhaps check against someone else's.

Undercarbonated bottles (after 2 weeks)
- Check priming quantity. Add more if needed.
- Strong beer? May need alcohol-tolerant yeast for bottling.
- Long aging before bottling? Needs fresh yeast.
- Temperature below 60°F/16°C? Move bottles to warmer place.

Overcarbonated bottles
- Check priming quantity.
- Fruit beer? Weird sugars ferment slowly.
- Can be symptomatic of wild yeast.
- Uncap, vent, recap. This may need to be done several times. Or, serve very cold in large glasses.

Undercarbonated kegs
- Leave on gas longer and/or raise pressure.
- Check regulator pressure; adjust if needed. (See Beer Priming and Carbonation chart, page 225.)
- Check against another regulator. Gauges are easily damaged, often inaccurate.

Overcarbonated kegs
- Pop vent, leave open a few hours. Re-check.

Foamy draft beer
- Usually a result of imbalanced draft systems. Add restriction (see Serving Draft Beer, page 230).
- Check regulator pressure, adjust if needed. (See Beer Priming and Carbonation chart, page 225).
- Check against another regulator. Gauges are easily damaged, often inaccurate.

RESOURCES

CONVERSION SCALES for COMMON UNITS of BREWING MEASUREMENT

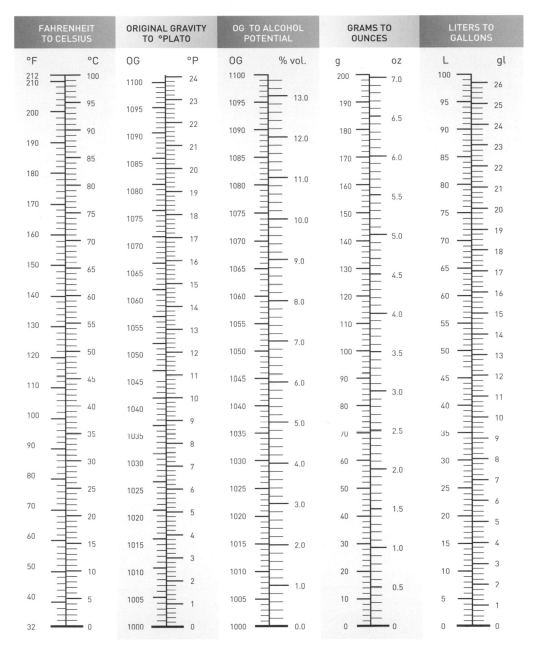

FAHRENHEIT TO CELSIUS		ORIGINAL GRAVITY TO °PLATO		OG TO ALCOHOL POTENTIAL		GRAMS TO OUNCES		LITERS TO GALLONS	
°F	°C	OG	°P	OG	% vol.	g	oz	L	gl
212	100	1100	24	1100		200	7.0	100	26
210			23	1095	13.0	190		95	25
200	95	1095	22	1090	12.0	180	6.5	90	24
	90	1090	21						23
190	85	1085	20	1085	11.0	170	6.0	85	22
180	80	1080	19	1080		160	5.5	80	21
170	75	1075	18	1075	10.0	150	5.0	75	20
160	70	1070	17	1070	9.0	140		70	19
150	65	1065	16	1065		130	4.5	65	18
			15						17
140	60	1060	14	1060	8.0	120	4.0	60	16
130	55	1055	13	1055	7.0	110		55	15
120	50	1050	12	1050		100	3.5	50	14
	45	1045	11	1045	6.0	90	3.0	45	13
110			10						12
100	40	1040	9	1040	5.0	80		40	11
	35	1035	8	1035		70	2.5	35	10
90	30	1030	7	1030	4.0	60	2.0	30	9
80									8
	25	1025	6	1025	3.0	50	1.5	25	7
70	20	1020	5	1020		40		20	6
	15	1015	4	1015	2.0	30	1.0	15	5
60			3						4
50	10	1010	2	1010	1.0	20	0.5	10	3
	5	1005	1	1005		10		5	2
40									1
32	0	1000	0	1000	0.0	0	0	0	0

Use these scales for a quick translation between various commonly used units of brewing/measurement. Find the number you wish to convert and read across the scale to the corresponding measurement unit.

WEIGHTS *and* MEASURES CONVERSIONS (U.S./U.K.)

hectoliter (hl)	100 liters 26.418 U.S. gallons 0.387 U.S. barrels 21.998 British gallons 0.611 British barrels	U.S. hundredweight (CWT)	100 pounds
		British hundredweight (CWT)	112 pounds
		ounce (Avdp)	0.0625 pound 28.35 grams
liter (L)	0.01 hectoliter 1000 milliliters 1 kilogram of water 33.815 U.S. fluid ounces 1.057 U.S. quart 0.2642 U.S. gallons 35.196 British fluid ounces 0.8799 British quart 0.2199 British gallons	grain	64.80 milligrams
		cubic foot	7.481 U.S. gallons 6.229 British gallons 28.317 liters
		1 bar (atmosphere) of pressure	14.70 pounds per square inch
		1 pound per square inch	0.068 bar (atmosphere) of pressure
kilogram (kg)	1000 grams 2.20462 pounds 35.274 ounces	bushel, U.S. malt	34 pounds
		bushel, U.S. barley	48 pounds
gram (g)	0.0022 pounds 0.03527 ounces 15.432 grains	bushel, U.K. malt	40 pounds
		bushel, U.K. barley	50 pounds
U.S. barrel	31 U.S. gallons 1.924 hectoliters 0.7291 British barrels	quarter of malt	336 pounds
		quarter of barley	448 pounds
U.S. gallon	128 ounces 3.7853 liters 0.8327 British gallons 8.345 pounds of water	alcohol % volume	1.267 × % weight
		alcohol % weight	0.789 × % volume
U.S. quart	32 U.S. ounces 0.9463 liters 946.3 milliliters 0.8327 British quarts	density of water	1.000 (specific gravity) 8.345 lb/3.78 kg per U.S. gallon 10.43 lb/4.73 kg per U.K. gallon 1 kilogram per liter
fluid ounce	0.03125 U.S. quart 0.025 British quart 0.02957 liters 29.57 milliliters	density of ethyl alcohol	0.789 (specific gravity) 6.58 lb/2.98 kg per U.S. gallon 8.23 lb/3.73 kg per U.K. gallon 789 grams per liter
British barrel	36 British gallons 43.2 U.S. gallons 1.6365 hectoliters 2 kilderkins/4 firkins (10.8 U.S. gallons)	alcohol boiling point	173°F/78.5°C
		°F to °C	subtract 32, then multiply by 5/9
		°C to °F	multiply by 9/5, then add 32
British (imperial) gallon	160 British fluid ounces 1.201 U.S. gallons 4.546 liters		
British (imperial) quart	1.201 U.S. quart 1.365 liters		
butt (big barrel)	2 hogsheads (64.85 U.S. gallons, 54 U.K. gallons) 3 British barrels		
pound	0.45359 kilogram 453.59 grams 256 drams 7000 grains 0.1198 gallons of water		

GLOSSARY of BEER and BREWING TERMS

A

ACETALDEHYDE Chemical present in beer that has a coarse grassy/appley aroma.

ACROSPIRE The shoot of the barley grain, which develops during malting.

ADJUNCT Any source of sugars added to barley malt for beermaking: wheat, oats, rye, rice, corn, sugar, and more.

ADSORPTION Physical process involving adherence of particles to one another at the microscopic level; important in fining and other processes.

ALCOHOL An organic compound containing one or more hydroxyl (OH) groups. Ethanol is the type found in fermented beverages. Other types (*see* fusels) occur in beer and other fermented products, but in small quantities.

ALDEHYDE A group of important flavor chemicals found in beer and other foodstuffs. Most common in beer as acetaldehyde and as a group of chemicals present in stale, oxidized beer.

ALE Any beer produced with top-fermenting yeast; in the old days, a strong unhopped beer.

ALKALINITY A measure of water hardness, expressed as ppm of calcium carbonate.

ALPHA ACID A group of substances that form the bitter component of hop flavor. Analyses of hops are given in percentage of alpha acid, which may be used to estimate the bitterness for a particular beer.

AMINO ACIDS A group of complex organic chemicals that form the building blocks of protein; important in yeast nutrition.

AMYLASE (ALPHA AND BETA) Primary starch-converting enzymes present in barley and malt. They both break the long chains of starch molecules into shorter, fermentable, sugars.

ASBC (AMERICAN SOCIETY OF BREWING CHEMISTS) The standards-setting organization for beer analysis in North America.

ATTENUATION The degree to which residual sugars have been fermented out of a finished beer.

AUTOLYSIS The self-digestion and disintegration of yeast cells. This can give rise to "soapy" off-flavors if beer is not racked off dead yeast after primary fermentation.

B

°BALLING Antiquated European measurement of specific gravity based on the percentage of pure sugar in the wort. Still used in Czech Republic (Karl Balling was Czech).

BARLEY Cereal grain; member of the genus *Hordeum*. When malted, the primary ingredient in beer.

BARREL The standard unit in commercial brewing. U.S. barrel is 31 gallons/117 L; British barrel is 43.2 U.S. gallons/163.5 L.

BAUME A specific gravity scale seldom used in brewing, but often found on hydrometer scales. It corresponds with the potential alcohol scale.

BEAD The bubbles in beer. Important qualities are fineness and persistence.

BEER A broad term that correctly describes any fermented beverage made from barley malt or other cereal grains. Originally denoted products containing hops instead of other herbs.

BETA GLUCANS A group of gummy carbohydrates in malt. Some grain varieties have an excess of beta glucans, which can cause problems with runoff and during fermentation, where they may precipitate as a sticky goo.

BITTERING UNITS (BU) International measure of bitterness, expressed as the ppm of isomerized alpha acids in the finished beer.

BODY A quality of beer, largely determined by the presence of colloidal protein complexes. To a lesser extent due to the presence of unfermentable sugars (dextrins) or glucans in the finished beer.

BREAK The sudden precipitation of proteins and resins in wort. The *hot break* occurs during the boil, and the *cold break* occurs during rapid chilling.

BUNG A wooden plug for a beer barrel. Generally used in connection with real ale in casks.

BURTON SALTS A mixture of minerals added to brewing water to approximate the water of Burton-on-Trent, England, famous for the production of pale ales.

BURTONIZE To treat with Burton salts, a mix of calcium and magnesium sulfates.

C

CAMPDEN TABLETS Pellets of sodium metabisulfite used to inhibit wild yeast. Not technically a sanitizer. Used more in the making of wine, mead, and cider than brewing, but useful for removing chloramine from brewing water.

CANDI SUGAR An imprecise term that may mean large crystals of rock sugar or, more likely in Belgium, special caramel syrups made for brewers.

CARAMEL A sugar syrup cooked until very dark, and used as a coloring and flavoring ingredient in beer and many other foods and drinks. Most traditional in some Belgian beer styles.

CARAMEL MALT A specially processed type of malt used to add body and caramel color and flavor to amber and dark beers. It is heated to mashing temperatures when wet, causing starch to be converted to sugars while still in the husk. These sugars crystallize when cooling and contain large amounts of unfermentable sugars. Comes in several shades of color.

CARA-PILS Trade name for a specially processed malt used to add body to pale beers. Similar to caramel malt but not roasted. Also called dextrine malt.

CARBOHYDRATES The class of chemicals such as sugars and their polymers, including starch and dextrins.

CARBOY A large glass jug used to ferment beer or wine. Available in 2-, 5-, and 6.5-gallon and other sizes.

CARRAGEEN Alternate name for Irish moss.

CASK The term for any size of cooperage used for real ale in England. Don't ever call it a keg.

CATTINESS A term describing the aroma of some high-alpha hops, especially North American ones that have notes of cat urine among their floral and grapefruit-like flavors.

CELSIUS European thermometer scale, formerly called centigrade.

CENTIGRADE *See* Celsius.

CEREAL The broad term for a group of grass plant species cultivated as food grains. Also used in brewing to refer to adjuncts, especially rice or corn.

CHILL HAZE A cloudy residue of protein that precipitates when beer is chilled. Occurs when the protein rest stage of the mash is inadequate, especially with high-protein malt such as six-row.

CHIT MALT A type of malt sometimes used in Europe that is malted for a very short time, and thus highly undermodified. It must be treated like raw grain.

CHOCOLATE (MALT) Medium-brown roasted malt with a sharp coffee flavor.

COLD BREAK A rapid precipitation of proteins, which occurs when boiled wort is rapidly chilled.

COLLOID A state of matter involving very minute particles suspended in a liquid. Beer is a colloid, as is gelatin. Many reactions in beer involve the colloidal state, especially those affecting haze and stability.

CONDITIONING The process of maturation of beer, whether in bottles or in kegs. During this phase, complex sugars are slowly fermented, CO_2 is dissolved, and yeast settles to the bottom while unpleasant fermentation aromas like diacetyl and acetaldehyde are reabsorbed by the yeast.

CONE The fluffy catkins of the hop plant used in brewing.

CONVERSION In the mash, this refers to starch changing to sugar.

COPPER The brewing kettle, named for its traditional material of construction.

CORN SUGAR Also called dextrose or glucose. A simple sugar, sometimes used in beermaking, derived from corn.

CORNY Abbreviation for "Cornelius," meaning a soda keg that is the preferred draft keg for home-brewers, most commonly in a 5-gallon/19-L size.

CRYSTAL MALT *See* caramel malt.

DECOCTION A continental mashing technique that involves removing a portion of the mash, boiling it, then returning it to the mash to raise its temperature.

DEXTRIN, DEXTRINE A family of long-chain sugars not normally fermentable by yeast. Contributes somewhat to body in beer.

DEXTROSE Also called glucose or corn sugar. A simple sugar, easily fermented by yeast, sometimes used in beermaking.

DIACETYL A powerful flavor chemical with the aroma of butter; created during fermentation and also by wild organisms, especially *Lactobacillus* and *Pediococcus*.

DIASTASE An enzyme complex present in barley and malt that is responsible for the conversion of starch into sugars.

DIASTATIC ACTIVITY An analytical measure expressed in degrees Lintner of the power of malt or other grains to convert starches to sugars in the mash.

DISACCHARIDE Sugars formed by the combination of two simple sugar units. Maltose is an example.

DMS (DIMETHYL SULFIDE) A powerful flavor chemical found in beer, with the aroma of cooked corn.

DOUGH-IN The process of mixing the crushed malt with water in the beginning of the mash operation.

DRAFT, DRAUGHT Beer from a cask or a keg, as opposed to bottled beer. Generally unpasteurized.

DRY-HOPPING A method of adding hops directly to the secondary, to increase hop aroma without adding bitterness.

DUNKEL German word for "dark," as in dark beer. Usually refers to Munich dark style.

EBC (EUROPEAN BREWING CONVENTION) Continental standards-setting organization for brewing.

ENDOSPERM The starchy middle of a cereal grain that serves as the food reserve for the young plant. It is the source of fermentable material for brewing.

ENTIRE An old term meaning to combine the first, middle, and last runnings into one batch of beer. This was begun in the large mechanized porter breweries in London during the 1700s, and is the standard practice today.

ENZYME Proteins that act as catalysts for most reactions crucial to brewing, including starch conversion, proteolysis, and yeast metabolism. Highly dependent upon conditions such as temperature, time, and pH.

EPSOM SALTS Magnesium sulfate. A common mineral found in water, sometimes added to brewing water in a quest for perfect Burton water, but rarely beneficial.

ESB Extra special bitter, or ESB, is a trade term sometimes used to mean the strongest version of a bitter in a brewer's lineup. In the United States, ESB is often seen as a richer, maltier type of bitter, owing to the presence of Fuller's ESB, which has those characteristics.

ESTERS A large class of compounds formed from the oxidation of various alcohols, including many flavor components commonly found in fruits. Created in beer as a by-product of yeast metabolism. Especially prominent in top-fermented beers.

ETHANOL The main alcohol found in beer; its intoxicating component.

EXTRACT The term used to refer to sugars and other solids derived from malt, dissolved in wort or beer. Also, the commercially prepared malt extract in syrup or dried form.

F

FAN (FREE AMINO NITROGEN) Small nitrogen-bearing molecules, mainly protein breakdown products including amino acids. Important in the wort as a source of yeast nutrition.

FINING A process of beer clarification that uses gelatinous or other types of compounds to settle out particulates, proteins, and other haze-forming materials.

FLAKED A type of grain processing that presses the cereals between hot rollers, flattening as well as gelatinizing them, making them easier to use in brewing.

FUSEL ALCOHOL, OILS Higher (more complex) alcohols, found in all fermented beverages.

G

GELATIN Used in beermaking as a fining agent.

GELATINIZATION The cooking of corn or other unmalted cereals to break down the cell walls of the starch granules. The resulting starch is in a colloidal state, making it accessible for enzymatic conversion into sugars. Occurs in barley at 140°F/ 60°C, but is higher in grains, such as corn and rice.

GLUCAN A type of carbohydrate found in barley and other sources that can interfere with lautering by creating a gelatinous texture in the mash.

GLUCOSE Corn sugar or dextrose. A simple sugar sometimes used in brewing.

GOODS The stuff being mashed.

GRANT A small vessel that serves as a temporary holding tank for wort that is running off the lauter en route to the boil kettle.

GRAVITY *See* original gravity.

GRITS Ground, de-germed corn or rice used in brewing.

GRUIT A medieval herb mixture used in beer.

GYLE A single batch of beer.

GYPSUM Calcium sulfate—CaSO4. A common groundwater mineral. Often added to water in the production of pale ales.

H

HARDNESS A common measurement of water mineral levels, especially sulfates and carbonates. Expressed as parts-per-million of calcium carbonate.

HEAD Foam on the surface of beer or fermenting wort.

HEFEWEIZEN Translates literally to "yeast-wheat" and is the German term for Bavarian wheat beer that is packaged with yeast in the bottle, which produces the beer's characteristically cloudy appearance.

HERM Heat Exchange Recirculating Mash, a type of mashing that continually runs off the mash and circulates it through a coil submerged in the hot liquor tank in order to raise or maintain the mash temperature.

HEXOSE A category of simple sugars containing 6 carbon atoms per molecule. Dextrose is an example.

HOP A climbing vine of the family Cannibicinae, whose flower cones are used to give beer its bitterness and characteristic aroma.

HOP BACK A strainer tank used in commercial brewing to filter hops and trub from boiled wort before it is chilled.

HOT BREAK The rapid coagulation of proteins and resins, assisted by the hops, which occurs after a sustained period of boiling.

HUMULENE One of the most plentiful of the many chemicals that give hops their characteristic aroma.

HUSK The outer covering of barley or other grains. May impart a rough, bitter taste to beer if sparging is carried out incorrectly.

HYDROLYSIS A chemical process in which the addition of water to a molecule breaks bonds, usually as part of a degradation of a substance. It may be enzyme-driven. In brewing, saccharification involves hydrolysis.

HYDROMETER Glass instrument used in brewing to measure the specific gravity of beer and wort.

I

IBU (INTERNATIONAL BITTERING UNIT) *See* bittering units.

INFUSION A mash technique of the simplest type used to make all kinds of English ales and stouts. Features a single temperature rest, rather than a series of gradually increasing steps common in other mashing styles.

IODINE TEST Used to determine if a mash in progress has reached starch conversion. An iodine solution turns dark blue or black in the presence of unconverted starch.

ION An electrically charged component of a molecule, which may be one atom, or a combination of atoms. When calcium sulfate, CaSO4, is dissolved in water, it breaks into the ions Ca++ and SO4.

IPA India Pale Ale, a typically hoppier and often paler variant of pale ale.

IRISH MOSS A marine alga, *Chrondus crispus*, that is used during wort boiling to enhance the hot break. Also called carrageen.

ISINGLASS A type of gelatin obtained from the swim bladder of certain types of fish (usually sturgeon), used as a fining agent in ales.

ISO International Organization for Standardization, a global standards-setting association.

ISOMERIZATION In brewing, the structural chemical change that takes place in hop bittering resins that allows them to become soluble in wort. Boiling is the agent of this change.

K

KETTLE Boiling vessel, also known as a copper.

KILNING The process of heating grains to dry them out, or to roast them to varying degrees of darkness. Also applied to the drying of hops.

KRÄUSEN The thick foamy head on fermenting beer.

KRÄUSENING The practice of adding vigorously fermenting young beer to beer in the secondary.

LACTIC ACID An organic acid sometimes used to assist the acidification of the mash. Also, a by-product of *Lactobacillus*, responsible for the tart flavor of Berliner weisse and some Belgian ales.

LACTOBACILLUS A large class of aerobic bacteria. May be either a spoilage organism, or a consciously added fermenting agent in such products as yogurt, Kölsch, or Berliner weisse.

LACTOSE Milk sugar. Unfermentable by yeast; used as a sweetener in milk stout.

LAGER Beers made with bottom-fermenting yeast and aged at near-freezing temperatures.

LAUTER TUN German term for a sparging vessel.

LEES Sludgy mix of dead yeast, protein, and other detritus in the bottom of a fermenter.

LIGHT-STRUCK An off-flavor in beer that develops from exposure to short-wavelength (blue) light. Even a short exposure to sunlight can cause this "skunky" odor to develop. Often occurs in beer in green or clear bottles sold from fluorescent-lighted cooler cases. Brown bottles are good protection.

°LINTNER The commonly used European standard measurement of diastatic activity.

LOCK A small water-filled device used on a carboy to let CO_2 gas escape, without allowing air to enter.

°LOVIBOND Beer and grain color measurement, now superseded by the newer SRM method, but still used in reference to malt color in the United States.

LUPULIN The sticky substance in hops containing all the resins and aromatic oils.

MAILLARD BROWNING The chemical reaction, also known as nonenzymic browning, responsible for most of the roasted color and flavor in beer.

MALT Barley or other grain that has been allowed to sprout, then is dried or roasted.

MALT EXTRACT Concentrated commercial preparations of wort. Available as syrup or powder, in a wide range of colors, hopped or unhopped.

MALTODEXTRIN A purified long-chain sugar (dextrin) that is unfermentable by yeast. Used as an additive in extract beers to add body and richness; 6 to 8 ounces/180 to 240 ml per 5-gl/19-L batch is typical.

MALTOSE A simple sugar that is by far the predominant fermentable material in wort.

MALTOTETRAOSE A type of sugar molecule consisting of four molecules of glucose hooked together. Fermentable by some more attenuative brewers' yeast strains.

MALTOTRIOSE Type of sugar molecule consisting of three molecules of glucose hooked together.

MASH The cooking procedure central to brewing in which starch is converted into sugars, among other things. Various enzyme reactions occur between 110 to 175°F/43 to 79°C.

MASH-IN The act of beginning a mash.

MASH-OUT The final step of mashing that involves a temperature rise to 170°F/77°C to inactivate the enzymes and make sparging easier.

MASH TUN The vessel in which mashing is carried out. A mash/lauter has a perforated false bottom to allow liquid to drain through.

MEAD Wine made from honey, sometimes with the addition of malt, fruit, spices, etc.

MELANOIDINS A group of complex color compounds formed by heating sugars and starches in the presence of proteins. Created in brewing during grain roasting and wort boiling.

MILLING The term for grain grinding or crushing.

MILLIVAL Measurement of chemicals or minerals expressed relative to actual numbers of molecules rather than weight. This allows calculations of equivalent amounts involved in reactions, which can then be converted back to actual weight.

MODIFICATION The degree to which malting has been allowed to progress. More modification means more accessible starch.

MONOSACCHARIDE Simple sugars, such as glucose, having only one sugar unit.

MOUTHFEEL Sensory qualities of a beverage other than flavor, such as body and carbonation.

NITROGEN The element used as a measure of protein level in malt. Important in a free amino state as a yeast nutrient. Also used to pressurize stout.

OLIGOSACCHARIDES Sugars that contain a few molecules of a monosaccharide, joined.

ORIGINAL GRAVITY (OG) The specific gravity of wort before fermentation as an indicator of potential strength. It is expressed as a ratio; 1.050 wort is 1.05 times as dense as pure water. Sometimes the decimal point is omitted.

OXIDATION A chemical reaction that often involves oxygen but can also happen in other ways. In beer it is quite complex, involving everything from brewhouse procedure to oxygen trapped in bottled beer. Oxidized off-flavors most often smell of wet paper or cardboard.

OXYGEN Element important in yeast metabolism, especially during startup. Also may cause problems in long-term storage. *See also* oxidation.

PARTI-GYLE Antiquated brewhouse practice in England. The first and strongest runnings become strong ale, second runnings become ordinary beer, and the last and weakest runnings become small beer. It's a useful technique for homebrewers, who can get two beers of different strengths from the same brewing session.

PELLICLE A film that forms on the surface of liquids fermented with certain wild yeast and bacteria. A sign of infection in beer, but technically speaking, top-fermenting yeast has a pellicle, too.

PENTOSANS Polymers of pentose, a five-sided sugar, found in barley as gums.

PEPTIDASE An enzyme that breaks apart proteins during the early stages of the mash. Most effective around 122°F/50°C.

PEPTIDE A short fragment of a protein. Also the bond holding amino acids into chains of protein.

PET Polyethylene Terepthalate, a plastic used to make soda bottles, among many other things.

pH Logarithmic scale of hydrogen ion concentration, used to express the level of acidity and alkalinity in a solution. 7 = neutral; 0 = most acid; 14 = most alkaline. Each step on the scale represents a tenfold change from the previous one.

PHENOL A large group of chemicals often present in beer, with aromas from spicy to peppery to smoky to electrical fire and bandage. May or may not be desirable.

PITCHING The act of adding yeast to wort to start fermentation.

°PLATO A scale of wort gravity based on a percentage of pure sugar in the wort. It is a newer, more accurate version of the Balling scale.

POLYCLAR The trade name for a material (PVPP) used to clear beer. Consists of microscopic plastic beads that remove chill haze by adsorption.

POLYMER Chemical molecule made of the repetition of smaller basic units. In brewing, they are common as polysaccharides and polypeptides.

POLYPHENOL A class of molecules that includes tannins, important in beer in connection with protein coagulation and chill haze.

POLYSACCHARIDES Polymers of simple sugars. Includes a range from complex sugars through dextrins, up to starches.

PPB (PARTS PER BILLION) 1 microgram per liter.

PPM (PARTS PER MILLION) 1 milligram per liter.

PRECIPITATION A chemical process, involving a material coming out of solution.

PRIMARY FERMENTATION Initial rapid stage of yeast activity when maltose and other simple sugars are metabolized. Lasts about a week.

PRIMING The process of adding sugar to beer before bottling or racking to kegs. Restarts fermentation, which produces CO_2 gas, carbonating the beer.

PROTEIN Complex nitrogenous organic molecules important in all living matter. In beer, involved in enzyme activity, yeast nutrition, head retention, and colloidal stability. During mashing, boiling, and cooling, they may be broken apart and/or precipitated.

PROTEINASE Enzyme complex that breaks proteins apart into smaller, more soluble units. Most active at 122°F/50°C.

PROTEIN REST During mashing, a 120 to 125°F/49 to 52°C temperature rest for 20 minutes or more to eliminate proteins that cause chill haze.

PROTEOLYSIS The breaking up or digestion of proteins by enzymes that occurs in the mash around 122°F/50°C.

PROTEOLYTIC ENZYMES Enzymes naturally present in barley and malt that have the power to break up proteins in the mash.

PVPP *See* Polyclar.

QUARTER An English measure of malt equal to 336 pounds/152 kg; and of barley, 448 pounds/203 kg. Only the Queen knows why.

RACKING Transferring the fermenting beer from one vessel to another to avoid tainting by extended contact with dead yeast and trub.

REINHEITSGEBOT The Bavarian beer purity law, enacted in 1516, that limits lager beer ingredients to malt, water, hops, and yeast.

RIMS Recirculating Infusion Mash System, a type of mashing that continually runs off mash and flows it through a heat exchanger typically heated by gas flame or an electric element in order to raise or maintain the mash temperature.

RO Reverse osmosis, a type of water purification that removes virtually all minerals from water.

ROCKY The term used to describe the texture of head on beer, especially during primary fermentation.

ROLLER MILL The preferred malt grinding device. Crushes the starchy middle of malt between rollers without pulverizing the husks.

ROPINESS Spoilage condition causing beer to be thick and slimy. Certain bacteria produce gums that cause this condition.

RUNNINGS Wort that is drained from the mash during sparging.

RUNOFF The draining of wort from the mash during sparging.

SACCHARIFICATION The conversion of starch to sugars in the mash through enzyme activity.

SACCHAROMYCES The scientific genus name of yeast used in brewing. Two species are used: *Saccharomyces cerevesiae*, which is top-fermenting yeast, and *Saccharomyces pastorianus*, which is bottom-fermenting, or lager, yeast.

SALT Minerals present in water that have various effects on the brewing process.

SECONDARY FERMENTATION Outdated term for the conditioning of beer.

SET MASH Condition that sometimes develops during sparging that makes runoff difficult. Grains with high protein or glucans, insufficient husks for filtering, or improper grinding may be the culprit. Mashes with a high percentage of unmalted grains often have this problem.

SIX-ROW A type of barley with high protein and therefore high diastatic activity, making it ideal for the mashing of unmalted adjuncts, which have no starch-converting power of their own.

SKUNKY An aroma caused by overexposure of beer to light. *See also* light-struck.

SMM S-Methyl Methionone, a chemical found in barley and other grains that is a precursor to DMS, which can add cooked corn aroma to beer if brewing is not conducted properly.

SPARGE Process of rinsing mashed grains with hot water to recover all available wort sugars.

SPECIFIC GRAVITY A measurement of density, expressed relative to the density of water. Used in brewing to follow the course of fermentation.

SRM (STANDARD REFERENCE METHOD) Measurement of beer color, expressed as ten times the optical density (absorbance) of beer, as measured at 346 nm in a spectrophotometer. Nearly the same as the older Lovibond color series, measured with a set of specially colored glass samples.

STARCH Complex carbohydrates, long polymers of sugars, that are converted into sugars during mashing.

STARCH HAZE Cloudiness in beer due to suspended starch particles. Usually caused by incorrect mash temperature resulting in incomplete saccharification; or sparging temperatures over 180°F/82°C, which can dissolve residual starch from the mash. Desirable only in witbier.

STARTER A small amount of fermenting beer, prepared in advance, then added to the main batch. Allows for a quicker beginning of fermentation.

STEELY A quality of raw or undermodified malt in which portions of the grains are hard and "flinty." These hard ends resist milling and saccharification.

STEEP The process of soaking barley or wheat in water to begin malting.

STEINBIER A type of beer brewed in Germany using hot stones to boil the wort.

STEP MASH Mashing technique using controlled temperature steps.

STRIKE The addition of hot water to the crushed malt to raise the temperature and begin mashing.

SUCROSE A disaccharide consisting of one unit of glucose/dextrose and one unit of fructose, typically derived from beets or sugarcane. Passable, but not particularly well suited to brewing.

TANNIN Polyphenols, which are complex organic materials with a characteristic astringent flavor, extracted from hops and the husks of barley. Most noticeable in the last runnings.

TEIG Gray sludgy protein material that settles on top of the mash during sparging.

TERPENES A group of flavor chemicals forming the main component of hop oils.

TORREFICATION The process of rapidly heating grain so it puffs up like popcorn. Commonly applied to barley and wheat. Often used in British pale ales.

TRISACCHARIDE Sugar molecule consisting of three simple sugars linked together.

TRUB Coagulated protein and hop resin sludge that precipitates out of wort during boiling and again at chilling.

TUN *See* lauter tun.

TWO-ROW A type of barley with a lower protein content and proportionately less husk than six-row, making it better suited to brewing all-malt beers.

UNDERLET The addition of water to a mash-in-progress from below so the grains float a bit. Encourages quicker and more thorough mixing.

UNDERMODIFIED Applies to malt that has not been allowed to grow to an advanced stage.

VERLAUFING The act of recirculating the first runnings of the mash back through the grains to remove any chunks or cloudiness. Typically, this is perhaps 10 percent of the total runoff.

WEISS General term applied to wheat ales.

WEISSE German word meaning "white"; applied to the tart wheat beers of the Berliner style.

WEIZEN German word for "wheat." Usually applied to Bavarian-style wheat ale.

WHIRLPOOL Device used to separate hops and trub from wort after boiling. Wort is stirred in a circular motion and collects in the center of the whirlpool. Clear wort is drained from the edge.

WITBIER Dutch/Belgian term literally meaning "white beer," referring to the classic style associated with Louvain and Hoegaarde, Belgium.

WORT Unfermented beer, the sugar-laden liquid obtained from the mash.

WORT CHILLER Heat exchanger used to rapidly cool wort from near boiling to pitching temperature.

YEAST Large class of microscopic fungi, several species of which are used in brewing.

ZYMURGY The science of fermentation, used as the name of the magazine of the American Homebrew Association. The last, and coolest, word in my dictionary.

FURTHER READING
MODERN BOOKS on BEER STYLES and BREWING

Bennett, Judith M. *Ale, Beer and Brewsters in England: Women's Work in a Changing World*. Oxford, UK: Oxford University Press, 1996.

Briggs, Dennis, and others. *Brewing Science and Practice*. Oxford, UK: Woodhead Publishing Ltd, 2004.

Clerck, Jean de. *A Textbook of Brewing*. Translated by Kathleen Barton-Wright. London, UK: Chapman & Hall Ltd., 1987.

Cornell, Martyn. *Beer: The Story of the Pint*. London, UK: Headline Book Publishing, 2003.

Corran, H. S. *A History of Brewing*. London, UK: David & Charles Ltd. 1975.

Eckhardt, Fred. *Essentials of Beer Style*. Portland, OR: Fred Eckhardt Associates, 1989.

———. *A Treatise on Lager Beers*. Portland, OR: Hobby Wine-maker, n.d.

Fix, George. *An Analysis of Brewing Techniques*. Boulder, CO: Brewers Publications, 1998.

———. *Principles of Brewing Science: A Study of Serious Brewing Issues*. Boulder, CO: Brewers Publications, 1999.

Heath, Henry B., and Gary Reineccius. *Flavor Chemistry and Technology*. Westport, CT: AVI Publishing, 1986.

Hieronymous, Stan. *Brewing with Wheat*. Boulder, CO: Brewers Publications, 2010.

———. *Brew Like a Monk*. Boulder, CO: Brewers Publications, 2005.

Hind, H. Lloyd. *Brewing, Science & Practise*. London, UK: Chapman & Hall Ltd., 1948.

Hornsey, Ian. *A History of Beer and Brewing*. London, UK: The Royal Society of Chemistry, 2004.

Hough, J. S. *The Biotechnology of Malting and Brewing*. Cambridge, UK: Cambridge University Press, 1972.

Hough, J. S., D. E. Briggs, and R. Stevens. *Malting and Brewing Science*. London, UK: Chapman and Hall, 1971.

Jackson, Michael. *Beer Companion*. Philadelphia: Running Press, 1993.

———. *The Great Beers of Belgium*. Boulder, CO: Brewers Publications, 2009.

———. *The New World Guide to Beer*. Philadelphia: Running Press, 1988.

———. *The Simon and Schuster Pocket Guide to Beer*. New York: Simon & Schuster, n.d.

———. *Ultimate Beer*. New York: DK Publishing, 1998.

Kunze, Wolfgang. *Technology: Brewing and Malting*. Berlin, Germany: VLB, 2008.

Lender, Mark Edward, and James Kirby Martin. *Drinking in America: A History*. Second Edition. New York: The Free Press, 1987.

Line, Dave. *The Big Book of Brewing*. Andover, Hants, UK: Standard Press Ltd., 1974.

———. *Brewing Beers Like Those You Buy*. Andover, Hants, UK: Standard Press Ltd., 1977.

Markowski, Phil. *Farmhouse Ales: Culture and Craftsmanship in the Belgian Tradition*. Springfield, IL: Charles C. Thomas, n.d.

Mc Govern, Patrick E. *Uncorking the Past*. Berkeley: University of California Press, 2010.

Mosher, Randy. *Radical Brewing*. Boulder, CO: Brewers Publications, 2004.

———. *Tasting Beer*. North Adams, MA: Storey Publishing, 2009.

Noonan, Gregory J. *New Brewing Lager Beer*. Boulder, CO: Brewers Publications, 2003.

Ogle, Maureen. *Ambitious Brew: The Story of America's Beer*. Orlando, FL: Harcourt, 2006.

Oliver, Garrett, editor. *The Brewmaster's Table*. New York: HarperCollins, 2003.

———. *The Oxford Companion to Beer*. Oxford, UK: Oxford University Press, 2011.

Papazian, Charlie. *The New Complete Joy of Homebrewing*. New York: Avon Books, 1991.

Perrier-Robert, Annie and Charles Fontaine. *Beer by Belgium, Belgium by Beer*. Luxembourg: Esch/Alzette, 1996.

Protz, Roger. *The Ale Trail: A Celebration of the Revival of the World's Oldest Style*. Orpington, Kent, UK: Eric Dobby Publishing Ltd, 1995.

Sambrook, Pamela. *Country House Brewing in England 1500–1900*. London, UK, and Rio Grande, OH: The Hambledon Press, 1996.

Shepherd, Gordon M. *Neurogastronomy: How the Brain Creates Flavor and Why it Matters*. New York: Columbia University Press, 2011.

Sparrow, Jeff. *Wild Brews: Culture and Craftsmanship in the Belgian Tradition*. Boulder, CO: Brewers Publications, n.d.

Steiner, S. S. *Steiner's Guide to American Hops*. S. S. Steiner [self-published], 1986.

Tierney-Jones, Adrian, editor. *1001 Beers to Try Before You Die*. London, UK: Quintessence, 2010.

Wahl, Robert, and Max Henius. *A Handy Book of Brewing*. Chicago: Wahl-Henius Institute, 1901.

White, Chris, with Zaiasheff, Jamil. *Yeast: The Practical Guide to Beer Fermentation*. Boulder, CO: Brewers Publications, 2011.

HISTORICAL BREWING TEXTS

Original copies of these books are highly coveted by collectors, can command very high prices, and are correspondingly scarce. Fortunately, many old books are available in reprint editions or for free online at sites like Google Books and Project Gutenberg. Starting about 1700, the recipes make sense enough to be brewed, often with surprisingly delicious results. Here are some I find particularly engaging.

Arnold, John P. *Origin and History of Beer and Brewing*. Chicago: Alumni Association of the Wahl-Henius Institute, 1911. Wide-ranging academic view of early beer history with an overwhelming amount of detail, although much of the science has been vastly improved in the 100 years since its publication.

Bickerdyke, John. *The Curiosities of Ale and Beer*. London, UK: Spring House. Reprinted in 1965 from the original 1889 edition, widely available and inexpensive. A lively and engaging romp, mainly through the beer traditions of Jolly Old England.

Brown, Bob. *Let There Be Beer*. New York: Harrison Smith and Robert Haas, 1932. Lyrical paean to beer at the twilight of Prohibition written by a pal of H. L. Mencken, to whom it is dedicated. A series of remembrances: coming of drinking age in Chicago, pub-crawling in New York City, and even a "beer cure." Some of the most beautiful writing on beer I've seen.

Combrune, Michael. *The Theory and Practice of Brewing*. London, England: Vernon and Hood, 1804. Groundbreaking work, a highly systematic approach to brewing in as scientific a manner as was possible for the time.

Ellis, William, attributed to. Circa 1736 *The London & Country Brewer*, also known as *The Town & Country Brewer*. A fascinating bunch of books with a complex publishing history; many editions in the first half of the eighteenth century. One of the earliest books with usable recipes.

MacKenzie, Colin. *MacKenzie's 5000 Reciepts in All the Useful and Domestic Arts*. Philadelphia: Kay & Co., 1851. A great example of a domestic formulating book covering everything from beer to varnish.

Morrice, Alexander. *A Practical Treatise on Brewing the Various Sorts of Malt Liquor with Examples of Each Species, and the Mode of Using the Thermometer and Saccharometer*. London, UK: Sherwood, Neely and Jones, 1819. Quite readable and well-organized with some excellent historical recounting, plus lots of detailed recipes.

Richardson, John. *Philosophical Principles of the Art of Brewing*. London, UK: self-published, 1784–1805. Groundbreaking work detailing investigations of brewing using a hydrometer, so some of the earliest measured details of beer. His investigations changed beer forever.

Sykes, Walter J., and Arthur R. Ling. *The Principles & Practice of Brewing*. Glasgow, Scotland: C. Griffin and Company, Ltd, 1907. Scientific treatise, heavily slanted toward analytical methods.

Thausing, Julius E. *The Theory & Practice of the Preparation of Malt and the Fabrication of Beer*. Vienna, Austria: Henry Carey Baird & Co., 1882. All-purpose brewing text in the Germanic tradition, one of the few that was published in English.

Tizard, William Littell. *The Theory and Practice of Brewing*, London, UK: Gilbert and Rivington, 1850. Comprehensive view of Victorian English brewing by a seasoned and highly opinionated brewer. Great read.

Wahl, Robert, and Max Henius. *American Handy Book of the Brewing, Malting and Auxiliary Trades*. Chicago: Wahl-Henius, 1902. Compact and information-dense two-volume series that is a great snapshot of American brewing at the beginning of the twentieth century. Lots of tables of detailed beer analyses and tidbits on lost beers like Pennsylvania Swankey and Kentucky Common Beer.

ORGANIZATIONS

AMERICAN BREWERIANA ASSOCIATION
Brewery collectibles club. P.O. Box 11157, Pueblo, CO 81001.

AMERICAN HOMEBREWERS ASSOCIATION
Part of the Brewers Association, this is the only significant national organization for homebrewers. Publishers of *Zymurgy*. P.O. Box 1679, Boulder, CO 80306.

AMERICAN SOCIETY OF BREWING CHEMISTS
Professional organization forcused on analytical and quality standards for the brewing industry. 3340 Pilot Knob Road, St. Paul, MN 55121.

ASSOCIATION OF BREWERS
Microbrewery trade association. P.O. Box 1670, Boulder, CO 80306. *BrewersAssociation.com*; *craftbeer.com*

BEER CAN COLLECTORS OF AMERICA
Brewery collectibles not strictly limited to cans. 747 Merus Court, Fenton, MO 63026.

BEER JUDGE CERTIFICATION PROGRAM (BJCP)
Administers homebrew judges in a tested, ranked system. *BJCP.org*

CAMPAIGN FOR REAL ALE (CAMRA)
British ale devotee group. Good newsletter, *What's Brewing*. 34 Alma Road, St. Albans, Hertfordshire AL1 3BW, UK.

CICERONE
Beer professional certification in three levels run by Ray Daniels. *Cicerone.org*

INSTITUTE OF BREWING
Venerable brewing institute and publishers. 33 Clarges Street, London W1Y 7EE, UK.

MASTER BREWERS ASSOCIATION OF THE AMERICAS
Professional technical society, publishes *MBAA Technical Quarterly*. 4513 Vernon Blvd., Suite 202, Madison, WI 53705.

SCHOOLS

AMERICAN BREWERS GUILD
Mostly Web-based training with some in-person classes. 1001 Maple St., Salisbury, VT 05769. *www.abgbrew.com*

AMERICAN SCHOOL FOR MALTING AND BREWING SCIENCE AND TECHNOLOGY
University of California, Davis. A variety of short and long sessions focusing on all aspects of brewing practice and theory. Some sessions are appropriate for homebrewers. Contact the Registration Office, University Extension, University of California, Davis, CA 95616–8727. *www.extension.ucdavis.edu/brewing*

THE SIEBEL INSTITUTE OF TECHNOLOGY
Comprehensive program of brewing education. Short and long classes, as well as shorter seminars. Some classes suitable for advanced homebrewers. Also offers brewing analytical lab services. 4055 West Peterson Avenue, Chicago, IL 60646. *www.siebelinstitute.com*

HERB *and* SPICE RESOURCES

GERNOT KATZER'S SPICE PAGES
A great site with detailed information on a large range of spices and herbs, but nothing for sale. *www.uni-graz.at/~katzer/engl/index.html*

MONTEAGLE HERB FARM
Another botanical supplier. *www.monteagleherbs.com*

PENZEYS SPICES
Culinary herbs and spices. Retail stores in many cities. *www.penzeys.com*

SAN FRANCISCO HERB COMPANY
Large culinary herb supplier. *www.sfherb.com*

THE SPICE HOUSE
Culinary herbs and spices, including bitter orange and grains of paradise. Retail stores in many cities. *www.spicehouse.com*

WILD WEEDS
Botanical/herbal supplier with a big list. They have *Myrica gale*. *www.wildweeds.com*

INDEX